# Beginner Database Design & SQL Programming Using Microsoft SQL Server

Kalman Toth

# Beginner Database Design & SQL Programming

# Using Microsoft SQL Server

## Copyright © 2012 by Kalman Toth

# Beginner Database Design & SQL Programming
# Using Microsoft SQL Server

# Contents at a Glance

# About the Author

Kalman Toth has been working with relational database technology since 1990 when one day his boss, at a commodity brokerage firm in Greenwich, Connecticut, had to leave early and gave his SQL Server login & password to Kalman along with a small SQL task. Kalman was a C/C++ developer fascinated by SQL, therefore, he studied a Transact-SQL manual 3 times from start to end "dry", without any server access. His boss was satisfied with the execution of SQL task and a few days later Kalman's dream came true: he got his very own SQL Server login. His relational database career since then includes database design, database development, database administration, OLAP architecture and Business Intelligence development. Applications included enterprise-level general ledger & financial accounting, bond funds auditing, international stock market feeds processing, broker-dealer firm risk management, derivative instruments analytics, consumer ecommerce database management for online dating, personal finance, physical fitness, diet and health. Currently he is Principal Trainer at www.sqlusa.com. His MSDN forum participation in the Transact-SQL and SQL Server Tools was rewarded with the Microsoft Community Contributor award. Kalman has a Master of Arts degree in Physics from Columbia University and a Master of Philosophy degree in Computing Science also from Columbia. Microsoft certifications in database administration, development and Business Intelligence. The dream SQL career took him across United States & Canada as well as South America & Europe. SQL also involved him in World History. At one time he worked for Deloitte & Touche on the 96th floor of World Trade Center North. On September 11, 2001, he was an RDBMS consultant at Citibank on 111 Wall Street. After escaping at 10:30 on that fateful Tuesday morning in the heavy dirt smoke, it took 10 days before he could return to his relational database development job just 1/2 mile from the nearly three thousand victims buried under steel. What Kalman loves about SQL is that the same friendly, yet powerful, commands can process 2 records or 2 million records or 200 million records the same easy way. His current interest is Artificial Intelligence. He is convinced that machine intelligence will not only replace human intelligence but surpass it million times in the near future. His hobby is flying gliders & vintage fighter planes. Accessibility: @dbdesign1 at Twitter; http://twitter.com/dbdesign1, http://twitter.com/sqlusa, http://www.sqlusa.com/contact2005/.

# CONTENTS

# VII

# XV

This page is intentionally left blank.

# INTRODUCTION

**Developers across the world** are facing database issues daily. While they are immersed in procedural languages with loops , RDBMS forces them to think in terms of sets without loops. It takes transition. It takes training. It takes experience. Developers are exposed also to Excel worksheets or spreadsheets as they were called in the not so distant past. So if you know worksheets how hard databases can be? After all worksheets look pretty much like database tables? The big difference is connections among well-designed tables. A database is a set of connected tables which represent entities in the real world. A database can be 100 connected tables or 3000. The connection is very simple: row A in table Alpha has affiliated data with row B in table Beta. But even with 200 tables and 300 connections (FOREIGN KEY references), it takes a good amount of time to familiarize to the point of acceptable working knowledge.

"The Cemetery of Computer Languages" is expanding. You can see tombstones like PL/1, Forth, Ada, Pascal, LISP, RPG, APL, SNOBOL, JOVIAL, Algol and the list goes on. For some, the future is in question: PowerBuilder, ColdFusion, FORTRAN & COBOL. SQL on the other hand running strong after 3 decades of glorious existence. What is the difference? The basic difference is that SQL can handle large datasets in a consistent manner based on mathematical foundations. You can throw together a computer language easy: assignment statements, looping, if-then conditional, 300 library functions, and voila! Here is the new language: Mars/1, named after the red planet to be fashionable with NASA's new Mars robot. But can Mars/1 JOIN a table of 1 million rows with a table of 10 million rows in a second? The success of SQL language is so compelling that other technologies are tagged onto it like XML/XQuery which deals with semi-structured information objects.

In SQL you are thinking at a high level. In C# or Java, you are dealing with details, lots of them. That is the big difference. Why is so much of the book dedicated to database design? Why not plunge into SQL coding and sooner or later the developer will get a hang of the design? Because high level thinking requires thinking at the database design level. A farmer has 6 mules, how do we model it in the database? We design the Farmer and FarmAnimal tables, then connect them with FarmerID FOREIGN KEY in FarmAnimal referencing the FarmerID PRIMARY KEY in the Farmer table. What is the big deal about it, looks so simple? In fact, how about just calling the tables Table1 & Table2 to be more generic? Ouch... meaningful naming is the very basis of good database design. Relational database design is truly simple for simple well-understood models. The challenge starts in modeling complex objects such as financial derivative instruments, airplane passenger scheduling or social network website. When you need to add 5 new tables to a 1000 tables database and hook them in (define FOREIGN KEY references) correctly, it is a huge challenge. To begin with, some of the 5 new tables may already be redundant, but you don't know that until you understand what the 1000 tables are really storing. Frequently, learning the application area is the biggest challenge for a developer when starting a new job.

The SQL language is simple to program and read even if when touching 10 tables. Complexities are abound though. The very first one: does the SQL statement touch the right data set? 999 records and 1000 or 998? T-SQL statements are turned into Transact-SQL scripts, stored procedures, user-defined functions and triggers, server-side database objects. They can be 5 statements or 1000 statements long programs. The style of Transact-SQL programming is different from the style in procedural programming languages. There are no arrays, only tables or table variables. Typically there is no looping, only set-based operations. Error control is different. Testing & debugging is relatively simple in Transact-SQL due to the interactive environment and the magic of selecting & executing a part without recompiling the whole.

## WHO THIS BOOK IS FOR

Developers, programmers and systems analysts who are new to relational database technology. Also developers, designers and administrators, who know some SQL programming and database design,  wish to expand their RDBMS design & development technology horizons. Familiarity with other computer language is assumed. The book has lots of queries, lots of T-SQL scripts, plenty to learn. The best way to learn it is to type in the query in your own SQL Server copy and test it, examine it, change it. Wouldn't it be easier just to copy & paste it? It would but the learning value would diminish. You need to feel the SQL language in your fingers. SQL queries must "pour" out from your fingers into the keyboard. Why is that so important? After everything can be found on the web and just copy & paste? Well not exactly. If you want to be an expert, it has to be in your head not on the web. Second, when your supervisor is looking over your shoulder, "Charlie, can you tell me what is the total revenue for March?", you have to be able to type in the query without SQL forum search and provide the results to your superior promptly.

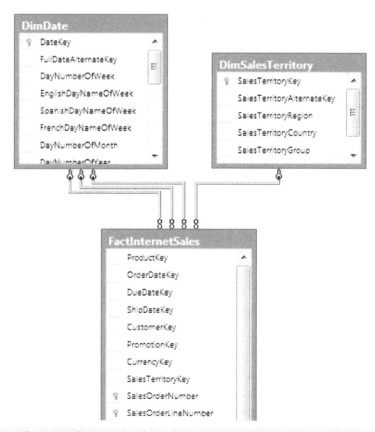

# ABOUT THIS BOOK

Beginning relational database design and beginning Transact-SQL programming. It is not a reference manual, rather learn by examples: there are over 1,100 SELECT queries in the book. Instead of imaginary tables, the book uses the SQL Server sample databases for explanations and examples: pubs (PRIMARY KEYs 9, FOREIGN KEYs 10) , Northwind (PRIMARY KEYs 13, FOREIGN KEYs 13) and the AdventureWorks family. Among them: AdventureWorks, AdventureWorks2008, AdventureWorks2012 (PRIMARY KEYs 71, FOREIGN KEYs 90), & AdventureWorksDW2012 (PRIMARY KEYs 27, FOREIGN KEYs 44). The book introduces relational database design concepts, then reinforces them again and again, not to bore the reader, rather indoctrinate with relational database design principles. Light weight SQL starts at the beginning of the book, because working with database metadata (not the content of the database, rather data which describes the database) is essential for understanding database design. By the time the reader gets to T-SQL programming, already knows basic SQL programming from the database design section of the book. The book was designed to be readable in any environment, even on the beach laptop around or no laptop in sight at all. All queries are followed by results row count and /or full/partial results listing in tabular (grid) format. For full benefits though, the reader should try out the T-SQL queries and scripts as he progresses from page to page, topic to topic. Example for SQL Server 2012 T-SQL query and results presentation.

```
SELECT          V.Name                              AS Vendor,
                FORMAT(SUM(POH.TotalDue), 'c', 'en-US')  AS [Total Purchase],
                FORMAT(AVG(POH.TotalDue), 'c', 'en-US')  AS [Average Purchase]
FROM AdventureWorks.Purchasing.Vendor AS V
   INNER JOIN AdventureWorks.Purchasing.PurchaseOrderHeader AS POH
       ON V.VendorID = POH.VendorID
GROUP BY V.Name  ORDER BY Vendor;
-- (79 row(s) affected) - Partial results.
```

| Vendor | Total Purchase | Average Purchase |
|---|---|---|
| Advanced Bicycles | $28,502.09 | $558.86 |
| Allenson Cycles | $498,589.59 | $9,776.27 |
| American Bicycles and Wheels | $9,641.01 | $189.04 |
| American Bikes | $1,149,489.84 | $22,539.02 |

## CONVENTIONS USED IN THIS BOOK

The Transact-SQL queries and scripts (sequence of statements) are shaded.

The number of resulting rows is displayed as a comment line: -- (79 row(s) affected) .

The results of the queries is usually displayed in grid format.

Less frequently the results are enclosed in comment markers: /*...... */ .

When a query is a trivial variation of a previous query, no result is displayed.

While the intention of the book is database design & database development, SQL Server installation and some database administration tasks are included.

This page is intentionally left blank.

This page is intentionally left blank.

# CHAPTER 1: SQL Server Sample & System Databases

## AdventureWorks Series of OLTP Databases

AdventureWorks sample On Line Transaction Processing (OLTP) database has been introduced with SQL Server 2005 to replace the previous sample database Northwind, a fictional gourmet food items distributor. The intent of the AdventureWorks sample database is to support the business operations of AdventureWorks Cycles, a fictitious mountain, touring and road bike manufacturer. The company sells through dealer network and online on the web. In addition to bikes, it sells frames and parts as well as accessories such as helmets, biking clothes and water bottles. The AdventureWorks2012 database image of Touring-1000 Blue, 50 bike in Production.ProductPhoto table.

T-SQL query to generate the list of tables of AdventureWorks2012 in 5 columns. The core query is simple. Presenting the results in 5 columns instead of 1 column adds a bit of complexity.

```
;WITH cteTableList AS (      SELECT CONCAT(SCHEMA_NAME(schema_id), '.', name)          AS  TableName,
  (( ROW_NUMBER() OVER( ORDER BY CONCAT(SCHEMA_NAME(schema_id),'.', name)) ) % 5)      AS  Remainder,
  (( ROW_NUMBER() OVER( ORDER BY CONCAT(SCHEMA_NAME(schema_id),'.', name)) - 1 )/ 5)   AS  Quotient
                      FROM AdventureWorks2012.sys.tables),
CTE AS (SELECT TableName, CASE WHEN Remainder=0 THEN 5 ELSE Remainder END AS Remainder, Quotient
        FROM cteTableList)
SELECT    MAX(CASE WHEN Remainder = 1 THEN TableName END),
          MAX(CASE WHEN Remainder = 2 THEN TableName END),
          MAX(CASE WHEN Remainder = 3 THEN TableName END),
          MAX(CASE WHEN Remainder = 4 THEN TableName END),
          MAX(CASE WHEN Remainder = 5 THEN TableName END)
FROM  CTE GROUP  BY Quotient ORDER  BY Quotient;
GO
```

## The query result set in grid format: tables in AdventureWorks2012

| | | | | |
|---|---|---|---|---|
| dbo.AWBuildVersion | dbo.DatabaseLog | dbo.ErrorLog | HumanResources.Department | HumanResources.Employee |
| HumanResources.EmployeeDepartmentHistory | HumanResources.EmployeePayHistory | HumanResources.JobCandidate | HumanResources.Shift | Person.Address |
| Person.AddressType | Person.BusinessEntity | Person.BusinessEntityAddress | Person.BusinessEntityContact | Person.ContactType |
| Person.CountryRegion | Person.EmailAddress | Person.Password | Person.Person | Person.PersonPhone |
| Person.PhoneNumberType | Person.StateProvince | Production.BillOfMaterials | Production.Culture | Production.Document |
| Production.Illustration | Production.Location | Production.Product | Production.ProductCategory | Production.ProductCostHistory |
| Production.ProductDescription | Production.ProductDocument | Production.ProductInventory | Production.ProductListPriceHistory | Production.ProductModel |
| Production.ProductModelIllustration | Production.ProductModelProductDescriptionCulture | Production.ProductPhoto | Production.ProductProductPhoto | Production.ProductReview |
| Production.ProductSubcategory | Production.ScrapReason | Production.TransactionHistory | Production.TransactionHistoryArchive | Production.UnitMeasure |
| Production.WorkOrder | Production.WorkOrderRouting | Purchasing.ProductVendor | Purchasing.PurchaseOrderDetail | Purchasing.PurchaseOrderHeader |
| Purchasing.ShipMethod | Purchasing.Vendor | Sales.CountryRegionCurrency | Sales.CreditCard | Sales.Currency |
| Sales.CurrencyRate | Sales.Customer | Sales.PersonCreditCard | Sales.SalesOrderDetail | Sales.SalesOrderHeader |
| Sales.SalesOrderHeaderSalesReason | Sales.SalesPerson | Sales.SalesPersonQuotaHistory | Sales.SalesReason | Sales.SalesTaxRate |
| Sales.SalesTerritory | Sales.SalesTerritoryHistory | Sales.ShoppingCartItem | Sales.SpecialOffer | Sales.SpecialOfferProduct |
| Sales.Store | NULL | NULL | NULL | NULL |

CHAPTER 1: SQL Server Sample & System Databases

## Diagram of Person.Person & Related Tables

Database diagram displays the Person.Person and related tables. PRIMARY KEYs are marked with a gold (in color display) key. The "oo-------->" line is interpreted as many-to-one relationship. For example a person (one) can have one or more (many) credit cards. The "oo" side is the table with **FOREIGN KEY** referencing the gold key side table with the **PRIMARY KEY**.

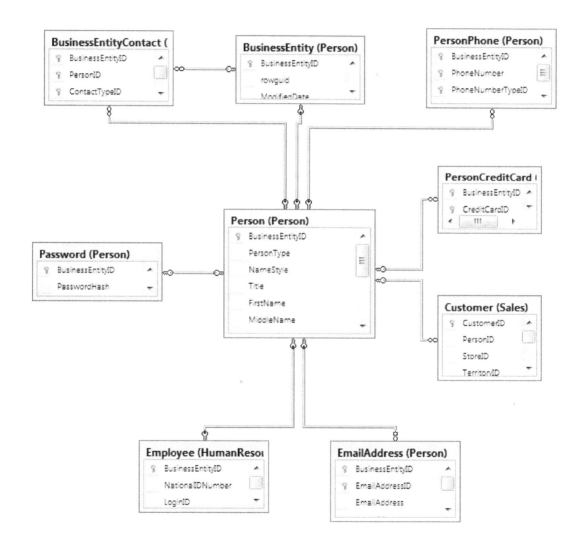

## Diagram of Sales.SalesOrderHeader and Related Tables

Database diagram displays Sales.SalesOrderHeader and all tables related with **FOREIGN KEY** constraints. The SalesOrderHeader table stores the general information about each order. Line items, e.g. 5 Helmets at $30 each,  are stored in the SalesOrderDetail table.

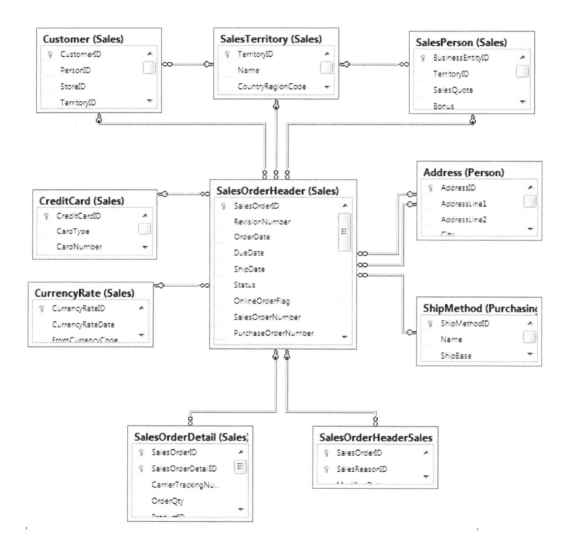

# SELECT Query Basics

We have to use "light-weight" SQL (Structured Query Language) in the database design lessons. The reason is that rather difficult to discuss any database related topic without demonstration T-SQL scripts, in fact it would not make sense. **Relational database** and the **SQL language** are "married" to each other forever and ever.

## The Simplest SELECT Statement

The simplest SELECT statement is "SELECT * FROM TableNameX" as demonstrated following. The "*" means wildcard inclusion of all columns in the table. Since there is no any other clause in the SELECT statement, it means also to retrieve all rows in the **table in no particular order**. Small tables which were populated in order are usually retrieved in order even though there is no ORDER BY clause. But this behaviour is purely coincidental. **Only ORDER BY clause can guarantee a sorted output.**

```
SELECT * FROM AdventureWorks2012.HumanResources.Department;
-- (16 row(s) affected)
```

| DepartmentID | Name | GroupName | ModifiedDate |
|---|---|---|---|
| 1 | Engineering | Research and Development | 2002-06-01 00:00:00.000 |
| 2 | Tool Design | Research and Development | 2002-06-01 00:00:00.000 |
| 3 | Sales | Sales and Marketing | 2002-06-01 00:00:00.000 |
| 4 | Marketing | Sales and Marketing | 2002-06-01 00:00:00.000 |
| 5 | Purchasing | Inventory Management | 2002-06-01 00:00:00.000 |
| 6 | Research and Development | Research and Development | 2002-06-01 00:00:00.000 |
| 7 | Production | Manufacturing | 2002-06-01 00:00:00.000 |
| 8 | Production Control | Manufacturing | 2002-06-01 00:00:00.000 |
| 9 | Human Resources | Executive General and Administration | 2002-06-01 00:00:00.000 |
| 10 | Finance | Executive General and Administration | 2002-06-01 00:00:00.000 |
| 11 | Information Services | Executive General and Administration | 2002-06-01 00:00:00.000 |
| 12 | Document Control | Quality Assurance | 2002-06-01 00:00:00.000 |
| 13 | Quality Assurance | Quality Assurance | 2002-06-01 00:00:00.000 |
| 14 | Facilities and Maintenance | Executive General and Administration | 2002-06-01 00:00:00.000 |
| 15 | Shipping and Receiving | Inventory Management | 2002-06-01 00:00:00.000 |
| 16 | Executive | Executive General and Administration | 2002-06-01 00:00:00.000 |

When tables are JOINed, SELECT * returns all the columns with all the data in the participant tables.

```
SELECT TOP 3 * FROM Sales.SalesOrderHeader H
            INNER JOIN Sales.SalesOrderDetail D
                ON H.SalesOrderID = D.SalesOrderID;
-- 121,317 rows in the JOIN
```

## *Query Result Set In Text Format*
If no grid format available, text format can be used. While it works, it is a challenge to read it, but computer geeks are used to this kind of data dump.

```
/* SalesOrderID RevisionNumber OrderDate        DueDate        ShipDate        Status
OnlineOrderFlag SalesOrderNumber        PurchaseOrderNumber    AccountNumber CustomerID
SalesPersonID TerritoryID BillToAddressID ShipToAddressID ShipMethodID CreditCardID
CreditCardApprovalCode CurrencyRateID SubTotal        TaxAmt        Freight        TotalDue
Comment                                                           rowguid
ModifiedDate        SalesOrderID SalesOrderDetailID CarrierTrackingNumber    OrderQty ProductID
SpecialOfferID UnitPrice        UnitPriceDiscount    LineTotal              rowguid
ModifiedDate
----------- -------------- ---------------------- ---------------------- ---------------------- ------ --------------- --------------------
------ ---------------------- --------------- ----------- ------------- ---------- --------------- --------------- --------------- ----------
- -------------------- ------------- ----------------- ---------------------- ----------------- -------------------- -------------------- ---------- --------------
--------------------------------------------------------------------- --------------------
---------- ---------------------- ----------- -------------- ---------------------- -------- -------------- ------------- -------------
-------- -------------------- ---------------------------------------------- ----------------------
43735    3       2005-07-10 00:00:00.000 2005-07-22 00:00:00.000 2005-07-17 00:00:00.000 5    1
SO43735        NULL        10-4030-016522 16522    NULL    9    25384    25384
1    6526    1034619Vi33896    119    3578.27    286.2616    89.4568
3953.9884    NULL                                98F80245-
C398-4562-BDAF-EA3E9A0DDFAC 2005-07-17 00:00:00.000 43735    391    NULL    1
749    1    3578.27    0.00    3578.270000        74838EF7-FDEB-4EB3-8978-
BA310FBA82E6 2005-07-10 00:00:00.000
43736    3       2005-07-10 00:00:00.000 2005-07-22 00:00:00.000 2005-07-17 00:00:00.000 5    1
SO43736        NULL        10-4030-011002 11002    NULL    9    20336    20336
1    1416    1135092Vi7270    119    3399.99    271.9992    84.9998
3756.989    NULL                                C14E29E7-
DB11-44EF-943E-143925A5A9AE 2005-07-17 00:00:00.000 43736    392    NULL    1
773    1    3399.99    0.00    3399.990000        3A0229FA-0A03-4126-
97CE-C3425968B670 2005-07-10 00:00:00.000
43737    3       2005-07-11 00:00:00.000 2005-07-23 00:00:00.000 2005-07-18 00:00:00.000 5    1
SO43737        NULL        10-4030-013261 13261    NULL    8    29772    29772
1    NULL    NULL    136    3578.27    286.2616    89.4568    3953.9884
NULL                                0B3E274D-E5A8-4E8C-A417-
0EAFABCFF162 2005-07-18 00:00:00.000 43737    393    NULL    1    750    1
3578.27    0.00    3578.270000        65AFCCE8-CA28-41C4-9A07-0265FB2DA5C8
2005-07-11 00:00:00.000

(3 row(s) affected)   */
```

## SELECT Query with WHERE Clause Predicate

Query to demonstrate how can we be selective with columns, furthermore, filter returned rows (WHERE clause) and sort them (ORDER BY clause).

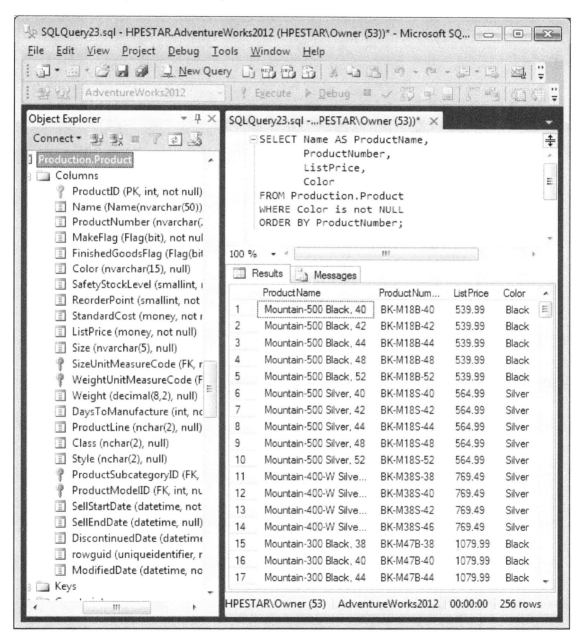

## Aggregating Data with GROUP BY Query

The second basic query is GROUP BY aggregation. It can be used to survey data at a high level.

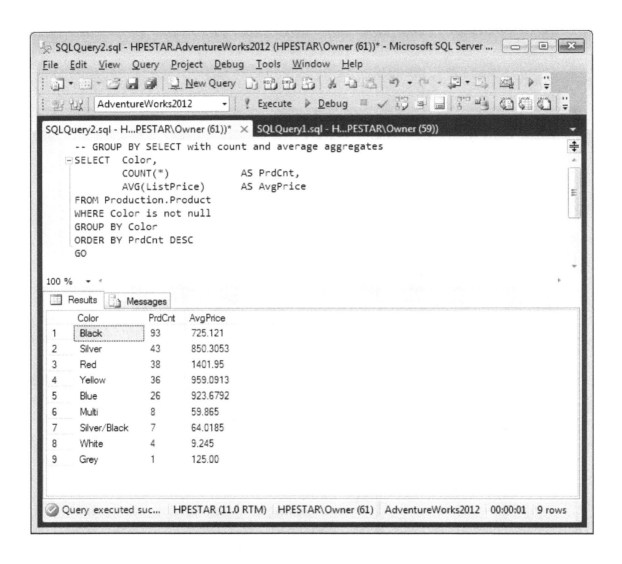

---

NOTE
GROUP BY aggregate queries can efficiently "fingerprint" (profile) data in tables, even millions of rows.
GROUP BY aggregates form the computational base of Business Intelligence.

---

## GROUP BY Query with 2 Tables & ORDER BY for Sorting

JOINing two tables on matching KEYs, FOREIGN KEY to PRIMARY KEY, to combine the data contents in a consistent fashion.

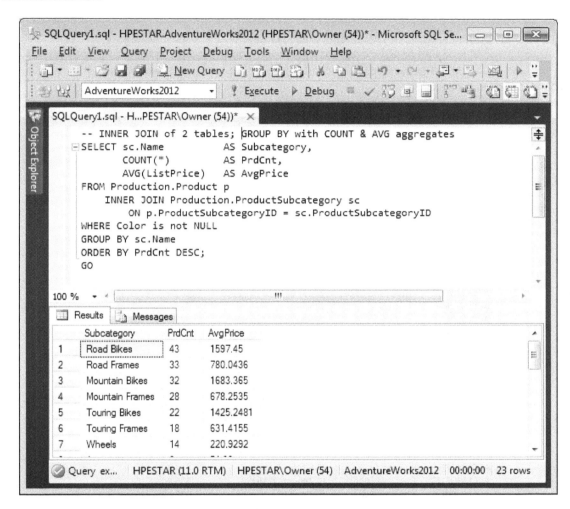

## LEN(), DATALENGTH(), LTRIM() & RTRIM() Functions

The LEN() function counts characters without the trailing spaces. DATALENGTH() counts storage bytes including trailing spaces. LTRIM() trims leading spaces, RTRIM() trims trailing spaces.

```
DECLARE @W varchar(32)= CHAR(32)+'Denver'+CHAR(32);
DECLARE @UW nvarchar(32) = CHAR(32)+N'MEGŐRZÉSE'+CHAR(32);  -- UNICODE 2 bytes per character
SELECT Length=LEN(@W), DLength=DATALENGTH (@W);                              -- 7  8
SELECT Length=LEN(@UW), DLength=DATALENGTH (@UW);                           -- 10 22
SELECT Length=LEN(LTRIM(RTRIM(@W))), DLength=DATALENGTH (LTRIM(RTRIM(@W)));  -- 6  6
SELECT Length=LEN(LTRIM(RTRIM(@UW))), DLength=DATALENGTH (LTRIM(RTRIM(@UW))); -- 9 18
```

**CHAPTER 1:  SQL Server Sample & System Databases**

## Finding All Accessories in Production.Product Table

Query to list all accessories ( a category) for sale.

USE AdventureWorks2012;

```
SELECT          UPPER(PC.Name) AS Category, PSC.Name          AS Subcategory,
                P.Name AS Product, FORMAT(ListPrice, 'c', 'en-US')  AS ListPrice,
                FORMAT(StandardCost, 'c', 'en-US')               AS StandardCost
FROM Production.Product AS P
   INNER JOIN Production.ProductSubcategory AS PSC
           ON PSC.ProductSubcategoryID = P.ProductSubcategoryID
   INNER JOIN Production.ProductCategory AS PC
           ON PC.ProductCategoryID = PSC.ProductCategoryID
WHERE PC.Name = 'Accessories'
ORDER BY Category, Subcategory, Product;
```

| Category | Subcategory | Product | ListPrice | StandardCost |
|---|---|---|---|---|
| ACCESSORIES | Bike Racks | Hitch Rack - 4-Bike | $120.00 | $44.88 |
| ACCESSORIES | Bike Stands | All-Purpose Bike Stand | $159.00 | $59.47 |
| ACCESSORIES | Bottles and Cages | Mountain Bottle Cage | $9.99 | $3.74 |
| ACCESSORIES | Bottles and Cages | Road Bottle Cage | $8.99 | $3.36 |
| ACCESSORIES | Bottles and Cages | Water Bottle - 30 oz. | $4.99 | $1.87 |
| ACCESSORIES | Cleaners | Bike Wash - Dissolver | $7.95 | $2.97 |
| ACCESSORIES | Fenders | Fender Set - Mountain | $21.98 | $8.22 |
| ACCESSORIES | Helmets | Sport-100 Helmet, Black | $34.99 | $13.09 |
| ACCESSORIES | Helmets | Sport-100 Helmet, Blue | $34.99 | $13.09 |
| ACCESSORIES | Helmets | Sport-100 Helmet, Red | $34.99 | $13.09 |
| ACCESSORIES | Hydration Packs | Hydration Pack - 70 oz. | $54.99 | $20.57 |
| ACCESSORIES | Lights | Headlights - Dual-Beam | $34.99 | $14.43 |
| ACCESSORIES | Lights | Headlights - Weatherproof | $44.99 | $18.56 |
| ACCESSORIES | Lights | Taillights - Battery-Powered | $13.99 | $5.77 |
| ACCESSORIES | Locks | Cable Lock | $25.00 | $10.31 |
| ACCESSORIES | Panniers | Touring-Panniers, Large | $125.00 | $51.56 |
| ACCESSORIES | Pumps | Minipump | $19.99 | $8.25 |
| ACCESSORIES | Pumps | Mountain Pump | $24.99 | $10.31 |
| ACCESSORIES | Tires and Tubes | HL Mountain Tire | $35.00 | $13.09 |
| ACCESSORIES | Tires and Tubes | HL Road Tire | $32.60 | $12.19 |
| ACCESSORIES | Tires and Tubes | LL Mountain Tire | $24.99 | $9.35 |
| ACCESSORIES | Tires and Tubes | LL Road Tire | $21.49 | $8.04 |
| ACCESSORIES | Tires and Tubes | ML Mountain Tire | $29.99 | $11.22 |
| ACCESSORIES | Tires and Tubes | ML Road Tire | $24.99 | $9.35 |
| ACCESSORIES | Tires and Tubes | Mountain Tire Tube | $4.99 | $1.87 |
| ACCESSORIES | Tires and Tubes | Patch Kit/8 Patches | $2.29 | $0.86 |
| ACCESSORIES | Tires and Tubes | Road Tire Tube | $3.99 | $1.49 |
| ACCESSORIES | Tires and Tubes | Touring Tire | $28.99 | $10.84 |
| ACCESSORIES | Tires and Tubes | Touring Tire Tube | $4.99 | $1.87 |

## How Can SQL Work without Looping?

Looping is implicit in the SQL language. The commands are set oriented and carried out for each member of the set be it 5 or 500 millions in an unordered manner.

SELECT * FROM AdventureWorks2012.Sales.SalesOrderDetail;     (121317 row(s) affected)

SQL Server database engine looped through internally on all rows in SalesOrderDetail table in an unordered way. In fact the database engine may have used some ordering for efficiency, but that behaviour is a blackbox as far as programming concerned. Implicit looping makes SQL statements so simple, yet immensely powerful for information access from low level to high level.

## Single-Valued SQL Queries

Single-valued SQL queries are very important because **we can use them where ever the T-SQL syntax requires a single value just by enclosing the query in parenthesis.**  The next T-SQL query returns a single value, a cell from the table which is the intersection of a row and a column.

SELECT ListPrice FROM AdventureWorks2012.Production.Product  WHERE ProductID = 800;
-- (1 row(s) affected)

| ListPrice |
| --- |
| 1120.49 |

**The ">" comparison operator requires a single value on the right hand side** so we plug in the single-valued query. The WHERE condition is evaluated for each row (implicit looping).

SELECT ProductID, Name AS ProductName, ListPrice
FROM AdventureWorks2012.Production.Product                              -- 504 rows
WHERE ListPrice > 2 *      (
                    **SELECT ListPrice FROM AdventureWorks2012.Production.Product**
                    **WHERE ProductID = 800**
                    **)**
ORDER BY ListPrice DESC, ProductName;
-- (35 row(s) affected) - Partial results.

| ProductID | ProductName | ListPrice |
| --- | --- | --- |
| 750 | Road-150 Red, 44 | 3578.27 |
| 751 | Road-150 Red, 48 | 3578.27 |
| 752 | Road-150 Red, 52 | 3578.27 |
| 753 | Road-150 Red, 56 | 3578.27 |
| 749 | Road-150 Red, 62 | 3578.27 |
| 771 | Mountain-100 Silver, 38 | 3399.99 |

CHAPTER 1:  SQL Server Sample & System Databases

## Data Dictionary Description of Tables in the Sales Schema

It is not easy to understand a database with 70 tables, even harder with 2,000 tables. Documentation is very helpful, if not essential, for any database. SQL Server provides Data Dictionary facility for documenting tables and other objects in the database. Data which describes the design & structure of a database is called **metadata**. Here is the high level documentation of tables in the Sales schema using the fn_listextendedproperty system function.

```
SELECT
        CONCAT('Sales.', objname COLLATE DATABASE_DEFAULT)      AS TableName,
        value                                                  AS [Description]
FROM fn_listextendedproperty (NULL, 'schema', 'Sales', 'table', default, NULL, NULL)
ORDER BY TableName;
```

| TableName | Description |
|---|---|
| Sales.ContactCreditCard | Cross-reference table mapping customers in the Contact table to their credit card information in the CreditCard table. |
| Sales.CountryRegionCurrency | Cross-reference table mapping ISO currency codes to a country or region. |
| Sales.CreditCard | Customer credit card information. |
| Sales.Currency | Lookup table containing standard ISO currencies. |
| Sales.CurrencyRate | Currency exchange rates. |
| Sales.Customer | Current customer information. Also see the Individual and Store tables. |
| Sales.CustomerAddress | Cross-reference table mapping customers to their address(es). |
| Sales.Individual | Demographic data about customers that purchase Adventure Works products online. |
| Sales.SalesOrderDetail | Individual products associated with a specific sales order. See SalesOrderHeader. |
| Sales.SalesOrderHeader | General sales order information. |
| Sales.SalesOrderHeaderSalesReason | Cross-reference table mapping sales orders to sales reason codes. |
| Sales.SalesPerson | Sales representative current information. |
| Sales.SalesPersonQuotaHistory | Sales performance tracking. |
| Sales.SalesReason | Lookup table of customer purchase reasons. |
| Sales.SalesTaxRate | Tax rate lookup table. |
| Sales.SalesTerritory | Sales territory lookup table. |
| Sales.SalesTerritoryHistory | Sales representative transfers to other sales territories. |
| Sales.ShoppingCartItem | Contains online customer orders until the order is submitted or cancelled. |
| Sales.SpecialOffer | Sale discounts lookup table. |
| Sales.SpecialOfferProduct | Cross-reference table mapping products to special offer discounts. |
| Sales.Store | Customers (resellers) of Adventure Works products. |
| Sales.StoreContact | Cross-reference table mapping stores and their employees. |

## NULL Values in Tables & Query Results

**NULL means no value**. If so why do we capitalize it? We don't have to. Somehow, it became a custom in the RDBMS industry, nobody knows anymore how it started. Since the U.S. default collation for server and databases are case insensitive, we can just use "null" as well. **NULL value is different from empty string (") or 0 (zero) which can be tested by the "=" or "!=" operators.** If a database table does not have a value in a cell for whatever reason, it is marked (flagged) as NULL by the database engine. When a value is entered, the NULL marking goes away. **NULL values can be tested by "IS NULL" or "IS NOT NULL" operators, but not the "=" or "!=" operators.**

The likelihood is high that the color attribute is not applicable to items like tire tube, that is the reason that some cell values were left unassigned (null).

```
SELECT TOP 5     Name                        AS ProductName,
                 ProductNumber,
                 ListPrice,
                 Color
FROM AdventureWorks2012.Production.Product  WHERE Color IS NULL
ORDER BY ProductName DESC;
```

| ProductName | ProductNumber | ListPrice | Color |
|---|---|---|---|
| Water Bottle - 30 oz. | WB-H098 | 4.99 | NULL |
| Touring Tire Tube | TT-T092 | 4.99 | NULL |
| Touring Tire | TI-T723 | 28.99 | NULL |
| Touring Rim | RM-T801 | 0.00 | NULL |
| Touring End Caps | EC-T209 | 0.00 | NULL |

We can do random selection as well and get a mix of products with color and null value.

```
SELECT TOP 5     Name AS ProductName, ProductNumber, ListPrice, Color
FROM AdventureWorks2012.Production.Product
ORDER BY NEWID();        -- Random sort
```

| ProductName | ProductNumber | ListPrice | Color |
|---|---|---|---|
| Touring-1000 Yellow, 46 | BK-T79Y-46 | 2384.07 | Yellow |
| HL Spindle/Axle | SD-9872 | 0.00 | NULL |
| ML Mountain Tire | TI-M602 | 29.99 | NULL |
| Road-650 Red, 60 | BK-R50R-60 | 782.99 | Red |
| Pinch Bolt | PB-6109 | 0.00 | NULL |

## NULL Values Generated by Queries

NULL values can be generated by queries as well. Typically, LEFT JOIN, RIGHT JOIN and some functions generate NULLs. The meaning of OUTER JOINs: include no-match rows from the left or right table in addition to the matching rows.

```
SELECT TOP 5
           PS.Name                    AS Category,
           P.Name                     AS ProductName,
           ProductNumber,
           ListPrice,
           Color
FROM AdventureWorks2012.Production.Product P
   RIGHT JOIN AdventureWorks2012.Production.ProductSubcategory PS
        ON PS.ProductSubcategoryID = P.ProductSubcategoryID
     AND ListPrice >= 3500.0
ORDER BY newid();
GO
```

| Category | ProductName | ProductNumber | ListPrice | Color |
|----------|-------------|---------------|-----------|-------|
| Road Bikes | Road-150 Red, 62 | BK-R93R-62 | 3578.27 | Red |
| Road Bikes | Road-150 Red, 52 | BK-R93R-52 | 3578.27 | Red |
| Bib-Shorts | NULL | NULL | NULL | NULL |
| Socks | NULL | NULL | NULL | NULL |
| Cranksets | NULL | NULL | NULL | NULL |

Some system functions, like the brand new TRY_CONVERT(), can generate NULL values as well. If the PostalCode cannot be converted into an integer, TRY_CONVERT() returns NULL.

```
SELECT TOP 5    ConvertedZip = TRY_CONVERT(INT, PostalCode),
         AddressLine1,    City, PostalCode
FROM Person.Address
ORDER by newid();
```

| ConvertedZip | AddressLine1 | City | PostalCode |
|--------------|-------------|------|------------|
| 91945 | 5979 El Pueblo | Lemon Grove | 91945 |
| NULL | 7859 Green Valley Road | London | W1V 5RN |
| 3220 | 6004 Peabody Road | Geelong | 3220 |
| NULL | 6713 Eaker Way | Burnaby | V3J 6Z3 |
| NULL | 5153 Hackamore Lane | Shawnee | V8Z 4N5 |

## The SOUNDEX() Function to Check Sound Alikes

The soundex() function is very interesting for testing different spelling of words such as names.

```
USE AdventureWorks2012;
GO

SELECT DISTINCT LastName FROM Person.Person
WHERE soundex(LastName)  = soundex('Steel');
GO
```

| LastName |
| --- |
| Seidel |
| Sotelo |
| Stahl |
| Steel |
| Steele |

```
SELECT DISTINCT LastName FROM Person.Person
WHERE soundex(LastName)  = soundex('Brown');
GO
```

| LastName |
| --- |
| Bourne |
| Brian |
| Brown |
| Browne |
| Bruno |

```
SELECT DISTINCT FirstName FROM Person.Person
WHERE soundex(FirstName)  = soundex('Mary');
GO
```

| FirstName |
| --- |
| Mari |
| Maria |
| María |
| Mariah |
| Marie |
| Mario |
| Mary |
| Mary Lou |
| Mayra |

# Building an FK-PK Diagram in AdventureWorks2012

The **FOREIGN KEY - PRIMARY KEY** diagram of AdventureWorks2012 database with over 70 tables can be built just by adding the tables to the diagram. The FK-PK lines are automatically drawn. An FK-PK line represents a predefined referential constraint.

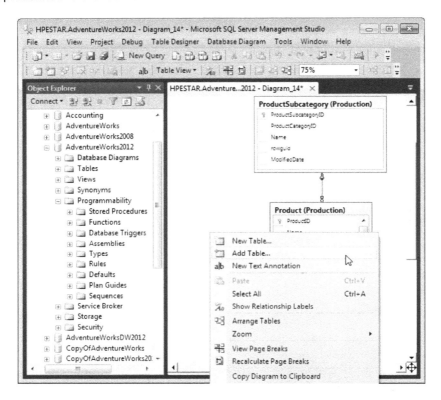

While all tables are important in a database, tables with the most connections play central roles, in a way analogous to the Sun with planets around it.

```
-- PRIMARY KEY tables with the most FOREIGN KEY references
SELECT          schema_name(schema_id)          AS SchemaName,
                o.name                           AS PKTable,
                count(*)                         AS FKCount
FROM sys.sysforeignkeys s   INNER JOIN sys.objects o      ON s.rkeyid = o.object_id
GROUP BY schema_id, o.name    HAVING count(*) >= 5    ORDER BY FKCount DESC;
```

| SchemaName | PKTable | FKCount |
|---|---|---|
| Production | Product | 14 |
| Person | Person | 7 |
| HumanResources | Employee | 6 |
| Person | BusinessEntity | 5 |
| Sales | SalesTerritory | 5 |

**CHAPTER 1:  SQL Server Sample & System Databases**

# AdventureWorksDW Data Warehouse Database

AdventureWorksDW contains second hand data only since it is a Data Warehouse database. All the data originates from other sources such as the AdventureWorks OLTP database and Excel worksheets. The tables in the data warehousing database are divided between two groups: dimension tables and fact tables.

## Diagram of a Star Schema in AdventureWorksDW2012

The high level star schema diagram in AdventureWorksDW2012 Data Warehouse database with FactResellerSales fact table and related dimension tables. The temporal dimension table DimDate plays a central role in Business Intelligence data analytics.

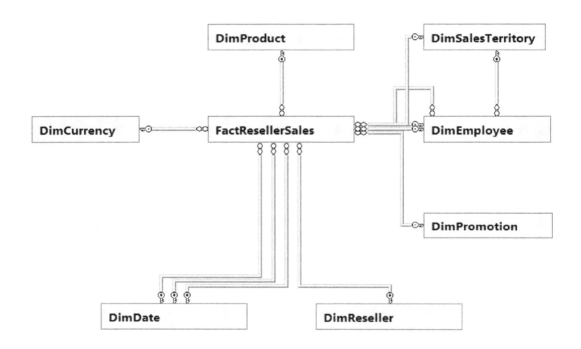

Distribution of **PRIMARY KEY - FOREIGN KEY** relationships can be generated from metadata (system views) for the entire Data Warehouse.

```
SELECT   schema_name(schema_id) AS SchemaName, o.name AS PKTable,  count(*) AS FKCount
FROM sys.sysforeignkeys s   INNER JOIN sys.objects o    ON s.rkeyid = o.object_id
GROUP BY schema_id, o.name  HAVING COUNT(*) > 2 ORDER BY FKCount DESC;
```

| SchemaName | PKTable | FKCount |
|---|---|---|
| dbo | DimDate | 12 |
| dbo | DimCurrency | 4 |
| dbo | DimSalesTerritory | 4 |
| dbo | DimEmployee | 3 |
| dbo | DimProduct | 3 |

# AdventureWorks2008 Sample Database

There were substantial changes made from the prior version of the sample database. Among them demonstration use of the **hierarchyid** data type which has been introduced with SS 2008 to support sophisticated tree hierarchy processing. In addition employee, customer and dealer PRIMARY KEYs are pooled together and called BusinessEntityID.

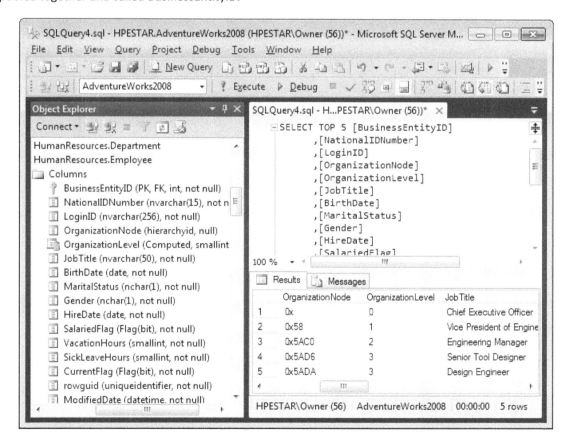

# AdventureWorks2012 Sample Database

There were no apparent design changes made from the prior version of the sample database. A significant content change: dates were advanced 4 years. An OrderDate (Sales.SalesOrderHeader table) of 2004-02-01 in previous versions is now 2008-02-01.

The OrderDate statistics in the two sample databases.

```
SELECT  [Year]              = YEAR(OrderDate),      OrderCount      = COUNT(*)
FROM AdventureWorks2008.Sales.SalesOrderHeader GROUP BY YEAR(OrderDate)
ORDER BY [Year];
```

| Year | OrderCount |
|------|------------|
| 2001 | 1379 |
| 2002 | 3692 |
| 2003 | 12443 |
| 2004 | 13951 |

```
SELECT  [Year]              = YEAR(OrderDate),      OrderCount      = COUNT(*)
FROM AdventureWorks2012.Sales.SalesOrderHeader GROUP BY YEAR(OrderDate)
ORDER BY [Year];
```

| Year | OrderCount |
|------|------------|
| 2005 | 1379 |
| 2006 | 3692 |
| 2007 | 12443 |
| 2008 | 13951 |

Starting with SQL Server 2012, numeric figures, among others, can be formatted with the FORMAT function.

```
SELECT  [Year]              = YEAR(OrderDate),
             OrderCount      = FORMAT(COUNT(*), '###,###')
FROM AdventureWorks2012.Sales.SalesOrderHeader
GROUP BY YEAR(OrderDate)  ORDER BY [Year];
```

| Year | OrderCount |
|------|------------|
| 2005 | 1,379 |
| 2006 | 3,692 |
| 2007 | 12,443 |
| 2008 | 13,951 |

## Production.Product and Related Tables

The Product table is the "center" of the database. The reason is that AdventureWorks Cycles is a product base company selling through dealers and directly to consumers through the internet. You may wonder why are we pushing **FOREIGN KEY - PRIMARY KEY** relationship so vehemently? Because there is nothing else to a database just **well-designed tables and their connections which are FK-PK constraints**.

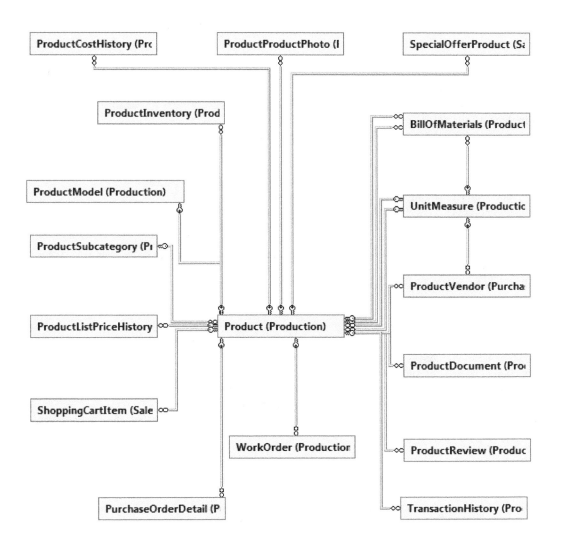

## Descriptions of Columns in Production.Product Table

Queries to list the description of table and columns from Extended Property (data dictionary).

```
USE AdventureWorks2012;
SELECT          objname AS TableName, value      AS [Description]
FROM fn_listextendedproperty(    NULL, 'schema', 'Production', 'table', 'Product', NULL, NULL);
```

| TableName | Description |
|---|---|
| Product | Products sold or used in the manfacturing of sold products. |

```
SELECT          'Production.Product'          AS TableName,            -- String literal
                objname                       AS ColumnName,
                value                         AS [Description]
FROM fn_listextendedproperty(    NULL, 'schema', 'Production', 'table',
                'Product', 'column', default);
```

| TableName | ColumnName | Description |
|---|---|---|
| Production.Product | ProductID | Primary key for Product records. |
| Production.Product | Name | Name of the product. |
| Production.Product | ProductNumber | Unique product identification number. |
| Production.Product | MakeFlag | 0 = Product is purchased, 1 = Product is manufactured in-house. |
| Production.Product | FinishedGoodsFlag | 0 = Product is not a salable item. 1 = Product is salable. |
| Production.Product | Color | Product color. |
| Production.Product | SafetyStockLevel | Minimum inventory quantity. |
| Production.Product | ReorderPoint | Inventory level that triggers a purchase order or work order. |
| Production.Product | StandardCost | Standard cost of the product. |
| Production.Product | ListPrice | Selling price. |
| Production.Product | Size | Product size. |
| Production.Product | SizeUnitMeasureCode | Unit of measure for Size column. |
| Production.Product | WeightUnitMeasureCode | Unit of measure for Weight column. |
| Production.Product | Weight | Product weight. |
| Production.Product | DaysToManufacture | Number of days required to manufacture the product. |
| Production.Product | ProductLine | R = Road, M = Mountain, T = Touring, S = Standard |
| Production.Product | Class | H = High, M = Medium, L = Low |
| Production.Product | Style | W = Womens, M = Mens, U = Universal |
| Production.Product | ProductSubcategoryID | Product is a member of this product subcategory. Foreign key to ProductSubCategory.ProductSubCategoryID. |
| Production.Product | ProductModelID | Product is a member of this product model. Foreign key to ProductModel.ProductModelID. |
| Production.Product | SellStartDate | Date the product was available for sale. |
| Production.Product | SellEndDate | Date the product was no longer available for sale. |
| Production.Product | DiscontinuedDate | Date the product was discontinued. |
| Production.Product | rowguid | ROWGUIDCOL number uniquely identifying the record. Used to support a merge replication sample. |
| Production.Product | ModifiedDate | Date and time the record was last updated. |

## Mountain Bikes in Production.Product Table

Query to list all mountain bikes offered for sale by AdventureWorks Cycles with category, subcategory, list price and standard cost information.

```
USE AdventureWorks2012;
GO
SELECT  UPPER(PC.Name) AS Category, PSC.Name AS Subcategory,
        P.Name AS Product, FORMAT(ListPrice, 'c', 'en-US') AS ListPrice,
        FORMAT(StandardCost, 'c', 'en-US') AS StandardCost
FROM Production.Product AS P
   INNER JOIN Production.ProductSubcategory AS PSC
           ON PSC.ProductSubcategoryID = P.ProductSubcategoryID
   INNER JOIN Production.ProductCategory AS PC
           ON PC.ProductCategoryID = PSC.ProductCategoryID
WHERE PSC.Name = 'Mountain Bikes'
ORDER BY Category, Subcategory, Product;
```

| Category | Subcategory | Product | ListPrice | StandardCost |
|---|---|---|---|---|
| BIKES | Mountain Bikes | Mountain-100 Black, 38 | $3,374.99 | $1,898.09 |
| BIKES | Mountain Bikes | Mountain-100 Black, 42 | $3,374.99 | $1,898.09 |
| BIKES | Mountain Bikes | Mountain-100 Black, 44 | $3,374.99 | $1,898.09 |
| BIKES | Mountain Bikes | Mountain-100 Black, 48 | $3,374.99 | $1,898.09 |
| BIKES | Mountain Bikes | Mountain-100 Silver, 38 | $3,399.99 | $1,912.15 |
| BIKES | Mountain Bikes | Mountain-100 Silver, 42 | $3,399.99 | $1,912.15 |
| BIKES | Mountain Bikes | Mountain-100 Silver, 44 | $3,399.99 | $1,912.15 |
| BIKES | Mountain Bikes | Mountain-100 Silver, 48 | $3,399.99 | $1,912.15 |
| BIKES | Mountain Bikes | Mountain-200 Black, 38 | $2,294.99 | $1,251.98 |
| BIKES | Mountain Bikes | Mountain-200 Black, 42 | $2,294.99 | $1,251.98 |
| BIKES | Mountain Bikes | Mountain-200 Black, 46 | $2,294.99 | $1,251.98 |
| BIKES | Mountain Bikes | Mountain-200 Silver, 38 | $2,319.99 | $1,265.62 |
| BIKES | Mountain Bikes | Mountain-200 Silver, 42 | $2,319.99 | $1,265.62 |
| BIKES | Mountain Bikes | Mountain-200 Silver, 46 | $2,319.99 | $1,265.62 |
| BIKES | Mountain Bikes | Mountain-300 Black, 38 | $1,079.99 | $598.44 |
| BIKES | Mountain Bikes | Mountain-300 Black, 40 | $1,079.99 | $598.44 |
| BIKES | Mountain Bikes | Mountain-300 Black, 44 | $1,079.99 | $598.44 |
| BIKES | Mountain Bikes | Mountain-300 Black, 48 | $1,079.99 | $598.44 |
| BIKES | Mountain Bikes | Mountain-400-W Silver, 38 | $769.49 | $419.78 |
| BIKES | Mountain Bikes | Mountain-400-W Silver, 40 | $769.49 | $419.78 |
| BIKES | Mountain Bikes | Mountain-400-W Silver, 42 | $769.49 | $419.78 |
| BIKES | Mountain Bikes | Mountain-400-W Silver, 46 | $769.49 | $419.78 |
| BIKES | Mountain Bikes | Mountain-500 Black, 40 | $539.99 | $294.58 |
| BIKES | Mountain Bikes | Mountain-500 Black, 42 | $539.99 | $294.58 |
| BIKES | Mountain Bikes | Mountain-500 Black, 44 | $539.99 | $294.58 |
| BIKES | Mountain Bikes | Mountain-500 Black, 48 | $539.99 | $294.58 |
| BIKES | Mountain Bikes | Mountain-500 Black, 52 | $539.99 | $294.58 |
| BIKES | Mountain Bikes | Mountain-500 Silver, 40 | $564.99 | $308.22 |
| BIKES | Mountain Bikes | Mountain-500 Silver, 42 | $564.99 | $308.22 |
| BIKES | Mountain Bikes | Mountain-500 Silver, 44 | $564.99 | $308.22 |
| BIKES | Mountain Bikes | Mountain-500 Silver, 48 | $564.99 | $308.22 |
| BIKES | Mountain Bikes | Mountain-500 Silver, 52 | $564.99 | $308.22 |

# Prior SQL Server Sample Databases

There are two other sample databases used in the releases of SQL Server: **Northwind** and **pubs**. Northwind has been introduced with SQL Server 7.0 in 1998. That SQL Server version had very short lifetime, replaced with SQL Server 2000 in year 2000. The pubs sample database originates from the time Microsoft & Sybase worked jointly on the database server project around 1990. Despite the relative simplicity of pre-2005 sample databases, they were good enough to demonstrate basic RDBMS SQL queries.

Book sales summary GROUP BY aggregation query.

```
USE pubs;

SELECT pub_name              AS Publisher,
    au_lname                 AS Author,
    title                    AS Title,
    SUM(qty)                 AS SoldQty
FROM  authors
    INNER JOIN titleauthor
        ON authors.au_id = titleauthor.au_id
    INNER JOIN titles
        ON titles.title_id = titleauthor.title_id
    INNER JOIN publishers
        ON publishers.pub_id = titles.pub_id
    INNER JOIN sales
        ON sales.title_id = titles.title_id
GROUP  BY pub_name,   au_lname,      title
ORDER BY Publisher, Author, Title;
-- (23 row(s) affected) - Partial results.
```

| Publisher | Author | Title |
|---|---|---|
| Algodata Infosystems | Bennet | The Busy Executive's Database Guide |
| Algodata Infosystems | Carson | But Is It User Friendly? |
| Algodata Infosystems | Dull | Secrets of Silicon Valley |
| Algodata Infosystems | Green | The Busy Executive's Database Guide |
| Algodata Infosystems | Hunter | Secrets of Silicon Valley |
| Algodata Infosystems | MacFeather | Cooking with Computers: Surreptitious Balance Sheets |
| Algodata Infosystems | O'Leary | Cooking with Computers: Surreptitious Balance Sheets |
| Algodata Infosystems | Straight | Straight Talk About Computers |
| Binnet & Hardley | Blotchet-Halls | Fifty Years in Buckingham Palace Kitchens |
| Binnet & Hardley | DeFrance | The Gourmet Microwave |

# Northwind Sample Database

The Northwind sample database contains well-prepared sales data for a fictitious company called Northwind Traders, which imports & exports specialty gourmet foods & drinks from wholesale suppliers around the world. The company's sales offices are located in Seattle and London. Among the gourmet food item products: Carnarvon Tigers, Teatime Chocolate Biscuits, Sir Rodney's Marmalade, Sir Rodney's Scones, Gustaf's Knäckebröd, Tunnbröd & Guaraná Fantástica.

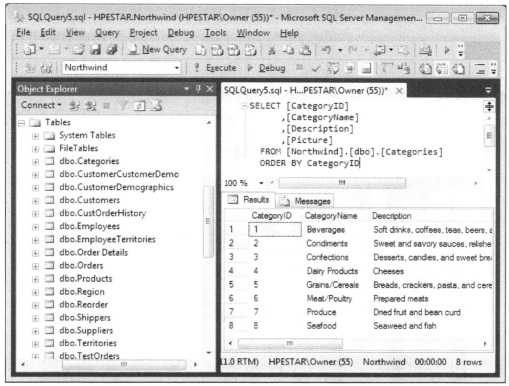

## Diagram of Northwind Database

The basic diagram of Northwind database excluding a few ancillary tables. The Orders table is central since the business is wholesale distribution (reselling) of high-end food products.

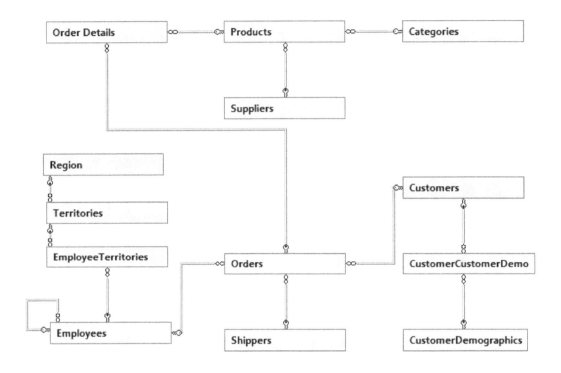

CHAPTER 1: SQL Server Sample & System Databases

# pubs  Sample Database

The pubs database is a very small and simple publishing database, yet it demonstrates the main features of database design such as PRIMARY KEYs, FOREIGN KEYs, and junction table reflecting many-to-many relationship. The main entities (tables) are: (book) titles, authors, titleauthor (junction table), publishers, sales & royalties.

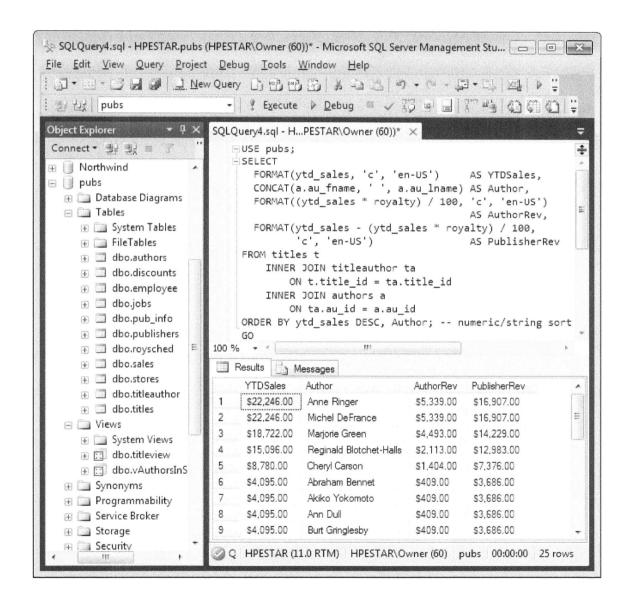

## Book Titles in pubs Database

The titles table has the most interesting content in the pubs database as demonstrated by the following T-SQL query.

```
SELECT  TOP 4 title_id AS TitleID, title AS Title, type                   AS Type,
        pub_id AS PubID, FORMAT(price, 'c','en-US')                       AS Price,
        FORMAT(advance, 'c','en-US')                                      AS  Advance,
        FORMAT(royalty/100.0, 'p') AS Royalty, FORMAT(ytd_sales, 'c', 'en-US')  AS YTDSales,
        Notes
FROM pubs.dbo.titles ORDER BY title;
```

| TitleID | Title | Type | PubID | Price | Advance | Royalty | YTDSales | Notes |
|---------|-------|------|-------|-------|---------|---------|----------|-------|
| PC1035 | But Is It User Friendly? | popular_comp | 1389 | $22.95 | $7,000.00 | 16.00 % | $8,780.00 | A survey of software for the naive user, focusing on the 'friendliness' of each. |
| PS1372 | Computer Phobic AND Non-Phobic Individuals: Behavior Variations | psychology | 0877 | $21.59 | $7,000.00 | 10.00 % | $375.00 | A must for the specialist, this book examines the difference between those who hate and fear computers and those who don't. |
| BU1111 | Cooking with Computers: Surreptitious Balance Sheets | business | 1389 | $11.95 | $5,000.00 | 10.00 % | $3,876.00 | Helpful hints on how to use your electronic resources to the best advantage. |
| PS7777 | Emotional Security: A New Algorithm | psychology | 0736 | $7.99 | $4,000.00 | 10.00 % | $3,336.00 | Protecting yourself and your loved ones from undue emotional stress in the modern world. Use of computer and nutritional aids emphasized. |

# Diagram of pubs Database

Since pubs is a small database, the diagram conveniently fits on a page.

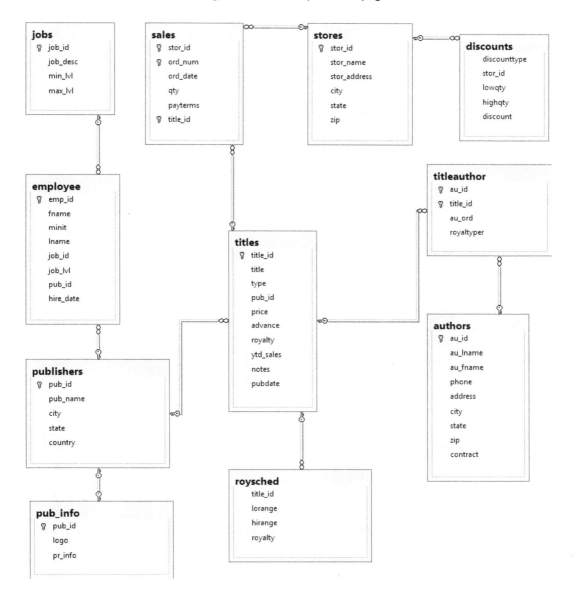

# SQL Server System Databases

The master, model, tempdb and msdb are system databases for special database server operations purposes.

SSMS Object Explorer drill-down listing of system databases.

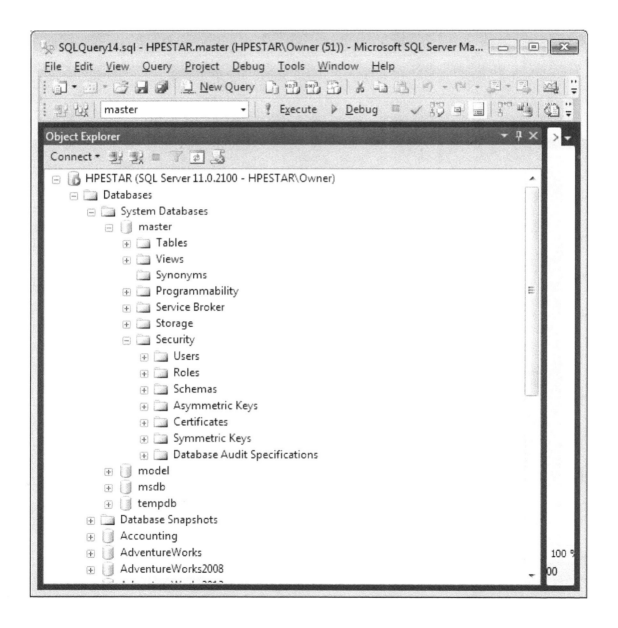

# The master Database

The master system database is the nerve center of SQL Server. It contains tables and db objects essential for server operations. System tables are accessible only through read-only views, they cannot be changed by users.  A subset of the system views are called Dynamic Management Views (DMV) which return server state information for monitoring the operational aspects of a SQL Server instance, diagnosing problems, and  performance tuning.  Dynamic Management Functions (DMF) are applied in conjunction with DMVs.

```
SELECT TOP 5 ST.text, EQS.*
FROM master.sys.dm_exec_query_stats AS EQS              -- DMV
CROSS APPLY master.sys.dm_exec_sql_text(EQS.sql_handle) as ST      -- DMF
ORDER BY last_worker_time DESC;
```

Object Explorer display of some objects in the master database and query listing of databases.

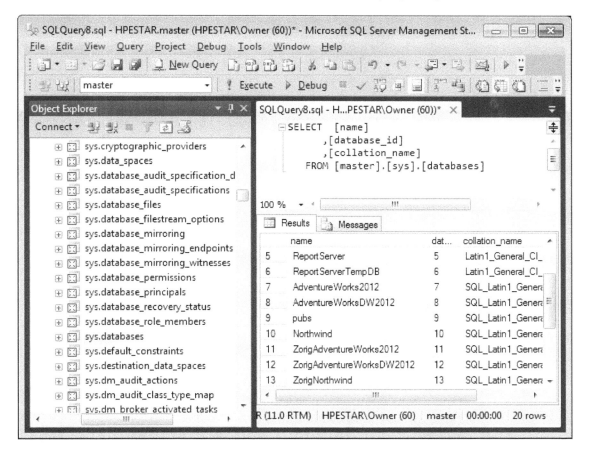

*An Important System View In master Database: sys.databases*

SELECT TOP (10) name, database_id FROM master.sys.databases ORDER BY database_id;

| name | database_id |
|------|-------------|
| master | 1 |
| tempdb | 2 |
| model | 3 |
| msdb | 4 |
| ReportServer | 5 |
| ReportServerTempDB | 6 |
| AdventureWorks2012 | 7 |
| AdventureWorksDW2012 | 8 |
| pubs | 9 |
| Northwind | 10 |

The spt_values table in the master database can be used for integer sequence with a range of 0 - 2047.

-- End of the range - BOTTOM
SELECT TOP 5 number FROM master.dbo.spt_values WHERE TYPE='P' ORDER BY number DESC;

| number |
|--------|
| 2047 |
| 2046 |
| 2045 |
| 2044 |
| 2043 |

Example for using the sequence in spt_values to generate DATE and MONTH sequences.

SELECT TOP 5 number,     dateadd(day, number, '20000101')          AS "Date",
                         dateadd(mm, number, '20000101')           AS "Month"
FROM **master.dbo.spt_values** WHERE type = 'P' ORDER BY number;

| number | Date | Month |
|--------|------|-------|
| 0 | 2000-01-01 00:00:00.000 | 2000-01-01 00:00:00.000 |
| 1 | 2000-01-02 00:00:00.000 | 2000-02-01 00:00:00.000 |
| 2 | 2000-01-03 00:00:00.000 | 2000-03-01 00:00:00.000 |
| 3 | 2000-01-04 00:00:00.000 | 2000-04-01 00:00:00.000 |
| 4 | 2000-01-05 00:00:00.000 | 2000-05-01 00:00:00.000 |

## The model Database

The model database serves as prototype for a new database and tempdb when the SQL Server instance started. Upon server shutdown or restart everything is wiped out of tempdb, it starts with a clean slate as a copy of the model database.

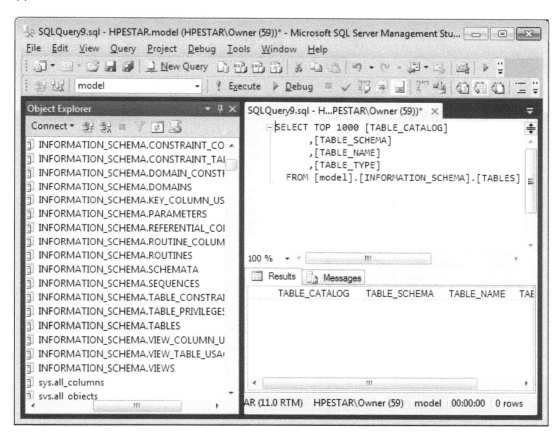

## The msdb Database

The msdb database is used for server internal operations such as support for SQL Server Agent job scheduling facility or keeping track of database the all important backups and restores.

## The tempdb Database

The tempdb serves as temporary database for system operations such as sorting. Temporary tables (#temp1) and global temporary tables ( ##globaltemp1) are stored in the tempdb as well. "Permanent" tables can be created  in tempdb with a short lifetime which lasts till shutdown or restart.

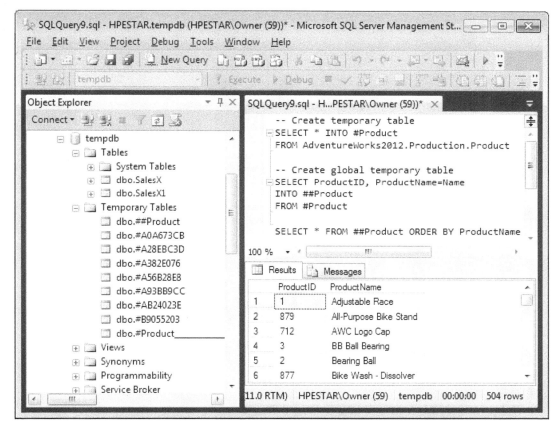

CHAPTER 1:  SQL Server Sample & System Databases

## *Sudden Death in tempdb When Server Restarts*

Even though a temporary table and a global temporary table are created and queried in the context setting for AdventureWorks2012 database, they are placed into tempdb automatically. Same consideration when a temporary table is created from a stored procedure which is compiled in an application database. Upon server restart everything is wiped out of tempdb, rebirth follows as a copy of model db.

# CHAPTER 3:  Structure of the SELECT Statement

## The SELECT Clause

The SELECT clause is the only required clause in a SELECT statement, all the other clauses are optional. The SELECT columns can be literals (constants), expressions, table columns and even subqueries. Lines can be commented with "--".

```
SELECT 15 * 15;                          -- 225

SELECT Today = convert(DATE, getdate());    -- 2016-07-27

SELECT          Color,
                ProdCnt          = COUNT(*),
                AvgPrice         = FORMAT(AVG(ListPrice),'c','en-US')
FROM AdventureWorks2012.Production.Product p
WHERE Color is not null
GROUP BY Color   HAVING count(*) > 10
ORDER BY AvgPrice DESC;
GO
```

| Color  | ProdCnt | AvgPrice   |
|--------|---------|------------|
| Yellow | 36      | $959.09    |
| Blue   | 26      | $923.68    |
| Silver | 43      | $850.31    |
| Black  | 93      | $725.12    |
| Red    | 38      | $1,401.95  |

```
-- Equivalent with column aliases on the right
SELECT          Color,
                COUNT(*)                              AS ProdCnt,
                FORMAT(AVG(ListPrice),'c','en-US')    AS AvgPrice
FROM AdventureWorks2012.Production.Product p
WHERE Color is not null  GROUP BY Color
HAVING count(*) > 10
ORDER BY AvgPrice DESC;
GO
```

## SELECT with Search Expression

SELECT statement can have complex expressions for text or numbers as demonstrated in the next T-SQL query for finding the street name in AddressLine1 column.

```
SELECT  AddressID,
        SUBSTRING(AddressLine1, CHARINDEX(' ', AddressLine1+' ', 1) +1,
        CHARINDEX(' ', AddressLine1+' ', CHARINDEX(' ', AddressLine1+' ', 1) +1) -
        CHARINDEX(' ', AddressLine1+' ', 1) -1)                                    AS StreetName,
        AddressLine1,
        City
FROM AdventureWorks2012.Person.Address
WHERE ISNUMERIC (LEFT(AddressLine1,1))=1
  AND City = 'Seattle'
ORDER BY AddressLine1;
-- -- (141 row(s) affected)- Partial results.
```

| AddressID | StreetName | AddressLine1 | City |
|---|---|---|---|
| 13079 | boulevard | 081, boulevard du Montparnasse | Seattle |
| 859 | Oak | 1050 Oak Street | Seattle |
| 110 | Slow | 1064 Slow Creek Road | Seattle |
| 113 | Ravenwood | 1102 Ravenwood | Seattle |
| 95 | Bradford | 1220 Bradford Way | Seattle |
| 32510 | Steven | 1349 Steven Way | Seattle |
| 118 | Balboa | 136 Balboa Court | Seattle |
| 32519 | Mazatlan | 137 Mazatlan | Seattle |
| 25869 | Calle | 1386 Calle Verde | Seattle |
| 114 | Yorba | 1398 Yorba Linda | Seattle |
| 15657 | Book | 151 Book Ct | Seattle |
| 105 | Stillman | 1619 Stillman Court | Seattle |
| 18002 | Carmel | 1635 Carmel Dr | Seattle |
| 19813 | Acardia | 1787 Acardia Pl. | Seattle |
| 16392 | Orchid | 1874 Orchid Ct | Seattle |
| 18053 | Green | 1883 Green View Court | Seattle |
| 13035 | Mt. | 1887 Mt. Diablo St | Seattle |
| 29864 | Valley | 1946 Valley Crest Drive | Seattle |
| 13580 | Hill | 2030 Hill Drive | Seattle |
| 106 | San | 2144 San Rafael | Seattle |

## SELECT Statement with Subquery

Two Northwind category images, Beverages & Dairy Products, from the dbo.Categories table.

The following SELECT statement involves a subquery which is called a derived table. It also demonstrates that INNER JOIN can be performed with a GROUP BY subquery as well not only with another table or view.

```
USE Northwind;
SELECT   c.CategoryName                        AS Category,
              cnum.NoOfProducts                AS CatProdCnt,
              p.ProductName                    AS Product,
              FORMAT(p.UnitPrice,'c', 'en-US') AS UnitPrice
 FROM    Categories c
              INNER JOIN Products p
                  ON c.CategoryID = p.CategoryID
              INNER JOIN (    SELECT  c.CategoryID,
                                      NoOfProducts = count(* )
                         FROM    Categories c
                         INNER JOIN Products p
                                  ON c.CategoryID = p.CategoryID
                         GROUP BY c.CategoryID
                  ) cnum                                -- derived table
              ON c.CategoryID = cnum.CategoryID
ORDER BY Category, Product;
-- (77 row(s) affected) - Partial results.
```

| Category | CatProdCnt | Product | UnitPrice |
|---|---|---|---|
| Dairy Products | 10 | Mozzarella di Giovanni | $34.80 |
| Dairy Products | 10 | Queso Cabrales | $21.00 |
| Dairy Products | 10 | Queso Manchego La Pastora | $38.00 |
| Dairy Products | 10 | Raclette Courdavault | $55.00 |
| Grains/Cereals | 7 | Filo Mix | $7.00 |
| Grains/Cereals | 7 | Gnocchi di nonna Alice | $38.00 |
| Grains/Cereals | 7 | Gustaf's Knäckebröd | $21.00 |
| Grains/Cereals | 7 | Ravioli Angelo | $19.50 |
| Grains/Cereals | 7 | Singaporean Hokkien Fried Mee | $14.00 |
| Grains/Cereals | 7 | Tunnbröd | $9.00 |

**CHAPTER 3: Structure of the SELECT Statement**

# Creating Delimited String List (CSV) with XML PATH

The XML PATH clause , the text() function and correlated subquery is used to create a comma delimited string within the SELECT columns. Note: it cannot be done using traditional (without XML) SQL single statement, it can be done with multiple SQL statements only. STUFF() string function is applied to replace the leading comma with an empty string

.

```
USE AdventureWorks;

SELECT   Territory = st.[Name],
         SalesYTD =  FORMAT(floor(SalesYTD), 'c', 'en-US'), -- currency format
         SalesStaffAssignmentHistory =

         STUFF((SELECT CONCAT(', ', c.FirstName, SPACE(1), c.LastName)        AS [text()]
             FROM   Person.Contact c
             INNER JOIN Sales.SalesTerritoryHistory sth
             ON c.ContactID = sth.SalesPersonID
             WHERE  sth.TerritoryID =  st.TerritoryID
             ORDER  BY StartDate
             FOR XML Path ('')), 1, 1, SPACE(0))

FROM   Sales.SalesTerritory st
ORDER  BY SalesYTD DESC;
GO
```

| Territory | SalesYTD | SalesStaffAssignmentHistory |
|---|---|---|
| Southwest | $8,351,296.00 | Shelley Dyck, Jauna Elson |
| Canada | $6,917,270.00 | Carla Eldridge, Michael Emanuel, Gail Erickson |
| Northwest | $5,767,341.00 | Shannon Elliott, Terry Eminhizer, Martha Espinoza |
| Central | $4,677,108.00 | Linda Ecoffey, Maciej Dusza |
| France | $3,899,045.00 | Mark Erickson |
| Northeast | $3,857,163.00 | Maciej Dusza, Linda Ecoffey |
| United Kingdom | $3,514,865.00 | Michael Emanuel |
| Southeast | $2,851,419.00 | Carol Elliott |
| Germany | $2,481,039.00 | Janeth Esteves |
| Australia | $1,977,474.00 | Twanna Evans |

## Logical Processing Order of the SELECT Statement

The results from the previous step will be available to the next step. The logical processing order for a SELECT statement is the following. Actual processing by the database engine may be different due to performance and other considerations.

| | |
|---|---|
| 1. | FROM |
| 2. | ON |
| 3. | JOIN |
| 4. | WHERE |
| 5. | GROUP BY |
| 6. | WITH CUBE or WITH ROLLUP |
| 7. | HAVING |
| 8. | SELECT |
| 9. | DISTINCT |
| 10. | ORDER BY |
| 11. | TOP |

As an example, it is logical to filter with the WHERE clause prior to applying GROUP BY. It is also logical to sort when the final result set is available.

SELECT Color, COUNT(*) AS ColorCount  FROM AdventureWorks2012.Production.Product
WHERE Color is not NULL  GROUP BY Color ORDER BY ColorCount DESC;

| Color | ColorCount |
|---|---|
| Black | 93 |
| Silver | 43 |
| Red | 38 |
| Yellow | 36 |
| Blue | 26 |
| Multi | 8 |
| Silver/Black | 7 |
| White | 4 |
| Grey | 1 |

**CHAPTER 3:  Structure of the SELECT Statement**

# The TOP Clause

The TOP clause filters results according the sorting specified in an ORDER BY clause, otherwise random filtering takes place.

Simple TOP usage to return 10 rows only.

SELECT TOP 10 SalesOrderID, OrderDate,  TotalDue
FROM AdventureWorks2012.Sales.SalesOrderHeader  ORDER BY TotalDue DESC;

| SalesOrderID | OrderDate | TotalDue |
|---|---|---|
| 51131 | 2007-07-01 00:00:00.000 | 187487.825 |
| 55282 | 2007-10-01 00:00:00.000 | 182018.6272 |
| 46616 | 2006-07-01 00:00:00.000 | 170512.6689 |
| 46981 | 2006-08-01 00:00:00.000 | 166537.0808 |
| 47395 | 2006-09-01 00:00:00.000 | 165028.7482 |
| 47369 | 2006-09-01 00:00:00.000 | 158056.5449 |
| 47355 | 2006-09-01 00:00:00.000 | 145741.8553 |
| 51822 | 2007-08-01 00:00:00.000 | 145454.366 |
| 44518 | 2005-11-01 00:00:00.000 | 142312.2199 |
| 51858 | 2007-08-01 00:00:00.000 | 140042.1209 |

Complex TOP function usage: not known in advance how many rows will be returned due to "TIES".

SELECT   TOP 1 WITH TIES  coalesce(Color, 'N/A')                    AS Color,
          FORMAT(ListPrice, 'c', 'en-US')                    AS ListPrice,
          Name                                              AS ProductName,
          ProductID
FROM     AdventureWorks2012.Production.Product
ORDER BY ROW_NUMBER()  OVER(PARTITION BY Color ORDER BY ListPrice DESC);
.

| Color | ListPrice | ProductName | ProductID |
|---|---|---|---|
| N/A | $229.49 | HL Fork | 804 |
| Black | $3,374.99 | Mountain-100 Black, 38 | 775 |
| Red | $3,578.27 | Road-150 Red, 62 | 749 |
| Silver | $3,399.99 | Mountain-100 Silver, 38 | 771 |
| Blue | $2,384.07 | Touring-1000 Blue, 46 | 966 |
| Grey | $125.00 | Touring-Panniers, Large | 842 |
| Multi | $89.99 | Men's Bib-Shorts, S | 855 |
| Silver/Black | $80.99 | HL Mountain Pedal | 937 |
| White | $9.50 | Mountain Bike Socks, M | 709 |
| Yellow | $2,384.07 | Touring-1000 Yellow, 46 | 954 |

# The DISTINCT Clause to Omit Duplicates

The DISTINCT clause returns only unique results, omitting duplicates in the result set.

```
USE AdventureWorks2012;
SELECT DISTINCT Color FROM Production.Product
WHERE Color is not NULL
ORDER BY Color;
GO
```

| Color |
|-------|
| Black |
| Blue |
| Grey |
| Multi |
| Red |
| Silver |
| Silver/Black |
| White |
| Yellow |

```
SELECT DISTINCT ListPrice
FROM Production.Product
 WHERE ListPrice > 0.0
ORDER BY ListPrice DESC;
GO
-- (102 row(s) affected) - Partial results.
```

| ListPrice |
|-----------|
| 3578.27 |
| 3399.99 |
| 3374.99 |
| 2443.35 |

```
-- Using DISTINCT in COUNT - NULL is counted
SELECT          COUNT(*)                    AS TotalRows,
                COUNT(DISTINCT Color)       AS ProductColors,
                COUNT(DISTINCT Size)        AS ProductSizes
FROM AdventureWorks2012.Production.Product;
```

| TotalRows | ProductColors | ProductSizes |
|-----------|---------------|--------------|
| 504 | 9 | 18 |

CHAPTER 3:  Structure of the SELECT Statement

## The CASE Conditional Expression

The CASE conditional expression evaluates to a **single value of the same data type**, therefore **it can be used anywhere in a query where a single value is required.**

```
SELECT    CASE ProductLine
                        WHEN 'R' THEN 'Road'
                        WHEN 'M' THEN 'Mountain'
                        WHEN 'T' THEN 'Touring'
                        WHEN 'S' THEN 'Other'
                        ELSE 'Parts'
                END                             AS Category,
                Name                            AS ProductName,
                ProductNumber
FROM AdventureWorks2012.Production.Product
ORDER BY ProductName;
GO
-- (504 row(s) affected) - Partial results.
```

| Category | ProductName | ProductNumber |
|----------|-------------|---------------|
| Touring | Touring-3000 Blue, 62 | BK-T18U-62 |
| Touring | Touring-3000 Yellow, 44 | BK-T18Y-44 |
| Touring | Touring-3000 Yellow, 50 | BK-T18Y-50 |
| Touring | Touring-3000 Yellow, 54 | BK-T18Y-54 |
| Touring | Touring-3000 Yellow, 58 | BK-T18Y-58 |
| Touring | Touring-3000 Yellow, 62 | BK-T18Y-62 |
| Touring | Touring-Panniers, Large | PA-T100 |
| Other | Water Bottle - 30 oz. | WB-H098 |
| Mountain | Women's Mountain Shorts, L | SH-W890-L |

Query to return different result sets for repeated execution due to newid().

```
SELECT  TOP 3 CompanyName,   City=CONCAT(City, ', ', Country),          PostalCode,
        [IsNumeric] =   CASE        WHEN PostalCode like '[0-9][0-9][0-9][0-9][0-9]'
                                    THEN '5-Digit Numeric'   ELSE 'Other' END
FROM    Northwind.dbo.Suppliers
ORDER BY NEWID();                           -- random sort
GO
```

| CompanyName | City | PostalCode | IsNumeric |
|-------------|------|------------|-----------|
| PB Knäckebröd AB | Göteborg, Sweden | S-345 67 | Other |
| Gai pâturage | Annecy, France | 74000 | 5-Digit Numeric |
| Heli Süßwaren GmbH & Co. KG | Berlin, Germany | 10785 | 5-Digit Numeric |

*CHAPTER 3: Structure of the SELECT Statement*

*Same query as above expanded with ROW_NUMBER() and another CASE expression column.*

```
SELECT   ROW_NUMBER() OVER (ORDER BY Name)          AS RowNo,
               CASE ProductLine
                 WHEN 'R' THEN 'Road'
                 WHEN 'M' THEN 'Mountain'
                 WHEN 'T' THEN 'Touring'
                 WHEN 'S' THEN 'Other'
                 ELSE 'Parts'
               END                                  AS Category,
               Name                                 AS ProductName,
               CASE WHEN Color is null THEN 'N/A'
                       ELSE Color END               AS Color,
               ProductNumber
FROM Production.Product   ORDER BY ProductName;
-- (504 row(s) affected) - Partial results.
```

| RowNo | Category | ProductName | Color | ProductNumber |
|-------|----------|-------------|-------|---------------|
| 1 | Parts | Adjustable Race | N/A | AR-5381 |
| 2 | Mountain | All-Purpose Bike Stand | N/A | ST-1401 |
| 3 | Other | AWC Logo Cap | Multi | CA-1098 |
| 4 | Parts | BB Ball Bearing | N/A | BE-2349 |
| 5 | Parts | Bearing Ball | N/A | BA-8327 |
| 6 | Other | Bike Wash - Dissolver | N/A | CL-9009 |
| 7 | Parts | Blade | N/A | BL-2036 |
| 8 | Other | Cable Lock | N/A | LO-C100 |
| 9 | Parts | Chain | Silver | CH-0234 |
| 10 | Parts | Chain Stays | N/A | CS-2812 |

Testing PostalCode with  ISNUMERIC  and generating a flag with CASE expression.

```
SELECT  TOP (4) AddressID,   City,    PostalCode                    AS Zip,
        CASE WHEN ISNUMERIC(PostalCode) = 1 THEN 'Y'  ELSE 'N'  END    AS IsZipNumeric
FROM    AdventureWorks2008.Person.Address  ORDER BY NEWID();
```

| AddressID | City | Zip | IsZipNumeric |
|-----------|------|-----|--------------|
| 16704 | Paris | 75008 | Y |
| 26320 | Grossmont | 91941 | Y |
| 27705 | Matraville | 2036 | Y |
| 18901 | Kirkby | KB9 | N |

**CHAPTER 3:  Structure of the SELECT Statement**

# The OVER Clause

The OVER clause defines the partitioning and sorting of a rowset (intermediate result set) preceding the application of an associated window function, such as ranking. Window functions are also dubbed as ranking functions.

```
USE AdventureWorks2012;
-- Query with three different OVER clauses
SELECT  ROW_NUMBER() OVER ( ORDER BY SalesOrderID, ProductID)            AS RowNum
        ,SalesOrderID, ProductID, OrderQty
        ,RANK() OVER(PARTITION BY SalesOrderID ORDER BY OrderQty DESC)    AS Ranking
        ,SUM(OrderQty) OVER(PARTITION BY SalesOrderID)                    AS TotalQty
        ,AVG(OrderQty) OVER(PARTITION BY SalesOrderID)                    AS AvgQty
        ,COUNT(OrderQty) OVER(PARTITION BY SalesOrderID)  AS "Count"  -- T-SQL keyword, use "" or []
        ,MIN(OrderQty) OVER(PARTITION BY SalesOrderID)                    AS "Min"
        ,MAX(OrderQty) OVER(PARTITION BY SalesOrderID)                    AS "Max"
FROM Sales.SalesOrderDetail
WHERE SalesOrderID BETWEEN 61190 AND 61199  ORDER BY RowNum;
-- (143 row(s) affected) - Partial results.
```

| RowNum | SalesOrderID | ProductID | OrderQty | Ranking | TotalQty | AvgQty | Count | Min | Max |
|--------|--------------|-----------|----------|---------|----------|--------|-------|-----|-----|
| 1 | 61190 | 707 | 4 | 13 | 159 | 3 | 40 | 1 | 17 |
| 2 | 61190 | 708 | 3 | 18 | 159 | 3 | 40 | 1 | 17 |
| 3 | 61190 | 711 | 5 | 8 | 159 | 3 | 40 | 1 | 17 |
| 4 | 61190 | 712 | 12 | 2 | 159 | 3 | 40 | 1 | 17 |
| 5 | 61190 | 714 | 3 | 18 | 159 | 3 | 40 | 1 | 17 |
| 6 | 61190 | 715 | 5 | 8 | 159 | 3 | 40 | 1 | 17 |
| 7 | 61190 | 716 | 5 | 8 | 159 | 3 | 40 | 1 | 17 |
| 8 | 61190 | 858 | 4 | 13 | 159 | 3 | 40 | 1 | 17 |
| 9 | 61190 | 859 | 7 | 6 | 159 | 3 | 40 | 1 | 17 |
| 10 | 61190 | 864 | 8 | 4 | 159 | 3 | 40 | 1 | 17 |
| 11 | 61190 | 865 | 3 | 18 | 159 | 3 | 40 | 1 | 17 |
| 12 | 61190 | 870 | 9 | 3 | 159 | 3 | 40 | 1 | 17 |
| 13 | 61190 | 876 | 4 | 13 | 159 | 3 | 40 | 1 | 17 |
| 14 | 61190 | 877 | 5 | 8 | 159 | 3 | 40 | 1 | 17 |
| 15 | 61190 | 880 | 1 | 34 | 159 | 3 | 40 | 1 | 17 |
| 16 | 61190 | 881 | 5 | 8 | 159 | 3 | 40 | 1 | 17 |
| 17 | 61190 | 883 | 2 | 26 | 159 | 3 | 40 | 1 | 17 |
| 18 | 61190 | 884 | 17 | 1 | 159 | 3 | 40 | 1 | 17 |
| 19 | 61190 | 885 | 3 | 18 | 159 | 3 | 40 | 1 | 17 |
| 20 | 61190 | 886 | 1 | 34 | 159 | 3 | 40 | 1 | 17 |
| 21 | 61190 | 889 | 2 | 26 | 159 | 3 | 40 | 1 | 17 |
| 22 | 61190 | 892 | 4 | 13 | 159 | 3 | 40 | 1 | 17 |
| 23 | 61190 | 893 | 3 | 18 | 159 | 3 | 40 | 1 | 17 |
| 24 | 61190 | 895 | 1 | 34 | 159 | 3 | 40 | 1 | 17 |

# FROM Clause: Specifies the Data Source

The FROM clause specifies the source data sets for the query such as tables, views, derived tables and table-valued functions. Typically the tables are JOINed together. The most common JOIN is INNER JOIN which is based on equality between FOREIGN KEY and PRIMARY KEY values in the two tables.

| PERFORMANCE NOTE |
|---|
| All FOREIGN KEYs should be indexed. PRIMARY KEYs are indexed automatically with unique index. |

```
USE AdventureWorks2012;
GO
SELECT
  ROW_NUMBER() OVER(ORDER BY SalesYTD DESC)                        AS RowNo,
  ROW_NUMBER() OVER(PARTITION BY PostalCode ORDER BY SalesYTD DESC)  AS SeqNo,
              CONCAT(p.FirstName, SPACE(1), p.LastName)             AS SalesStaff,
              FORMAT(s.SalesYTD,'c','en-US')                        AS YTDSales,
              City,
              a.PostalCode                                          AS ZipCode
FROM Sales.SalesPerson AS s
  INNER JOIN Person.Person AS p
    ON s.BusinessEntityID = p.BusinessEntityID
  INNER JOIN Person.Address AS a
    ON a.AddressID = p.BusinessEntityID
WHERE  TerritoryID IS NOT NULL   AND SalesYTD <> 0 ORDER BY ZipCode, SeqNo;
```

| RowNo | SeqNo | SalesStaff | YTDSales | City | ZipCode |
|---|---|---|---|---|---|
| 1 | 1 | Linda Mitchell | $4,251,368.55 | Issaquah | 98027 |
| 3 | 2 | Michael Blythe | $3,763,178.18 | Issaquah | 98027 |
| 4 | 3 | Jillian Carson | $3,189,418.37 | Issaquah | 98027 |
| 8 | 4 | Tsvi Reiter | $2,315,185.61 | Issaquah | 98027 |
| 12 | 5 | Garrett Vargas | $1,453,719.47 | Issaquah | 98027 |
| 14 | 6 | Pamela Ansman-Wolfe | $1,352,577.13 | Issaquah | 98027 |
| 2 | 1 | Jae Pak | $4,116,871.23 | Renton | 98055 |
| 5 | 2 | Ranjit Varkey Chudukatil | $3,121,616.32 | Renton | 98055 |
| 6 | 3 | José Saraiva | $2,604,540.72 | Renton | 98055 |
| 7 | 4 | Shu Ito | $2,458,535.62 | Renton | 98055 |
| 9 | 5 | Rachel Valdez | $1,827,066.71 | Renton | 98055 |
| 10 | 6 | Tete Mensa-Annan | $1,576,562.20 | Renton | 98055 |
| 11 | 7 | David Campbell | $1,573,012.94 | Renton | 98055 |
| 13 | 8 | Lynn Tsoflias | $1,421,810.92 | Renton | 98055 |

# The WHERE Clause to Filter Records (Rows)

The WHERE clause filters the rows generated by the query. Only rows satisfying (TRUE) the WHERE clause predicates are returned.

| PERFORMANCE NOTE |
| --- |
| All columns in WHERE clause should be indexed. |

USE AdventureWorks2012;

String equal match predicate - equal is TRUE, not equal is FALSE.

SELECT ProductID, Name, ListPrice, Color
FROM Production.Product  WHERE Name = 'Mountain-100 Silver, 38' ;

| ProductID | Name | ListPrice | Color |
| --- | --- | --- | --- |
| 771 | Mountain-100 Silver, 38 | 3399.99 | Silver |

-- Function equality predicate
SELECT * FROM Sales.SalesOrderHeader WHERE YEAR(OrderDate) = 2008;
-- (13951 row(s) affected)

| PERFORMANCE NOTE |
| --- |
| When a column is used as a parameter in a function ( e.g. YEAR(OrderDate) ), index (if any) usage is voided. |
| Instead of random SEEK, all rows are SCANned in the table.  The predicate is not SARGable. |

-- String wildcard match predicate
SELECT ProductID, Name, ListPrice, Color
FROM Production.Product  WHERE Name LIKE ('%touring%');

-- Integer range predicate
SELECT ProductID, Name, ListPrice, Color
FROM Production.Product  WHERE ProductID >= 997 ;

-- Double string wildcard match predicate
SELECT ProductID, Name, ListPrice, Color
FROM Production.Product  WHERE Name LIKE ('%bike%')  AND Name LIKE ('%44%');

-- String list match predicate
SELECT ProductID, Name, ListPrice, Color  FROM Production.Product
WHERE Name IN ('Mountain-100 Silver, 44', 'Mountain-100 Black, 44');

**CHAPTER 3:  Structure of the SELECT Statement**

# The GROUP BY Clause to Aggregate Results

The GROUP BY clause is applied to partition the rows and calculate aggregate values. An extremely powerful way of looking at the data from a summary point of view.

```
SELECT
                V.Name                                  AS Vendor,
                FORMAT(SUM(TotalDue), 'c', 'en-US')     AS TotalPurchase,
                A.City,
                SP.Name                                 AS State,
                CR.Name                                 AS Country
FROM Purchasing.Vendor AS V
   INNER JOIN Purchasing.VendorAddress AS VA
                ON VA.VendorID = V.VendorID
   INNER JOIN Person.Address AS A
                ON A.AddressID = VA.AddressID
   INNER JOIN Person.StateProvince AS SP
                ON SP.StateProvinceID =  A.StateProvinceID
   INNER JOIN Person.CountryRegion AS CR
                ON CR.CountryRegionCode = SP.CountryRegionCode
  INNER JOIN Purchasing.PurchaseOrderHeader POH
                ON POH.VendorID = V.VendorID
GROUP BY  V.Name, A.City, SP.Name, CR.Name
ORDER BY SUM(TotalDue) DESC,  Vendor;   -- TotalPurchase does a string sort instead of numeric
GO
-- (79 row(s) affected) - Partial results.
```

| Vendor | TotalPurchase | City | State | Country |
|---|---|---|---|---|
| Superior Bicycles | $5,034,266.74 | Lynnwood | Washington | United States |
| Professional Athletic Consultants | $3,379,946.32 | Burbank | California | United States |
| Chicago City Saddles | $3,347,165.20 | Daly City | California | United States |
| Jackson Authority | $2,821,333.52 | Long Beach | California | United States |
| Vision Cycles, Inc. | $2,777,684.91 | Glendale | California | United States |
| Sport Fan Co. | $2,675,889.22 | Burien | Washington | United States |
| Proseware, Inc. | $2,593,901.31 | Lebanon | Oregon | United States |
| Crowley Sport | $2,472,770.05 | Chicago | Illinois | United States |
| Greenwood Athletic Company | $2,472,770.05 | Lemon Grove | Arizona | United States |
| Mitchell Sports | $2,424,284.37 | Everett | Washington | United States |
| First Rate Bicycles | $2,304,231.55 | La Mesa | New Mexico | United States |
| Signature Cycles | $2,236,033.80 | Coronado | California | United States |
| Electronic Bike Repair & Supplies | $2,154,773.37 | Tacoma | Washington | United States |
| Vista Road Bikes | $2,090,857.52 | Salem | Oregon | United States |
| Victory Bikes | $2,052,173.62 | Issaquah | Washington | United States |
| Bicycle Specialists | $1,952,375.30 | Lake Oswego | Oregon | United States |

# The HAVING Clause to Filter Aggregates

The HAVING clause is similar to the WHERE clause filtering but applies to GROUP BY aggregates.

```
USE AdventureWorks;
SELECT
                V.Name                                    AS Vendor,
                FORMAT(SUM(TotalDue), 'c', 'en-US')       AS TotalPurchase,
                A.City,
                SP.Name                                   AS State,
                CR.Name                                   AS Country
FROM Purchasing.Vendor AS V
   INNER JOIN Purchasing.VendorAddress AS VA
            ON VA.VendorID = V.VendorID
   INNER JOIN Person.Address AS A
            ON A.AddressID = VA.AddressID
   INNER JOIN Person.StateProvince AS SP
            ON SP.StateProvinceID =   A.StateProvinceID
   INNER JOIN Person.CountryRegion AS CR
            ON CR.CountryRegionCode = SP.CountryRegionCode
   INNER JOIN Purchasing.PurchaseOrderHeader POH
            ON POH.VendorID = V.VendorID
GROUP BY  V.Name, A.City, SP.Name, CR.Name
HAVING SUM(TotalDue) < $26000    -- HAVING clause predicate
ORDER BY SUM(TotalDue) DESC,  Vendor;
```

| Vendor | TotalPurchase | City | State | Country |
|---|---|---|---|---|
| Speed Corporation | $25,732.84 | Anacortes | Washington | United States |
| Gardner Touring Cycles | $25,633.64 | Altadena | California | United States |
| National Bike Association | $25,513.90 | Sedro Woolley | Washington | United States |
| Australia Bike Retailer | $25,060.04 | Bellingham | Washington | United States |
| WestAmerica Bicycle Co. | $25,060.04 | Houston | Texas | United States |
| Ready Rentals | $23,635.06 | Kirkland | Washington | United States |
| Morgan Bike Accessories | $23,146.99 | Albany | New York | United States |
| Continental Pro Cycles | $22,960.07 | Long Beach | California | United States |
| American Bicycles and Wheels | $9,641.01 | West Covina | California | United States |
| Litware, Inc. | $8,553.32 | Santa Cruz | California | United States |
| Business Equipment Center | $8,497.80 | Everett | Montana | United States |
| Bloomington Multisport | $8,243.95 | West Covina | California | United States |
| International | $8,061.10 | Salt Lake City | Utah | United States |
| Wide World Importers | $8,025.60 | Concord | California | United States |
| Midwest Sport, Inc. | $7,328.72 | Detroit | Michigan | United States |
| Wood Fitness | $6,947.58 | Philadelphia | Pennsylvania | United States |
| Metro Sport Equipment | $6,324.53 | Lebanon | Oregon | United States |
| Burnett Road Warriors | $5,779.99 | Corvallis | Oregon | United States |
| Lindell | $5,412.57 | Lebanon | Oregon | United States |
| Consumer Cycles | $3,378.17 | Torrance | California | United States |
| Northern Bike Travel | $2,048.42 | Anacortes | Washington | United States |

# The ORDER BY  Clause to Sort Results

The ORDER BY clause sorts the result set. It guarantees ordering according to the columns or expressions listed from major to minor keys. Unique ordering requires a set of keys which generate unique data rows. The major key, YEAR(HireDate), in the first example is not sufficient for uniqueness.

```
USE AdventureWorks2012;
-- Sort on 2 keys
SELECT BusinessEntityID AS EmployeeID, JobTitle, HireDate
FROM HumanResources.Employee  ORDER BY YEAR(HireDate) DESC, EmployeeID;
-- (290 row(s) affected) - Partial results.
```

| EmployeeID | JobTitle | HireDate |
|---|---|---|
| 285 | Pacific Sales Manager | 2007-04-15 |
| 286 | Sales Representative | 2007-07-01 |
| 288 | Sales Representative | 2007-07-01 |
| 284 | Sales Representative | 2006-11-01 |
| 287 | European Sales Manager | 2006-05-18 |
| 289 | Sales Representative | 2006-07-01 |
| 290 | Sales Representative | 2006-07-01 |
| 11 | Senior Tool Designer | 2005-01-05 |
| 13 | Tool Designer | 2005-01-23 |
| 14 | Senior Design Engineer | 2005-01-30 |

```
-- Sort on CASE conditional expression
SELECT   BusinessEntityID AS SalesStaffID, CONCAT(LastName, ', ', FirstName) AS FullName,
        CASE CountryRegionName WHEN 'United States' THEN TerritoryName
            ELSE '' END AS TerritoryName, CountryRegionName
FROM Sales.vSalesPerson   WHERE TerritoryName IS NOT NULL        -- view
ORDER BY CASE WHEN CountryRegionName != 'United States' THEN  CountryRegionName
        ELSE TerritoryName  END;
```

| SalesStaffID | FullName | TerritoryName | CountryRegionName |
|---|---|---|---|
| 286 | Tsoflias, Lynn | | Australia |
| 278 | Vargas, Garrett | | Canada |
| 282 | Saraiva, José | | Canada |
| 277 | Carson, Jillian | Central | United States |
| 290 | Varkey Chudukatil, Ranjit | | France |
| 288 | Valdez, Rachel | | Germany |
| 275 | Blythe, Michael | Northeast | United States |
| 283 | Campbell, David | Northwest | United States |
| 284 | Mensa-Annan, Tete | Northwest | United States |
| 280 | Ansman-Wolfe, Pamela | Northwest | United States |
| 279 | Reiter, Tsvi | Southeast | United States |
| 276 | Mitchell, Linda | Southwest | United States |
| 281 | Ito, Shu | Southwest | United States |
| 289 | Pak, Jae | | United Kingdom |

# CTE - Common Table Expression

CTE helps with structured programming by the definition of named subqueries at the beginning of the query. It supports nesting and recursion.

```
USE AdventureWorks;
-- Testing CTE
WITH CTE (SalesPersonID, NumberOfOrders, MostRecentOrderDate)
   AS (        SELECT SalesPersonID, COUNT(*), CONVERT(date, MAX(OrderDate))
               FROM Sales.SalesOrderHeader
               GROUP BY SalesPersonID   )
SELECT * FROM CTE;
-- (18 row(s) affected) - Partial results.
```

| SalesPersonID | NumberOfOrders | MostRecentOrderDate |
|---|---|---|
| 284 | 39 | 2004-05-01 |
| 278 | 234 | 2004-06-01 |
| 281 | 242 | 2004-06-01 |

```
-- Using CTE in a query
;WITH CTE (SalesPersonID, NumberOfOrders, MostRecentOrderDate)
   AS ( SELECT SalesPersonID, COUNT(*), CONVERT(date, MAX(OrderDate))
        FROM Sales.SalesOrderHeader   GROUP BY SalesPersonID        )
-- Start of outer (main) query
 SELECT E.EmployeeID,
               OE.NumberOfOrders              AS EmpOrders,
               OE.MostRecentOrderDate         AS EmpLastOrder,
               E.ManagerID,
               OM.NumberOfOrders              AS MgrOrders,
               OM.MostRecentOrderDate         AS MgrLastOrder
 FROM  HumanResources.Employee AS E
        INNER JOIN CTE AS OE          ON E.EmployeeID = OE.SalesPersonID
        LEFT OUTER JOIN CTE AS OM     ON E.ManagerID = OM.SalesPersonID
ORDER BY EmployeeID;
-- (17 row(s) affected) - Partial results.
```

| EmployeeID | EmpOrders | EmpLastOrder | ManagerID | MgrOrders | MgrLastOrder |
|---|---|---|---|---|---|
| 268 | 48 | 2004-06-01 | 273 | NULL | NULL |
| 275 | 450 | 2004-06-01 | 268 | 48 | 2004-06-01 |
| 276 | 418 | 2004-06-01 | 268 | 48 | 2004-06-01 |
| 277 | 473 | 2004-06-01 | 268 | 48 | 2004-06-01 |
| 278 | 234 | 2004-06-01 | 268 | 48 | 2004-06-01 |

CHAPTER 3: Structure of the SELECT Statement

## Combining Results of Multiple Queries with UNION

UNION and UNION ALL (no duplicates elimination) operators can be used to **stack result sets from two or more queries into a single result set**.

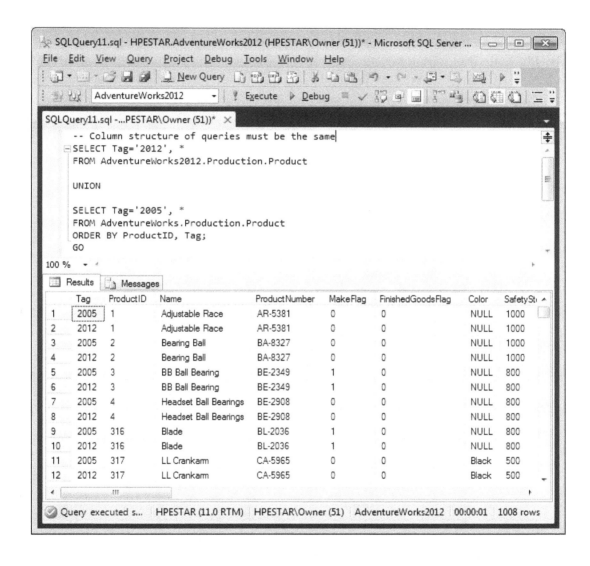

## TOP n by Group Query with OVER PARTITION BY

OVER PARTITION BY method is very convenient for TOP n by group selection. List of top 3 orders placed by resellers (customers of AdventureWorks Cycles).

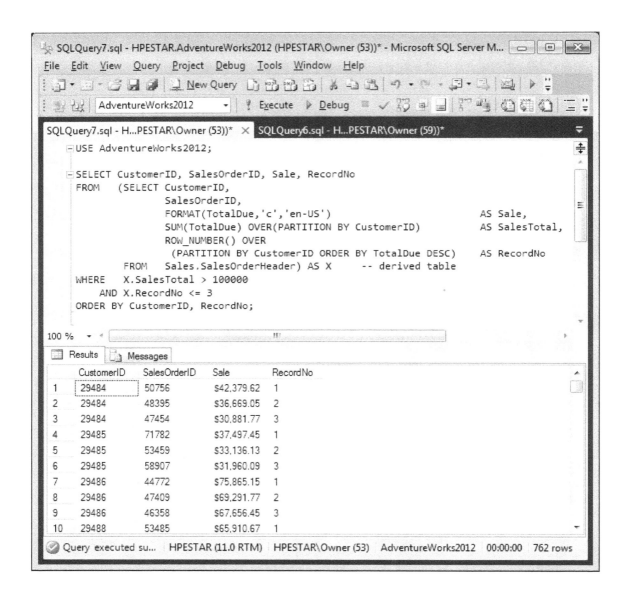

# CHAPTER 4: SQL Server Management Studio

## SQL Server Programming, Administration & Management Tool

SQL Server Management Studio (SSMS) is a GUI (Graphical User Interface) tool for accessing, configuring, managing, administering, and developing all major components of SQL Server with the exception of Business Intelligence components: SSAS (Analysis Services), SSRS (Reporting Services) & SSIS (Integration Services). The two main environments in SSMS: Object Explorer and Query Editor. Object Explorer is used to access servers, databases and db objects. Query Editor is to develop and execute queries. SSMS is used by a DBA (Data Base Administrator) for administrative and programming functions. SSMS can also be used by a database developer to develop application related db objects such as stored procedures, functions and triggers. Some developers prefer to stay in Visual Studio environment which has features to support database development albeit not as extensive as Management Studio. A typical screen display of Management Studio.

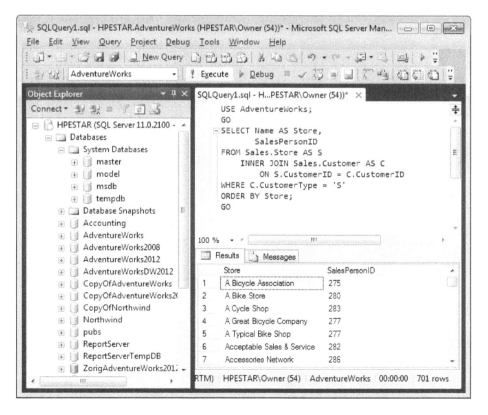

**CHAPTER 4: SQL Server Management Studio**

# Query Editor

The Query Editor is used to type in queries, edit them and submit them for execution by the server. Queries can also be loaded from a disk file, typically with .sql extension. In addition to textual query development, a number of special tools available such as graphical query designer, debugger, execution plan display and query analysis in the Database Engine Tuning Advisor.

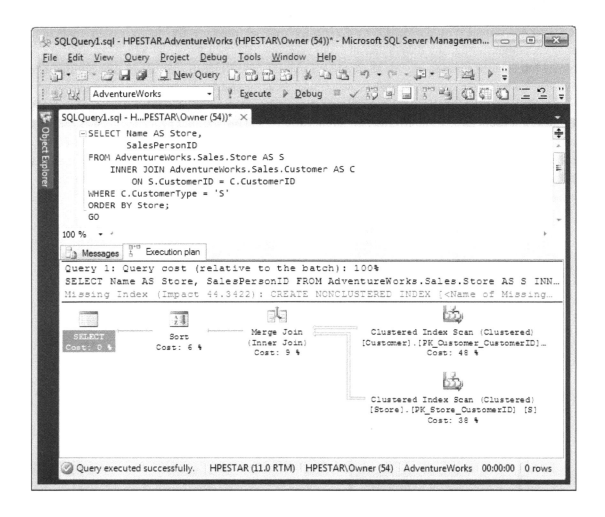

## Execute All Batches in Query Editor

The entire content of the Query Editor is executed when we click on the Execute button. Batches typically separated by "GO" on a separate line.

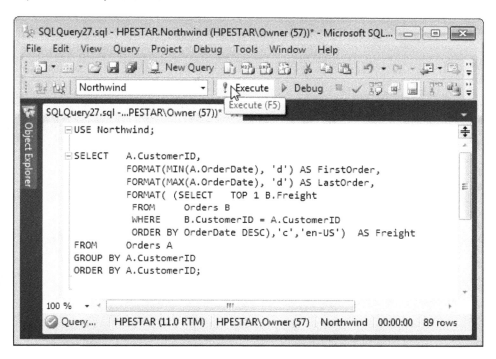

## The Significance of GO in T-SQL Scripts

"GO" is not transmitted to SQL Server. "GO" indicates the end of batch to the client software such as SSMS. "GO" also indicates the end of a logical unit to the human reader. Certain statements must be the first line, or have "GO" preceding them.

```
USE AdventureWorks2012;
CREATE FUNCTION Z () RETURNS TABLE AS
RETURN  SELECT * FROM Production.ProductSubcategory;
GO
/* Msg 111, Level 15, State 1, Line 2   'CREATE FUNCTION' must be the first statement in a query batch. */

USE AdventureWorks2012;
GO
CREATE FUNCTION Z () RETURNS TABLE AS RETURN SELECT * FROM Production.ProductSubcategory;
GO
-- Command(s) completed successfully.
```

*The Results Pane contains the result rows of the query. It is currently set to Grid format.*

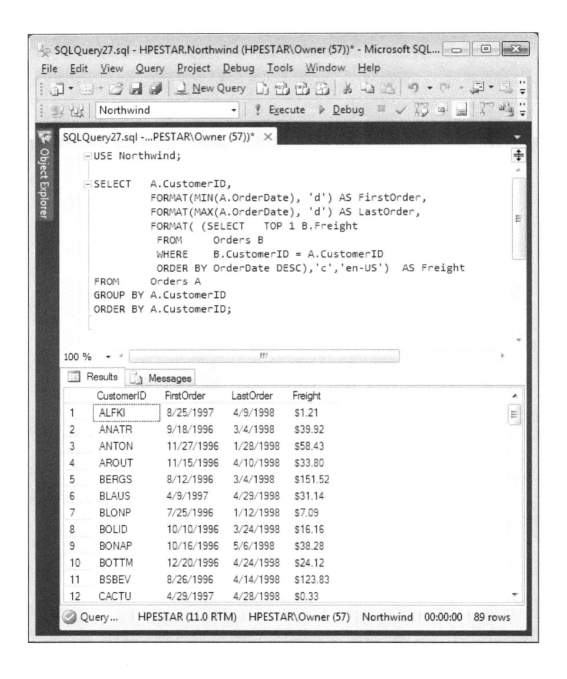

*The Messages Pane gets the row count values, warning & error messages as well as the output of the PRINT & RAISERROR statements if any.*

The client software also gets the same messages following query execution.

## Routing Results to Grid, Text or File

Results can be routed to Grid, Text or File from the right-click menu or the Query drop-down menu.

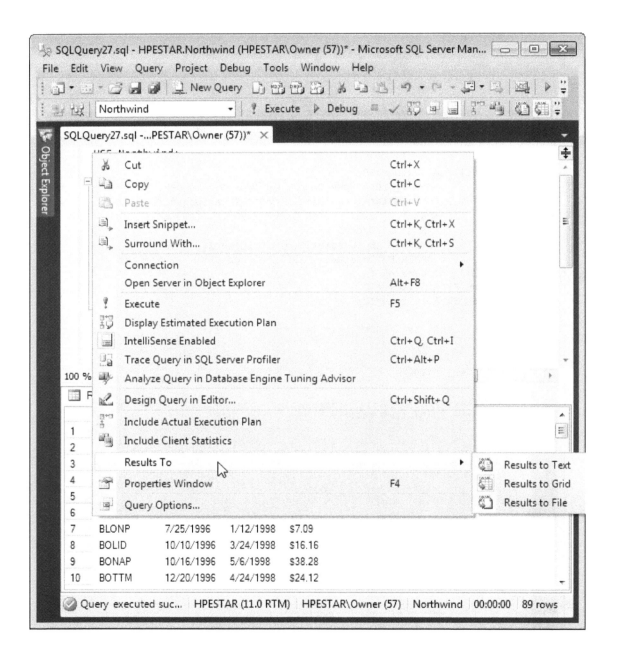

## Routing  Results to Text

The following screen window image displays results in text format. Messages also come to the Results window, following the results rows.

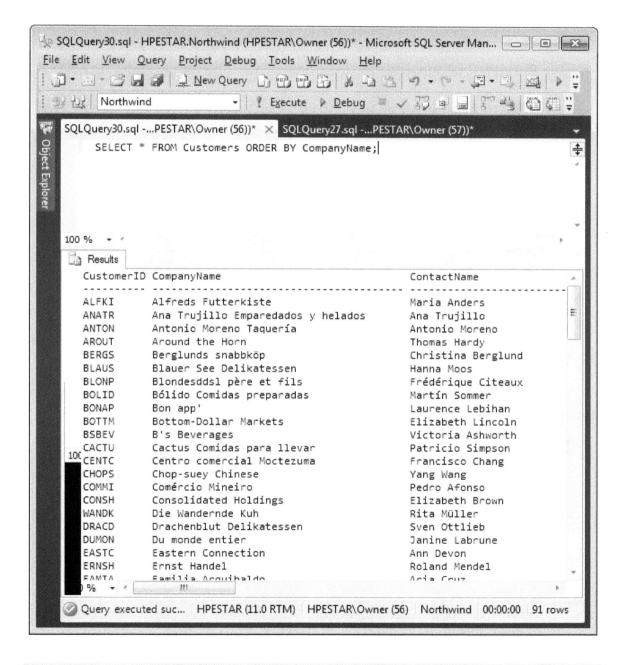

## Routing Results to File

When the routing option is file, the file save window pops up upon query execution.

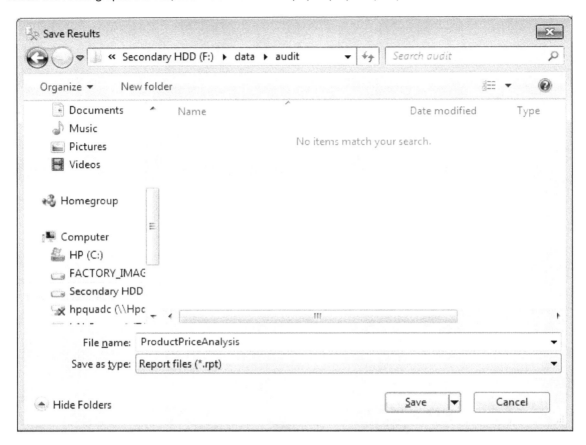

Part of the file in Notepad.

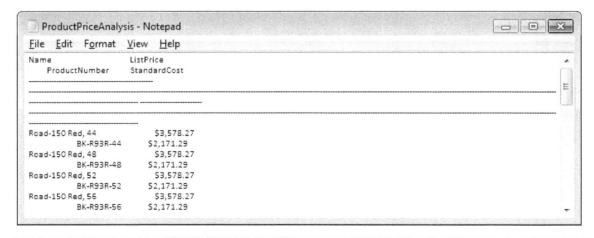

## Saving Results in CSV Flat File Format

Results can also be saved in CSV (comma separated values) format which can be read by Excel and other software.

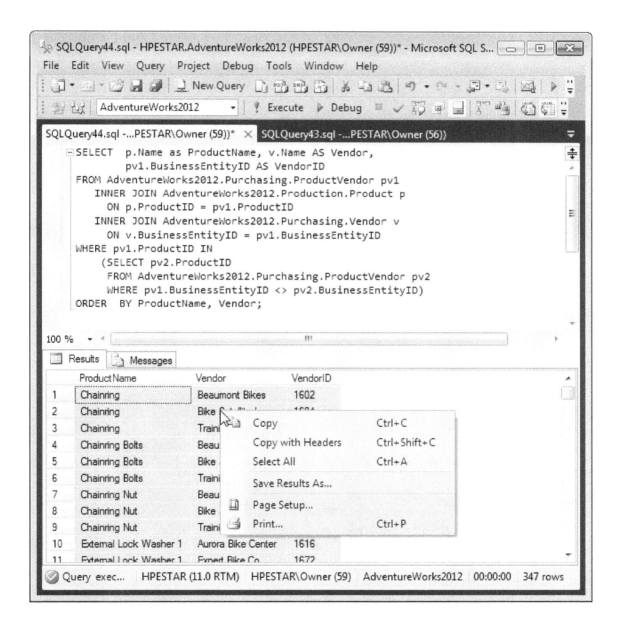

*The saving file dialog box is configured automatically to csv saving.*

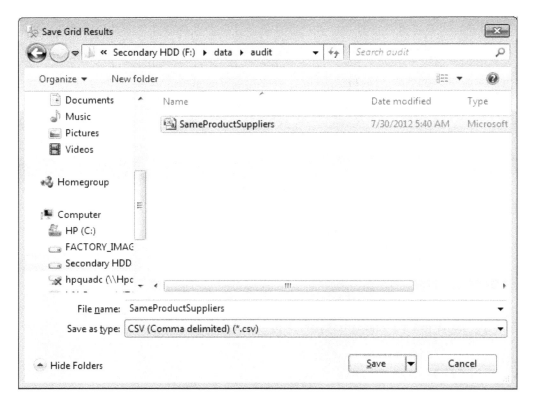

Part of the file in Notepad window.

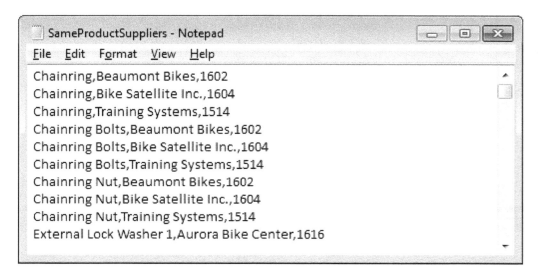

**CHAPTER 4:  SQL Server Management Studio**

## Copy & Paste Results to Excel

Using the copy / copy with headers option in SSMS result window, the query results can simply be pasted into an Excel worksheet. Excel may do implicit conversions on some columns.

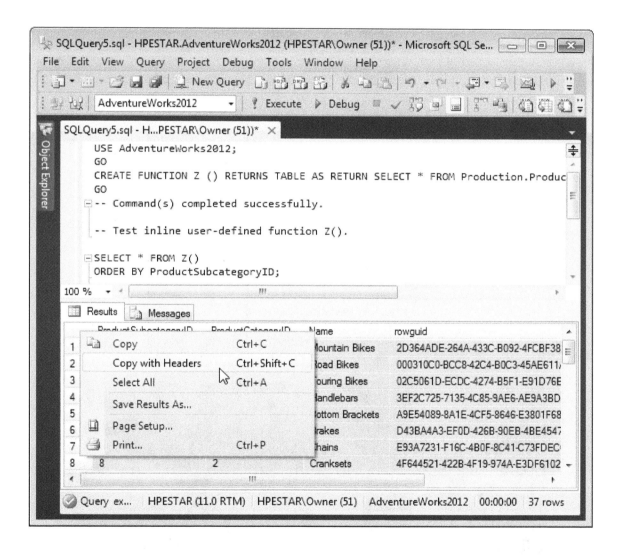

*After pasting into an Excel worksheet some formatting may be necessary such as for datetime columns.*

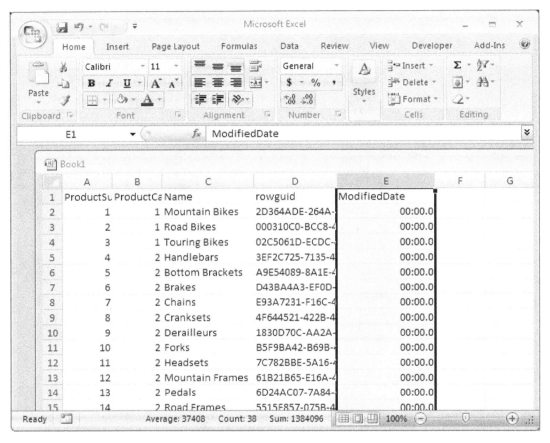

CHAPTER 4: SQL Server Management Studio

## Error Handling & Debugging

Error handling and debugging is a major part of database development work. When there is an error, it is displayed in the Messages area ( or returned to the application client software ) which automatically becomes active. In the following example, we introduced an invalid column name which resulted in error. The error message line reference starts with the top line of the batch which is the first line after the first "GO" which indicates a new batch. The red wave-underlining comes from optional IntelliSense and not related to the execution attempt error message. IntelliSense gives warning ahead of time if it detects a potential error. Simple errors can be corrected with help from the error message. Complex errors may required web search and/or examining the query in parts.

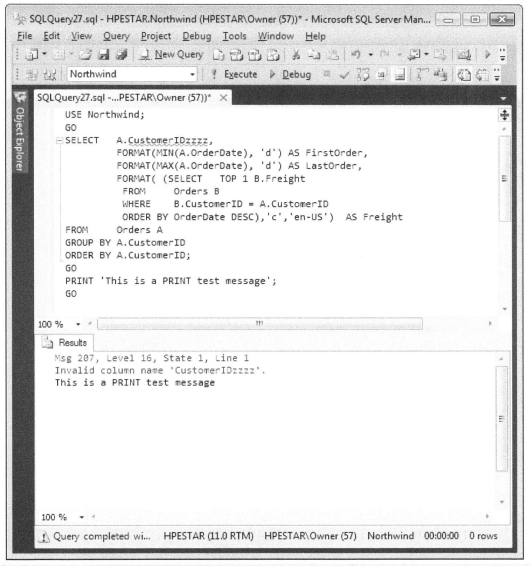

## Locating the Error Line  in a Query

Position the cursor on the error and double click. The error line will be highlighted. This method does not work for all errors.

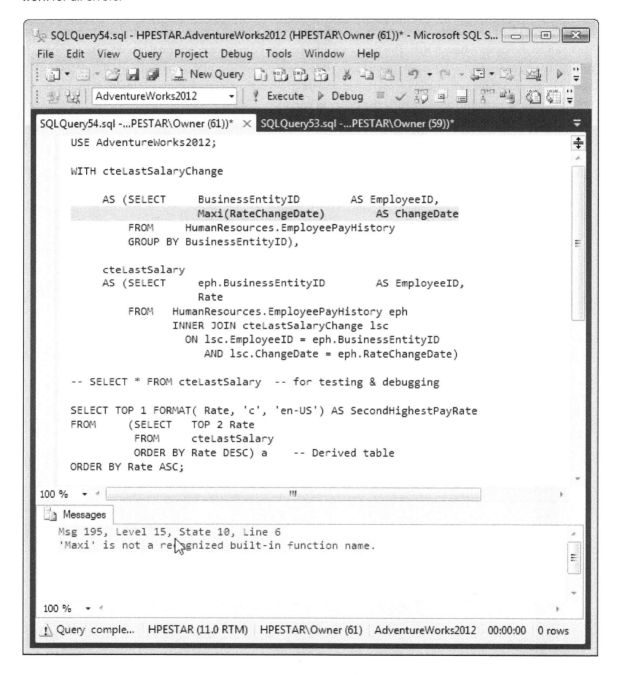

## Error Message Pointing to the Wrong Line

For some errors, the first line of the query (3) is returned by the database engine not the actual error line (13). The error message is still very helpful though in this instance.

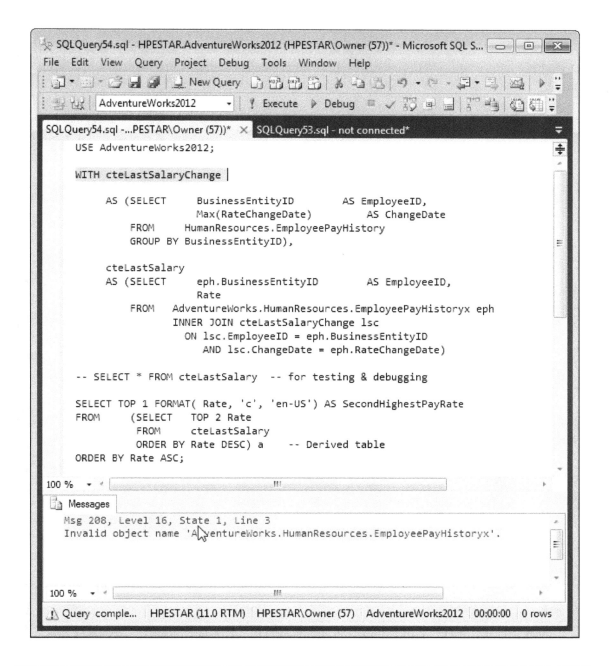

## Parsing a Query for Syntax Errors

A query (or one or more batches) can be parsed for syntax errors. Parsing catches syntax errors such as using "ORDER" instead of "ORDER BY" for sorting.

```
USE AdventureWorks2012;

WITH cteLastSalaryChange

    AS (SELECT      BusinessEntityID        AS EmployeeID,
                    Max(RateChangeDate)        AS ChangeDate
        FROM      HumanResources.EmployeePayHistory
        GROUP BY BusinessEntityID),

    cteLastSalary
    AS (SELECT      eph.BusinessEntityID        AS EmployeeID,
                    Rate
        FROM      HumanResources.EmployeePayHistory eph
                  INNER JOIN cteLastSalaryChange lsc
                    ON lsc.EmployeeID = eph.BusinessEntityID
                    AND lsc.ChangeDate = eph.RateChangeDate)

-- SELECT * FROM cteLastSalary  -- for testing & debugging

SELECT TOP 1 FORMAT( Rate, 'c', 'en-US') AS SecondHighestPayRate
FROM      (SELECT    TOP 2 Rate
           FROM      cteLastSalary
           ORDER  Rate DESC) a     -- Derived table
ORDER BY Rate ASC;
```

```
Msg 102, Level 15, State 1, Line 23
Incorrect syntax near 'Rate'.
```

CHAPTER 4: SQL Server Management Studio

## Deferred Name Resolution Process

Deferred Name Resolution Process: Only syntax errors are caught when parsed, not execution (runtime) errors as shown in the following demo which has an invalid table reference (EmployeePayHistoryx). Similarly, **stored procedures can be compiled without errors with invalid table references**. A table need not exist for stored procedure compilation, only for execution.

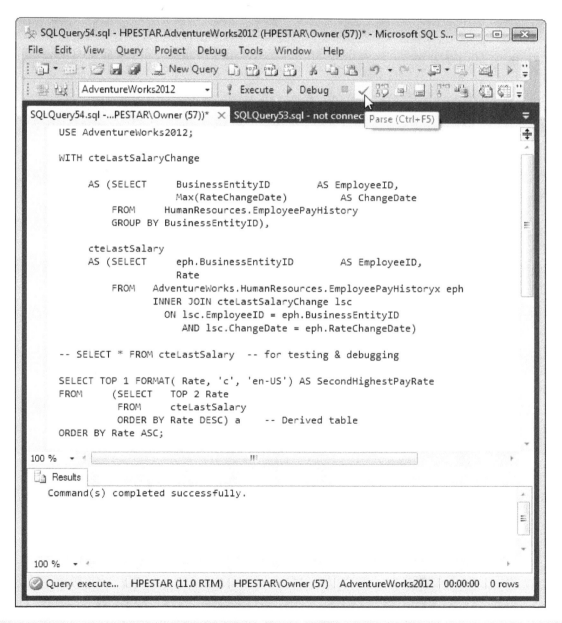

## Executing Single Batch Only

A single batch can be executed by selecting (highlighting) it and clicking on Execute.

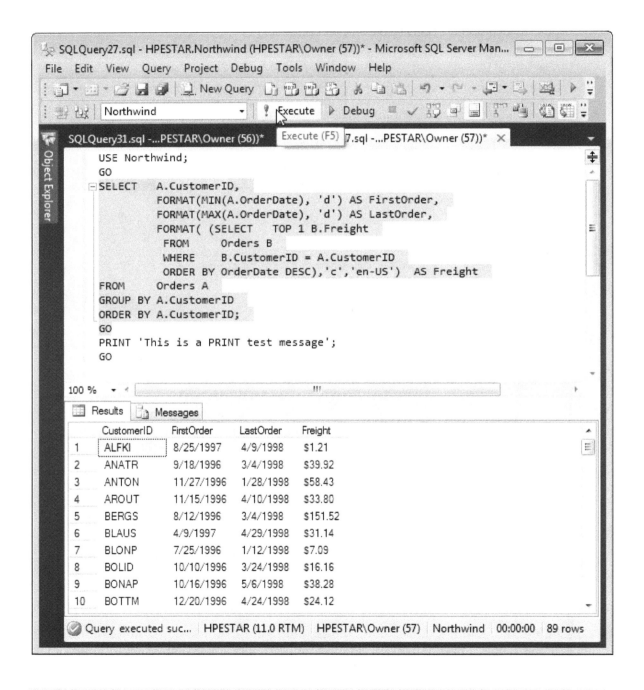

## Executing Part of a Query

A part of a query can be executed as long as it is a valid query, otherwise error results.  The query part has to be selected (highlighted) and the Execute button has to be pushed. The selected part of the query is considered a batch which is sent to the server. In this example, we executed the subquery (inner query) in the WHERE clause predicate.

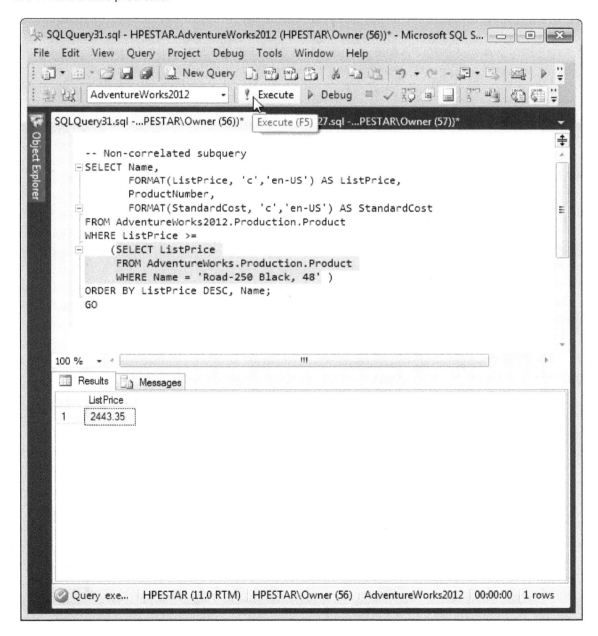

# Object Explorer

SSMS Object Explorer functions as:

- ➤ A tree-based directory of all database objects
- ➤ A launching base for graphical user-interface tools
- ➤ An access way to object properties

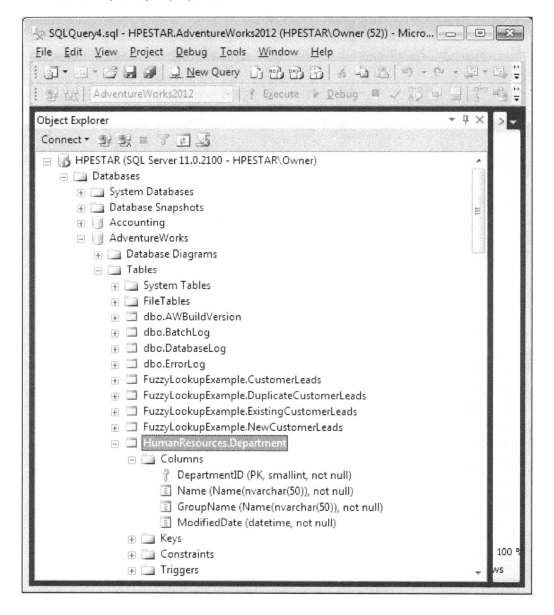

## Context-Sensitive Right-Click Menu

Based on what object the cursor is on, right-click menu changes accordingly, it is context-sensitive. In the following demo the cursor is on table object when we right click on the mouse.

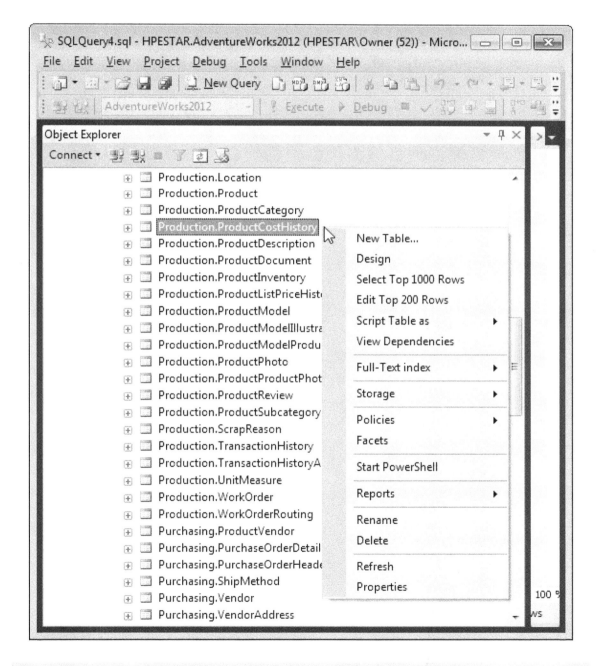

## Server Administration & Management Tools

All the available SQL Server administration and management tools can be accessed from the Object Explorer. Usually the Database Administrator (DBA) uses these tools.

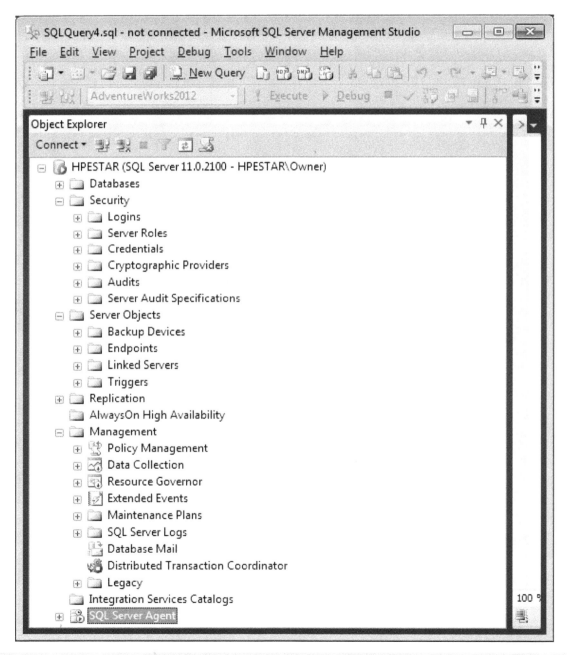

## SQL Server Agent Jobs to Automate Administration Tasks

SQL Server Agent is a job creation and scheduling facility with notification features. For example, database backup job can be scheduled to execute 2:15AM every night as shown on the following dialog box. Stored procedure execution can also be setup as a job and scheduled for periodic execution.

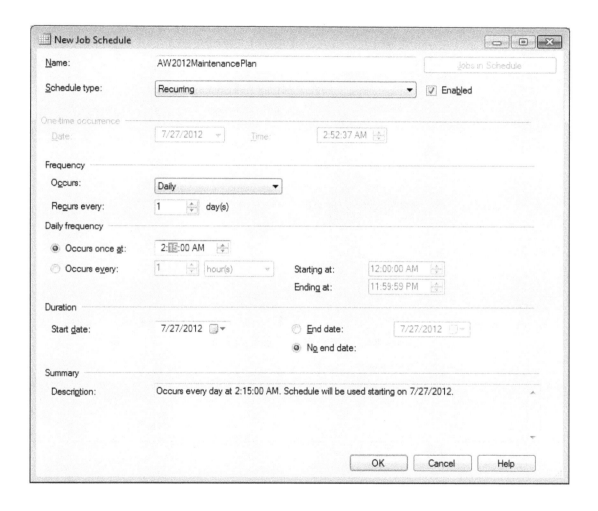

*Job properties panel can be used to create and manage jobs with multiple job steps and multiple schedules.*

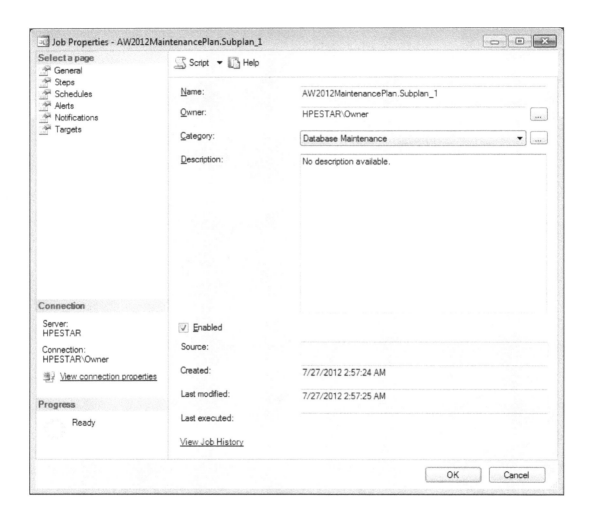

# Graphical Query Designer

The Design Query in Editor entry on the Query drop-down menu launches the graphical Query Designer which can be used to design the query with GUI method and the T-SQL SELECT code will be generated automatically upon completion.

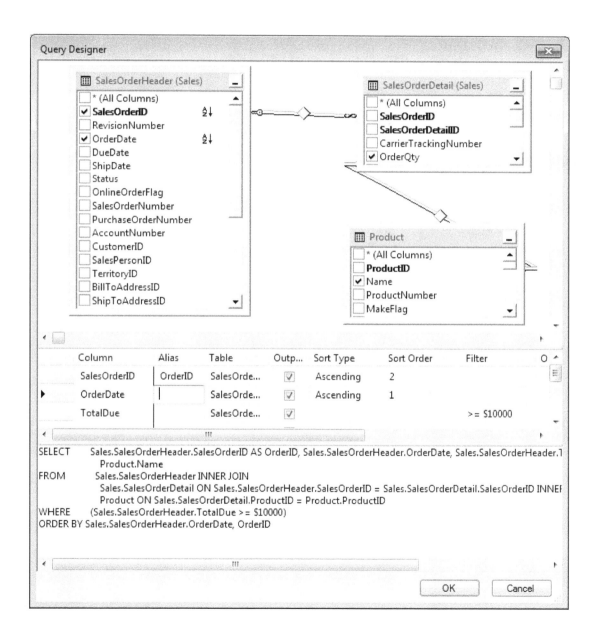

## Designing a GROUP BY Query in Query Designer

Query Designer can be used to design from simple to complex queries. It can also serve as a starter query for a more complex query. It is really easy to get the tables JOINs graphically.

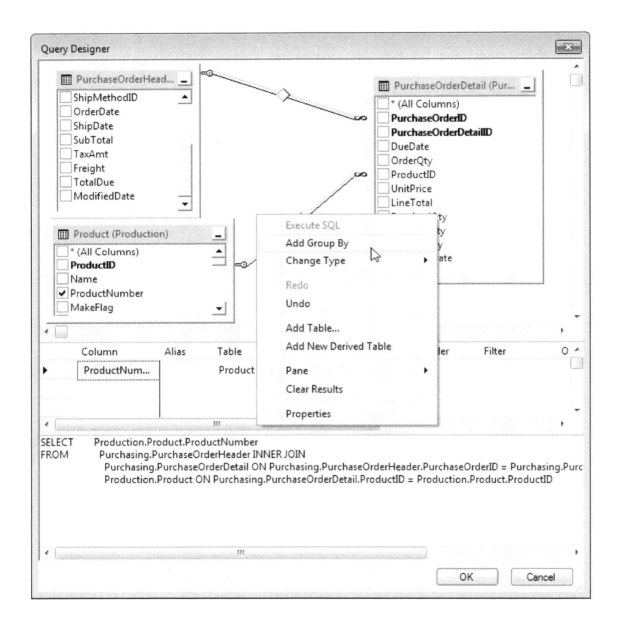

*The Production.Product.Name column will also be configured as GROUP BY (drop-down default).*

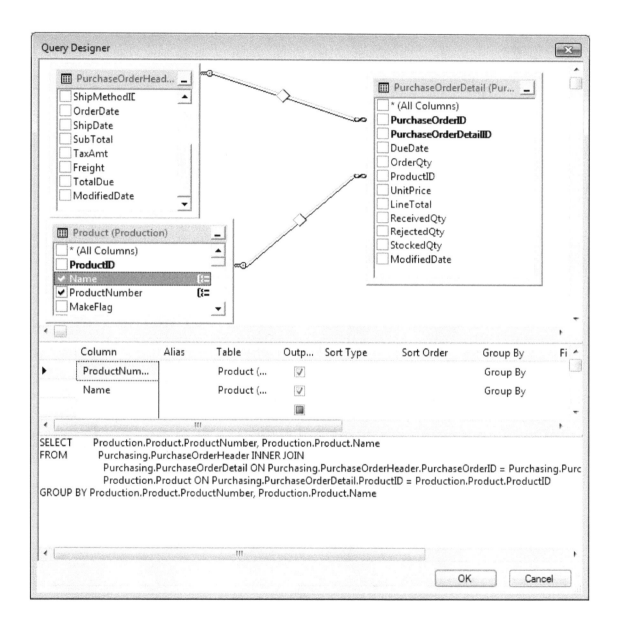

*We add the TotalDue column and change the summary function to "SUM" from "Group by" and configure sorting on the first column.*

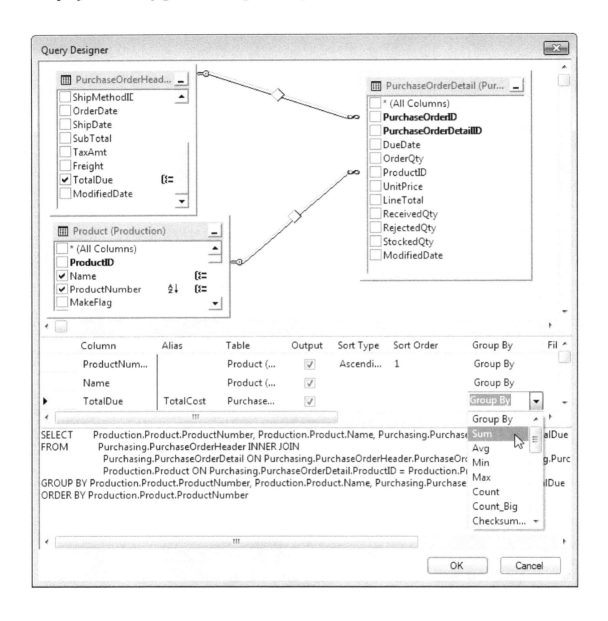

*After pressing OK, the query is moved into the Query Editor window. Frequently it requires reformatting.*

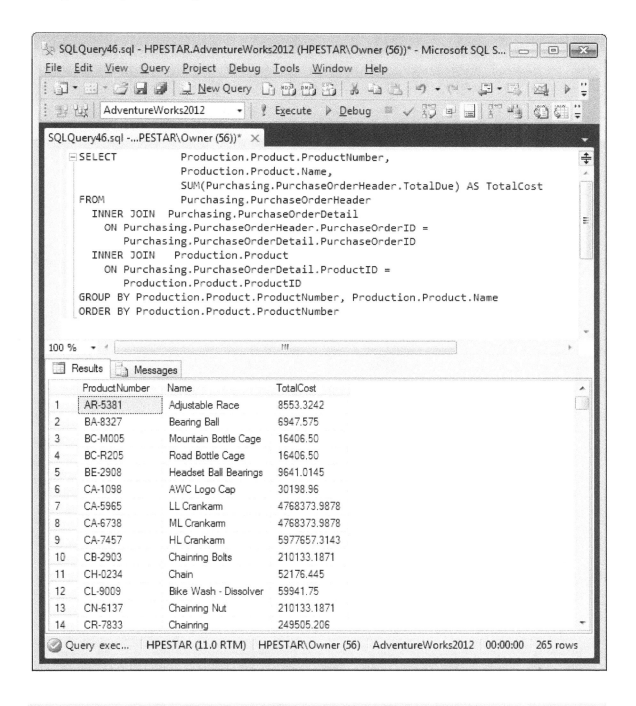

*The only remaining issue with the query is the 3-part column references which is hard to read. We can change the query for readability improvement by using table aliases.*

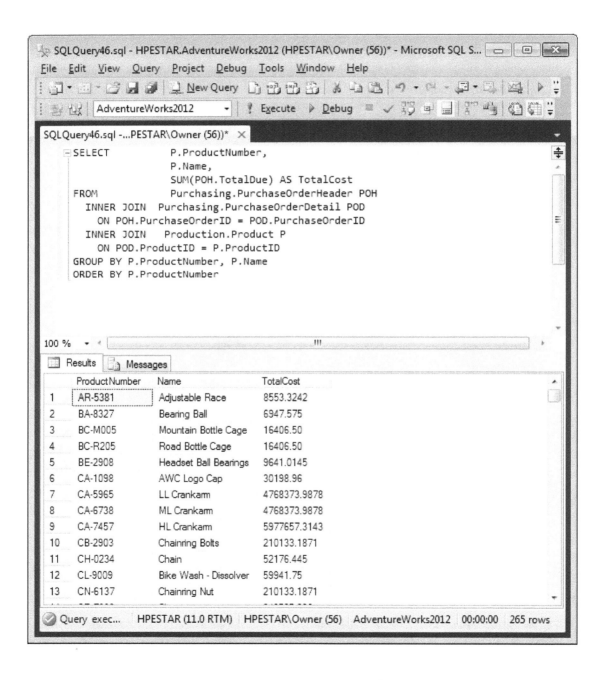

## Graphically Editing of an Existing Query

An existing query, exception certain complex queries, can be uploaded into the Graphical Query Designer the following way: select (highlight) the query and right-click for the drop-down menu; click on Design Query in Editor.

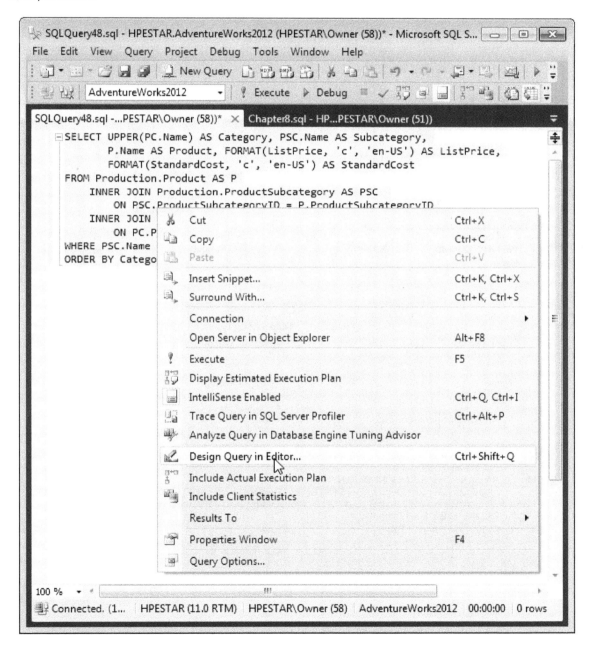

*Following screen image shows the query in the Graphical Query Designer after some manual beautifying such as moving the tables for better display.*

The query can be edited graphically and upon clicking on "OK", the query text is updated in the Query Editor window.

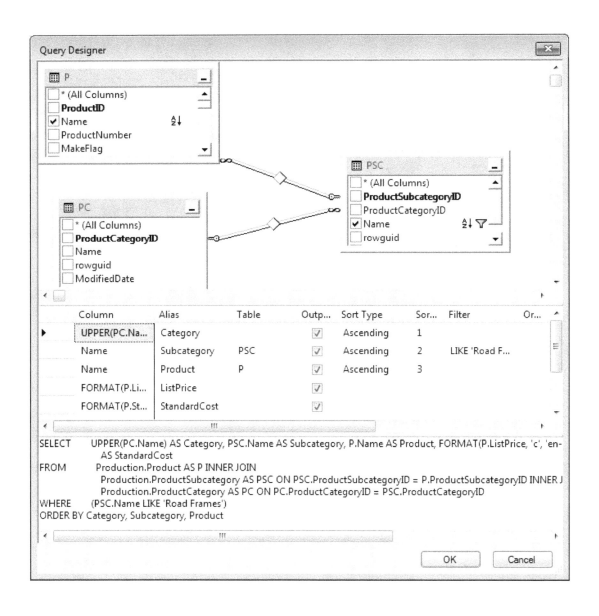

# Configuring Line Numbers in Query Editor

Line numbering is an option which is off by default. Line numbers are helpful to find errors in large queries or T-SQL scripts (a sequence of T-SQL statements) when the error references a line number. Following is an example an error which includes the line number.

*The Display Line Numbers option in the query editor can be activated from Options.*

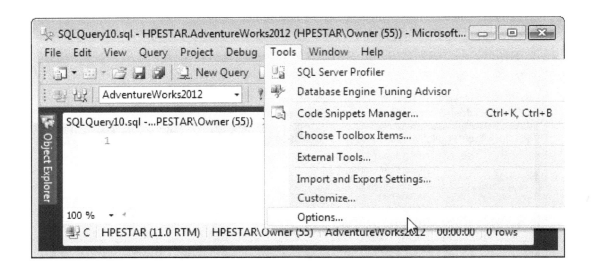

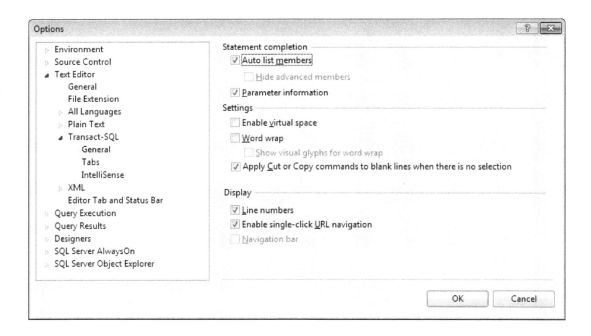

# IntelliSense - Your Smart Assistant

IntelliSense is a smart agent in Query Editor. It helps completing long object names and pointing out potential errors by red wave-lining them.

The Options configuration screen for IntelliSense.

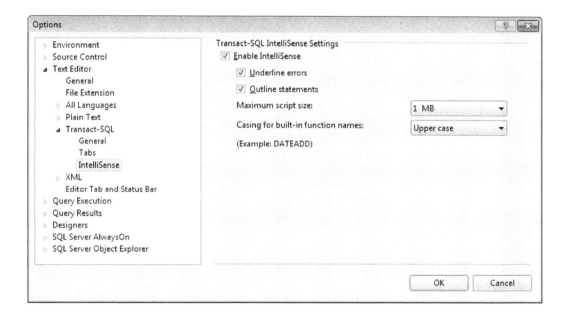

Underlining with red wave-line potential errors such as misspelling of a column name.

```
SELECT TOP 1000 [BillOfMaterialsID]
      ,[ProductAssemblyID]
      ,[ComponentID]
      ,[StartDate]
      ,[EndDate]
      ,[UnitMeasureCodex]
      ,[BOMLevel]
      ,[PerAssemblyQty]
      ,[ModifiedDate]
  FROM [AdventureWorks2012].[Production].[BillOfMaterials]
```

100 %

## IntelliSense Guessing and Completing Object Names

Screenshots show IntelliSense in action when typing queries.

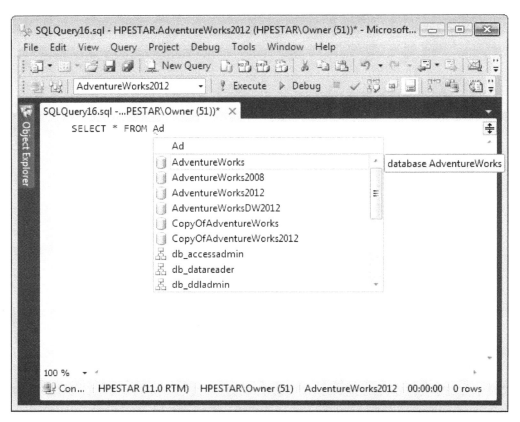

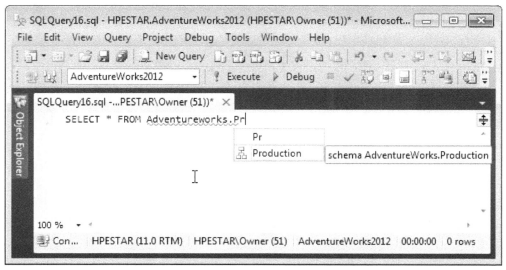

*IntelliSense drop-down menu for "Prod".*

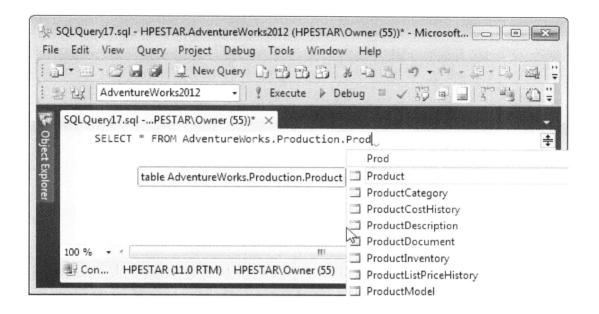

IntelliSense drop-down menu for "ProductS".

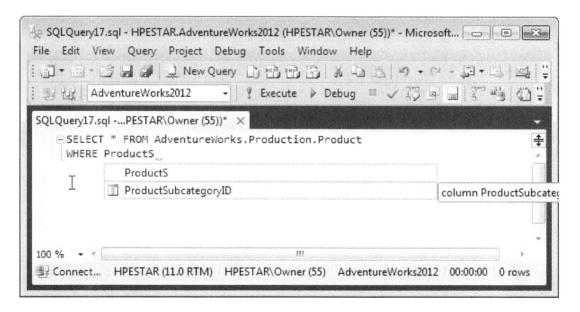

**CHAPTER 4: SQL Server Management Studio**

*IntelliSense completion assistance for "ProductN"*

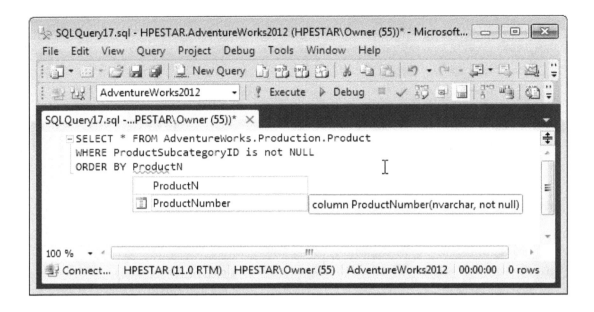

IntelliSense completion assistance for "Produ"

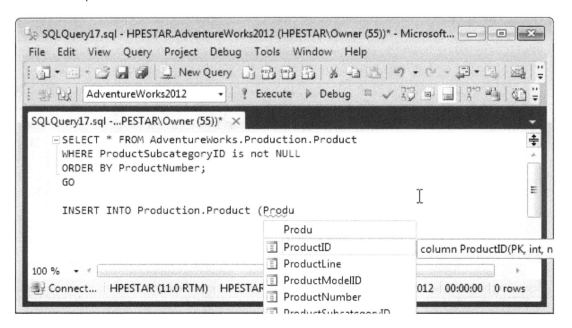

## IntelliSense Assisting with User-Defined Objects

IntelliSense helps out with a user-defined stored procedure execution.

```
SQLQuery75.sql - HPESTAR.AdventureWorks2012 (HPESTAR\Owner (58))* - Microsoft SQL S...

File   Edit   View   Query   Project   Debug   Tools   Window   Help

New Query                                                    Execute   Debug

AdventureWorks2012

SQLQuery75.sql -...PESTAR\Owner (58))*  ×

    USE AdventureWorks2012;
    GO
    CREATE PROCEDURE sprocProductPaging
      (
        @PageNumber int,
        @RowsPerPage int
      )
      AS
    BEGIN
    SELECT   ProductNumber,
             Name              AS ProductName,
             ListPrice,
             Color
      FROM Production.Product p
      WHERE ProductSubcategoryID is not NULL
      ORDER BY ProductNumber
      OFFSET (@PageNumber-1) * @RowsPerPage ROWS
      FETCH NEXT @RowsPerPage ROWS ONLY;
    END;
    GO
    -- Command(s) completed successfully.

    EXEC sprocProductPaging 10
    ┌──────────────────────────────────────────────────────────────────────┐
    │ AdventureWorks2012.dbo.sprocProductPaging@PageNumber int,@RowsPerPage int │
    │ Stored procedures always return INT.                                    │
    └──────────────────────────────────────────────────────────────────────┘

100 %

Query ex...   HPESTAR (11.0 RTM)   HPESTAR\Owner (58)   AdventureWorks2012   00:00:00   20 rows
```

## IntelliSense Smart Guessing Partial Word in Middle of Object Names

You don't have to remember how an object name starts. You just have to remember some part of the name.  Looking for the system view associated with "waits".

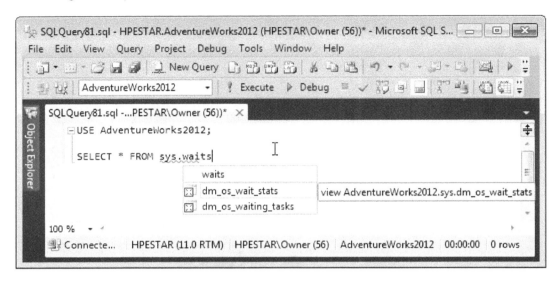

Looking for the SalesOrderHeader table but only remembering "head".

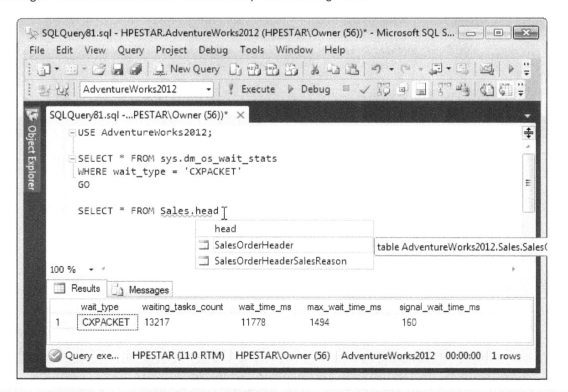

**CHAPTER 4:  SQL Server Management Studio**

## Hovering over Red Squiggly Underline Errors for Explanation

IntelliSense red wave (squiggly) underlining of errors which is caused, actually, by a single invalid table reference.

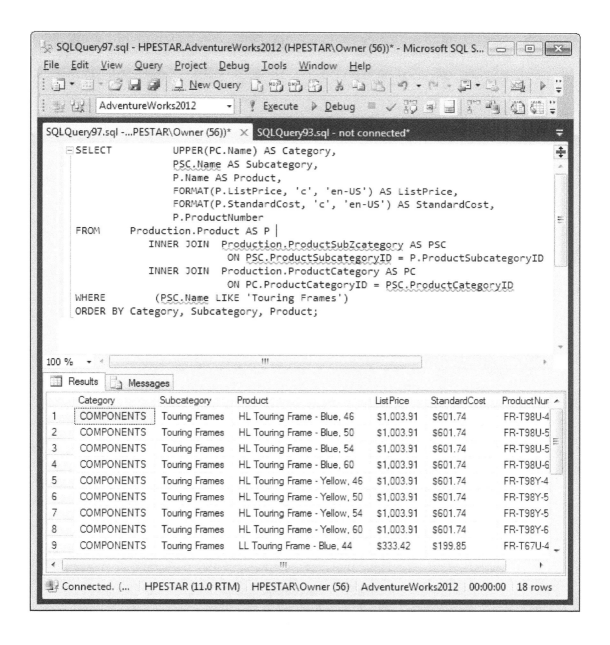

## Common Error: The multi-part identifier "abc" could not be bound.

Hovering over the first error results in an explanation pop-up. This is a distant error, the kind usually the hardest to solve, because, actually, it is a secondary error caused by the primary error which is located on a different line. In this instance, there are few lines difference only, but in a large stored procedure the difference can be 200 lines as an example.

```
PSC.Name AS Subcategory,
    The multi-part identifier "PSC.Name" could not be bound.
```

Hovering over the second error yields the cause of all errors: "ProductSubZcategory".

```
Production.ProductSubZcategory AS PSC
    Invalid object name 'Production.ProductSubZcategory'.
```

The remaining error messages are all "multi-part..." caused by the solitary invalid table reference.

```
PSC.ProductSubcategoryID = P.ProductSubcategoryID
    The multi-part identifier "PSC.ProductSubcategoryID" could not be bound.
```

After fixing the table name, all errors are gone.

```
SELECT          UPPER(PC.Name)                          AS Category,
                PSC.Name                                AS Subcategory,
                P.Name                                  AS Product,
                FORMAT(P.ListPrice, 'c', 'en-US')       AS ListPrice,
                FORMAT(P.StandardCost, 'c', 'en-US')    AS StandardCost,
                P.ProductNumber
FROM       Production.Product AS P
           INNER JOIN  Production.ProductSubcategory AS PSC
                       ON PSC.ProductSubcategoryID = P.ProductSubcategoryID
           INNER JOIN  Production.ProductCategory AS PC
                       ON PC.ProductCategoryID = PSC.ProductCategoryID
WHERE          (PSC.Name LIKE 'Touring Frames')
ORDER BY Category, Subcategory, Product;
```

# Refreshing IntelliSense Cache for New DB Objects

IntelliSense cache is not updated real-time. If new objects are created in another connection ( session ), they will not be seen until exit SSMS/reenter or IntelliSense cache is updated.  No red-wave underline for the **newly created object SOD** in the same connection.

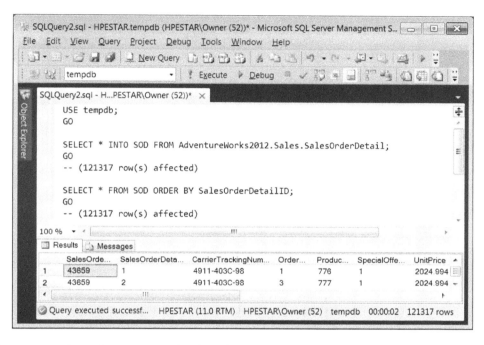

In another connection, the query works, but there are red squiggly underlining for the new table & column.

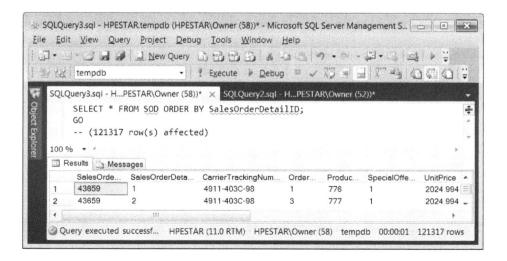

## *Refreshing IntelliSense Local Cache*

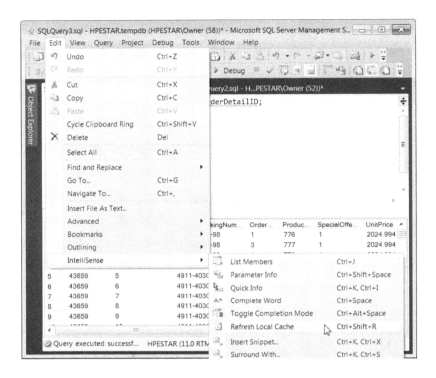

Squiggly red line goes away in all connections for the new database objects.

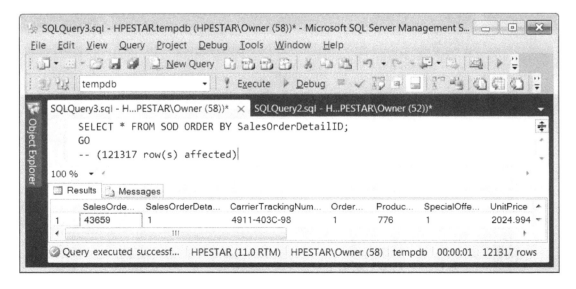

# CHAPTER 5: Basic Concepts of Client-Server Computing

## Client - Server Relational Database Management System

The "server" is SQL Server, operating on a powerful hardware platform, managing databases and related items. The client is application software. The real client is naturally a human user who runs the application software. Automated software which uses the database for one thing or another is also considered a "client". The client computer, in the next room or thousands of miles away, is connected to the server through communications link. The client software sends a request, a query, to SQL Server, after execution the server returns the results to the client. An example for a query sent by the client to the server:

SELECT ListPrice FROM AdventureWorks2012.Production.Product WHERE ProductID = 800;

SQL Server executes the query and returns "1120.49" to the client with a flag indicating successful query execution. A tempting analogy is a restaurant: kitchen is the server, patrons are the clients and the communications / delivery done by waiters & waitresses.

Screenshot displays SQL Server (highlighted) along with other related software such as SQL Server Agent (job scheduling facility) , SSIS ( data transformation & transfer), SSRS (Reporting), SSAS (OLAP Cube) and other auxiliary software.

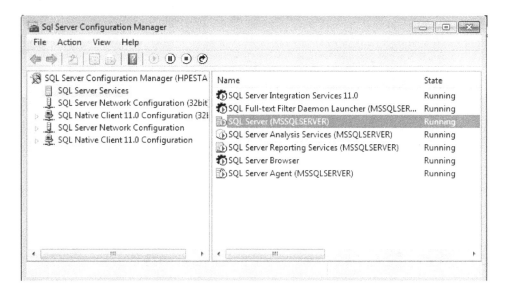

# Database Objects on Server-Side

Screenshot of Object Explorer displays almost all important database objects with the exception of constraints, triggers and indexes.

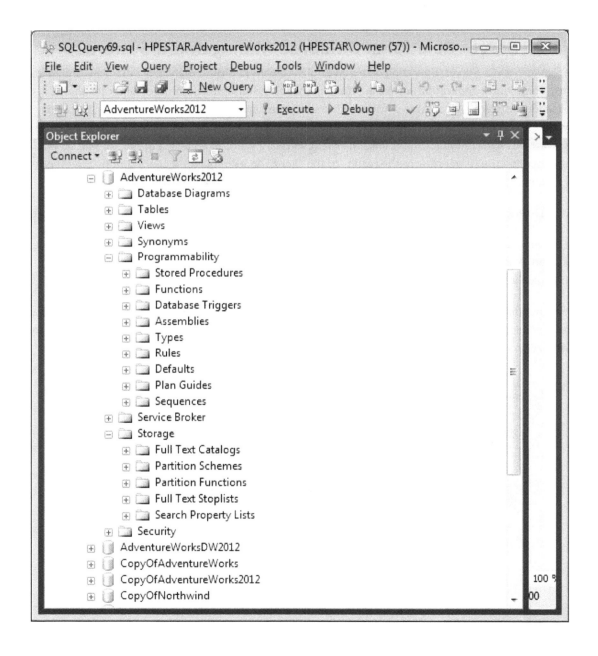

# Database Related Items on Client-Side

On the client side the following items:

- SQL Server client libraries to access the server and database
- SQL queries imbedded in application programs
- Stored procedure calls imbedded in application software

Queries by themselves are not database object. To make them database objects we have to build stored procedures, functions or views around them.

The following code segment illustrates database connection and query from ASP to Inventory database. In ANSI SQL terminology catalog means database.

```
' Connect
<%
Dim StrConnInventory
Dim ConnInventory

StrConnInventory = "Provider=SQLOLEDB.1;Data Source=LONDONHEADOFFICE;Initial
Catalog=Inventory;User ID=finance;Password=fa$nAnCe#9*"

Set ConnInventory = Server.CreateObject("ADODB.Connection")

ConnInventory.ConnectionTimeout = 4000
ConnInventory.CommandTimeout = 4000
ConnInventory.Open StrConnInventory

' Query
Dim YourQuery As String = "SELECT Name, Price FROM Product"
 Dim YourCommand As New SqlCommand(YourQuery)
 YourCommand.Connection = ConnInventory
 YourConnection.Open()
 YourCommand.ExecuteNonQuery()
 Response.Write(YourCommand)
 YourCommand.Connection.Close()
%>

' Disconnect
<%
ConnInventory.Close
Set ConnInventory = Nothing
%>
```

# SQL Server Profiler to Monitor Client-Server Communications

SQL Server Profiler, a tool in SSMS, has two modes of operations: interactive GUI and silent T-SQL script based operation. The simplest use of the Profiler is to check what queries are sent to the server (SQL Server) from the client and how long does processing take (duration). The client software sending the queries is SSMS.  Even though SSMS appears as the "face of SQL Server", it is only a client software.

```
USE pubs;
GO
SELECT * FROM titles;
GO


USE Northwind;
GO
SELECT * FROM Products ORDER BY ProductName;
GO


USE AdventureWorks2012;
GO
SELECT * FROM Sales.SalesOrderHeader WHERE OrderDate='20080201';
GO
```

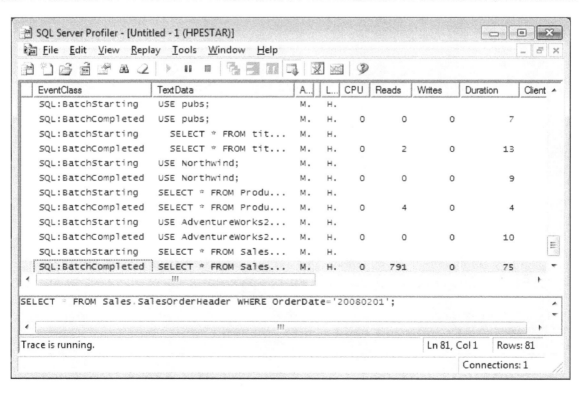

# Table - Database Object

A database table holds data in tabular format by rows and columns. The main method of connecting tables is  FOREIGN KEY referencing  PRIMARY KEY. A set of connected tables makes up the database. Screenshot displays the structure and partial content of Northwind database Products table.

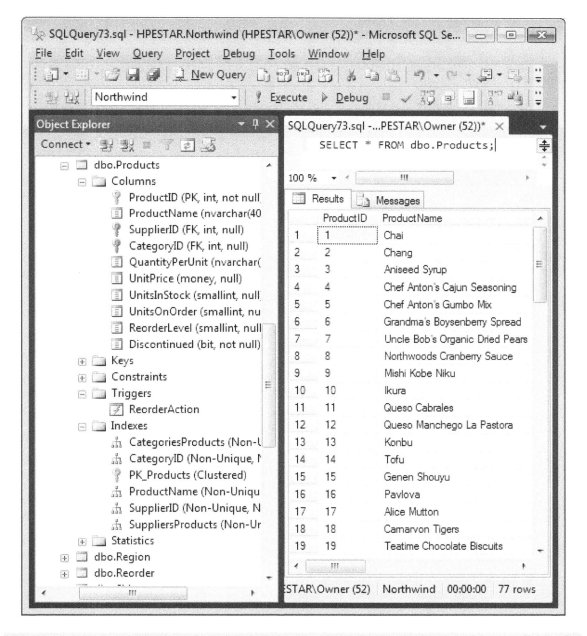

**CHAPTER 5:  Basic Concepts of Client-Server Computing**

## Tables in Production Schema

The listing and data dictionary description of tables in AdventureWorks2012 Production schema.

```
USE AdventureWorks2012;

SELECT   CONCAT('Production.', objname COLLATE DATABASE_DEFAULT)          AS TableName,
         value                                                           AS [Description]
FROM fn_listextendedproperty (    NULL,
                                  'schema', 'Production',
                                  'table', default,
                                   NULL, NULL)
ORDER BY TableName;
```

| TableName | Description |
| --- | --- |
| Production.BillOfMaterials | Items required to make bicycles and bicycle subassemblies. It identifies the hierarchical relationship between a parent product and its components. |
| Production.Culture | Lookup table containing the languages in which some AdventureWorks data is stored. |
| Production.Document | Product maintenance documents. |
| Production.Illustration | Bicycle assembly diagrams. |
| Production.Location | Product inventory and manufacturing locations. |
| Production.Product | Products sold or used in the manfacturing of sold products. |
| Production.ProductCategory | High-level product categorization. |
| Production.ProductCostHistory | Changes in the cost of a product over time. |
| Production.ProductDescription | Product descriptions in several languages. |
| Production.ProductDocument | Cross-reference table mapping products to related product documents. |
| Production.ProductInventory | Product inventory information. |
| Production.ProductListPriceHistory | Changes in the list price of a product over time. |
| Production.ProductModel | Product model classification. |
| Production.ProductModelIllustration | Cross-reference table mapping product models and illustrations. |
| Production.ProductModelProductDescriptionCulture | Cross-reference table mapping product descriptions and the language the description is written in. |
| Production.ProductPhoto | Product images. |
| Production.ProductProductPhoto | Cross-reference table mapping products and product photos. |
| Production.ProductReview | Customer reviews of products they have purchased. |
| Production.ProductSubcategory | Product subcategories. See ProductCategory table. |
| Production.ScrapReason | Manufacturing failure reasons lookup table. |
| Production.TransactionHistory | Record of each purchase order, sales order, or work order transaction year to date. |
| Production.TransactionHistoryArchive | Transactions for previous years. |
| Production.UnitMeasure | Unit of measure lookup table. |
| Production.WorkOrder | Manufacturing work orders. |
| Production.WorkOrderRouting | Work order details. |

# Index - Database Object

An index on a table is a B-tree based structure which speeds up random searches. **Typically PRIMARY KEY (automatic), FOREIGN KEY and WHERE clause columns have indexes.** If the index is constructed on more than one column, it is called **composite index**. If all the columns in a query are in the index, it is called **covering index**. Properties dialog box displays the PRIMARY KEY composite index of the EmployeeDepartmentHistory table.

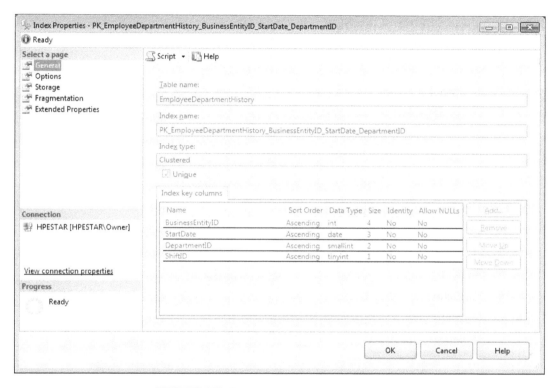

CHAPTER 5: Basic Concepts of Client-Server Computing

## Diagram of EmployeeDepartmentHistory and Related Tables

EmployeeDepartmentHistory is a simple junction table with three FOREIGN KEYS to the Employee, Shift and Department tables respectively.

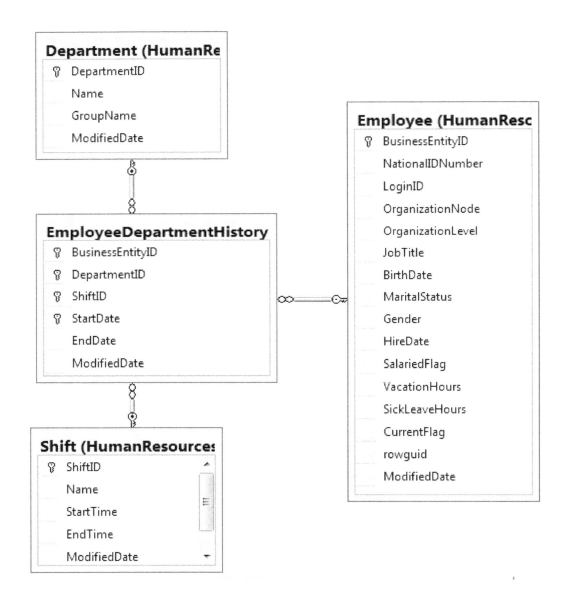

## Index Description in Data Dictionary

The indexes listing for Product, SalesOrderHeader & SalesOrderDetail tables.

```
USE AdventureWorks2012;
GO


SELECT   objtype                          AS ObjectType,
         'Sales.SalesOrderHeader'         AS TableName,
         objname                          AS ObjectName,
         value                            AS [Description]
FROM fn_listextendedproperty (NULL, 'schema', 'Sales', 'table', 'SalesOrderHeader', 'index', default)


UNION


SELECT objtype, 'Sales.SalesOrderDetail', objname, value
FROM fn_listextendedproperty (NULL, 'schema', 'Sales', 'table', 'SalesOrderDetail', 'index', default)


UNION


SELECT objtype, 'Production.Product', objname,  value
FROM fn_listextendedproperty (NULL, 'schema', 'Production', 'table', 'Product', 'index', default)
ORDER BY TableName;
GO
```

| ObjectType | TableName | ObjectName | Description |
|---|---|---|---|
| INDEX | Production.Product | AK_Product_Name | Unique nonclustered index. |
| INDEX | Production.Product | AK_Product_ProductNumber | Unique nonclustered index. |
| INDEX | Production.Product | AK_Product_rowguid | Unique nonclustered index. Used to support replication samples. |
| INDEX | Production.Product | PK_Product_ProductID | Clustered index created by a primary key constraint. |
| INDEX | Sales.SalesOrderDetail | AK_SalesOrderDetail_rowguid | Unique nonclustered index. Used to support replication samples. |
| INDEX | Sales.SalesOrderDetail | IX_SalesOrderDetail_ProductID | Nonclustered index. |
| INDEX | Sales.SalesOrderDetail | PK_SalesOrderDetail_SalesOrderID_SalesOrderDetailID | Clustered index created by a primary key constraint. |
| INDEX | Sales.SalesOrderHeader | AK_SalesOrderHeader_rowguid | Unique nonclustered index. Used to support replication samples. |
| INDEX | Sales.SalesOrderHeader | AK_SalesOrderHeader_SalesOrderNumber | Unique nonclustered index. |
| INDEX | Sales.SalesOrderHeader | IX_SalesOrderHeader_CustomerID | Nonclustered index. |
| INDEX | Sales.SalesOrderHeader | IX_SalesOrderHeader_SalesPersonID | Nonclustered index. |
| INDEX | Sales.SalesOrderHeader | PK_SalesOrderHeader_SalesOrderID | Clustered index created by a primary key constraint. |

## Constraint - Database Object

The **PRIMARY KEY constraint ensures that each row has a unique ID. The FOREIGN KEY constraint ensures that the FK points to (references) a valid PK. CHECK constraint enforces formulas (check clauses) defined for a column such as OrderQty > 0.** If the formula evaluates to TRUE, the CHECK constraint satisfied, otherwise ERROR condition is generated by the database engine. SSMS screenshot shows a CHECK constraints listing query and results in the Northwind database.

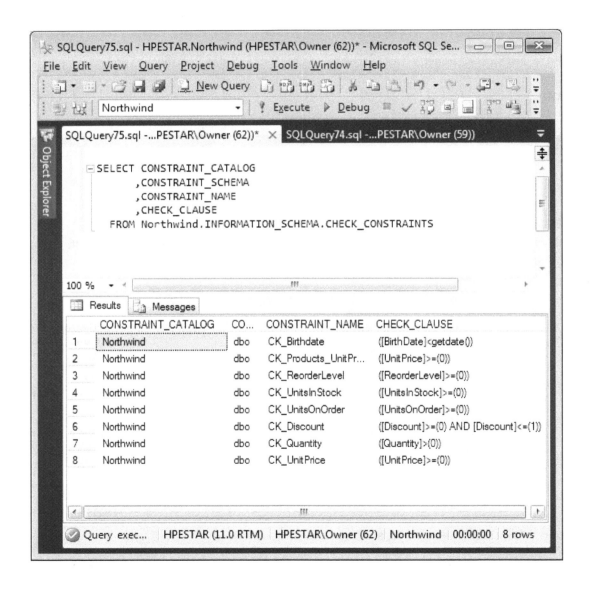

## PRIMARY KEY & FOREIGN KEY Constraint Descriptions in Data Dictionary

Query to retrieve constraint descriptions (extended properties) for Product, SalesOrderHeader & SalesOrderDetail tables. Note: *description* not definition.

```
USE AdventureWorks2012;
-- UNION of 3 result sets
SELECT objtype AS ObjectType, 'Sales.SalesOrderHeader' AS TableName,
        objname as ObjectName, value AS [Description]
FROM fn_listextendedproperty (NULL, 'schema', 'Sales', 'table', 'SalesOrderHeader', 'constraint', default)
WHERE left(convert(varchar,value),7)='Foreign' or left(convert(varchar,value),7)='Primary'
UNION
SELECT objtype, 'Sales.SalesOrderDetail', objname,  value
FROM fn_listextendedproperty (NULL, 'schema', 'Sales', 'table', 'SalesOrderDetail', 'constraint', default)
WHERE left(convert(varchar,value),7)='Foreign' or left(convert(varchar,value),7)='Primary'
UNION
SELECT objtype, 'Production.Product', objname,  value
FROM fn_listextendedproperty (NULL, 'schema', 'Production', 'table', 'Product', 'constraint', default)
WHERE left(convert(varchar,value),7)='Foreign' or left(convert(varchar,value),7)='Primary'
ORDER BY TableName, ObjectName DESC;
GO
```

| ObjectType | TableName | ObjectName | Description |
|---|---|---|---|
| CONSTRAINT | Production.Product | PK_Product_ProductID | Primary key (clustered) constraint |
| CONSTRAINT | Production.Product | FK_Product_UnitMeasure_WeightUnitMeasureCode | Foreign key constraint referencing UnitMeasure.UnitMeasureCode. |
| CONSTRAINT | Production.Product | FK_Product_UnitMeasure_SizeUnitMeasureCode | Foreign key constraint referencing UnitMeasure.UnitMeasureCode. |
| CONSTRAINT | Production.Product | FK_Product_ProductSubcategory_ProductSubcategoryID | Foreign key constraint referencing ProductSubcategory.ProductSubcategoryID. |
| CONSTRAINT | Production.Product | FK_Product_ProductModel_ProductModelID | Foreign key constraint referencing ProductModel.ProductModelID. |
| CONSTRAINT | Sales.SalesOrderDetail | PK_SalesOrderDetail_SalesOrderID_SalesOrderDetailID | Primary key (clustered) constraint |
| CONSTRAINT | Sales.SalesOrderDetail | FK_SalesOrderDetail_SpecialOfferProduct_SpecialOfferIDProductID | Foreign key constraint referencing SpecialOfferProduct.SpecialOfferIDProductID. |
| CONSTRAINT | Sales.SalesOrderDetail | FK_SalesOrderDetail_SalesOrderHeader_SalesOrderID | Foreign key constraint referencing SalesOrderHeader.PurchaseOrderID. |
| CONSTRAINT | Sales.SalesOrderHeader | PK_SalesOrderHeader_SalesOrderID | Primary key (clustered) constraint |
| CONSTRAINT | Sales.SalesOrderHeader | FK_SalesOrderHeader_ShipMethod_ShipMethodID | Foreign key constraint referencing ShipMethod.ShipMethodID. |
| CONSTRAINT | Sales.SalesOrderHeader | FK_SalesOrderHeader_SalesTerritory_TerritoryID | Foreign key constraint referencing SalesTerritory.TerritoryID. |
| CONSTRAINT | Sales.SalesOrderHeader | FK_SalesOrderHeader_SalesPerson_SalesPersonID | Foreign key constraint referencing SalesPerson.SalesPersonID. |
| CONSTRAINT | Sales.SalesOrderHeader | FK_SalesOrderHeader_Customer_CustomerID | Foreign key constraint referencing Customer.CustomerID. |
| CONSTRAINT | Sales.SalesOrderHeader | FK_SalesOrderHeader_CurrencyRate_CurrencyRateID | Foreign key constraint referencing CurrencyRate.CurrencyRateID. |
| CONSTRAINT | Sales.SalesOrderHeader | FK_SalesOrderHeader_CreditCard_CreditCardID | Foreign key constraint referencing CreditCard.CreditCardID. |
| CONSTRAINT | Sales.SalesOrderHeader | FK_SalesOrderHeader_Address_ShipToAddressID | Foreign key constraint referencing Address.AddressID. |
| CONSTRAINT | Sales.SalesOrderHeader | FK_SalesOrderHeader_Address_BillToAddressID | Foreign key constraint referencing Address.AddressID. |

# View - Database Object

A SELECT query, with some restrictions, can be repackaged as view and thus become a server-side object, a coveted status, from "homeless" to "mansion". The creation of view is very simple, basically a name assignment is required as shown in the following demonstration. As soon as the CREATE VIEW statement is executed successfully the query, unknown to the SQL Server so far, becomes an "official" SQL Server database object, stored in the database.  A view, a virtual table,  can be used just like a table in SELECT queries.  A note about the query: **the column aliases FirstAuthor and SecondAuthor cannot be used in the WHERE clause, only in the ORDER BY clause if present.**

SELECT results from views require ORDER BY if sorting is desired.  There is no way around it.

```
USE pubs;
GO


CREATE VIEW vAuthorsInSameCity
AS
SELECT          FirstAuthor       = CONCAT(au1.au_fname,' ', au1.au_lname),
                SecondAuthor      = CONCAT(au2.au_fname,' ', au2.au_lname),
                FirstCity         = au1.city,
                SecondCity        = au2.city
FROM    authors au1
     INNER JOIN authors au2
       ON au1.city = au2.city
WHERE   CONCAT(au1.au_fname,' ', au1.au_lname) < CONCAT(au2.au_fname,' ', au2.au_lname)
GO


SELECT * FROM vAuthorsInSameCity
ORDER BY FirstAuthor, SecondAuthor
GO
-- (13 row(s) affected) - Partial results.
```

| FirstAuthor | SecondAuthor | FirstCity | SecondCity |
|---|---|---|---|
| Abraham Bennet | Cheryl Carson | Berkeley | Berkeley |
| Albert Ringer | Anne Ringer | Salt Lake City | Salt Lake City |
| Ann Dull | Sheryl Hunter | Palo Alto | Palo Alto |
| Dean Straight | Dirk Stringer | Oakland | Oakland |
| Dean Straight | Livia Karsen | Oakland | Oakland |
| Dean Straight | Marjorie Green | Oakland | Oakland |
| Dean Straight | Stearns MacFeather | Oakland | Oakland |
| Dirk Stringer | Livia Karsen | Oakland | Oakland |

## View Descriptions in Data Dictionary
Query to list view descriptions in selected schemas.

```
USE AdventureWorks2012;
SELECT
        CONCAT('Sales.', objname COLLATE DATABASE_DEFAULT)            AS ViewName,
        value                                                        AS [Description]
FROM fn_listextendedproperty (NULL, 'schema', 'Sales', 'view', default, NULL, NULL)
UNION
SELECT
        CONCAT('Production.', objname COLLATE DATABASE_DEFAULT),
        value
FROM fn_listextendedproperty (NULL, 'schema', 'Production', 'view', default, NULL, NULL)
UNION
SELECT
        CONCAT('HumanResources.', objname COLLATE DATABASE_DEFAULT),
        value
FROM fn_listextendedproperty (NULL, 'schema', 'HumanResources', 'view', default, NULL, NULL)
UNION
SELECT
        CONCAT('Person.', objname COLLATE DATABASE_DEFAULT),
        value
FROM fn_listextendedproperty (NULL, 'schema', 'Person', 'view', default, NULL, NULL)   ORDER BY
ViewName;
```

| ViewName | Description |
| --- | --- |
| HumanResources.vEmployee | Employee names and addresses. |
| HumanResources.vEmployeeDepartment | Returns employee name, title, and current department. |
| HumanResources.vEmployeeDepartmentHistory | Returns employee name and current and previous departments. |
| HumanResources.vJobCandidate | Job candidate names and resumes. |
| HumanResources.vJobCandidateEducation | Displays the content from each education related element in the xml column Resume in the HumanResources.JobCandidate table. The content has been localized into French, Simplified Chinese and Thai. Some data may not display correctly unless supplemental language support is installed. |
| HumanResources.vJobCandidateEmployment | Displays the content from each employment history related element in the xml column Resume in the HumanResources.JobCandidate table. The content has been localized into French, Simplified Chinese and Thai. Some data may not display correctly unless supplemental language support is installed. |
| Person.vAdditionalContactInfo | Displays the contact name and content from each element in the xml column AdditionalContactInfo for that person. |
| Person.vStateProvinceCountryRegion | Joins StateProvince table with CountryRegion table. |
| Production.vProductAndDescription | Product names and descriptions. Product descriptions are provided in multiple languages. |
| Production.vProductModelCatalogDescription | Displays the content from each element in the xml column CatalogDescription for each product in the Production.ProductModel table that has catalog data. |
| Production.vProductModelInstructions | Displays the content from each element in the xml column Instructions for each product in the Production.ProductModel table that has manufacturing instructions. |
| Sales.vIndividualCustomer | Individual customers (names and addresses) that purchase Adventure Works Cycles products online. |
| Sales.vPersonDemographics | Displays the content from each element in the xml column Demographics for each customer in the Person.Person table. |
| Sales.vSalesPerson | Sales representatives (names and addresses) and their sales-related information. |
| Sales.vSalesPersonSalesByFiscalYears | Uses PIVOT to return aggregated sales information for each sales representative. |
| Sales.vStoreWithAddresses | Stores (including store addresses) that sell Adventure Works Cycles products to consumers. |
| Sales.vStoreWithContacts | Stores (including store contacts) that sell Adventure Works Cycles products to consumers. |
| Sales.vStoreWithDemographics | Stores (including demographics) that sell Adventure Works Cycles products to consumers. |

## Graphical View Designer

A view can be designed graphically or an existing view altered by using the Design option on the View drop-down menu in SSMS Object Explorer. First we create a view, then enter the graphical view designer to take a look.

```
USE [Northwind];
GO
CREATE VIEW [dbo].[ListOfProducts] AS
SELECT Categories.CategoryName as Category, ProductName, CompanyName AS Supplier
FROM Categories           INNER JOIN Products  ON Categories.CategoryID = Products.CategoryID
                          INNER JOIN Suppliers  ON Suppliers.SupplierID = Products.SupplierID
WHERE (((Products.Discontinued)=0));
GO
```

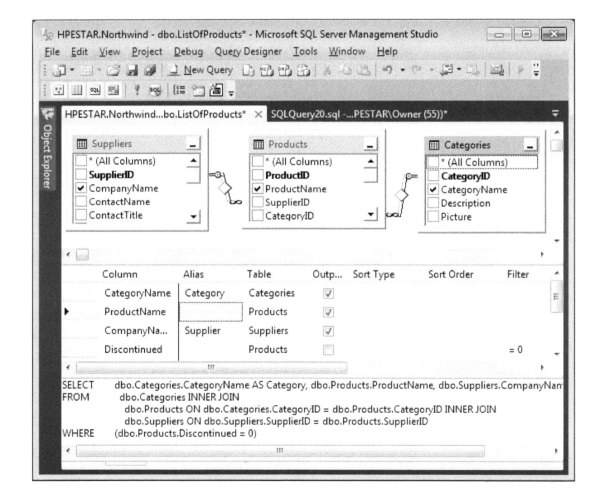

# Stored Procedures: Server-Side Programs

Stored procedures are T-SQL programs with optional input/output parameters. They vary from very simply to extremely complex. Following is the query which we will transform into a stored procedure, a server-side database object. Typical stored procedure returns table-like results to the client application software just like a SELECT query. That is though not a requirement.

```
USE AdventureWorks2012;
GO
SELECT          P.Name                          AS Product,
                L.Name                          AS [Inventory Location],
                SUM(PI.Quantity)                AS [Qty Available]
FROM Production.Product AS P
   INNER JOIN Production.ProductInventory AS PI
              ON P.ProductID = PI.ProductID
   INNER JOIN Production.Location AS L
              ON PI.LocationID = L.LocationID
   INNER JOIN Production.ProductSubcategory SC
              ON P.ProductSubcategoryID = SC.ProductSubcategoryID
WHERE SC.Name = 'Touring Bikes'
GROUP BY P.Name, L.Name
ORDER BY P.Name;
GO
-- (44 row(s) affected) - Partial results.
```

| Product | Inventory Location | Qty Available |
|---------|-------------------|---------------|
| Touring-1000 Blue, 46 | Final Assembly | 86 |
| Touring-1000 Blue, 46 | Finished Goods Storage | 99 |
| Touring-1000 Blue, 50 | Final Assembly | 81 |
| Touring-1000 Blue, 50 | Finished Goods Storage | 67 |
| Touring-1000 Blue, 54 | Final Assembly | 60 |
| Touring-1000 Blue, 54 | Finished Goods Storage | 73 |
| Touring-1000 Blue, 60 | Final Assembly | 99 |
| Touring-1000 Blue, 60 | Finished Goods Storage | 30 |
| Touring-1000 Yellow, 46 | Final Assembly | 83 |
| Touring-1000 Yellow, 46 | Finished Goods Storage | 65 |
| Touring-1000 Yellow, 50 | Final Assembly | 62 |
| Touring-1000 Yellow, 50 | Finished Goods Storage | 75 |
| Touring-1000 Yellow, 54 | Final Assembly | 40 |
| Touring-1000 Yellow, 54 | Finished Goods Storage | 35 |
| Touring-1000 Yellow, 60 | Final Assembly | 100 |

## Stored Procedure with Input Parameters

To make the stored procedure even more useful, we replace the literal 'Touring Bikes' with an input parameter.

```
CREATE PROC uspProductInventoryLocation @Subcategory nvarchar(50)
AS
BEGIN
SELECT          P.Name                    AS Product,
                L.Name                    AS [Inventory Location],
                SUM(PI.Quantity)          AS [Qty Available]
FROM Production.Product AS P
   INNER JOIN Production.ProductInventory AS PI
            ON P.ProductID = PI.ProductID
   INNER JOIN Production.Location AS L
            ON PI.LocationID = L.LocationID
   INNER JOIN Production.ProductSubcategory SC
            ON P.ProductSubcategoryID = SC.ProductSubcategoryID
WHERE SC.Name = @Subcategory
GROUP BY P.Name, L.Name
ORDER BY P.Name;
END
GO


-- Execute stored procedure with parameter
EXEC uspProductInventoryLocation 'Touring Bikes';
-- (44 row(s) affected)

EXEC uspProductInventoryLocation 'Mountain Bikes';          -- (64 row(s) affected) - Partial results.
```

| Product | Inventory Location | Qty Available |
| --- | --- | --- |
| Mountain-100 Black, 38 | Final Assembly | 56 |
| Mountain-100 Black, 38 | Finished Goods Storage | 99 |
| Mountain-100 Black, 42 | Final Assembly | 116 |
| Mountain-100 Black, 42 | Finished Goods Storage | 78 |
| Mountain-100 Black, 44 | Final Assembly | 100 |
| Mountain-100 Black, 44 | Finished Goods Storage | 49 |
| Mountain-100 Black, 48 | Final Assembly | 65 |
| Mountain-100 Black, 48 | Finished Goods Storage | 88 |
| Mountain-100 Silver, 38 | Final Assembly | 100 |
| Mountain-100 Silver, 38 | Finished Goods Storage | 49 |
| Mountain-100 Silver, 42 | Final Assembly | 65 |
| Mountain-100 Silver, 42 | Finished Goods Storage | 88 |
| Mountain-100 Silver, 44 | Final Assembly | 75 |
| Mountain-100 Silver, 44 | Finished Goods Storage | 83 |
| Mountain-100 Silver, 48 | Final Assembly | 102 |

## Stored Procedure Descriptions in Data Dictionary

Query to list stored procedure descriptions in selected schemas.

```
USE AdventureWorks2012;

SELECT
        CONCAT('dbo.', objname COLLATE DATABASE_DEFAULT)          AS SprocName,
        value                                                     AS [Description]
FROM fn_listextendedproperty (NULL, 'schema', 'dbo', 'procedure', default, NULL, NULL)
WHERE LEN(convert(nvarchar(max),value)) > 4
UNION
SELECT
        CONCAT('dbo.', objname COLLATE DATABASE_DEFAULT),
        value
FROM fn_listextendedproperty (NULL, 'schema', 'HumanResources', 'procedure', default, NULL, NULL)
ORDER BY SprocName;
```

| SprocName | Description |
| --- | --- |
| dbo.uspGetBillOfMaterials | Stored procedure using a recursive query to return a multi-level bill of material for the specified ProductID. |
| dbo.uspGetEmployeeManagers | Stored procedure using a recursive query to return the direct and indirect managers of the specified employee. |
| dbo.uspGetManagerEmployees | Stored procedure using a recursive query to return the direct and indirect employees of the specified manager. |
| dbo.uspGetWhereUsedProductID | Stored procedure using a recursive query to return all components or assemblies that directly or indirectly use the specified ProductID. |
| dbo.uspLogError | Logs error information in the ErrorLog table about the error that caused execution to jump to the CATCH block of a TRY...CATCH construct. Should be executed from within the scope of a CATCH block otherwise it will return without inserting error information. |
| dbo.uspPrintError | Prints error information about the error that caused execution to jump to the CATCH block of a TRY...CATCH construct. Should be executed from within the scope of a CATCH block otherwise it will return without printing any error information. |
| dbo.uspUpdateEmployeeHireInfo | Updates the Employee table and inserts a new row in the EmployeePayHistory table with the values specified in the input parameters. |
| dbo.uspUpdateEmployeeLogin | Updates the Employee table with the values specified in the input parameters for the given BusinessEntityID. |
| dbo.uspUpdateEmployeePersonalInfo | Updates the Employee table with the values specified in the input parameters for the given EmployeeID. |

# Trigger: Event Fired Server-Side Program

Trigger is like a stored procedure with four differences:

- ➤ Trigger is fired by an event such as table insert not by a call like a stored procedure.
- ➤ Trigger has the deleted (old row copy) and inserted (new row copy) tables available.
- ➤ Trigger does not have input/output parameter option.
- ➤ Trigger never returns table-like results.

Trigger to synchronize data in StateTaxFreeBondArchive table if data is inserted or updated in the StateTaxFreeBond table.

```
CREATE TRIGGER trgFillInMissingCouponRate

ON [dbo].StateTaxFreeBond

FOR INSERT,UPDATE

AS

BEGIN

    UPDATE StateTaxFreeBondArchive

        SET CouponRate = isnull(i.CouponRate,m.CouponRate)

    FROM StateTaxFreeBondArchive m

        INNER JOIN inserted i

            ON m.MBCID = i.MBCID

END

GO
```

Once a trigger is compiled, it is active and working silently in the background whenever insert, update or delete event fires it up.

**It is important to note that there is a downside to the trigger** "stealth" operation: if a trigger is dropped , it may not be noticed as part of the day-to-day operation. This behaviour is unlike  stored procedure whereby if dropped, it causes error in the calling application software which can be noticed by users.

# Functions: Read-Only Server-Side Programs

A user-defined function is also a program like a stored procedure, however, **no database change can be performed within a function, read only**. The database can be changed both in a trigger and a stored procedure. The following T-SQL script demonstrates the creation and use of a table-valued user-defined function. The other function type is scalar-valued, returns only a single value.

```
CREATE FUNCTION dbo.ufnSplitCommaDelimitedIntegerString (@NumberList nvarchar(max))
RETURNS @SplitList TABLE ( Element INT )
AS
 BEGIN
   DECLARE @Pointer   int,
        @Element nvarchar(32)
   SET @NumberList = LTRIM(RTRIM(@NumberList))
   IF ( RIGHT(@NumberList, 1) != ',' )
    SET @NumberList=@NumberList + ','
   SET @Pointer = CHARINDEX(',', @NumberList, 1)
   IF REPLACE(@NumberList, ',', '') <> ''
    BEGIN
      WHILE ( @Pointer > 0 )
       BEGIN
         SET @Element = LTRIM(RTRIM(LEFT(@NumberList, @Pointer - 1)))
         IF ( @Element <> '' )
          INSERT INTO @SplitList
          VALUES    (CONVERT(int, @Element))
         SET @NumberList = RIGHT(@NumberList,
                 LEN(@NumberList) - @Pointer  )
         SET @Pointer = CHARINDEX(',', @NumberList, 1)
       END
     END
   RETURN
 END;
GO
```

SELECT * FROM  dbo.ufnSplitCommaDelimitedIntegerString ('1, 2, 4, 8, 16, 32, 64, 128, 256');

| Element |
| --- |
| 1 |
| 2 |
| 4 |
| 8 |
| 16 |
| 32 |
| 64 |
| 128 |
| 256 |

**CHAPTER 5:  Basic Concepts of Client-Server Computing**

## User-Defined Function Descriptions in Data Dictionary

Query to list user-defined function descriptions in the default "dbo" schema. "dbo" stands for database owner, a database role.

```
USE AdventureWorks2012;
GO

SELECT
        CONCAT('dbo.', objname COLLATE DATABASE_DEFAULT)             AS UDFName,
        value                                                       AS [Description]
FROM fn_listextendedproperty (NULL, 'schema', 'dbo', 'function', default, NULL, NULL)
WHERE LEN(convert(nvarchar(max),value)) > 4
ORDER BY UDFName;
GO
```

| UDFName | Description |
| --- | --- |
| dbo.ufnGetAccountingEndDate | Scalar function used in the uSalesOrderHeader trigger to set the starting account date. |
| dbo.ufnGetAccountingStartDate | Scalar function used in the uSalesOrderHeader trigger to set the ending account date. |
| dbo.ufnGetContactInformation | Table value function returning the first name, last name, job title and contact type for a given contact. |
| dbo.ufnGetDocumentStatusText | Scalar function returning the text representation of the Status column in the Document table. |
| dbo.ufnGetProductDealerPrice | Scalar function returning the dealer price for a given product on a particular order date. |
| dbo.ufnGetProductListPrice | Scalar function returning the list price for a given product on a particular order date. |
| dbo.ufnGetProductStandardCost | Scalar function returning the standard cost for a given product on a particular order date. |
| dbo.ufnGetPurchaseOrderStatusText | Scalar function returning the text representation of the Status column in the PurchaseOrderHeader table. |
| dbo.ufnGetSalesOrderStatusText | Scalar function returning the text representation of the Status column in the SalesOrderHeader table. |
| dbo.ufnGetStock | Scalar function returning the quantity of inventory in LocationID 6 (Miscellaneous Storage)for a specified ProductID. |
| dbo.ufnLeadingZeros | Scalar function used by the Sales.Customer table to help set the account number |

# Sequence - Database Object

The INT IDENTITY(1,1) function commonly used as **SURROGATE PRIMARY KEY** is limited to the host table. Sequence object, new in SQL Server 2012, can be shared by tables and programs.  T-SQL script to demonstrate how two tables can share an integer sequence.

```
USE AdventureWorks2012;
GO
CREATE SEQUENCE CustomerSequence as INT
START WITH 1  INCREMENT BY 1;
GO
CREATE TABLE LONDONCustomer
(
        CustomerID      INT PRIMARY KEY,
        Name            NVARCHAR(64) UNIQUE,
        ModifiedDate    DATE default (CURRENT_TIMESTAMP)    );
GO
CREATE TABLE NYCCustomer
(
        CustomerID      INT PRIMARY KEY,
        Name            NVARCHAR(64) UNIQUE,
        ModifiedDate    DATE default (CURRENT_TIMESTAMP)    );
GO
INSERT NYCCustomer (CustomerID, Name)
VALUES
        (NEXT VALUE FOR CustomerSequence, 'Richard Blackstone'),
        (NEXT VALUE FOR CustomerSequence, 'Anna Smithfield');
GO
SELECT * FROM NYCCustomer;
```

| CustomerID | Name | ModifiedDate |
|---|---|---|
| 1 | Richard Blackstone | 2016-07-18 |
| 2 | Anna Smithfield | 2016-07-18 |

```
INSERT LONDONCustomer (CustomerID, Name)
VALUES
        (NEXT VALUE FOR CustomerSequence, 'Kevin Lionheart'),
        (NEXT VALUE FOR CustomerSequence, 'Linda Wakefield');
GO

SELECT * FROM LONDONCustomer;
```

| CustomerID | Name | ModifiedDate |
|---|---|---|
| 3 | Kevin Lionheart | 2016-07-18 |
| 4 | Linda Wakefield | 2016-07-18 |

**CHAPTER 5:  Basic Concepts of Client-Server Computing**

# ROW_NUMBER() and Ranking Functions

Ranking functions (window functions), introduced with SQL Server 2005, provide sequencing and ranking items in a partition or all.  ROW_NUMBER() (sequence) function is the most used.

```
SELECT  CustomerID,
        CONVERT(date, OrderDate)                          AS OrderDate,
        RANK() OVER (    PARTITION BY CustomerID
                         ORDER BY OrderDate DESC)          AS RankNo
FROM   AdventureWorks2012.Sales.SalesOrderHeader
ORDER  BY CustomerID,  RankNo;
GO
-- (31465 row(s) affected) - Partial results.
```

| CustomerID | OrderDate | RankNo |
|---|---|---|
| 11014 | 2007-11-01 | 1 |
| 11014 | 2007-09-24 | 2 |
| 11015 | 2007-07-22 | 1 |
| 11016 | 2007-08-13 | 1 |
| 11017 | 2008-04-16 | 1 |
| 11017 | 2007-07-05 | 2 |
| 11017 | 2005-07-15 | 3 |
| 11018 | 2008-04-26 | 1 |
| 11018 | 2007-07-20 | 2 |
| 11018 | 2005-07-20 | 3 |
| 11019 | 2008-07-15 | 1 |
| 11019 | 2008-07-14 | 2 |
| 11019 | 2008-06-12 | 3 |
| 11019 | 2008-06-02 | 4 |
| 11019 | 2008-06-01 | 5 |
| 11019 | 2008-04-28 | 6 |
| 11019 | 2008-04-19 | 7 |
| 11019 | 2008-03-22 | 8 |
| 11019 | 2008-03-11 | 9 |
| 11019 | 2008-02-23 | 10 |
| 11019 | 2008-01-24 | 11 |
| 11019 | 2007-11-26 | 12 |
| 11019 | 2007-11-09 | 13 |
| 11019 | 2007-10-30 | 14 |
| 11019 | 2007-09-14 | 15 |
| 11019 | 2007-09-05 | 16 |
| 11019 | 2007-08-16 | 17 |
| 11020 | 2007-07-02 | 1 |

*Partition data by CustomerID and rank it OrderDate DESC (most recent orders first).*

```
SELECT *
FROM   (SELECT CustomerID,
           CONVERT(date, OrderDate)        AS OrderDate,
           RANK()  OVER (
              PARTITION BY CustomerID
              ORDER BY OrderDate DESC)       AS RankNo
       FROM   AdventureWorks2012.Sales.SalesOrderHeader)  x -- derived table
WHERE  RankNo  BETWEEN 1 AND 4
ORDER  BY CustomerID;
GO
-- (29383 row(s) affected)  - Partial results.
```

| CustomerID | OrderDate | RankNo |
|---|---|---|
| 11675 | 2007-08-13 | 1 |
| 11675 | 2006-04-27 | 2 |
| 11676 | 2008-06-11 | 1 |
| 11676 | 2008-02-21 | 2 |
| 11677 | 2008-06-02 | 1 |
| 11677 | 2008-03-24 | 2 |
| 11677 | 2008-03-17 | 3 |
| 11677 | 2008-03-07 | 4 |
| 11678 | 2007-08-09 | 1 |
| 11678 | 2006-04-12 | 2 |
| 11679 | 2008-06-01 | 1 |
| 11679 | 2008-04-15 | 2 |
| 11680 | 2008-07-22 | 1 |
| 11680 | 2008-03-04 | 2 |
| 11681 | 2008-05-28 | 1 |
| 11681 | 2007-09-08 | 2 |
| 11682 | 2008-06-11 | 1 |
| 11682 | 2008-03-08 | 2 |
| 11683 | 2007-08-11 | 1 |
| 11683 | 2006-04-07 | 2 |
| 11684 | 2008-06-14 | 1 |
| 11684 | 2008-01-02 | 2 |
| 11685 | 2008-06-15 | 1 |
| 11685 | 2007-09-12 | 2 |
| 11686 | 2007-10-26 | 1 |
| 11686 | 2007-09-09 | 2 |
| 11687 | 2007-12-23 | 1 |
| 11687 | 2007-10-14 | 2 |
| 11688 | 2007-08-18 | 1 |
| 11688 | 2006-04-04 | 2 |
| 11689 | 2008-03-05 | 1 |
| 11689 | 2008-02-27 | 2 |

## *Query to compare RANK, DENSE_RANK and NTILE.*

USE AdventureWorks;

```
SELECT  c.AccountNumber                          AS CustAccount,
    FLOOR(h.SubTotal / 1000)                     AS [SubTotal (Thousands $)],
    ROW_NUMBER() OVER(
        ORDER BY FLOOR(h.SubTotal /1000) DESC)    AS RowNumber,
    RANK()  OVER(
        ORDER BY FLOOR(h.SubTotal /1000) DESC)   AS Rank,
    DENSE_RANK()  OVER(
        ORDER BY FLOOR(h.SubTotal /1000) DESC)   AS DenseRank,
    NTILE(5)  OVER(
        ORDER BY FLOOR(h.SubTotal /1000) DESC)   AS NTile
FROM   Sales.Customer c
    INNER JOIN Sales.SalesOrderHeader h
        ON c.CustomerID = h.CustomerID
    INNER JOIN Sales.SalesTerritory t
        ON h.TerritoryID = t.TerritoryID
WHERE  t.Name = 'Germany'
        AND OrderDate >= '20040101' AND OrderDate  <  DATEADD(yy, 1, '20040101' )
        AND SubTotal >= 4000.0
ORDER  BY RowNumber;
```

| CustAccount | SubTotal (Thousands $) | RowNumber | Rank | DenseRank | NTile |
|---|---|---|---|---|---|
| AW00000230 | 100.00 | 1 | 1 | 1 | 1 |
| AW00000230 | 88.00 | 2 | 2 | 2 | 1 |
| AW00000302 | 77.00 | 3 | 3 | 3 | 1 |
| AW00000320 | 68.00 | 4 | 4 | 4 | 1 |
| AW00000536 | 68.00 | 5 | 4 | 4 | 1 |
| AW00000536 | 64.00 | 6 | 6 | 5 | 1 |
| AW00000266 | 58.00 | 7 | 7 | 6 | 1 |
| AW00000302 | 44.00 | 8 | 8 | 7 | 2 |
| AW00000687 | 43.00 | 9 | 9 | 8 | 2 |
| AW00000482 | 36.00 | 10 | 10 | 9 | 2 |
| AW00000176 | 36.00 | 11 | 10 | 9 | 2 |
| AW00000464 | 35.00 | 12 | 12 | 10 | 2 |
| AW00000320 | 35.00 | 13 | 12 | 10 | 2 |
| AW00000176 | 34.00 | 14 | 14 | 11 | 2 |
| AW00000464 | 34.00 | 15 | 14 | 11 | 3 |

**CHAPTER 5:  Basic Concepts of Client-Server Computing**

# Dynamic SQL To Soar Beyond the Limits of Static SQL

Static (regular) T-SQL syntax does not accept variables at all places in a query. With dynamic SQL we can overcome the  limitation. Dynamic SQL script uses table list metadata from the INFORMATION_SCHEMA.TABLES system view to build a COUNT() query for all tables. COUNT(*) returns 4 bytes integer. For large values COUNT_BIG() returns an 8 bytes integer.

```
DECLARE @SQL nvarchar(max) = '', @Schema sysname, @Table sysname;
SELECT TOP 20 @SQL = CONCAT(@SQL , 'SELECT ''',QUOTENAME(TABLE_SCHEMA),'.',
      QUOTENAME(TABLE_NAME),'''',
        '= COUNT(*) FROM ', QUOTENAME(TABLE_SCHEMA),'.',QUOTENAME(TABLE_NAME) , ';',
CHAR(10))
FROM AdventureWorks2012.INFORMATION_SCHEMA.TABLES WHERE TABLE_TYPE='BASE TABLE';
PRINT @SQL;          -- Test & debug - Partial results.
```

```
SELECT '[Production].[ScrapReason]'= COUNT(*) FROM [Production].[ScrapReason];
SELECT '[HumanResources].[Shift]'= COUNT(*) FROM [HumanResources].[Shift];
SELECT '[Production].[ProductCategory]'= COUNT(*) FROM [Production].[ProductCategory];
SELECT '[Purchasing].[ShipMethod]'= COUNT(*) FROM [Purchasing].[ShipMethod];
SELECT '[Production].[ProductCostHistory]'= COUNT(*) FROM [Production].[ProductCostHistory];
SELECT '[Production].[ProductDescription]'= COUNT(*) FROM [Production].[ProductDescription];
SELECT '[Sales].[ShoppingCartItem]'= COUNT(*) FROM [Sales].[ShoppingCartItem];
SELECT '[Production].[ProductDocument]'= COUNT(*) FROM [Production].[ProductDocument];
SELECT '[dbo].[DatabaseLog]'= COUNT(*) FROM [dbo].[DatabaseLog];
SELECT '[Production].[ProductInventory]'= COUNT(*) FROM [Production].[ProductInventory];
```

```
EXEC sp_executesql @SQL   -- Dynamic SQL query execution
-- Partial results.
```

```
[Production].[ScrapReason]
16


[HumanResources].[Shift]
3


[Production].[ProductCategory]
4


[Purchasing].[ShipMethod]
5
```

**CHAPTER 5:  Basic Concepts of Client-Server Computing**

# Built-in System Functions

SQL Server T-SQL language has a large collection of system functions such as date & time, string and math function. The nested REPLACE string function can be used to remove unwanted characters from a string.

```
DECLARE @text nvarchar(128) = '#1245! $99^@';
SELECT REPLACE(REPLACE(REPLACE(REPLACE(REPLACE(REPLACE(REPLACE(REPLACE(REPLACE(@text,
      '!',''),'@',''),'#',''),'$',''),'%',''),'^',''),'&',''),'*',''),' ','');    -- 124599
```

All the system function are listed in SSMS Object Explorer under the Programmability tab.

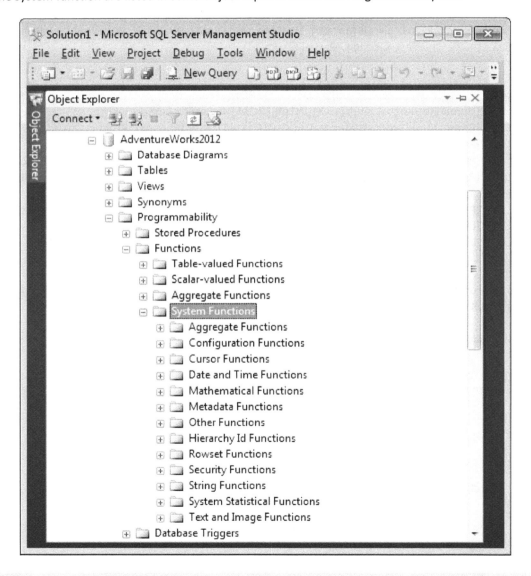

# Local Variables & Table Variables in T-SQL

Local variables with different data types have scope of a batch or a stored procedure/trigger/function. Note that a "GO" in T-SQL script indicates end of batch, therefore the end of scope for local variables. Table variable is a virtual table with similar scope to local variable. Script to demonstrate local and table variables.

```
DECLARE @i INT;  SET @i = 999;

SELECT @i + @i;
-- 1998

SELECT @i = 555;  -- assignment
SELECT @i + @i;
GO
-- 1110

DECLARE @i INT = 999;            -- new in SQL Server 2008
SET @i += 1;                     -- new in SQL Server 2008

SELECT @i;
GO
-- 1000

DECLARE @OrderShipperJunction TABLE              -- Table variable
 (
   ShipperID            SMALLINT IDENTITY ( 1, 1 ) PRIMARY KEY,
   ShipperName          NVARCHAR(64),
   PurchaseOrderID      INT,
   ShipDate             DATE DEFAULT (CURRENT_TIMESTAMP),
   FreightCost          SMALLMONEY
 ) ;
INSERT @OrderShipperJunction
   (ShipperName,
    PurchaseOrderID,
    FreightCost)
VALUES('Custom Motor Bike Distributor',      11111,    177.34)

SELECT * FROM   @OrderShipperJunction
GO
```

| ShipperID | ShipperName | PurchaseOrderID | ShipDate | FreightCost |
|---|---|---|---|---|
| 1 | Custom Motor Bike Distributor | 11111 | 2016-07-18 | 177.34 |

**CHAPTER 5:  Basic Concepts of Client-Server Computing**

## Metadata Visibility Through System Views

The system views provide SQL Server and database metadata which can be used just for viewing in SSMS Object Explorer or programmatically in T-SQL scripts. The system views are based on system tables which are no longer accessible since SQL Server 2005. The system view sys.objects contains all the basic info on each and every user objects in the database with the exception of indexes. Query to retrieve partial data form sys.objects system view.

```
select
    s.name              as [Schema],
    o.name              as [Name],
    o.type_desc         as [Type],
    o.create_date       as CreateDate
from    sys.objects o
        inner join sys.schemas s
            on s.schema_id = o.schema_id
where is_ms_shipped = 0
order by [Type], [Schema], [Name]
-- (722 row(s) affected)  -  Partial results.
```

| Schema | Name | Type | CreateDate |
|--------|------|------|------------|
| HumanResources | Department | USER_TABLE | 2012-03-14 13:14:19.267 |
| HumanResources | Employee | USER_TABLE | 2012-03-14 13:14:19.303 |
| HumanResources | EmployeeDepartmentHistory | USER_TABLE | 2012-03-14 13:14:19.313 |
| HumanResources | EmployeePayHistory | USER_TABLE | 2012-03-14 13:14:19.320 |
| HumanResources | JobCandidate | USER_TABLE | 2012-03-14 13:14:19.337 |
| HumanResources | Shift | USER_TABLE | 2012-03-14 13:14:19.593 |
| Person | Address | USER_TABLE | 2012-03-14 13:14:19.140 |
| Person | AddressType | USER_TABLE | 2012-03-14 13:14:19.150 |
| Person | BusinessEntity | USER_TABLE | 2012-03-14 13:14:19.183 |
| Person | BusinessEntityAddress | USER_TABLE | 2012-03-14 13:14:19.190 |
| Person | BusinessEntityContact | USER_TABLE | 2012-03-14 13:14:19.197 |
| Person | ContactType | USER_TABLE | 2012-03-14 13:14:19.207 |
| Person | CountryRegion | USER_TABLE | 2012-03-14 13:14:19.220 |
| Person | EmailAddress | USER_TABLE | 2012-03-14 13:14:19.290 |
| Person | Password | USER_TABLE | 2012-03-14 13:14:19.350 |
| Person | Person | USER_TABLE | 2012-03-14 13:14:19.357 |
| Person | PersonPhone | USER_TABLE | 2012-03-14 13:14:19.370 |
| Person | PhoneNumberType | USER_TABLE | 2012-03-14 13:14:19.377 |
| Person | StateProvince | USER_TABLE | 2012-03-14 13:14:19.623 |
| Production | BillOfMaterials | USER_TABLE | 2012-03-14 13:14:19.170 |
| Production | Culture | USER_TABLE | 2012-03-14 13:14:19.237 |

# Constructing T-SQL Identifiers

Identifiers are the names given to SQL Server & database objects such as linked servers, tables, views or stored procedures.

Very simple rule: **do not include any special character in an identifier other than single underscore (_). Double underscore in an identifier inevitably leads to confusion, loss of database developer productivity.**

Creating good identifiers helps with productivity in database development, administration and maintenance. Using names AccountsPayable1 and AccountsPayable2 as variations for AccountsPayable is not good because the 1,2 suffixes are meaningless. On the other hand AccountsPayableLondon & AccountsPayableNYC are good, meaningful names. The  list of identifiers can be enumerated from AdventureWorks2012.sys.objects.

SELECT name FROM AdventureWorks2012.sys.objects   ORDER BY name; -- (820 row(s) affected)

Selected results with comments.

| Identifier(name) | Style Comment |
|---|---|
| Account | single word |
| AddressType | double words CamelCase style |
| BillOfMaterials | CamelCase (also known as Pascal case) |
| BusinessEntityContact | CamelCase |
| CK__ImageStore__67152DD3 | double underscore separator, CK prefix for CHECK CONSTRAINT |
| CK_Document_Status | single underscore separator |
| CK_EmployeeDepartmentHistory_EndDate | mixed - CamelCase and underscore |
| DF__ImageStor__is_sy__75634D2A | database engine (system) generated name |
| sp_creatediagram | old-fashioned, sp prefix for system procedure |
| syscscolsegments | old-fashioned with abbreviations |
| ufnGetProductDealerPrice | Hungarian naming, ufn stands for user(-defined) function |
| vSalesPersonSalesByFiscalYears | Hungarian naming, v prefix is for view |

**CHAPTER 5:  Basic Concepts of Client-Server Computing**

# The Use of [] - Square Brackets in Identifiers

Each identifier can be enclosed in square brackets, but not required. If the identifier is the same as a T-SQL reserved keyword, then it is required. Square brackets are also required when the identifier includes a special character such as space. Double quotes can be used also but that becomes very confusing when single quotes are present. The use of brackets is demonstrated in the following T-SQL script.

```
USE Northwind;

-- Syntax error without brackets since table name has space
SELECT * FROM Order Details;
/* ERROR
Msg 156, Level 15, State 1, Line 3
Incorrect syntax near the keyword 'Order'.
*/

-- Valid statement with brackets around table name
SELECT * FROM [Order Details];
-- (2155 row(s) affected)

-- Create and populate table with SELECT INTO
-- Error since ORDER is a reserved keyword
SELECT * INTO Order FROM Orders;
/* ERROR
Msg 156, Level 15, State 1, Line 1
Incorrect syntax near the keyword 'Order'.
*/

-- With brackets, query is valid
SELECT * INTO [Order] FROM Orders;
-- (830 row(s) affected)
```

When a database object is scripted out in SSMS Object Explore, the identifiers are surrounded with square brackets even when not needed as shown in the following demonstration.

```
CREATE TABLE [dbo].[Order Details](
        [OrderID] [int] NOT NULL,
        [ProductID] [int] NOT NULL,
        [UnitPrice] [money] NOT NULL,
        [Quantity] [smallint] NOT NULL,
        [Discount] [real] NOT NULL,
 CONSTRAINT [PK_Order_Details] PRIMARY KEY CLUSTERED
(       [OrderID] ASC,
        [ProductID] ASC));
```

*CHAPTER 5:  Basic Concepts of Client-Server Computing*

# CHAPTER 6: Fundamentals of Relational Database Design

## Logical Data Modeling

Logical data modeling is the first step in database design. The task can be carried out by systems analysts, subject-matter experts, database designers or lead database developers. Small budget projects usually settle for an experienced database developer in the design role. The database design team spends time with the future users (stakeholders) of the database to find out the expectations and requirements for the new database. As soon as the design team has some basic idea of functional requirements, the iterative process continues with discussing entities (corresponds to tables in the database) and their relationships with the users. For example the Order entity has many to many relationship to the Product entity. A Product occurs in many orders, and an Order may hold many products.

## Physical Data Modeling

Physical Data Modeling is the process of translating the logical data model into actual database tables and related objects such as PRIMARY KEY and FOREIGN KEY constraints. If a software tool was used to design the logical data model then the forward engineering feature can be applied to generate SQL scripts to create tables and related database objects. **An important step in this process is the design of indexes to support SQL query performance**. Example for Data Warehouse dimension table implementation.

```
⊟ ▢ dbo.DimDate
   ⊟ ▢ Columns
        🔑 DateKey (PK, int, not null)
        ▤ FullDateAlternateKey (date, not null)
        ▤ DayNumberOfWeek (tinyint, not null)
        ▤ EnglishDayNameOfWeek (nvarchar(10), not null)
        ▤ SpanishDayNameOfWeek (nvarchar(10), not null)
        ▤ FrenchDayNameOfWeek (nvarchar(10), not null)
        ▤ DayNumberOfMonth (tinyint, not null)
        ▤ DayNumberOfYear (smallint, not null)
        ▤ WeekNumberOfYear (tinyint, not null)
        ▤ EnglishMonthName (nvarchar(10), not null)
        ▤ SpanishMonthName (nvarchar(10), not null)
        ▤ FrenchMonthName (nvarchar(10), not null)
        ▤ MonthNumberOfYear (tinyint, not null)
        ▤ CalendarQuarter (tinyint, not null)
        ▤ CalendarYear (smallint, not null)
        ▤ CalendarSemester (tinyint, not null)
        ▤ FiscalQuarter (tinyint, not null)
        ▤ FiscalYear (smallint, not null)
        ▤ FiscalSemester (tinyint, not null)
```

## Column Definitions for the FactInternetSales Table

Table columns for a fact table in AdventureWorksDW2012 database.

The screen image is from SSMS Object Explorer.

```
⊟ ▱ dbo.FactInternetSales
  ⊟ ▱ Columns
        🔑 ProductKey (FK, int, not null)
        🔑 OrderDateKey (FK, int, not null)
        🔑 DueDateKey (FK, int, not null)
        🔑 ShipDateKey (FK, int, not null)
        🔑 CustomerKey (FK, int, not null)
        🔑 PromotionKey (FK, int, not null)
        🔑 CurrencyKey (FK, int, not null)
        🔑 SalesTerritoryKey (FK, int, not null)
        🔑 SalesOrderNumber (PK, nvarchar(20), not null)
        🔑 SalesOrderLineNumber (PK, tinyint, not null)
        ▤ RevisionNumber (tinyint, not null)
        ▤ OrderQuantity (smallint, not null)
        ▤ UnitPrice (money, not null)
        ▤ ExtendedAmount (money, not null)
        ▤ UnitPriceDiscountPct (float, not null)
        ▤ DiscountAmount (float, not null)
        ▤ ProductStandardCost (money, not null)
        ▤ TotalProductCost (money, not null)
        ▤ SalesAmount (money, not null)
        ▤ TaxAmt (money, not null)
        ▤ Freight (money, not null)
        ▤ CarrierTrackingNumber (nvarchar(25), null)
        ▤ CustomerPONumber (nvarchar(25), null)
        ▤ OrderDate (datetime, null)
        ▤ DueDate (datetime, null)
        ▤ ShipDate (datetime, null)
```

# Table Column Data Types

### Exact Numerics

| | | |
|---|---|---|
| bigint | 8 byte signed integer | -- Exact Numerics |
| bit | Boolean | |
| decimal | 5 - 17 bytes decimal  number with variable precision | |
| int | 4 byte signed integer | |
| money | 8 byte with ten-thousandth accuracy | |
| numeric | Same as decimal | |
| smallint | 2 byte signed integer | |
| smallmoney | 4 byte with ten-thousandth accuracy | |
| tinyint | 1 byte signed integer | |

### Approximate Numerics

| | | |
|---|---|---|
| float | 4 - 8 byte floating point | -- Approximate Numerics |
| real | 4 byte floating point | |

### Date and Time

| | |
|---|---|
| date | 3 byte date only |
| datetime | 8 byte date & time |
| datetime2 | 6 - 8 byte date & time |
| datetimeoffset | 10 byte date & time with time zone |
| smalldatetime | 4 byte date & time |
| time | 5 byte time only |

### Character Strings

| | |
|---|---|
| char | Fixed length ASCII character storage - 1 byte for each character  -- Character String |
| text | Variable-length ASCII  data  with a maximum string length of 2^31-1 (deprecated) |
| varchar | Variable length ASCII character storage |

### Unicode Character Strings

| | |
|---|---|
| nchar | Fixed length UNICODE character storage - 2 bytes for each character |
| ntext | Variable-length UNICODE data  with a maximum string length of 2^30-1 (deprecated) |
| nvarchar | Variable length UNICODE character storage |

### Binary Strings

| | |
|---|---|
| binary | Fixed-length binary data with maximum storage size of 2^31-1 bytes   -- Binary String |
| image | Variable-length binary data  with maximum storage size of 2^31-1 bytes (deprecated) |
| varbinary | Variable-length binary data with maximum storage size of 2^31-1 bytes |

### Other Data Types

| | |
|---|---|
| cursor | Contains a reference to a cursor - not for column use |
| hierarchyid | Represents a position in a tree hierarchy, typically a few bytes up to 892 bytes |
| sql_variant | Stores values of various SQL Server data types, maximum length of 8016 bytes |
| table | Store a result set for processing at a later time, not for columns |
| timestamp | 8 byte generated binary number, mechanism for version-stamping table rows |
| uniqueidentifier | 16 byte GUID - Globally Unique Identifier |
| xml | Stores XML data up to 2GB in size |

# Date Type max_length, precision, scale & collation_name Listing

Database metadata on data types can be found in types system view.

SELECT          name, system_type_id, max_length, precision, scale,
                isnull(collation_name, SPACE(0)) AS collation_name
FROM AdventureWorks2012.sys.types WHERE schema_id = 4 ORDER BY name;

| name | system_type_id | max_length | precision | scale | collation_name |
|---|---|---|---|---|---|
| bigint | 127 | 8 | 19 | 0 | |
| binary | 173 | 8000 | 0 | 0 | |
| bit | 104 | 1 | 1 | 0 | |
| char | 175 | 8000 | 0 | 0 | SQL_Latin1_General_CP1_CI_AS |
| date | 40 | 3 | 10 | 0 | |
| datetime | 61 | 8 | 23 | 3 | |
| datetime2 | 42 | 8 | 27 | 7 | |
| datetimeoffset | 43 | 10 | 34 | 7 | |
| decimal | 106 | 17 | 38 | 38 | |
| float | 62 | 8 | 53 | 0 | |
| geography | 240 | -1 | 0 | 0 | |
| geometry | 240 | -1 | 0 | 0 | |
| hierarchyid | 240 | 892 | 0 | 0 | |
| image | 34 | 16 | 0 | 0 | |
| int | 56 | 4 | 10 | 0 | |
| money | 60 | 8 | 19 | 4 | |
| nchar | 239 | 8000 | 0 | 0 | SQL_Latin1_General_CP1_CI_AS |
| ntext | 99 | 16 | 0 | 0 | SQL_Latin1_General_CP1_CI_AS |
| numeric | 108 | 17 | 38 | 38 | |
| nvarchar | 231 | 8000 | 0 | 0 | SQL_Latin1_General_CP1_CI_AS |
| real | 59 | 4 | 24 | 0 | |
| smalldatetime | 58 | 4 | 16 | 0 | |
| smallint | 52 | 2 | 5 | 0 | |
| smallmoney | 122 | 4 | 10 | 4 | |
| sql_variant | 98 | 8016 | 0 | 0 | |
| sysname | 231 | 256 | 0 | 0 | SQL_Latin1_General_CP1_CI_AS |
| text | 35 | 16 | 0 | 0 | SQL_Latin1_General_CP1_CI_AS |
| time | 41 | 5 | 16 | 7 | |
| timestamp | 189 | 8 | 0 | 0 | |
| tinyint | 48 | 1 | 3 | 0 | |
| uniqueidentifier | 36 | 16 | 0 | 0 | |
| varbinary | 165 | 8000 | 0 | 0 | |
| varchar | 167 | 8000 | 0 | 0 | SQL_Latin1_General_CP1_CI_AS |
| xml | 241 | -1 | 0 | 0 | |

# U.S. Default Collation SQL_Latin1_General_CP1_CI_AS

Interpretation:

> ➢ SQL collation not Windows
> ➢ Latin 1 alphabet
> ➢ Code page 1 for sorting
> ➢ Case insensitive
> ➢ Accent sensitive

SQL_Latin1_General_CP1_CI_AS is the default collation of SQL Server 2012 in the United States. Only a handful of experts around the world really understand collations.  You first encounter with collation will probably be like the following error.

```
SELECT CONCAT('Production.', objname) AS TableName, value AS [Description]
FROM fn_listextendedproperty (NULL, 'schema', 'Production', 'table', default, NULL, NULL);
GO
/*  Msg 468, Level 16, State 9, Line 1
Cannot resolve the collation conflict between "SQL_Latin1_General_CP1_CI_AS" and
"Latin1_General_CI_AI" in the concat operation.
*/
```

The easiest fix in most collation error cases is placing COLLATE DATABASE_DEFAULT following the right most operator.

```
SELECT CONCAT('Production.', objname COLLATE DATABASE_DEFAULT) AS TableName,
                value AS [Description]
FROM fn_listextendedproperty (NULL, 'schema', 'Production', 'table', default, NULL, NULL);
GO
```

There are a number of articles on the web which deal extensively with collations.

Collation is a column level property. Server and database collations are only defaults. To change the collation of a column, use ALTER TABLE.

```
-- SQL Server Change Column Collation
SELECT * INTO Product FROM AdventureWorks2012.Production.Product;
GO
ALTER TABLE Product ALTER COLUMN Name nvarchar(50) COLLATE SQL_Latin1_General_CP1_CS_AS null;
GO  -- (504 row(s) affected)
```

**CHAPTER 6:  Fundamentals of Relational Database Design**

# DATE & DATETIME Temporal Data Types

DATE data type has been introduced with SQL Server 2008. DATETIME on the other hand is around since the inception of SQL Server. A good deal of programming effort goes into supporting hundreds of different string date & time formats. Each country has its own string date formats adding more to the general confusion. As an example in the United States the mdy string date format is used. In the United Kingdom, the dmy format is used. When one looks at a date like 10/11/2015, it is not apparent which date format is it. In a globalized world the data flows freely from one country to another, frequently without adequate documentation, hence the loss of database developer productivity as related to date & time data issues. List of century (CCYY or YYYY) datetime conversions styles (stylenumber >= 100).

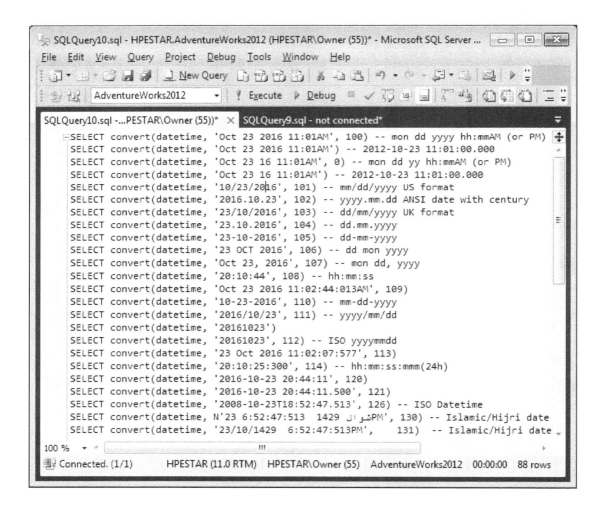

## Two Ways of Commenting in T-SQL Scripts

Line comment is prefixed by "--". Multiple lines comment has to be enclosed with "/*" and "*/".

# Exploring Database Schemas

A schema - introduced in SQL Server 2005 - is a single-level container of database objects to replace database object "owner" in previous SQL Server versions. **The default schema is "dbo", database owner**. Schemas can be used for functional separation of objects which may be essential in large databases with thousands of tables. The application schemas in AdventureWorks: HumanResources, Production, Purchasing, Sales, and Person. The word "schemas" also used in database terminology to mean table definition scripts or database diagram. Screenshot to display all the schemas in AdventureWorks2012 and to demonstrate the use of the CREATE SCHEMA statement. Database object reference in SQL Server 2012 is: "dbname.schemaname.objectname" like "AdventureWorks2012.Sales.SalesOrderheader".

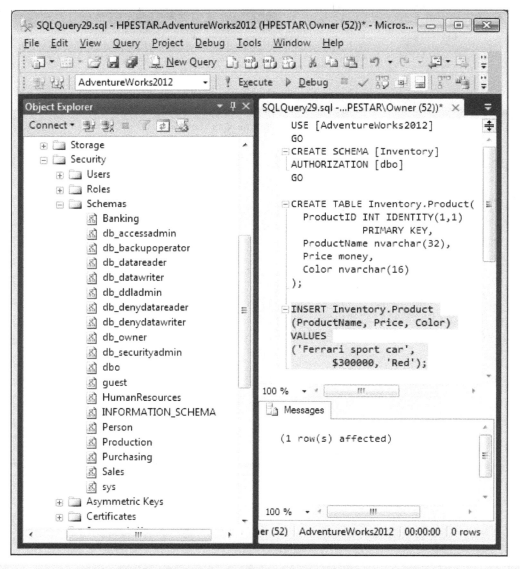

## SCHEMA_NAME() Function

The SCHEMA_NAME() function can be used to obtain the name of a schema based on the schema_id parameter. Query to list all 3 database objects with the name "Product" in 3 different schemas.

```
SELECT          CONCAT(SCHEMA_NAME(schema_id),'.',name) as ObjectName,
                name, object_id, schema_id, type, type_desc
FROM sys.objects
WHERE name = 'Product'
ORDER BY ObjectName;
```

| ObjectName | name | object_id | schema_id | type | type_desc |
|---|---|---|---|---|---|
| dbo.Product | Product | 264388011 | 1 | U | USER_TABLE |
| Inventory.Product | Product | 1533964541 | 11 | U | USER_TABLE |
| Production.Product | Product | 1973582069 | 7 | U | USER_TABLE |

T-SQL query to display all the schemas in AdventureWorks2012.

```
SELECT s.*,  p.name as PrincipalName
FROM AdventureWorks2012.sys.schemas s
  INNER JOIN AdventureWorks2012.sys.database_principals p     ON s.principal_id = p.principal_id
ORDER BY principal_id, s.name;
```

| name | schema_id | principal_id | PrincipalName |
|---|---|---|---|
| Banking | 10 | 1 | dbo |
| dbo | 1 | 1 | dbo |
| HumanResources | 5 | 1 | dbo |
| Inventory | 11 | 1 | dbo |
| Person | 6 | 1 | dbo |
| Production | 7 | 1 | dbo |
| Purchasing | 8 | 1 | dbo |
| Sales | 9 | 1 | dbo |
| guest | 2 | 2 | guest |
| INFORMATION_SCHEMA | 3 | 3 | INFORMATION_SCHEMA |
| sys | 4 | 4 | sys |
| db_owner | 16384 | 16384 | db_owner |
| db_accessadmin | 16385 | 16385 | db_accessadmin |
| db_securityadmin | 16386 | 16386 | db_securityadmin |
| db_ddladmin | 16387 | 16387 | db_ddladmin |
| db_backupoperator | 16389 | 16389 | db_backupoperator |
| db_datareader | 16390 | 16390 | db_datareader |
| db_datawriter | 16391 | 16391 | db_datawriter |
| db_denydatareader | 16392 | 16392 | db_denydatareader |
| db_denydatawriter | 16393 | 16393 | db_denydatawriter |

**CHAPTER 6:  Fundamentals of Relational Database Design**

## Tables in HumanResources, Person & Purchasing Schemas

Query to list tables in the above schemas with data dictionary description.

```
USE AdventureWorks2012;

SELECT   CONCAT('Purchasing.', objname COLLATE DATABASE_DEFAULT)        AS TableName,
         value                                                          AS [Description]
FROM fn_listextendedproperty (NULL, 'schema', 'Purchasing', 'table', default, NULL, NULL)
UNION
SELECT   CONCAT('Person.', objname COLLATE DATABASE_DEFAULT)            AS TableName,
         value                                                          AS [Description]
FROM fn_listextendedproperty (NULL, 'schema', 'Person', 'table', default, NULL, NULL)
UNION
SELECT   CONCAT('HumanResources.', objname COLLATE DATABASE_DEFAULT) AS TableName,
         value                                                          AS [Description]
FROM fn_listextendedproperty (NULL, 'schema', 'HumanResources', 'table', default, NULL, NULL)
ORDER BY TableName;
```

| TableName | Description |
| --- | --- |
| HumanResources.Department | Lookup table containing the departments within the Adventure Works Cycles company. |
| HumanResources.Employee | Employee information such as salary, department, and title. |
| HumanResources.EmployeeDepartmentHistory | Employee department transfers. |
| HumanResources.EmployeePayHistory | Employee pay history. |
| HumanResources.JobCandidate | Résumés submitted to Human Resources by job applicants. |
| HumanResources.Shift | Work shift lookup table. |
| Person.Address | Street address information for customers, employees, and vendors. |
| Person.AddressType | Types of addresses stored in the Address table. |
| Person.BusinessEntity | Source of the ID that connects vendors, customers, and employees with address and contact information. |
| Person.BusinessEntityAddress | Cross-reference table mapping customers, vendors, and employees to their addresses. |
| Person.BusinessEntityContact | Cross-reference table mapping stores, vendors, and employees to people |
| Person.ContactType | Lookup table containing the types of business entity contacts. |
| Person.CountryRegion | Lookup table containing the ISO standard codes for countries and regions. |
| Person.EmailAddress | Where to send a person email. |
| Person.Password | One way hashed authentication information |
| Person.Person | Human beings involved with AdventureWorks: employees, customer contacts, and vendor contacts. |
| Person.PersonPhone | Telephone number and type of a person. |
| Person.PhoneNumberType | Type of phone number of a person. |
| Person.StateProvince | State and province lookup table. |
| Purchasing.ProductVendor | Cross-reference table mapping vendors with the products they supply. |
| Purchasing.PurchaseOrderDetail | Individual products associated with a specific purchase order. See PurchaseOrderHeader. |
| Purchasing.PurchaseOrderHeader | General purchase order information. See PurchaseOrderDetail. |
| Purchasing.ShipMethod | Shipping company lookup table. |
| Purchasing.Vendor | Companies from whom Adventure Works Cycles purchases parts or other goods. |

# The CREATE TABLE Statement

Creates a table based on  column name,  data type & size specifications. Constraint and default information can be included  as well, or alternately given as a separate ALTER TABLE statement.

## Branch Banking Database with ON DELETE CASCADE

T-SQL script to create basic banking application tables. Preceding the first CREATE TABLE, we execute a CREATE  SCHEMA to group the tables within one schema.

```
USE AdventureWorks2012;
GO

CREATE SCHEMA Banking;
GO


CREATE TABLE Banking.Branch
 (
    BranchID    INT IDENTITY ( 1, 1 ),
    BranchName   CHAR(32) NOT NULL UNIQUE,
    BranchCity  CHAR(32) NOT NULL,
    Assets     MONEY NOT NULL,
    ModifiedDate DATETIME DEFAULT (getdate()),
    PRIMARY KEY ( BranchID ),
 );

CREATE TABLE Banking.Account
 (
    AccountID    INT IDENTITY ( 1, 1 ) UNIQUE,
    BranchID     INT NOT NULL,
    AccountNumber CHAR(20) NOT NULL UNIQUE,
    AccountType   CHAR(12) NOT NULL CONSTRAINT ATC CHECK (AccountType IN ('C',    'S')),
    Balance     MONEY NOT NULL,
    ModifiedDate  DATETIME DEFAULT (getdate()),
    PRIMARY KEY ( AccountID ),
    FOREIGN KEY ( BranchID ) REFERENCES Banking.Branch(BranchID) ON DELETE   CASCADE
 );
```

```
-- T-SQL script continued

CREATE TABLE Banking.[Transaction]
 (
   TransactionID INT IDENTITY ( 1, 1 ),
   AccountID    INT,
   TranType     CHAR(1),
   Amount       MONEY,
   ModifiedDate  DATETIME DEFAULT (getdate()),
   PRIMARY KEY ( TransactionID ),
   FOREIGN KEY ( AccountID ) REFERENCES Banking.Account(AccountID) ON DELETE    CASCADE
 );

CREATE TABLE Banking.Customer
 (
   CustomerID   INT IDENTITY ( 1, 1 ) UNIQUE,
   Name       CHAR(32) NOT NULL UNIQUE,
   [Type]     CHAR(20) NOT NULL,
   Street     VARCHAR(32) NOT NULL,
   City       CHAR(32) NOT NULL,
   [State]    CHAR(32) NOT NULL,
   Zip        CHAR(10) NOT NULL,
   Country    CHAR(32) NOT NULL,
   ModifiedDate DATETIME DEFAULT (getdate()),
   PRIMARY KEY ( CustomerID )
 );

CREATE TABLE Banking.Loan
 (
   LoanID      INT IDENTITY ( 1, 1 ) PRIMARY KEY,
   BranchID     INT NOT NULL REFERENCES Banking.Branch(BranchID) ON DELETE    CASCADE,
   LoanNumber   CHAR(20) NOT NULL UNIQUE,
   LoanType    VARCHAR(30) NOT NULL,
   Amount      MONEY NOT NULL,
   ModifiedDate DATETIME DEFAULT (getdate())
 );
```

CHAPTER 6:  Fundamentals of Relational Database Design

**-- T-SQL script continued**

```
CREATE TABLE Banking.Depositor
 (
   CustomerID   INT NOT NULL,
   AccountID    INT NOT NULL,
   ModifiedDate DATETIME DEFAULT (getdate()),
   PRIMARY KEY ( CustomerID, AccountID ),
   FOREIGN KEY ( AccountID ) REFERENCES Banking.Account(AccountID) ON DELETE   CASCADE,
   FOREIGN KEY ( CustomerID ) REFERENCES Banking.Customer(CustomerID)
 );

CREATE TABLE Banking.Borrower
 (
   CustomerID   INT NOT NULL,
   LoanID       INT NOT NULL,
   ModifiedDate DATETIME DEFAULT (getdate()),
   PRIMARY KEY ( CustomerID, LoanID ),
   FOREIGN KEY ( CustomerID ) REFERENCES Banking.Customer(CustomerID),
   FOREIGN KEY ( LoanID ) REFERENCES Banking.Loan(LoanID)
 );
```

# Temporary Tables: Workhorses of SQL Server

So much so that they even have their own database: tempdb. Temporary tables (example: #Product1) can be applied in queries just like permanent tables. The differences are:

➤   Temporary tables are created in tempdb.

➤   Temporary tables have limited life.

There are two versions:

➤   Temporary tables (#tempA) are multi-user automatically, cannot be shared among connections.

➤   Global temporary tables (##gtempB) is single-user, can be shared among connections.

Global temporary tables are used only for special purposes since they make stored procedures single user only.

Temporary tables can be created by CREATE TABLE or SELECT INTO methods.

```
USE AdventureWorks2012;
GO
-- Command(s) completed successfully.


-- Create temporary table with CREATE TABLE
CREATE TABLE #Product
 (
        ProductID INT,
        ProductName nvarchar(50),
        ListPrice money,
        Color varchar(16)
);
GO
-- Command(s) completed successfully.


INSERT INTO #Product
SELECT   ProductID,
         Name,
         ListPrice,
         Color
FROM Production.Product
ORDER BY Name;
GO
--(504 row(s) affected)
```

## Temporary Tables Are Handy When Developing Scripts Or Stored Procedures

```
SELECT TOP 10 * FROM #Product
ORDER BY ProductName;
GO
```

| ProductID | ProductName | ListPrice | Color |
|---|---|---|---|
| 1 | Adjustable Race | 0.00 | NULL |
| 879 | All-Purpose Bike Stand | 159.00 | NULL |
| 712 | AWC Logo Cap | 8.99 | Multi |
| 3 | BB Ball Bearing | 0.00 | NULL |
| 2 | Bearing Ball | 0.00 | NULL |
| 877 | Bike Wash - Dissolver | 7.95 | NULL |
| 316 | Blade | 0.00 | NULL |
| 843 | Cable Lock | 25.00 | NULL |
| 952 | Chain | 20.24 | Silver |
| 324 | Chain Stays | 0.00 | NULL |

```
DROP TABLE #Product;
GO

-- CREATE temporary table with SELECT INTO
SELECT ProductID, ProductName = Name, ListPrice, StandardCost, Color
INTO #ProductA
FROM Production.Product
ORDER BY ProductName;
GO

SELECT TOP 10 * FROM #ProductA
ORDER BY ProductName;
```

| ProductID | ProductName | ListPrice | StandardCost | Color |
|---|---|---|---|---|
| 1 | Adjustable Race | 0.00 | 0.00 | NULL |
| 879 | All-Purpose Bike Stand | 159.00 | 59.466 | NULL |
| 712 | AWC Logo Cap | 8.99 | 6.9223 | Multi |
| 3 | BB Ball Bearing | 0.00 | 0.00 | NULL |
| 2 | Bearing Ball | 0.00 | 0.00 | NULL |
| 877 | Bike Wash - Dissolver | 7.95 | 2.9733 | NULL |
| 316 | Blade | 0.00 | 0.00 | NULL |
| 843 | Cable Lock | 25.00 | 10.3125 | NULL |
| 952 | Chain | 20.24 | 8.9866 | Silver |
| 324 | Chain Stays | 0.00 | 0.00 | NULL |

```
DROP TABLE #ProductA;
GO
```

## CHAPTER 6:  Fundamentals of Relational Database Design

# ALTER TABLE for Changing Table Definition

An empty table can easily be altered by ALTER TABLE. A populated table change (alter) may require additional operations such as data conversion to the new column data type. Generally increasing the size of a column is a safe change even if the table is populated. If we were to change size from 25 to 10, truncation may occur (data loss), for which we would have to plan by examining what will be lost if any. When decreasing string column size, we can use the LEFT function to truncate the string. T-SQL script to increase the size of a column from 25 to 32, then decrease it 9.

```
 USE CopyOfAdventureWorks2012;
-- Sales.SalesOrderDetail columns
/*Name    Policy Health State
SalesOrderID (PK, FK, int, not null)
SalesOrderDetailID (PK, int, not null)
CarrierTrackingNumber (nvarchar(25), null) ..... */
```

```
-- Increase column size of CarrierTrackingNumber
ALTER TABLE Sales.SalesOrderDetail   ALTER COLUMN CarrierTrackingNumber nvarchar(32)  null;
```

```
/* Columns after ALTER TABLE
Name      Policy Health State
SalesOrderID (PK, FK, int, not null)
SalesOrderDetailID (PK, int, not null)
CarrierTrackingNumber (nvarchar(32), null) .....          */
```

```
SELECT TOP (1) SalesOrderID, CarrierTrackingNumber FROM  Sales.SalesOrderDetail ORDER BY
SalesOrderID;
```

| SalesOrderID | CarrierTrackingNumber |
|---|---|
| 43659 | 4911-403C-98 |

We shall now decrease the size to 9 characters, but first truncate the extra characters. Without the UPDATE, the following error happens.
/* Msg 8152, Level 16, State 13, Line 1 String or binary data would be truncated. The statement has been terminated.*/

```
UPDATE Sales.SalesOrderDetail SET CarrierTrackingNumber = LEFT (CarrierTrackingNumber,9);
-- (121317 row(s) affected)
```

```
-- Decrease column size of CarrierTrackingNumber
ALTER TABLE Sales.SalesOrderDetail   ALTER COLUMN CarrierTrackingNumber nvarchar(9)  null;
-- Command(s) completed successfully.
```

```
SELECT TOP (1) SalesOrderID, CarrierTrackingNumber FROM  Sales.SalesOrderDetail  ORDER BY
SalesOrderID;
```

| SalesOrderID | CarrierTrackingNumber |
|---|---|
| 43659 | 4911-403C |

CHAPTER 6: Fundamentals of Relational Database Design

## Renaming Tables & Columns with sp_rename

The system stored procedure sp_rename can be used to rename tables, columns and other user-created database objects.

```
USE tempdb;
GO
```

```
-- Create test table
SELECT * INTO Department FROM AdventureWorks2012.HumanResources.Department;
GO
-- (16 row(s) affected)
```

```
SELECT TOP 1 * FROM Department;
GO
```

| DepartmentID | Name | GroupName | ModifiedDate |
|---|---|---|---|
| 1 | Engineering | Research and Development | 2002-06-01 00:00:00.000 |

```
-- Rename table column
EXEC sp_rename "Department.Name", "Department";
GO
```

```
SELECT TOP 1 * FROM Department;
GO
```

| DepartmentID | Department | GroupName | ModifiedDate |
|---|---|---|---|
| 1 | Engineering | Research and Development | 2002-06-01 00:00:00.000 |

```
-- Rename table
EXEC sp_rename "dbo.Department", "ProfitCenter"
GO
```

```
SELECT * FROM ProfitCenter;
GO
```

| DepartmentID | Department | GroupName | ModifiedDate |
|---|---|---|---|
| 1 | Engineering | Research and Development | 2002-06-01 00:00:00.000 |

```
DROP TABLE tempdb.dbo.ProfitCenter;
GO
```

# DROP TABLE: A Dangerous Statement

The DROP TABLE statement is to delete a table, including content, for good. It is a very dangerous statement which we don't want to execute accidentally. Therefore, if appropriate we should comment it out in a T-SQL script to prevent unintentional execution.

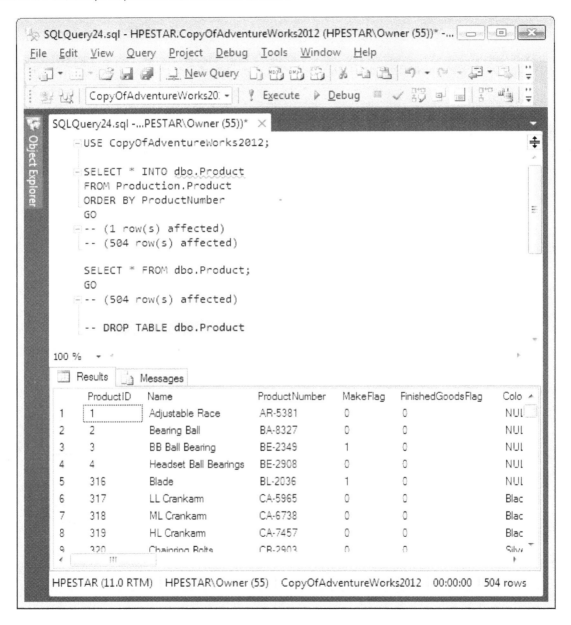

## Table Constraints Inclusion in CREATE TABLE

Table constraints are user-defined database objects that restricts the behaviors of columns. PRIMARY KEY, UNIQUE KEY, FOREIGN KEY, or CHECK constraint, or a DEFAULT constraint can be included in the CREATE TABLE statement on the same line as the column or added as a separate line. In the definition of the Banking.Branch table UNIQUE and DEFAULT constraints are included in the same line while the PRIMARY KEY constraint has its own line at the end of column list. In the definition of Banking.Loan table, the PRIMARY KEY constraint is included with the column definition. FOREIGN KEY constraint definition can include ON DELETE CASCADE action option, meaning if the PRIMARY KEY is deleted all FOREIGN KEYs in the table referencing it should also be deleted.

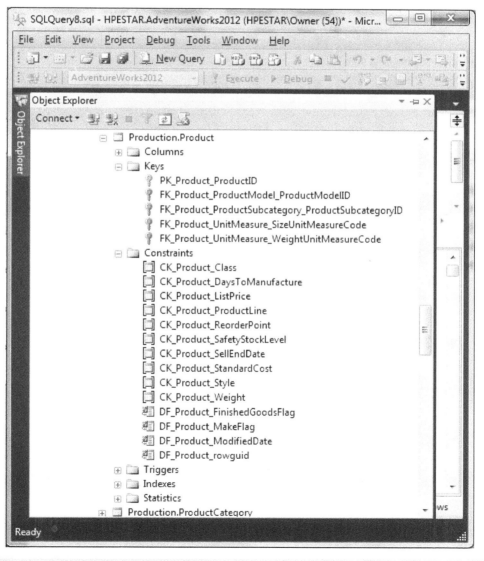

# Nullability Column-Level Constraints in CREATE TABLE

The default is NULL, the column can contain NULL entries, the column is nullable. We have to specifically declare NOT NULL on the column line in CREATE TABLE if we want to add the cardinality constraint to the column. The NULL / NOT NULL constraint cannot be declared on a separate line.  In the Production.Product table the Color column is nullable. The ListPrice column is not nullable instead has 0.0 price where there is no price.

## *PRIMARY KEY constraint on a column automatically implies NOT NULL*

The UNIQUE KEY CONSTRAINT allows only one NULL entry in a column since two or more NULL entries would not be unique.  Demonstration script:

```
USE tempdb;
CREATE TABLE Product     (   ProductID INT UNIQUE,
                             ProductName varchar(64) PRIMARY KEY
                        );


INSERT Product (ProductName) VALUES ('Mobile Phone xZing');
-- (1 row(s) affected)


-- One NULL is OK in ProductID column
-- Second NULL insert attempt errors out

INSERT Product (ProductName) VALUES ('Motor Bike');

/* Msg 2627, Level 14, State 1, Line 7
Violation of UNIQUE KEY constraint 'UQ__Product__B40CC6ECDF4DC6D3'.
Cannot insert duplicate key in object 'dbo.Product'.
The duplicate key value is (<NULL>).
The statement has been terminated. */


-- NULL value in PRIMARY KEY column not allowed

INSERT Product (ProductID) VALUES (2);

/* Msg 515, Level 16, State 2, Line 2
Cannot insert the value NULL into column
'ProductName', table 'tempdb.dbo.Product';
column does not allow nulls. INSERT fails.
The statement has been terminated. */

SELECT * FROM Product;
```

| ProductID | ProductName |
|-----------|-------------|
| NULL | Mobile Phone xZing |

The PRIMARY KEY constraint is a combination of UNIQUE and NOT NULL constraints.

## CHAPTER 6:  Fundamentals of Relational Database Design

# PRIMARY KEY & FOREIGN KEY Constraints

The PRIMARY KEY constraint is to ensure a referenceable unique address for each row in a table. PK column value cannot be NULL. The underlying mechanism to carry out the enforcement action is a unique index which is clustered by default but in can be nonclustered. PRIMARY KEY constraint can be considered as a UNIQUE constraint with NOT NULL on the column. The typical PRIMARY KEY is the SURROGATE PRIMARY KEY INT IDENTITY(1,1) column.  There can only be one PRIMARY KEY defined per table. A PRIMARY KEY can consist of multiple columns, a composite PRIMARY KEY. A PRIMARY KEY cannot be based on part of a column.  Production.ProductSubcategory table PRIMARY KEY setup.

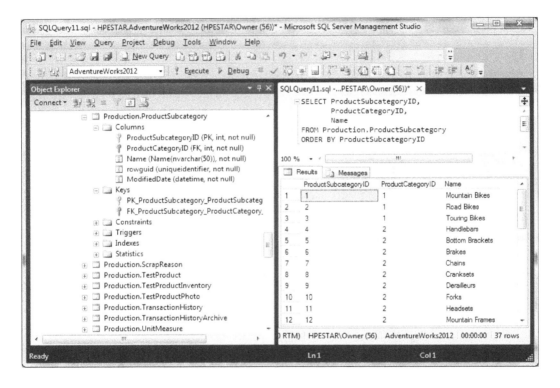

The ProductSubcategoryID is the PRIMARY KEY constraint. It is an INT IDENTITY(1,1) surrogate key. ProductCategoryID is a FOREIGN KEY referencing the Production.ProductCategory table ProductCategoryID column.  "Name" is the NATURAL KEY.  rowguid & ModifiedDate are row maintenance columns. The NATURAL KEY column Name has NOT NULL constraint and unique index defined.  As such it can serve as PRIMARY KEY for the table, but we shall see why a meaningless integer number (INT IDENTITY) is better for PRIMARY KEY. Related to this topic: A heap is a table without a clustered index. The implication is if we choose nonclustered PRIMARY KEY, we have to define a clustered index on other column(s) so that the database engine can work with the table as normal. Clustered index speeds up range searches.

## *FOREIGN KEY constraint requires that the referenced PK value exists.*

**FOREIGN KEY column is nullable. FOREIGN KEY can be named differently from the referenced PRIMARY KEY**, although for readability purposes usually the same. **Multiple FK columns can reference the same PK column**. In such a case only one FK column can have the same name as the PK column. Invalid FK reference results in error.

```
USE [AdventureWorks2012]
GO


INSERT INTO Production.ProductSubcategory
     (ProductCategoryID
     ,Name)
   VALUES
     (99
     ,'Inner Tube')


/*
Msg 547, Level 16, State 0, Line 2
The INSERT statement conflicted with the FOREIGN KEY constraint
"FK_ProductSubcategory_ProductCategory_ProductCategoryID".
The conflict occurred in database "AdventureWorks2012",
table "Production.ProductCategory", column 'ProductCategoryID'.
The statement has been terminated.
*/
```

DELETE attempt on a referenced PRIMARY KEY will give an error unless DELETE CASCADE is defined on the FK:

```
DELETE FROM Production.ProductSubcategory
WHERE ProductSubCategoryID = 4
GO


/* Msg 547, Level 16, State 0, Line 1
The DELETE statement conflicted with the REFERENCE constraint
"FK_Product_ProductSubcategory_ProductSubcategoryID".
The conflict occurred in database "AdventureWorks2012",
table "Production.Product", column 'ProductSubcategoryID'.
The statement has been terminated.  */
```

**CHAPTER 6:** Fundamentals of Relational Database Design

# Single Column & Composite PRIMARY KEY List with XML PATH

Query to form delimited list for composite PRIMARY KEY columns. STUFF function deletes the leading comma.

```
-- Show composite PRIMARY KEYs as a comma-delimited list
USE AdventureWorks2012;
SELECT   K.TABLE_SCHEMA,
         T.TABLE_NAME,
         PK_COLUMN_NAMES  =
                STUFF(( SELECT
                              CONCAT(', ',   KK.COLUMN_NAME)                    AS [text()]
                        FROM   INFORMATION_SCHEMA.KEY_COLUMN_USAGE kk
                        WHERE  K.CONSTRAINT_NAME = KK.CONSTRAINT_NAME
                        ORDER BY  KK.ORDINAL_POSITION
                        FOR XML Path ('')), 1, 1, '')
FROM   INFORMATION_SCHEMA.TABLE_CONSTRAINTS T
  INNER JOIN    INFORMATION_SCHEMA.KEY_COLUMN_USAGE K
        ON T.CONSTRAINT_NAME = K.CONSTRAINT_NAME
WHERE           T.CONSTRAINT_TYPE = 'PRIMARY KEY'
                AND K.ORDINAL_POSITION = 1
ORDER BY        K.TABLE_SCHEMA,
                T.TABLE_NAME;
-- (71 row(s) affected) - Partial results
```

| TABLE_SCHEMA | TABLE_NAME | PK_COLUMN_NAMES |
|---|---|---|
| dbo | AWBuildVersion | SystemInformationID |
| dbo | DatabaseLog | DatabaseLogID |
| dbo | ErrorLog | ErrorLogID |
| HumanResources | Department | DepartmentID |
| HumanResources | Employee | BusinessEntityID |
| HumanResources | EmployeeDepartmentHistory | BusinessEntityID, StartDate, DepartmentID, ShiftID |
| HumanResources | EmployeePayHistory | BusinessEntityID, RateChangeDate |
| HumanResources | JobCandidate | JobCandidateID |
| HumanResources | Shift | ShiftID |
| Person | Address | AddressID |
| Person | AddressType | AddressTypeID |
| Person | BusinessEntity | BusinessEntityID |
| Person | BusinessEntityAddress | BusinessEntityID, AddressID, AddressTypeID |
| Person | BusinessEntityContact | BusinessEntityID, PersonID, ContactTypeID |
| Person | ContactType | ContactTypeID |
| Person | CountryRegion | CountryRegionCode |
| Person | EmailAddress | BusinessEntityID, EmailAddressID |
| Person | Password | BusinessEntityID |
| Person | Person | BusinessEntityID |
| Person | PersonPhone | BusinessEntityID, PhoneNumber, PhoneNumberTypeID |

## SSMS GUI Table Designer

SSMS Object Explorer includes a GUI Table Designer which can be launched the following ways for new or existing table from the right-click drop-down menus.

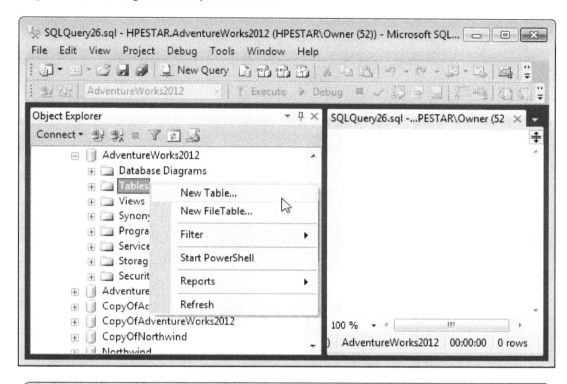

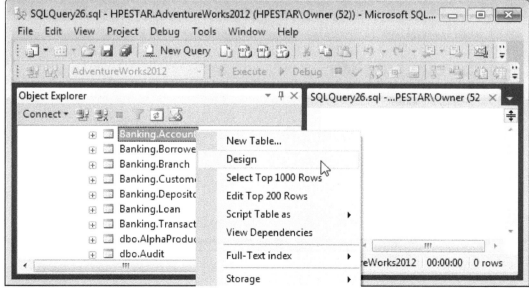

**CHAPTER 6: Fundamentals of Relational Database Design**

## Basic GUI Table Design

The Table Designer provides line-by-line row design including all properties (bottom of dialog box) such as defaults, computed columns, identity and so on.

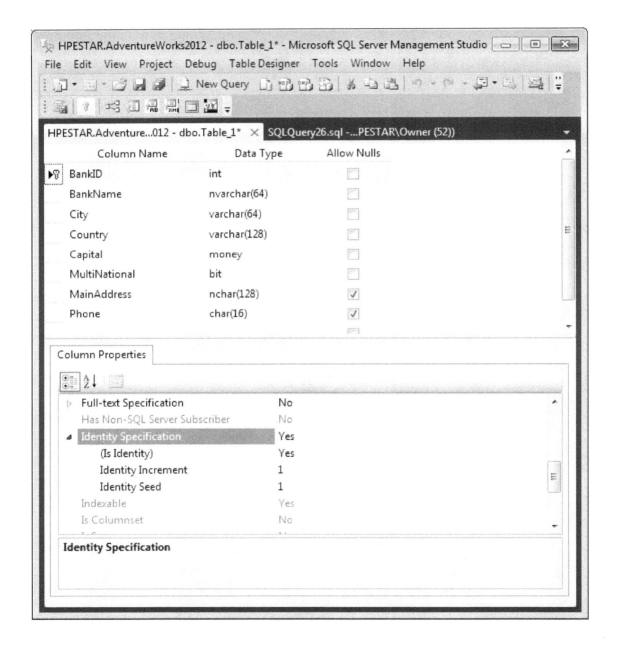

## CHECK Constraint Definition

CHECK Constraint design window can be launched from toolbox icon:  Manage Check Constraints or right-click drop-down menu. We create a constraint on Capital to be greater or equal to $5 billion.

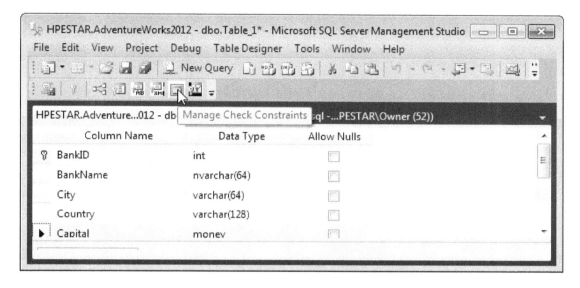

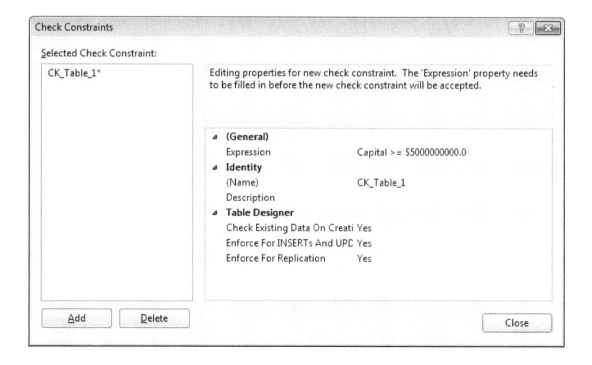

## Managing Indexes and Keys

The Manage Indexes and Keys window can be launched by toolbox icon or right-click menu. We add UNIQUE KEY property to the BankName column.

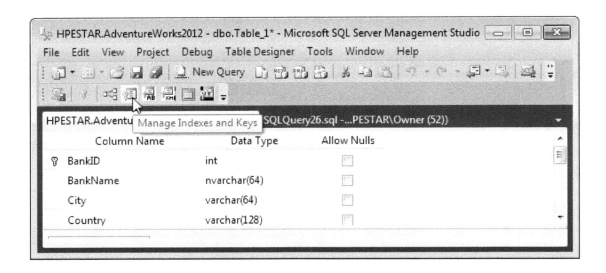

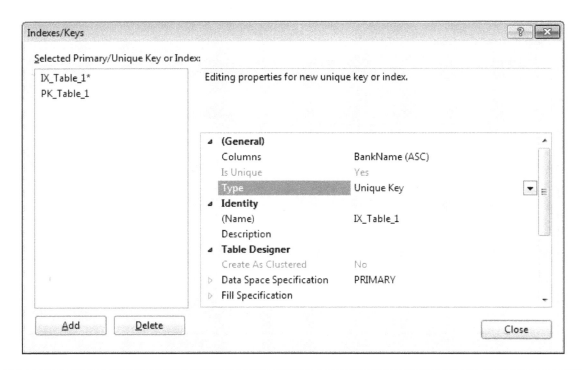

## Setting PRIMARY KEY with a Single Click

PRIMARY KEY can simply be configured just by clicking on the gold key icon. A PRIMARY KEY constraint is created automatically.

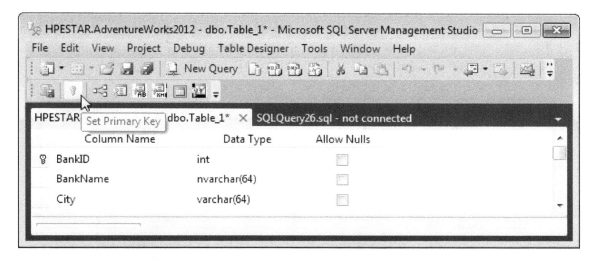

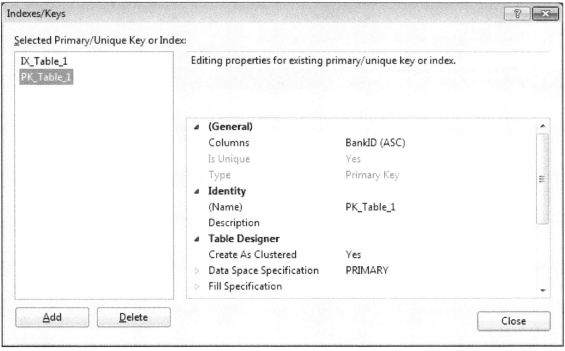

## Configuring FOREIGN KEY: Declarative Referential Integrity

The Relationships facility can be used to create a FOREIGN KEY link (constraint). NOTE: demo only, BusinessEntityID column in the demo table has no relationship to AdventureWorks tables.

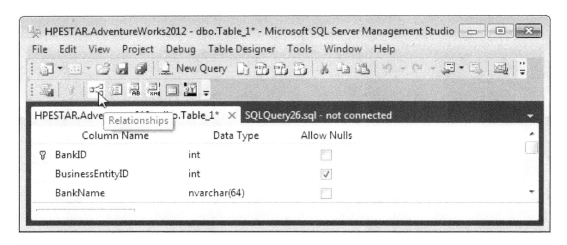

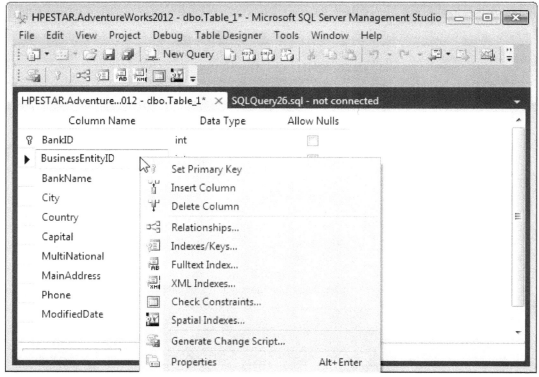

## Tables And Columns Specific Tab Is To Define Mapping From FK To PK

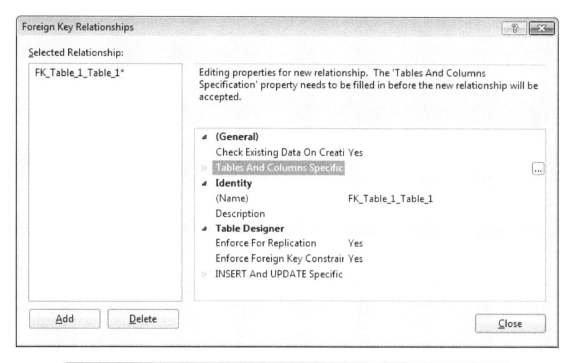

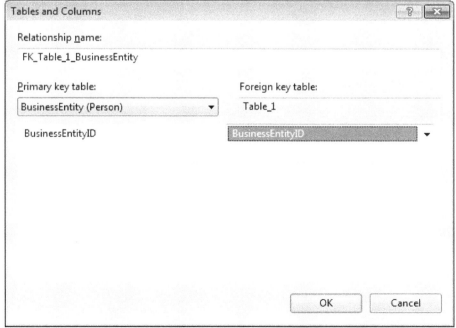

## T-SQL Script Generation from GUI Table Designer

T-SQL code can be generated any time prior to saving the changes.

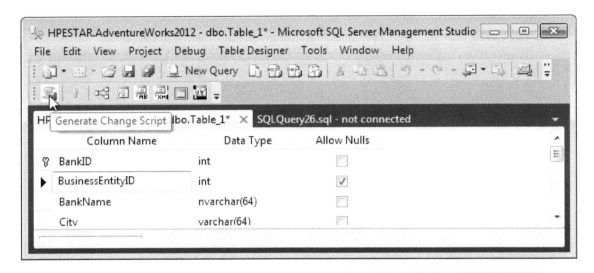

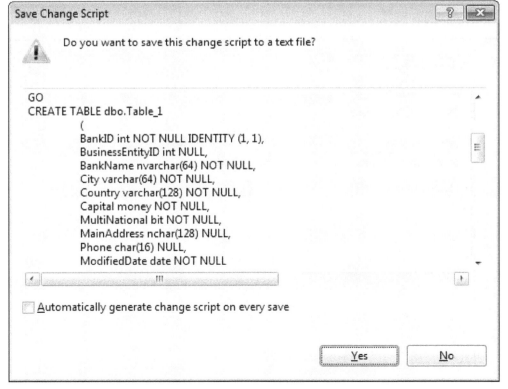

## Generated CREATE TABLE & Related Objects Script

Code generated by the Table Designer.

```
/* To prevent any potential data loss issues, you should review this script in detail before running it
outside the context of the database designer.*/
BEGIN TRANSACTION
SET QUOTED_IDENTIFIER ON
SET ARITHABORT ON
SET NUMERIC_ROUNDABORT OFF
SET CONCAT_NULL_YIELDS_NULL ON
SET ANSI_NULLS ON
SET ANSI_PADDING ON
SET ANSI_WARNINGS ON
COMMIT
BEGIN TRANSACTION
GO
CREATE TABLE dbo.Table_1
        (
        BankID int NOT NULL IDENTITY (1, 1),
        BusinessEntityID int NULL,
        BankName nvarchar(64) NOT NULL,
        City varchar(64) NOT NULL,
        Country varchar(128) NOT NULL,
        Capital money NOT NULL,
        MultiNational bit NOT NULL,
        MainAddress nchar(128) NULL,
        Phone char(16) NULL,
        ModifiedDate date NOT NULL
        ) ON [PRIMARY]
GO
ALTER TABLE dbo.Table_1 ADD CONSTRAINT
        CK_Table_1 CHECK (Capital >= $5000000000.0)
GO
ALTER TABLE dbo.Table_1 ADD CONSTRAINT
        DF_Table_1_ModifiedDate DEFAULT CURRENT_TIMESTAMP FOR ModifiedDate
GO
ALTER TABLE dbo.Table_1 ADD CONSTRAINT
        PK_Table_1 PRIMARY KEY CLUSTERED
        (
        BankID
        ) WITH( STATISTICS_NORECOMPUTE = OFF, IGNORE_DUP_KEY = OFF, ALLOW_ROW_LOCKS = ON,
ALLOW_PAGE_LOCKS = ON) ON [PRIMARY]

GO
```

**-- T-SQL script continues**

```
ALTER TABLE dbo.Table_1 ADD CONSTRAINT
        IX_Table_1 UNIQUE NONCLUSTERED
        (
        BankName
        ) WITH( STATISTICS_NORECOMPUTE = OFF, IGNORE_DUP_KEY = OFF, ALLOW_ROW_LOCKS = ON,
ALLOW_PAGE_LOCKS = ON) ON [PRIMARY]

GO
ALTER TABLE dbo.Table_1 ADD CONSTRAINT
        FK_Table_1_Table_1 FOREIGN KEY
        (
        BankID
        ) REFERENCES dbo.Table_1
        (
        BankID
        ) ON UPDATE  NO ACTION
         ON DELETE  NO ACTION

GO
ALTER TABLE dbo.Table_1 SET (LOCK_ESCALATION = TABLE)
GO
COMMIT
```

Upon Exit or Save, a name can be assigned to the table. In this instance, the Table_1 is changed to
MultiNationalBank. The Table Designer automatically replaces all the "Table_1" occurrences in the script
with "MultiNationalBank".

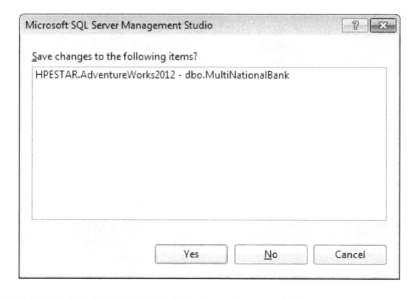

## One-to-Many Relationship Implementation

The cardinality of relationship implemented with PRIMARY KEY & FOREIGN KEY constraints is one-to-many. Many FKs can reference a single PK value.  In the following demo, many products map to a single subcategory value 'Touring Bike'. The matching is not done on the name between tables, rather on the surrogate PK value 3.

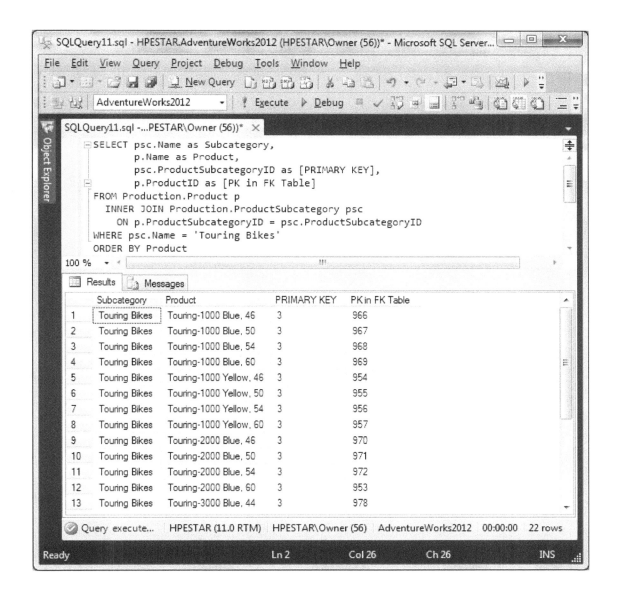

# FOREIGN KEY Referencing A UNIQUE KEY

A FOREIGN KEY can reference a UNIQUE KEY or UNIQUE index column in another table in addition to the PRIMARY KEY. In the following demonstration a FOREIGN KEY is created from ProdNumber column pointing to Production.Product ProductNumber (UNIQUE index) column.

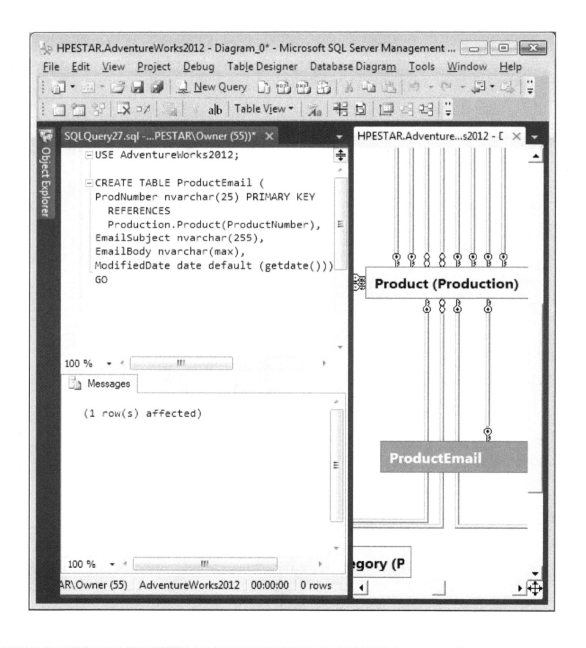

# FOREIGN KEY Relationship Without Constraint

A table can have a FOREIGN KEY which is not supported by server-side constraint. In such instance the client-side application software has to ensure that the relationship is valid. Generally it is undesirable. **Whatever can be done on the server-side should be done there because it is more efficient development wise, maintenance wise and performance wise.** Demonstration to remove the FK constraint on the ProductID column in the [Order Details] table of the CopyOfNorthwind database.

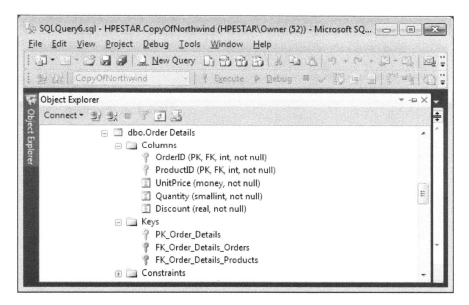

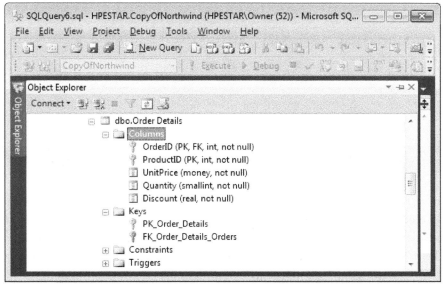

# Database Diagram Design Tool in SSMS

Management Studio Object Explorer includes a diagramming tool for tables and their relationships with each other. While not as sophisticated as independent database design tools, it is excellent for working with a small number of tables.

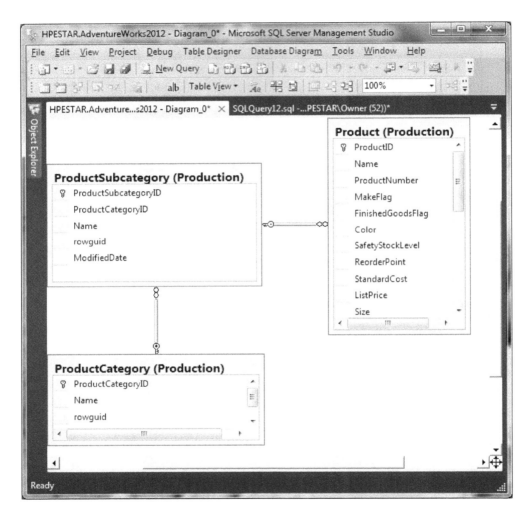

The diagramming tool has both reverse engineering and forward engineering features. **Reverse engineering**: it creates a diagram based on table and PK/FK constraints definitions. **Forward engineering**: it can change table and constraint setup in the database based on diagram changes. The Gold Key (PRIMARY KEY symbol) end of the connection line points to the PRIMARY KEY table, while the double "o" (infinite symbol in mathematics, here meaning many) end to the FOREIGN KEY table.

# PRIMARY KEY & FOREIGN KEY as JOIN ON Keys

When we need data from two related tables we have to JOIN the tables. The typical JOIN keys are the PRIMARY KEY and FOREIGN KEY. In the following demonstration, we want to display the subcategory for each Touring Bike product from the Product table. Since the 'Touring Bike' subcategory value is in the ProductSubcategory table, we have to JOIN it to the Product table. The JOIN keys are: ProductSubcategoryID PRIMARY KEY in the ProductSubcategory table and ProductSubcategoryID FOREIGN KEY in the Product table. Naming the FK same as the PK is helpful with readability, therefore developer productivity.

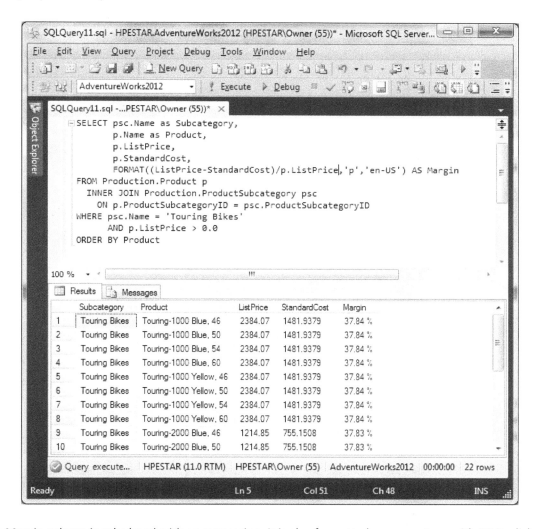

The Margin column is calculated with an expression. It is also formatted as percentage with US English culture.

## Composite & Indirect FOREIGN KEY

A composite (more than one column) PRIMARY KEY requires matching composite FOREIGN KEY references. In the Sales.SalesOrderDetail table SpecialOfferID & ProductID constitute a composite FOREIGN KEY which references the SpecialOfferProduct table composite PRIMARY KEY. Thus ProductID indirectly references the Production.Product table.

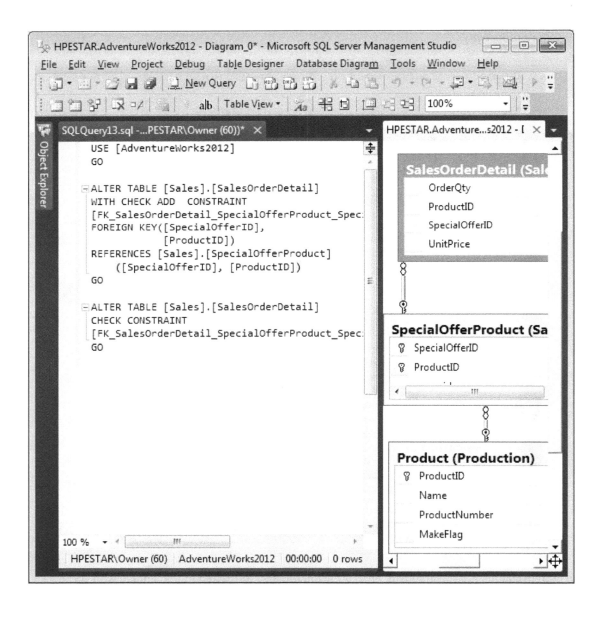

# NATURAL KEY is a Must in Every Table

NATURAL KEY is a unique key which can serve as PRIMARY KEY for identifying data. A product name is a natural key in a product table. A product number is also a NATURAL KEY in a product table. Note that product "number" should better be called product identification since it is frequently not a number rather it is alphanumeric like: AB342BL where BL stands for blue. The Name and ProductNumber columns are NATURAL KEYs in the Production.Product table. **Every table should have a NATURAL KEY**. If it does not, there is a definition problem. Naturally, test tables, work tables and staging tables are exceptions to this rule.

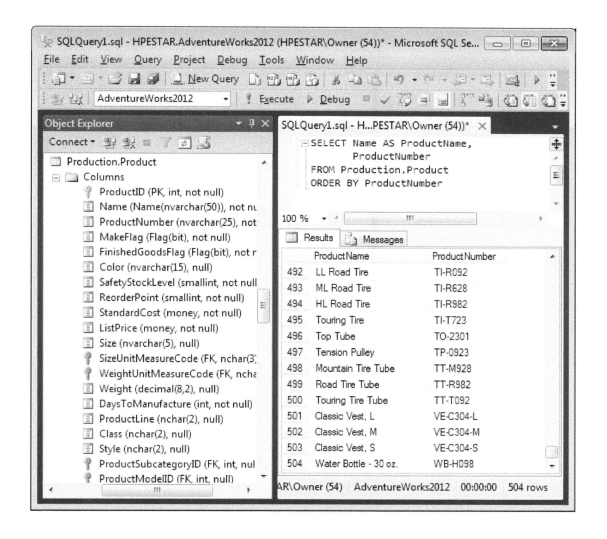

# CANDIDATE KEY

A CANDIDATE KEY can be any column or a combination of columns that can qualify as UNIQUE KEY in a table with no NULL value. The ProductID, Name, ProductNumber, rowguid ( 16 byte random value like FA3C65CD-0A22-47E3-BDF6-53F1DC138C43, hyphens are for readability) are all CANDIDATE KEYs in the Production.Product table. Only one of them can be the PRIMARY KEY. In this instance the selected PRIMARY KEY is ProductID, a SURROGATE (to NATURAL KEY) INT IDENTITY (1,1) PRIMARY KEY.

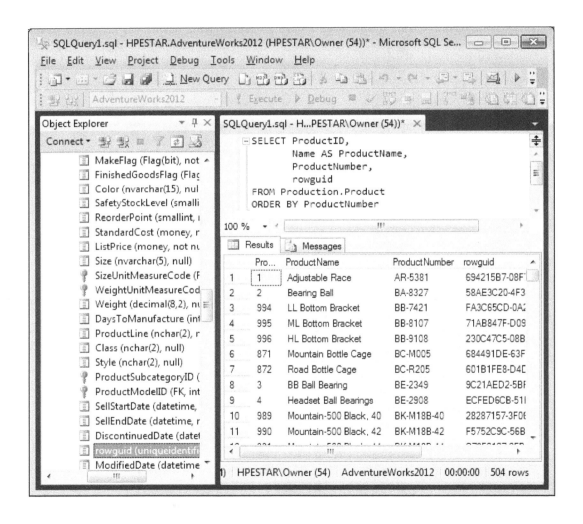

# Logical Data Modeling in Visio

The following screenshots demonstrate logical / conceptual data modeling in Visio using the ORM diagram tool.

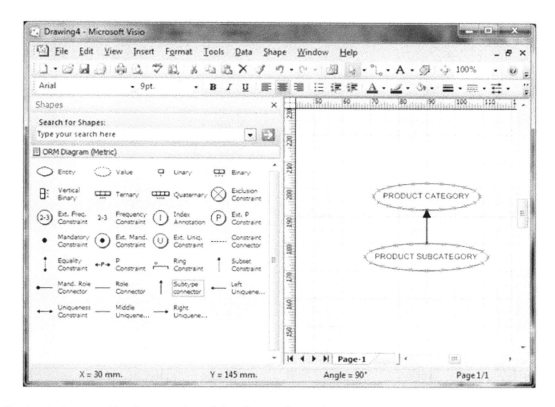

Following is the actual implementation of the above relationship.

```
CREATE TABLE [Production].[ProductCategory](
       [ProductCategoryID] [int] IDENTITY(1,1) PRIMARY KEY,
       [Name] [dbo].[Name] NOT NULL,
       [rowguid] [uniqueidentifier] ROWGUIDCOL  NOT NULL,
       [ModifiedDate] [datetime] NOT NULL          );

CREATE TABLE [Production].[ProductSubcategory](
       [ProductSubcategoryID] [int] IDENTITY(1,1) PRIMARY KEY,
       [ProductCategoryID] [int] NOT NULL REFERENCES
Production.ProductCategory(ProductCategoryID) ,
       [Name] [dbo].[Name] NOT NULL,
       [rowguid] [uniqueidentifier] ROWGUIDCOL  NOT NULL,
       [ModifiedDate] [datetime] NOT NULL          );
```

**CHAPTER 6:  Fundamentals of Relational Database Design**

*Branch Banking Conceptual Diagram Preparation In Visio ORM Diagram Tool*

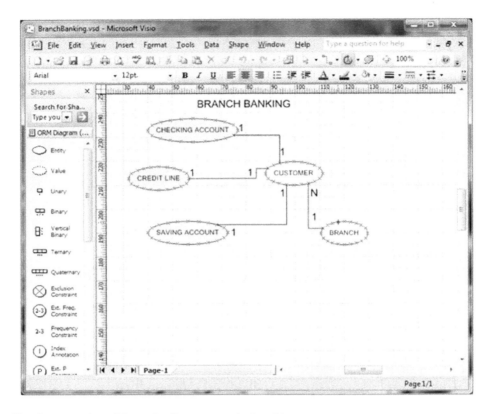

The actual implementation of Branch - Customer relationship.

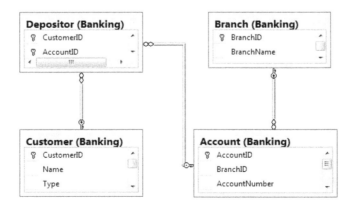

# Relational Database Design with Visio

Office Visio can be used for physical database modeling and design. Another widely used database modeling tool is ERWIN.

A sample database design diagram in Visio. Lines represent FOREIGN KEY constraints, arrowheads point to the referenced table.

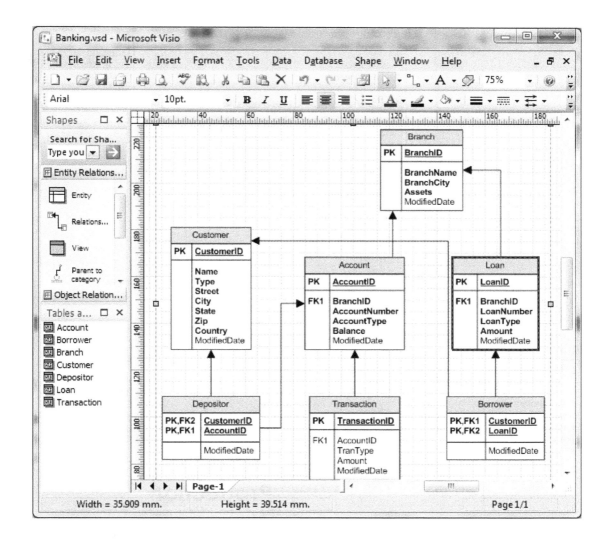

## AdventureWorks Database Model in Visio

A segment of the AdventureWorks database design model in Visio.

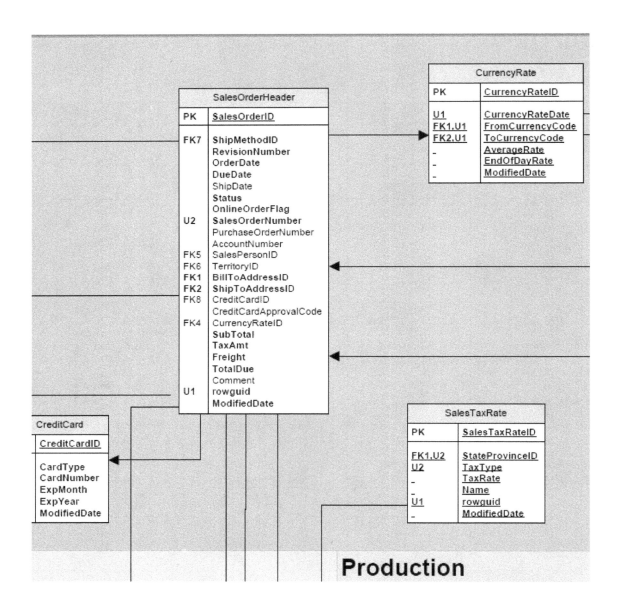

# Reverse Engineering a Database with Visio

Visio can reverse engineer a database. Based on PRIMARY KEY & FOREIGN KEY constraints and table definitions, it can construct a database diagram automatically. Here are the first and an intermediate steps.

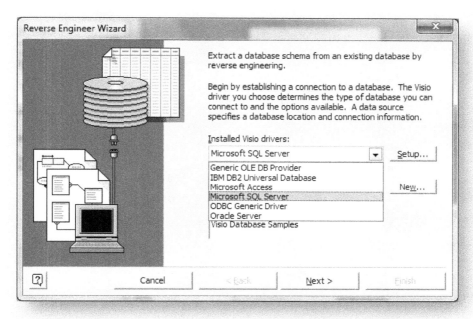

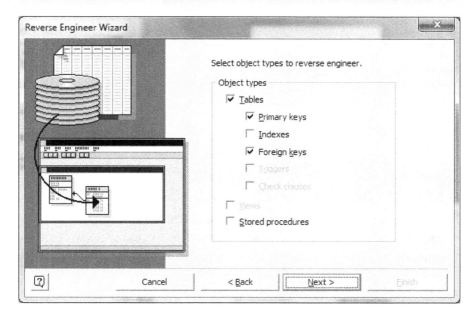

**CHAPTER 6: Fundamentals of Relational Database Design**

## Reverse Engineered Diagram of Northwind

A section display from the reverse engineered diagram of Northwind sample database:

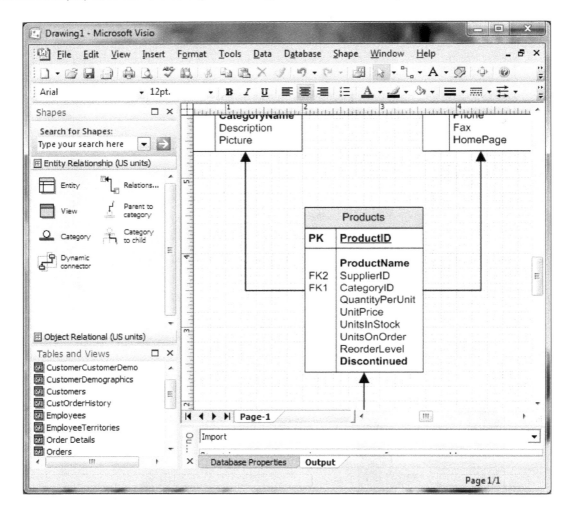

## Forward Engineering a Database with Visio

Visio product itself does not have forward engineering feature. Alberto Ferrari developed an Office Addin for generating database scripts from a Visio database model diagram: Visio Forward Engineer Addin for Office 2010 ( http://sqlblog.com/blogs/alberto_ferrari/archive/2010/04/16/visio-forward-engineer-addin-for-office-2010.aspx ).

Codeplex blog post and free download for the same: Visio Forward Engineer Addin ( http://forwardengineer.codeplex.com/ ).

# Forward Engineering from SSMS Diagram Tool

The Database Diagram Tool in SSMS Object Explorer support graphical design and forward engineering.

Screenshot to show the creation of a new table "Automobile" in the Diagram Tool.

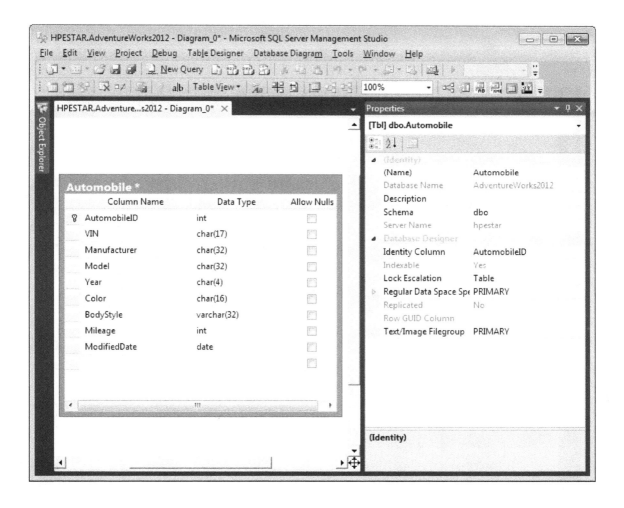

### The Properties Dialog Box Allows The Individual Configuration Of Each Column

The Right Click drop-down menu has options to add indexes, CHECK constraint and other table related database objects.

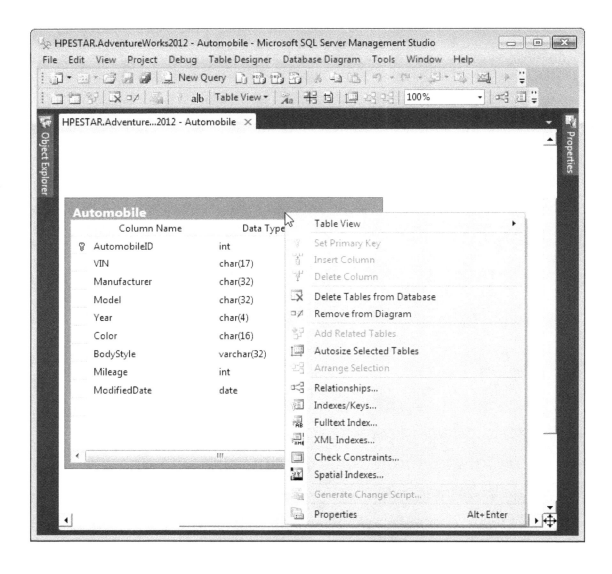

## Forward Engineering Can Be Initiated  By Exiting / Saving The Diagram
The save option dialog box activates automatically upon exit.

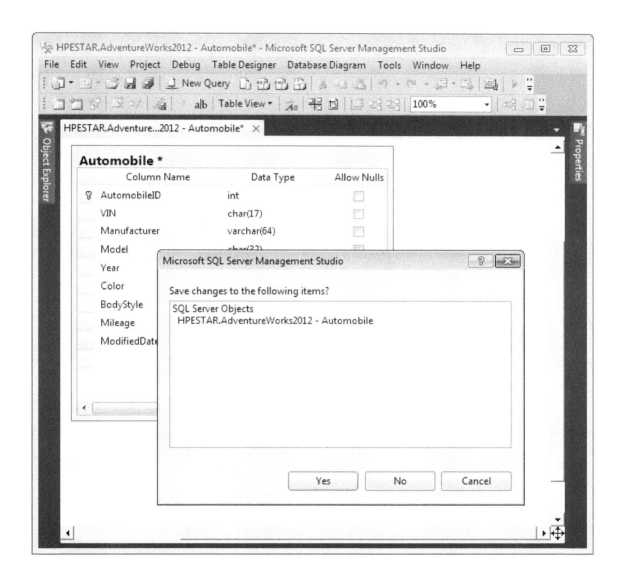

## *Save Change Script Panel Pops Up With The Generated T-SQL Change Script*

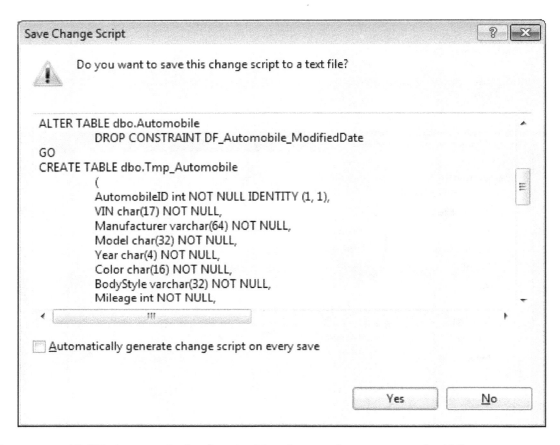

The generated T-SQL change script for changing Manufacturer data type to varchar(64).

```
/* To prevent any potential data loss issues, you should review this script in detail before running it
outside the context of the database designer.*/
BEGIN TRANSACTION
SET QUOTED_IDENTIFIER ON
SET ARITHABORT ON
SET NUMERIC_ROUNDABORT OFF
SET CONCAT_NULL_YIELDS_NULL ON
SET ANSI_NULLS ON
SET ANSI_PADDING ON
SET ANSI_WARNINGS ON
COMMIT
BEGIN TRANSACTION
GO
```

**-- T-SQL script continued**

```
ALTER TABLE dbo.Automobile
        DROP CONSTRAINT DF_Automobile_ModifiedDate
GO


CREATE TABLE dbo.Tmp_Automobile

        (
        AutomobileID int NOT NULL IDENTITY (1, 1),
        VIN char(17) NOT NULL,
        Manufacturer varchar(64) NOT NULL,
        Model char(32) NOT NULL,
        Year char(4) NOT NULL,
        Color char(16) NOT NULL,
        BodyStyle varchar(32) NOT NULL,
        Mileage int NOT NULL,
        ModifiedDate date NOT NULL )  ON [PRIMARY]
GO
ALTER TABLE dbo.Tmp_Automobile SET (LOCK_ESCALATION = TABLE)
GO
ALTER TABLE dbo.Tmp_Automobile ADD CONSTRAINT
        DF_Automobile_ModifiedDate DEFAULT (getdate()) FOR ModifiedDate
GO
SET IDENTITY_INSERT dbo.Tmp_Automobile ON
GO
IF EXISTS(SELECT * FROM dbo.Automobile)
        EXEC('INSERT INTO dbo.Tmp_Automobile (AutomobileID, VIN, Manufacturer, Model, Year,
Color, BodyStyle, Mileage, ModifiedDate)
                SELECT AutomobileID, VIN, CONVERT(varchar(64), Manufacturer), Model, Year, Color,
BodyStyle, Mileage, ModifiedDate FROM dbo.Automobile WITH (HOLDLOCK TABLOCKX)')
GO
SET IDENTITY_INSERT dbo.Tmp_Automobile OFF
GO
DROP TABLE dbo.Automobile
GO
EXECUTE sp_rename N'dbo.Tmp_Automobile', N'Automobile', 'OBJECT'
GO
ALTER TABLE dbo.Automobile ADD CONSTRAINT
        PK_Automobile PRIMARY KEY CLUSTERED
        ( AutomobileID
        ) WITH( STATISTICS_NORECOMPUTE = OFF, IGNORE_DUP_KEY = OFF, ALLOW_ROW_LOCKS = ON,
ALLOW_PAGE_LOCKS = ON) ON [PRIMARY]
GO
COMMIT
```

## Generate Change Script Option

Forward Engineering can also be initiated by the Generate Change Script option. The same option can be used when making any changes to the Diagram using the Diagram Tool.

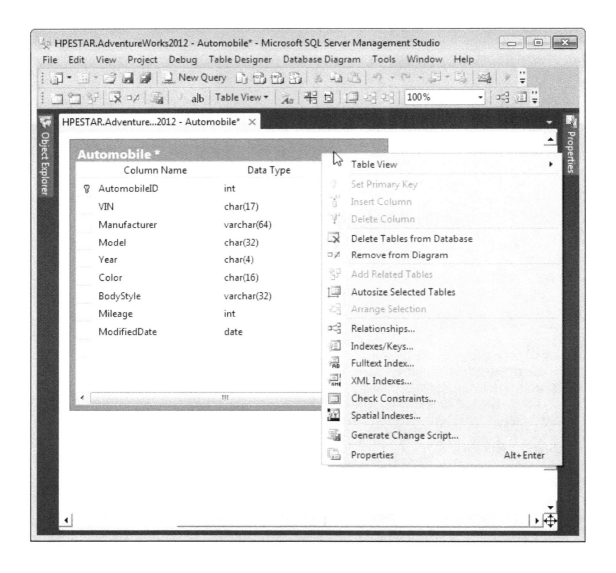

## The Generated Script Of The Automobile Table By The Diagram Tool

```
USE [AdventureWorks2012]
GO

/****** Object:  Table [dbo].[Automobile]    Script Date: 7/22/2016 11:20:17 AM ******/
SET ANSI_NULLS ON
GO

SET QUOTED_IDENTIFIER ON
GO

SET ANSI_PADDING ON
GO

CREATE TABLE [dbo].[Automobile](
        [AutomobileID] [int] IDENTITY(1,1) NOT NULL,
        [VIN] [char](17) NOT NULL,
        [Manufacturer] [char](32) NOT NULL,
        [Model] [char](32) NOT NULL,
        [Year] [char](4) NOT NULL,
        [Color] [char](16) NOT NULL,
        [BodyStyle] [varchar](32) NOT NULL,
        [Mileage] [int] NOT NULL,
        [ModifiedDate] [date] NOT NULL,
 CONSTRAINT [PK_Automobile] PRIMARY KEY CLUSTERED
(
        [AutomobileID] ASC
)WITH (PAD_INDEX = OFF, STATISTICS_NORECOMPUTE = OFF, IGNORE_DUP_KEY = OFF,
ALLOW_ROW_LOCKS = ON, ALLOW_PAGE_LOCKS = ON) ON [PRIMARY]
) ON [PRIMARY]

GO

SET ANSI_PADDING ON
GO

ALTER TABLE [dbo].[Automobile] ADD  CONSTRAINT [DF_Automobile_ModifiedDate]
DEFAULT (getdate()) FOR [ModifiedDate]
GO
```

# Scripting Single Database Object with Related Objects

The scripting feature works only through the graphical user interface (GUI) in SSMS Object Explorer. **There is no command to script a table.** Start with Right Click on the Banking.Account table.

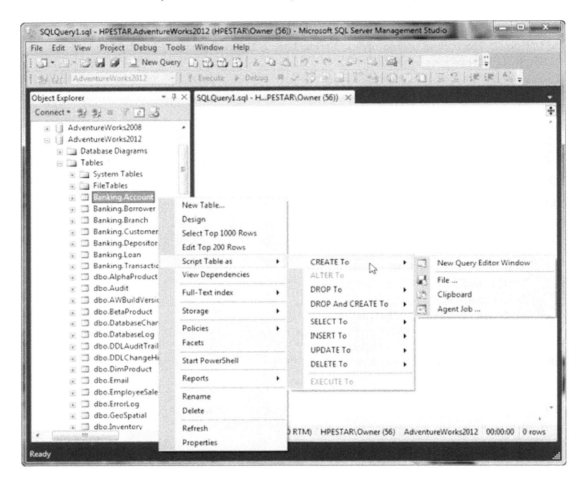

Generated script for the Banking.Account table and related objects.

```
USE [AdventureWorks2012]
GO
SET ANSI_NULLS ON
GO
SET QUOTED_IDENTIFIER ON
GO
SET ANSI_PADDING ON
GO
```

**CHAPTER 6:** *Fundamentals of Relational Database Design*

-- T-SQL script continued

```
CREATE TABLE [Banking].[Account](
        [AccountID] [int] IDENTITY(1,1) NOT NULL,
        [BranchID] [int] NOT NULL,
        [AccountNumber] [char](20) NOT NULL,
        [AccountType] [char](12) NOT NULL,
        [Balance] [money] NOT NULL,
        [ModifiedDate] [datetime] NULL,
PRIMARY KEY CLUSTERED
(
        [AccountID] ASC
)WITH  (PAD_INDEX  =  OFF,  STATISTICS_NORECOMPUTE  =  OFF,  IGNORE_DUP_KEY  =  OFF,
ALLOW_ROW_LOCKS = ON,
ALLOW_PAGE_LOCKS = ON) ON [PRIMARY],
UNIQUE NONCLUSTERED
(        [AccountID] ASC
)WITH  (PAD_INDEX  =  OFF,  STATISTICS_NORECOMPUTE  =  OFF,  IGNORE_DUP_KEY  =  OFF,
ALLOW_ROW_LOCKS = ON,
ALLOW_PAGE_LOCKS = ON) ON [PRIMARY],
UNIQUE NONCLUSTERED
(
        [AccountNumber] ASC
)WITH  (PAD_INDEX  =  OFF,  STATISTICS_NORECOMPUTE  =  OFF,  IGNORE_DUP_KEY  =  OFF,
ALLOW_ROW_LOCKS = ON,
ALLOW_PAGE_LOCKS = ON) ON [PRIMARY]   ) ON [PRIMARY]
GO
SET ANSI_PADDING ON
GO
ALTER TABLE [Banking].[Account] ADD  DEFAULT (getdate()) FOR [ModifiedDate]
GO


ALTER TABLE [Banking].[Account]  WITH CHECK ADD FOREIGN KEY([BranchID])
REFERENCES [Banking].[Branch] ([BranchID])
ON DELETE CASCADE
GO


ALTER TABLE [Banking].[Account]  WITH CHECK ADD  CONSTRAINT [ATC]
CHECK  (([AccountType]='S' OR [AccountType]='C'))
GO
```

**CHAPTER 6:  Fundamentals of Relational Database Design**

# Scripting DB Objects With Script Wizard

The Script Wizard is a sophisticated tool for scripting out multiple objects, in fact all objects can be scripted in a single setup and execution. The generated script can be saved to single/multiple files, new query window or the Clipboard. The launching sequence of menus starts with Right Click on the database.

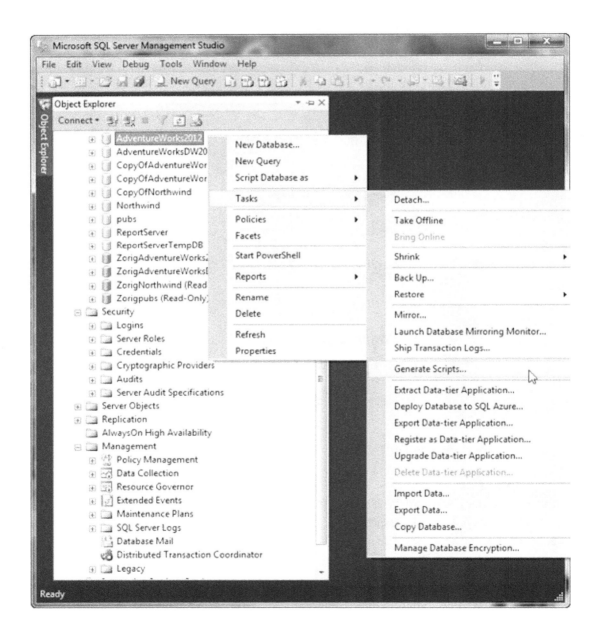

### *Script Wizard Optional Description Page*

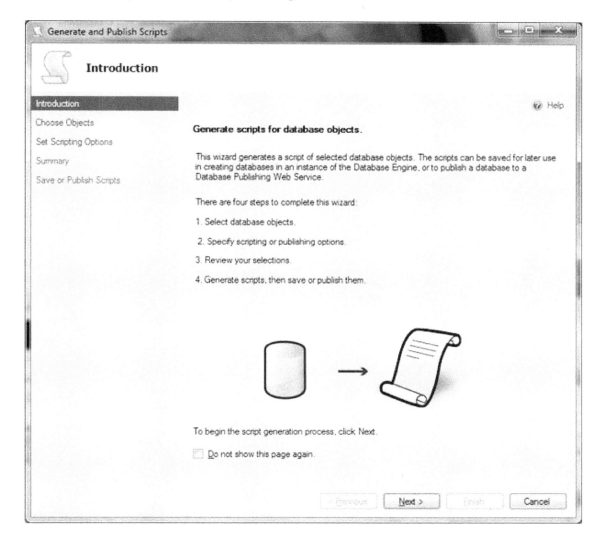

## *Object Selection Panel For Scripting*

*A number of options can be set for generation, including scripting of related objects.*

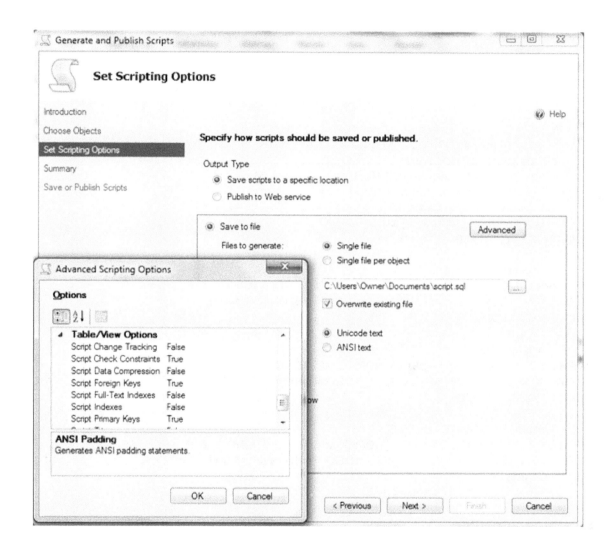

*The script generated by the Script Wizard for the Banking.Loan table and related objects*

```
USE [AdventureWorks2012]
GO
SET ANSI_NULLS ON
GO
SET QUOTED_IDENTIFIER ON
GO
SET ANSI_PADDING ON
GO
CREATE TABLE [Banking].[Loan](
        [LoanID] [int] IDENTITY(1,1) NOT NULL,
        [BranchID] [int] NOT NULL,
        [LoanNumber] [char](20) NOT NULL,
        [LoanType] [varchar](30) NOT NULL,
        [Amount] [money] NOT NULL,
        [ModifiedDate] [datetime] NULL,
PRIMARY KEY CLUSTERED
(
        [LoanID] ASC
)WITH (PAD_INDEX = OFF, STATISTICS_NORECOMPUTE = OFF, IGNORE_DUP_KEY = OFF,
ALLOW_ROW_LOCKS = ON, ALLOW_PAGE_LOCKS = ON) ON [PRIMARY],
UNIQUE NONCLUSTERED
(
        [LoanID] ASC
)WITH (PAD_INDEX = OFF, STATISTICS_NORECOMPUTE = OFF, IGNORE_DUP_KEY = OFF,
ALLOW_ROW_LOCKS = ON, ALLOW_PAGE_LOCKS = ON) ON [PRIMARY],
UNIQUE NONCLUSTERED
(
        [LoanNumber] ASC
)WITH (PAD_INDEX = OFF, STATISTICS_NORECOMPUTE = OFF, IGNORE_DUP_KEY = OFF,
ALLOW_ROW_LOCKS = ON, ALLOW_PAGE_LOCKS = ON) ON [PRIMARY]
) ON [PRIMARY]

GO
SET ANSI_PADDING ON
GO
ALTER TABLE [Banking].[Loan] ADD  DEFAULT (getdate()) FOR [ModifiedDate]
GO
ALTER TABLE [Banking].[Loan]  WITH CHECK ADD FOREIGN KEY([BranchID])
REFERENCES [Banking].[Branch] ([BranchID])
ON DELETE CASCADE
GO
```

## SEQUENCE Objects

Sequence objects are new in SQL Server 2012. They are similar to the INT IDENTITY(1,1) sequence, however, there is a big difference: they don't "live" inside a table. They are table independent database objects. T-SQL demonstration script displays the flexibility of the new method for sequence number management.

```
-- Create a sequence object similar to INT IDENTITY(1,1)
CREATE SEQUENCE seqPurchaseOrder
AS INT
START WITH 1   INCREMENT BY 1;
GO

SELECT NEXT VALUE FOR seqPurchaseOrder;
GO 50
/* 1  2  3  .... 50 */

SELECT NEXT VALUE FOR seqPurchaseOrder;
GO
-- 51

SELECT NextOrderNo = NEXT VALUE FOR seqPurchaseOrder;
-- 52

SELECT NEXT VALUE FOR seqPurchaseOrder as NextOrderNo;
-- 54

EXEC sp_help seqPurchaseOrder;
```

| Name | Owner | Type | Created_datetime |
|---|---|---|---|
| seqPurchaseOrder | dbo | sequence object | 2016-06-27 09:14:32.940 |

```
DECLARE @List TABLE (id int identity(1,1) primary key, i int);
INSERT @List(i) SELECT NEXT VALUE FOR seqPurchaseOrder;
INSERT @List(i) SELECT NEXT VALUE FOR seqPurchaseOrder;
INSERT @List(i) SELECT NEXT VALUE FOR seqPurchaseOrder;
INSERT @List(i) SELECT NEXT VALUE FOR seqPurchaseOrder;
INSERT @List(i) VALUES (NEXT VALUE FOR seqPurchaseOrder);
SELECT * FROM @List
```

| id | i |
|---|---|
| 1 | 55 |
| 2 | 56 |
| 3 | 57 |
| 4 | 58 |
| 5 | 59 |

CHAPTER 6:  Fundamentals of Relational Database Design

## SEQUENCE Object Sharing

SEQUENCE is visible in other connections/session as well not only now but until it exists.

Create a new connection to test NEXT VALUE for seqPurchaseOrder.

```
-- Check current value
SELECT current_value
FROM sys.sequences
WHERE name = 'seqPurchaseOrder';
-- 58
```

```
-- Check metadata
SELECT name, object_id, schema_name(schema_id) as SchemaName, type
FROM sys.sequences;
```

| name | object_id | SchemaName | type |
|------|-----------|------------|------|
| seqPurchaseOrder | 1338487847 | dbo | SO |

```
DECLARE @List TABLE (id int identity(1,1) primary key,
            i int default (NEXT VALUE FOR seqPurchaseOrder));
INSERT @List(i) DEFAULT VALUES;
INSERT @List(i) DEFAULT VALUES;
INSERT @List(i) DEFAULT VALUES;
INSERT @List(i) DEFAULT VALUES;
INSERT @List(i)DEFAULT VALUES;
SELECT * FROM @List
```

| id | i |
|----|-----|
| 1 | 59 |
| 2 | 60 |
| 3 | 61 |
| 4 | 62 |
| 5 | 63 |

```
DROP SEQUENCE seqPurchaseOrder;
GO
```

```
SELECT NEXT VALUE FOR seqPurchaseOrder;
```

```
/*  Msg 208, Level 16, State 1, Line 2

Invalid object name 'seqPurchaseOrder'.  */
```

## Cyclical Sequence Objects

We can create cyclical sequence objects as well for enumerating cyclical temporal objects such as weekdays or months.

```
CREATE SEQUENCE seqCycleSeven
AS TINYINT
START WITH 1  INCREMENT BY 1  MINVALUE  1   MAXVALUE  7  CYCLE
GO


CREATE TABLE #Weekdays ( ID INT IDENTITY(1,1) PRIMARY KEY, Weekday nchar(20));
GO


-- Populate table with days progressing by addition of cycle number to current day
INSERT INTO #Weekdays
SELECT DATENAME(dw, dateadd(dd,NEXT VALUE for seqCycleSeven,CURRENT_TIMESTAMP));
GO 20


SELECT * FROM #Weekdays ORDER BY ID;
GO
```

| ID | Weekday |
|----|-----------|
| 1  | Tuesday   |
| 2  | Wednesday |
| 3  | Thursday  |
| 4  | Friday    |
| 5  | Saturday  |
| 6  | Sunday    |
| 7  | Monday    |
| 8  | Tuesday   |
| 9  | Wednesday |
| 10 | Thursday  |
| 11 | Friday    |
| 12 | Saturday  |
| 13 | Sunday    |
| 14 | Monday    |
| 15 | Tuesday   |
| 16 | Wednesday |
| 17 | Thursday  |
| 18 | Friday    |
| 19 | Saturday  |
| 20 | Sunday    |

```
DROP SEQUENCE seqCycleSeven;  DROP TABLE #Weekdays;
```

## Getting the Source Code with sp_helptext

The sp_helptext system procedure can be applied to get the source code for some objects, but not all. **Table source code can only be obtained with GUI scripting in Object Explorer.**

```
EXEC sp_helptext 'sp_who'
GO
-- Command(s) completed successfully. - 94 rows - Partial results.

CREATE PROCEDURE sys.Sp_who --- 1995/11/28 15:48
 @loginame SYSNAME = NULL --or 'active'
AS
  DECLARE @spidlow  INT,
      @spidhigh INT,
      @spid    INT,
      @sid     VARBINARY(85)

  SELECT @spidlow = 0,
     @spidhigh = 32767

  IF ( @loginame IS NOT NULL
    AND Upper(@loginame COLLATE latin1_general_ci_as) = 'ACTIVE' )
   BEGIN
    SELECT spid,
        ecid,
        status,
        loginame=Rtrim(loginame),
        hostname,
        blk=CONVERT(CHAR(5), blocked),
        dbname = CASE
             WHEN dbid = 0 THEN NULL
             WHEN dbid <> 0 THEN Db_name(dbid)
           END,
        cmd,
        request_id
     FROM  sys.sysprocesses_ex
     WHERE  spid >= @spidlow
        AND spid <= @spidhigh
        AND Upper(cmd) <> 'AWAITING COMMAND'

    RETURN ( 0 )
  END
```

CHAPTER 6: *Fundamentals of Relational Database Design*

# CHAPTER 7:  Normal Forms & Database Normalization

## The Goals of Database Normalizaton

Database normalization is the design technique of logically organizing data in a database:

> ➢ Data should uniquely be addressable in a database by table, row and column identification - like x, y, z coordinates in 3D space.

> ➢ Data redundancy (storing the same data in more than one table) should be avoided.

> ➢ Data dependency ( a property is fully dependent on the PRIMARY KEY) should ensure that a piece of data gets into the right table or if there is none, a new one is created.

The first goal is relatively easy to achieve yet data duplication in a table is a constant issue plaguing database installations. The second goal is simple as well yet it conflicts with deep-seated human insecurity of not seeing all the data together. The third goal on the other hand requires careful design considerations, it can be quite challenging for complex data relationships or if the database designer is not familiar with the application.  If an OLTP database with many data access points is not normalized, the result is inefficiency in database application  development and maintenance which can be quite costly to a company for years to come. Metadata query to list all FOREIGN KEYs in NorthWind followed by a high level database diagram.

```
select    fkschema = fk.constraint_schema,  fktable = fk.table_name, fkcolumn = fk.column_name,
          pkcolumn = pk.column_name,   pktable = pk.table_name, pkschema = pk.table_schema,
          fkname = rc.constraint_name
from  northwind.information_schema.referential_constraints rc
        inner join northwind.information_schema.key_column_usage fk
              on fk.constraint_name = rc.constraint_name
        inner join northwind.information_schema.key_column_usage pk
              on pk.constraint_name = rc.unique_constraint_name
where   fk.ordinal_position = pk.ordinal_position order by fkschema, fktable, fkcolumn;
```

| fkschema | fktable | fkcolumn | pkcolumn | pktable | pkschema | fkname |
|---|---|---|---|---|---|---|
| dbo | CustomerCustomerDemo | CustomerID | CustomerID | Customers | dbo | FK_CustomerCustomerDemo_Customers |
| dbo | CustomerCustomerDemo | CustomerTypeID | CustomerTypeID | CustomerDemographics | dbo | FK_CustomerCustomerDemo |
| dbo | Employees | ReportsTo | EmployeeID | Employees | dbo | FK_Employees_Employees |
| dbo | EmployeeTerritories | EmployeeID | EmployeeID | Employees | dbo | FK_EmployeeTerritories_Employees |
| dbo | EmployeeTerritories | TerritoryID | TerritoryID | Territories | dbo | FK_EmployeeTerritories_Territories |
| dbo | Order Details | OrderID | OrderID | Orders | dbo | FK_Order_Details_Orders |
| dbo | Order Details | ProductID | ProductID | Products | dbo | FK_Order_Details_Products |
| dbo | Orders | CustomerID | CustomerID | Customers | dbo | FK_Orders_Customers |
| dbo | Orders | EmployeeID | EmployeeID | Employees | dbo | FK_Orders_Employees |
| dbo | Orders | ShipVia | ShipperID | Shippers | dbo | FK_Orders_Shippers |
| dbo | Products | CategoryID | CategoryID | Categories | dbo | FK_Products_Categories |
| dbo | Products | SupplierID | SupplierID | Suppliers | dbo | FK_Products_Suppliers |
| dbo | Territories | RegionID | RegionID | Region | dbo | FK_Territories_Region |

## Orders & Related Tables Diagram in Northwind

The database diagram clearly shows the central role of the Orders table at a company which is a reseller not a manufacturer.

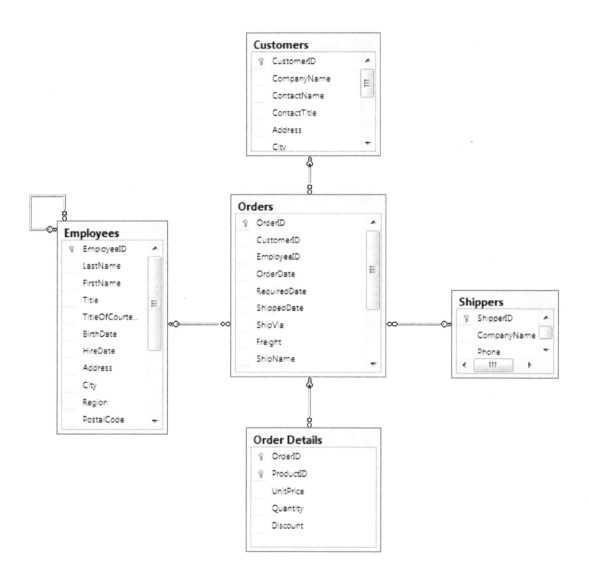

# First Normal Form (1NF)

The first normal form establishes RDBMS basics. The rules make common sense.

➢ Each group of related data (entity) should have its own table (no piggybacking data).

➢ Each column should be identified with a unique name in a table.

➢ Each row should be identified with a unique column or set of columns (PRIMARY KEY).

Selected tables (entities) in Northwind database.

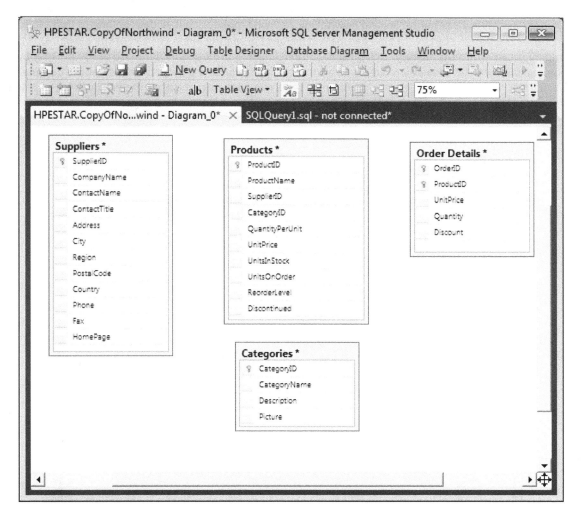

# Second Normal Form (2NF)

The Second Normal Form addresses the issue of piggybacking data on a related table.

> ➤ Tables are in  First Normal Form.

> ➤ Remove subsets of data that apply to multiple rows of a table and create a separate table for them.

> ➤ Create relationships between these new tables and their predecessors through the use of FOREIGN KEYs.

The tacit assumption here that there was no logical data modeling or that had a mistake. The database designer has created a set of tables and now taking a second look to see if all data belong to that table. Frequently the design starts with lead database developer preparing a first version of the design. Only big companies can afford the "luxury" of logical data modeling and professional database designer. That has to be qualified with a little known fact. Even a small company can hire a professional database designer for a month, surely money well spent.  Categories table can easily piggyback on the Products table. Being a separate table increases the usefulness, flexibility and expandability of the design.

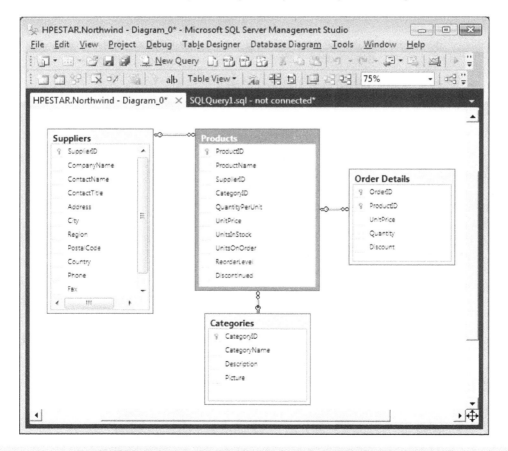

# Third Normal Form (3NF)

The Third Normal Form addresses the issue of storing the data in the appropriate table.

➢ Tables are in Second Normal Form.

➢ Remove columns that are not dependent upon the PRIMARY KEY and move them to the correct table.

The royalty and ytd_sales columns are not fully dependent on the title_id PRIMARY KEY. In fact royalty schedule is specified in the roysched table and the dependency includes quantity sold. A view (virtual table) can be setup to return the current royalties based on books sold and the royalty schedule. A more appropriate table for ytd_sales would be saleshist (SalesHistory).  The inclusion of  the time dependent dynamic ytd_sales column is suspicious right off the bat since all the other columns are static.

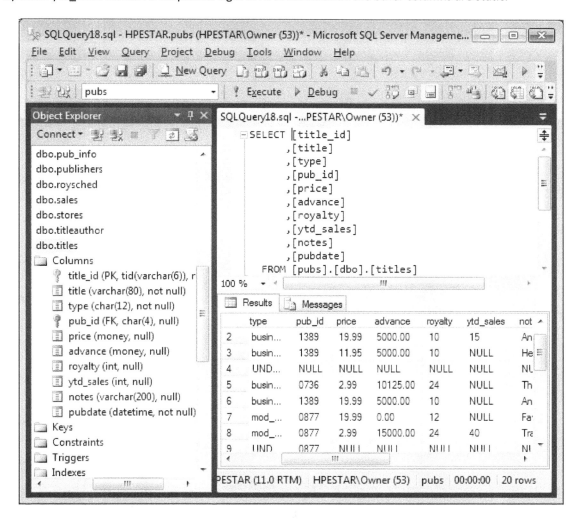

# Fourth Normal Form (4NF)

The Fourth Normal Form addresses the issue of subtle data dependency:

> ➤ Tables are in Third Normal Form.

> ➤ A relation should not have multi-valued dependencies.

If we look at "Road-650 Black, 44" and "Road-650 Red, 44" bikes in Production.Product we see that they are the same bike with different color. So it would be sufficient to store only a single row "Road-650, 44" and setup a junction table between the Product table and the (new) Color table to indicate the color variations and other dependent information. We can see that the color occurs in 3 columns: Name, ProductNumber (first letter of color) and Color. By doing 4NF normalization we can remove the color reference from the Name and ProductNumber columns.

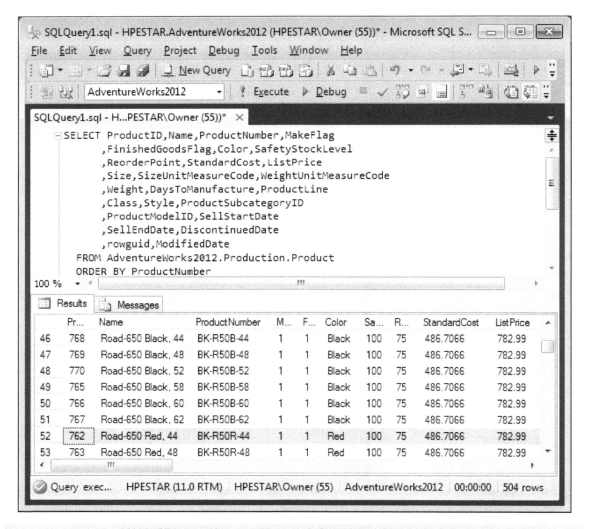

# Database Denormalizaton

Database denormalization is a technique to reduce the number of tables in a normalized database. The author personally disagrees with this process: why would you go into the trouble and expense of creating a normalized database and then ruin it? Regardless of the author's opinion, denormalization is an accepted notion in the database industry. Too many tables require too many JOINs, that is the underlying justification. The trouble with this process is two-fold:

➤ There is no guideline when to stop with denormalization, 10% table reduction, 50%?

➤ Also, there are no guidelines as to which tables to eliminate when denormalizing.

If you eliminate too many tables you may just end up with a messy database instead of the original neat & efficient 3NF database thus creating a potential disaster for your employer. Typically you would look at the small static tables as candidates for elimination which are not FOREIGN KEY referenced from many tables. There are precise guidelines how to achieve a normalized database. It is a scientific process. Denormalization is not. Performance is another reason mentioned for denormalization, but that is generally not a valid claim. There are much better ways to achieve good performance than denormalizing a well-designed database system. Hypothetically, let's take a look at low population tables in AdventureWorks2012, as candidates for denormalization.

```
SELECT  TOP 20 SCHEMA_NAME(schema_id)+'.'+o.name AS TableName, max(i.rows) AS Rows
FROM    sys.sysobjects o INNER JOIN sys.sysindexes i   ON o.id = i.id
     INNER JOIN sys.objects oo     ON o.id = oo.object_id
WHERE   xtype = 'u' AND OBJECTPROPERTY(o.id,N'IsUserTable') = 1
GROUP BY schema_id, o.name ORDER BY Rows ASC;
```

| TableName | Rows |
|---|---|
| dbo.ErrorLog | 0 |
| dbo.AWBuildVersion | 1 |
| Person.PhoneNumberType | 3 |
| HumanResources.Shift | 3 |
| Sales.ShoppingCartItem | 3 |
| Production.ProductCategory | 4 |
| Production.ProductReview | 4 |
| Production.Illustration | 5 |
| Purchasing.ShipMethod | 5 |
| Person.AddressType | 6 |
| Production.ProductModelIllustration | 7 |
| Production.Culture | 8 |
| Sales.SalesReason | 10 |
| Sales.SalesTerritory | 10 |
| Production.Document | 13 |
| HumanResources.JobCandidate | 13 |
| Production.Location | 14 |
| HumanResources.Department | 16 |
| Production.ScrapReason | 16 |
| Sales.SpecialOffer | 16 |

Tables like PhoneNumberType, Shift, Shipmethod and SalesReason can likely be eliminated without dire consequences. However, why ruin a well-designed 3NF database such as AdventureWorks2012 just to decrease the number of JOINs with one or two? Is it annoying to have 10 JOINs in a query? Not really. That is how SQL works. Is SQL Server going to be much faster with 8 JOINs as opposed to 10 JOINs? No, there is no such a rule in query optimization.

**CHAPTER 7:  Normal Forms & Database Normalization**

# Better Alternative to Denormalization

The best alternative is to use views for frequently used queries to avoid building JOINs again and again. The results of SELECT from a view must be sorted with ORDER BY just like the case for tables. There is no way around it. Demonstration of the powerful method.

```
USE AdventureWorks;
SELECT
              V.Name                                      AS Vendor,
              CONCAT(C.LastName, ', ', C.FirstName)       AS Contact,
              CT.Name                                     AS Title
FROM Person.Contact AS C
   INNER JOIN Purchasing.VendorContact VC
              ON C.ContactID = VC.ContactID
   INNER JOIN Person.ContactType CT
              ON CT.ContactTypeID = VC.ContactTypeID
   INNER JOIN Purchasing.Vendor V
              ON V.VendorID = VC.VendorID
ORDER BY Vendor, Contact;
-- (156 row(s) affected)


CREATE VIEW vVendorContact
AS
SELECT
              V.Name                                      AS Vendor,
              CONCAT(C.LastName, ', ', C.FirstName)       AS Contact,
              CT.Name                                     AS Title
FROM Person.Contact AS C
   INNER JOIN Purchasing.VendorContact VC      ON C.ContactID = VC.ContactID
   INNER JOIN Person.ContactType CT            ON CT.ContactTypeID = VC.ContactTypeID
   INNER JOIN Purchasing.Vendor V              ON V.VendorID = VC.VendorID
GO
```

SELECT TOP 5 * FROM vVendorContact ORDER BY Vendor, Contact;

| Vendor | Contact | Title |
|--------|---------|-------|
| A. Datum Corporation | Pellow, Frank | Assistant Sales Agent |
| A. Datum Corporation | Wilkie, Jay | Sales Agent |
| A. Datum Corporation | Yu, Wei | Sales Manager |
| Advanced Bicycles | Moeller, Jonathan | Sales Associate |
| Advanced Bicycles | Wilson, James | Sales Manager |

We have created from the 4 tables JOIN, a very simple to use, very easy to remember view.

*CHAPTER 7: Normal Forms & Database Normalization*

# Ten Most Common Database Design Mistakes

Along his database career the author found the following list of common design issues:

➢  Not involving systems analysts and/or subject matter experts in conceptual design.

➢  Not employing accomplished database designer / lead developer to implement 3NF design standards.

➢  Denormalizing a well-designed database.

➢  Not having NATURAL KEY in addition to INT IDENTITY(1,1) SURROGATE PRIMARY KEY.

➢  Poor documentation & lack of naming convention for the project.

➢  Not using PRIMARY KEY, FOREIGN KEY, UNIQUE , CHECK & DEFAULT constraints to protect data integrity.

➢  Using client programs for data management instead of server side stored procedures, functions & views.

➢  Using triggers to fix design or client software problems.

➢  Not following the solution implementation hierarchy:  constraints -> stored procedures -> triggers -> client SW.

➢  Lack of formal Quality Assurance process.

## Working for a Company with Messy Database Design

In your career you may work for companies with proper 3NF design databases, companies with messy databases or somewhere in the middle. It is a joy to work in 3NF environment. On the other hand, if the database is badly designed, or more accurately lacks design, you have to be careful in criticizing it because you can  pick up enemies quickly or even get fired. Badly designed database usually becomes an IT department political issue instead of remaining a technical issue. Most companies don't want to invest in redesigning the database properly. In such a situation you have to accept working with poorly designed databases, enjoy your nice paycheck and wait for an opportunity when new tables or database is needed to create proper 3NF design.

CHAPTER 7:  Normal Forms & Database Normalization

# Query to List All Table Sizes in a Database

T-SQL script to list all table sizes in AdventureWorks2012 database. Note: the tables are uniquely named in AdventureWorks databases, so there are no duplicates if the schema name is not used. This assumption though not true generally. Objects can be named the same in different schemas.

```
declare @TableSpace table (TableName sysname, RowsK varchar(32), -- table variable
        ReservedMB varchar(32), DataMB varchar(32),
        IndexMB varchar(32), UnusedMB varchar(32));


insert @TableSpace
exec sp_MSforeachtable @command1="exec sp_spaceused '?';" -- undocumented system procedure


update @TableSpace set RowsK = CONVERT(varchar,  1+convert(int, RowsK)/1024)
update @TableSpace set ReservedMB = CONVERT(varchar,
            1+convert(int,LEFT(ReservedMB, charindex(' K', ReservedMB,-1)))/1024);
update @TableSpace set DataMB = CONVERT(varchar,
            1+convert(int,LEFT(DataMB, charindex(' K', DataMB,-1)))/1024);
update @TableSpace set IndexMB = CONVERT(varchar,
            convert(int,LEFT(IndexMB, charindex(' K', IndexMB,-1)))/1024);
update @TableSpace set UnusedMB = CONVERT(varchar,
            convert(int,LEFT(UnusedMB, charindex(' K', UnusedMB,-1)))/1024);


select * from @TableSpace order by convert(int,DataMB) desc;
go
-- (71 row(s) affected) -- Partial results.
```

| TableName | RowsK | ReservedMB | DataMB | IndexMB | UnusedMB |
|---|---|---|---|---|---|
| Person | 20 | 84 | 30 | 51 | 2 |
| SalesOrderDetail | 119 | 18 | 10 | 6 | 1 |
| DatabaseLog | 2 | 7 | 7 | 0 | 0 |
| TransactionHistory | 111 | 11 | 7 | 3 | 0 |
| WorkOrderRouting | 66 | 8 | 6 | 1 | 0 |
| SalesOrderHeader | 31 | 9 | 6 | 2 | 0 |
| WorkOrder | 71 | 7 | 5 | 2 | 0 |
| TransactionHistoryArchive | 88 | 9 | 5 | 3 | 0 |
| ProductPhoto | 1 | 3 | 3 | 0 | 0 |
| Address | 20 | 6 | 3 | 2 | 0 |
| CreditCard | 19 | 3 | 2 | 0 | 0 |
| EmailAddress | 20 | 4 | 2 | 1 | 0 |
| Password | 20 | 2 | 2 | 0 | 0 |
| PersonPhone | 20 | 3 | 2 | 0 | 0 |
| SalesTerritory | 1 | 1 | 1 | 0 | 0 |
| PhoneNumberType | 1 | 1 | 1 | 0 | 0 |
| Product | 1 | 1 | 1 | 0 | 0 |
| SalesTerritoryHistory | 1 | 1 | 1 | 0 | 0 |
| SalesPersonQuotaHistory | 1 | 1 | 1 | 0 | 0 |
| Employee | 1 | 1 | 1 | 0 | 0 |

# CHAPTER 8: Functional Database Design

## Types of Table Relationships

The most frequent relationship is one-to-many ( or many-to-one) indicating many FOREIGN KEY references to a single PRIMARY KEY table row. Example: Products & ProductCategories; A product category may have 50 different products. The next most popular one is many-to-many relationship indicating that a single row in Table Alpha can reference multiple rows in Table Beta. Example: Classes & Students at a college; A class may have 20 students and a student may take 5 different classes. In the following pubs table relationship diagram we can see:

> ➢ many-to-many relationship ( oo - oo connectors): titleauthor table
> ➢ one-to-one relationship ( 2 gold keys): publishers & pub_info tables
> ➢ one-to-many: the remaining relationships

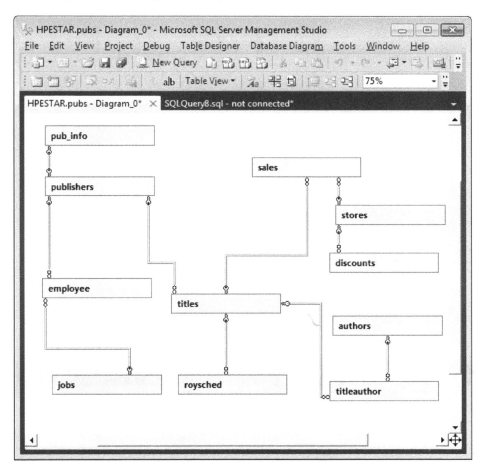

CHAPTER 8: Functional Database Design

## One-To-Many Relationship - FOREIGN KEY Reference

Northwind example shows that each product belongs to a category.

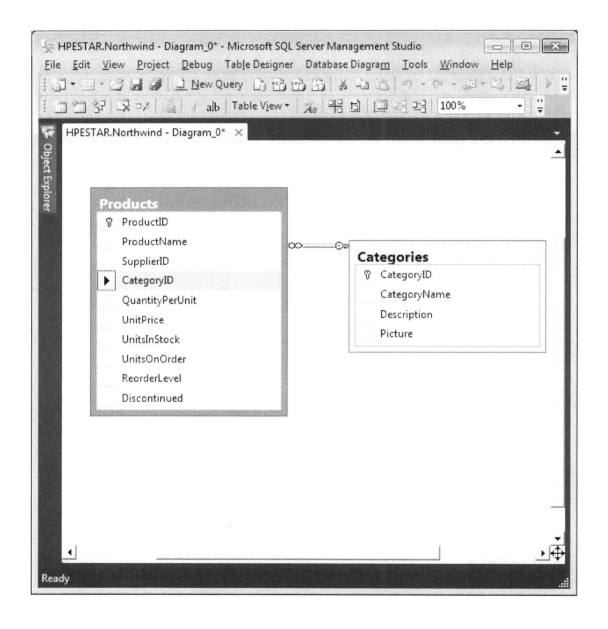

*CategoryID in the Products table is a FOREIGN KEY ( a pointer) to a PRIMARY KEY in the Categories table*

Therefore, we can safely JOIN the two tables using the two ON KEYs.

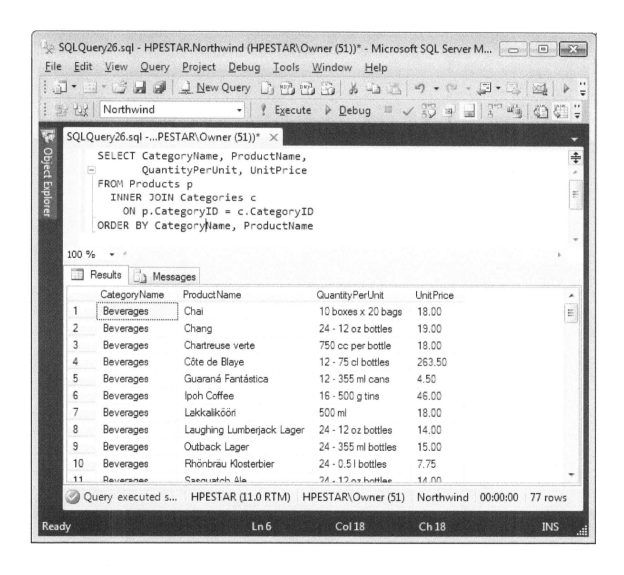

### The PRIMARY KEY and FOREIGN KEY should not be exposed to the database application user

The Business Intelligence consumer needs meaningful information not meaningless numbers. The software engineer can see the PK and FK values as part of his work.

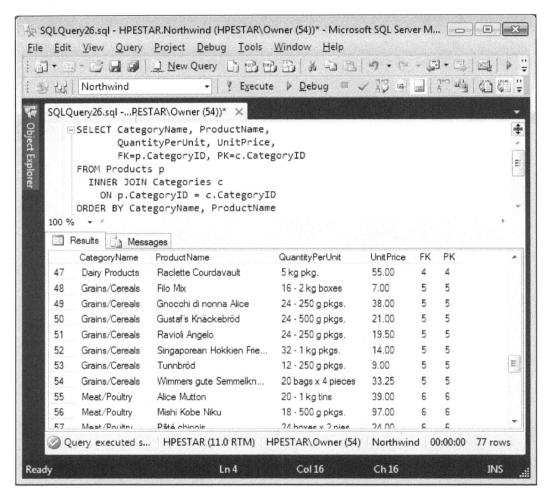

We could make the NATURAL KEY ProductName a PRIMARY KEY in the Products table. However, that is a string field (column) nvarchar(40) which can be 80 bytes in size ( each UNICODE character is 2 bytes). That would present increased space use and decreased performance in JOINs. It would also present increased maintenance cost if we have to change a product name, for example, "Ravioli Angelo" to "Ravioli Los Angeles". The change would have to be performed in the PRIMARY KEY table and each FOREIGN KEY table.  The 4-byte integer SURROGATE PRIMARY KEY ProductID solves all the problems above. Minimal space use, fast in JOINs and since a meaningless number (a database pointer), we never have to change it. If the ProductName changes, it is just a single UPDATE in the PRIMARY KEY table.

**CHAPTER 8:  Functional Database Design**

# Composite PRIMARY KEY

A composite PRIMARY KEY consists of two or more columns. Junction tables typically apply composite PRIMARY KEYs. An example is the Production.ProductProductPhoto junction table.

> ProductID (PK, FK, int, not null)
>
> ProductPhotoID (PK, FK, int, not null)
>
> Primary (Flag(bit), not null)
>
> ModifiedDate (datetime, not null)

The PRIMARY KEY is the composite of two FOREIGN KEYs: ProductID and ProductPhotoID.

T-SQL script definition of the above composite PRIMARY KEY.

```
USE [AdventureWorks2012];
GO

ALTER TABLE [Production].[ProductProductPhoto]
ADD  CONSTRAINT [PK_ProductProductPhoto_ProductID_ProductPhotoID]
PRIMARY KEY NONCLUSTERED
(
        [ProductID] ASC,
        [ProductPhotoID] ASC
);
```

**A FOREIGN KEY referencing a composite PRIMARY KEY must have the same column structure.** Query to display all the data in the table.

```
SELECT   ProductID
        ,ProductPhotoID
        ,[Primary]
        ,ModifiedDate
 FROM AdventureWorks2012.Production.ProductProductPhoto;
-- (504 row(s) affected) - Partial results.
```

| ProductID | ProductPhotoID | Primary | ModifiedDate |
|---|---|---|---|
| 813 | 1 | 1 | 2006-06-01 00:00:00.000 |
| 814 | 1 | 1 | 2006-06-01 00:00:00.000 |
| 815 | 160 | 1 | 2006-06-01 00:00:00.000 |
| 816 | 160 | 1 | 2006-06-01 00:00:00.000 |
| 817 | 160 | 1 | 2006-06-01 00:00:00.000 |
| 818 | 160 | 1 | 2006-06-01 00:00:00.000 |

## Parent-Child Hierarchy

When an employee's record includes the manager's ID, it is called self-reference since the manager is an employee also. A simple organizational chart (tree structure) can be established by self-referencing FOREIGN KEYs.

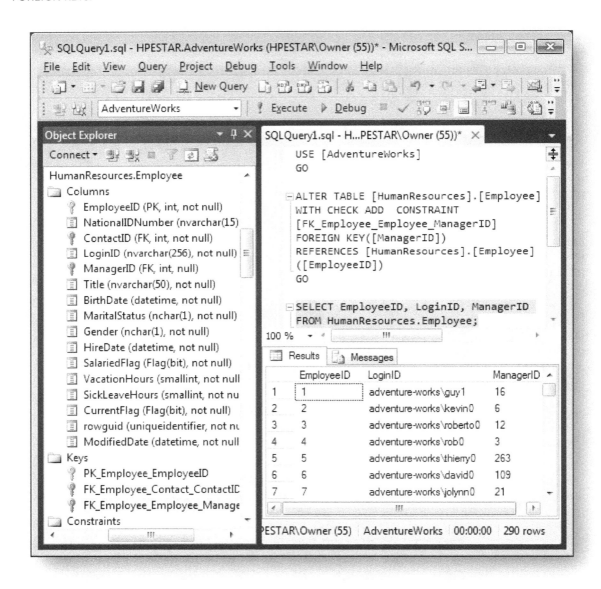

Reading the table:  david0 is the supervisor of kevin0, and roberto0 is the supervisor of rob0.

**CHAPTER 8:  Functional Database Design**

# Hierarchical Relationship - Multi-Level with FOREIGN KEYs

Product, ProductSubcategory and ProductCategory in AdventureWorks represent multi-level hierarchy which can be implemented with FOREIGN KEYs. To get the hierarchical information, we need to INNER JOIN the tables on the FOREIGN KEYS and PRIMARY KEYS. Column aliases are used to create meaningful column names from the 3 "Name"-s.

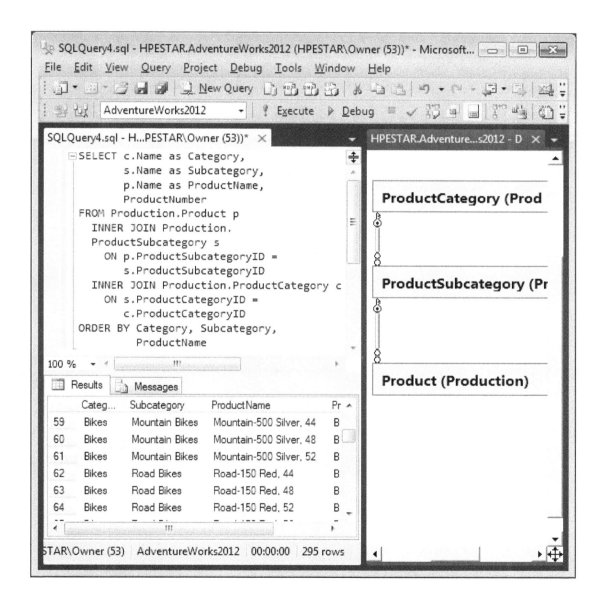

# Tree Hierarchy Representation with hierarchyid

An alternate to using self-referencing FOREIGN KEY is the application of hierarchyid data type introduced with SQL Server 2008.

We can read from the table that ken0 (Ken Sanchez, CEO) is the supervisor of terri0 who in turn is the supervisor of roberto0 who is the supervisor of rob0.

# Many-To-Many Relationship - Junction Table

Junction tables have many names, most popular among them are junction table, cross-reference table and bridge table. The titleauthor table in the pubs database is a junction table: a title (book ) can have many authors and an author can write many titles. The PRIMARY KEY is a composite of two FOREIGN KEYs referencing the titles and authors tables.

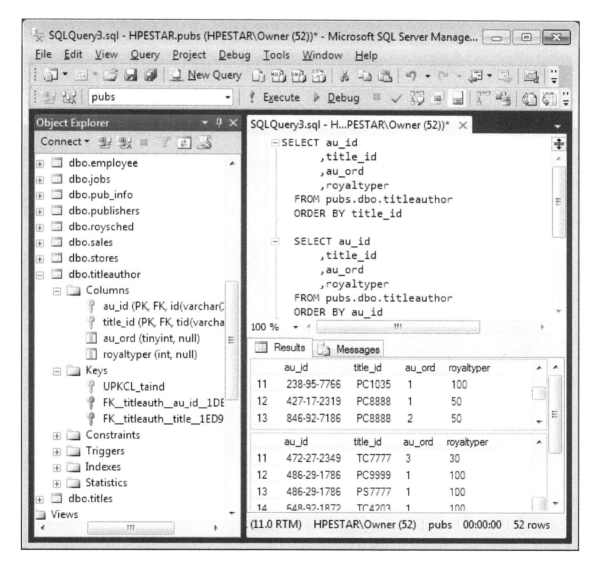

Reading the author - title junction table:  book title PC8888 has multiple (two) authors, while author 486-29-1786 wrote multiple (two) books.

**CHAPTER 8:  Functional Database Design**

# Parent-Child or Master-Detail Tables Design

In the AdventureWorks series of sample databases, Sales.SalesOrderHeader and Sales.SalesOrderDetail tables are implemented as master-detail tables. Similarly for Purchasing.PurchaseOrderHeader and Purchasing.PurchaseOrderDetail. The PRIMARY KEY of SalesOrderHeader is SalesOrderID (INT IDENTITY(1,1)). The PRIMARY KEY of SalesOrderDetail is composite of SalesOrderID FOREIGN KEY and SalesOrderDetailID (INT IDENTITY(1,1)). The business meaning is that an order from a bicycle reseller can have many line items such mountain bikes, helmets, touring frames and jerseys.

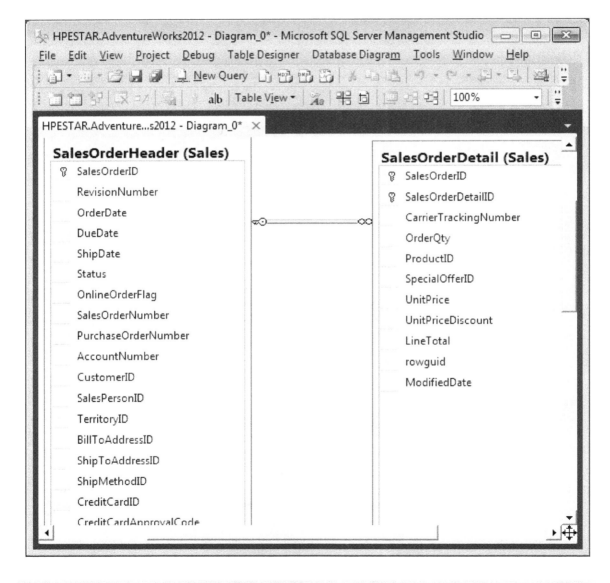

# Column Descriptions of SalesOrderHeader & SalesOrderDetail Tables

UNION query to lists  the column descriptions for the above master-detail tables from the data dictionary.

```
SELECT  'Sales.SalesOrderHeader' AS TableName, objname    AS ColumnName,
        value                                             AS [Description]
FROM fn_listextendedproperty (NULL, 'schema', 'Sales', 'table', 'SalesOrderHeader', 'Column', default)


UNION


SELECT  'Sales.SalesOrderDetail' AS TableName, objname    AS ColumnName,
        value                                             AS [Description]
FROM fn_listextendedproperty (NULL, 'schema', 'Sales', 'table', 'SalesOrderDetail', 'Column', default)


ORDER BY TableName DESC, ColumnName;
```

| TableName | ColumnName | Description |
| --- | --- | --- |
| Sales.SalesOrderHeader | AccountNumber | Financial accounting number reference. |
| Sales.SalesOrderHeader | BillToAddressID | Customer billing address. Foreign key to Address.AddressID. |
| Sales.SalesOrderHeader | Comment | Sales representative comments. |
| Sales.SalesOrderHeader | CreditCardApprovalCode | Approval code provided by the credit card company. |
| Sales.SalesOrderHeader | CreditCardID | Credit card identification number. Foreign key to CreditCard.CreditCardID. |
| Sales.SalesOrderHeader | CurrencyRateID | Currency exchange rate used. Foreign key to CurrencyRate.CurrencyRateID. |
| Sales.SalesOrderHeader | CustomerID | Customer identification number. Foreign key to Customer.BusinessEntityID. |
| Sales.SalesOrderHeader | DueDate | Date the order is due to the customer. |
| Sales.SalesOrderHeader | Freight | Shipping cost. |
| Sales.SalesOrderHeader | ModifiedDate | Date and time the record was last updated. |
| Sales.SalesOrderHeader | OnlineOrderFlag | 0 = Order placed by sales person. 1 = Order placed online by customer. |
| Sales.SalesOrderHeader | OrderDate | Dates the sales order was created. |
| Sales.SalesOrderHeader | PurchaseOrderNumber | Customer purchase order number reference. |
| Sales.SalesOrderHeader | RevisionNumber | Incremental number to track changes to the sales order over time. |
| Sales.SalesOrderHeader | rowguid | ROWGUIDCOL number uniquely identifying the record. Used to support a merge replication sample. |
| Sales.SalesOrderHeader | SalesOrderID | Primary key. |
| Sales.SalesOrderHeader | SalesOrderNumber | Unique sales order identification number. |
| Sales.SalesOrderHeader | SalesPersonID | Sales person who created the sales order. Foreign key to SalesPerson.BusinessEntityID. |
| Sales.SalesOrderHeader | ShipDate | Date the order was shipped to the customer. |
| Sales.SalesOrderHeader | ShipMethodID | Shipping method. Foreign key to ShipMethod.ShipMethodID. |
| Sales.SalesOrderHeader | ShipToAddressID | Customer shipping address. Foreign key to Address.AddressID. |
| Sales.SalesOrderHeader | Status | Order current status. 1 = In process; 2 = Approved; 3 = Backordered; 4 = Rejected; 5 = Shipped; 6 = Cancelled |
| Sales.SalesOrderHeader | SubTotal | Sales subtotal. Computed as SUM(SalesOrderDetail.LineTotal)for the appropriate SalesOrderID. |
| Sales.SalesOrderHeader | TaxAmt | Tax amount. |
| Sales.SalesOrderHeader | TerritoryID | Territory in which the sale was made. Foreign key to SalesTerritory.SalesTerritoryID. |
| Sales.SalesOrderHeader | TotalDue | Total due from customer. Computed as Subtotal + TaxAmt + Freight. |
| Sales.SalesOrderDetail | CarrierTrackingNumber | Shipment tracking number supplied by the shipper. |
| Sales.SalesOrderDetail | LineTotal | Per product subtotal. Computed as UnitPrice * (1 - UnitPriceDiscount) * OrderQty. |
| Sales.SalesOrderDetail | ModifiedDate | Date and time the record was last updated. |
| Sales.SalesOrderDetail | OrderQty | Quantity ordered per product. |
| Sales.SalesOrderDetail | ProductID | Product sold to customer. Foreign key to Product.ProductID. |
| Sales.SalesOrderDetail | rowguid | ROWGUIDCOL number uniquely identifying the record. Used to support a merge replication sample. |
| Sales.SalesOrderDetail | SalesOrderDetailID | Primary key. One incremental unique number per product sold. |
| Sales.SalesOrderDetail | SalesOrderID | Primary key. Foreign key to SalesOrderHeader.SalesOrderID. |
| Sales.SalesOrderDetail | SpecialOfferID | Promotional code. Foreign key to SpecialOffer.SpecialOfferID. |
| Sales.SalesOrderDetail | UnitPrice | Selling price of a single product. |
| Sales.SalesOrderDetail | UnitPriceDiscount | Discount amount. |

## Diagram of PurchaseOrderHeader and Related Tables

Database diagram to display the special relationship to the child table PurchaseOrderDetail and PK-FK relationships to other tables.

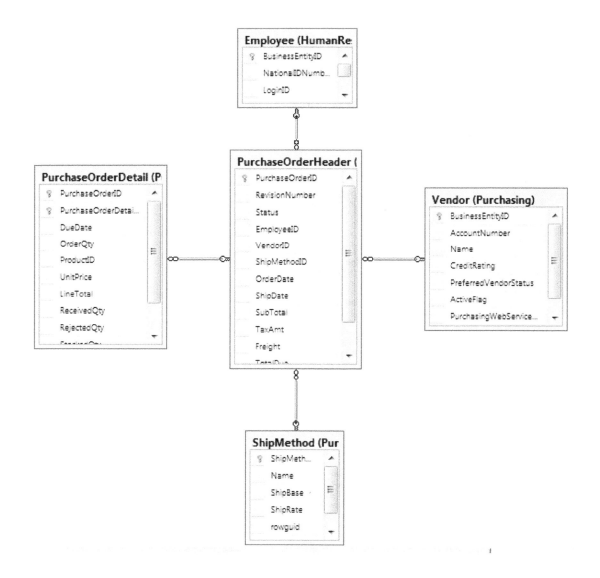

## Multiple FOREIGN KEYs from One Table to Another

Database diagram to illustrate the double FOREIGN KEYS from BillOfMaterials table to the Product table. The FOREIGN KEYS are named **ComponentID and ProductAssemblyID**. In the Product table **SizeUnitMeasureCode & WeightUnitMeasureCode** are double FOREIGN KEYs to the UnitMeasure table.

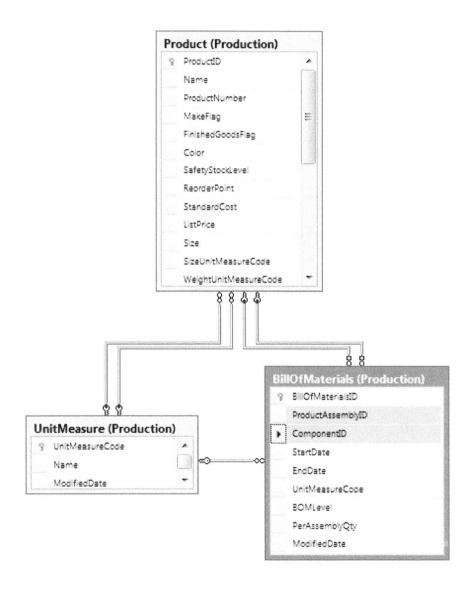

## Parent - Multiple Children Table Design

Database design & diagram to represent a parent table with two children table. Notice that in the children table the PRIMARY KEY is a FOREIGN KEY simultaneously.

```
CREATE TABLE Security  (
    Symbol              CHAR(7)  PRIMARY KEY,
    SecurityName        NVARCHAR(64),
    CUSIP               CHAR(9),
    ModifiedDate        DATETIME DEFAULT (CURRENT_TIMESTAMP)   );


CREATE TABLE Stock  (
    Symbol              CHAR(7)  PRIMARY KEY REFERENCES Security ON DELETE CASCADE,
    AuthShares          BIGINT,
    IssuedShares        BIGINT,
    ClosingPrice        DECIMAL(14, 2),
    ModifiedDate        DATETIME DEFAULT (CURRENT_TIMESTAMP)   );


CREATE TABLE Bond  (
    Symbol              CHAR(7)  PRIMARY KEY REFERENCES Security ON DELETE CASCADE,
    Rate                DECIMAL(14, 6),
    FaceValue           DECIMAL(14, 2),
    MaturityDate        DATE,
    ClosingPrice        DECIMAL(14, 2),
    ModifiedDate        DATETIME DEFAULT (CURRENT_TIMESTAMP)   );
```

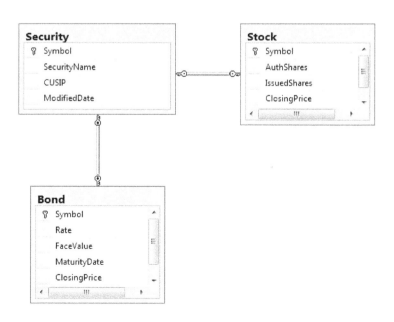

## LookupHeader & Lookup Tables for Storing All Lookups

T-SQL script to demonstrate a simple implementation of LookupHeader & Lookup (detail) tables to prevent database "pollution" by many small lookup (code/translate) tables.

```
USE AdventureWorks2012;

CREATE TABLE LookupHeader
(
        LookupHeaderID      INT IDENTITY(1, 1)      PRIMARY KEY,
        [Type]              VARCHAR(30)             UNIQUE,
        ModifiedDate        DATETIME                default ( CURRENT_TIMESTAMP)
);
go


CREATE TABLE Lookup
(
        LookupHeaderID      INT NOT NULL REFERENCES LookupHeader(LookupHeaderID),
        Code                VARCHAR(6) NOT NULL,
        [Description]       VARCHAR(255),
        ModifiedDate        DATETIME default ( CURRENT_TIMESTAMP)
);
go


-- composite PRIMARY KEY
ALTER TABLE dbo.Lookup
        ADD CONSTRAINT pk_lookup PRIMARY KEY CLUSTERED ( LookupHeaderID, Code );
go

INSERT LookupHeader  ([Type]) VALUES ('Country');

INSERT LookupHeader  ([Type]) VALUES ('Department');

SELECT * FROM   LookupHeader ;
go
```

| LookupHeaderID | Type | ModifiedDate |
|---|---|---|
| 1 | Country | 2016-08-08 07:34:59.077 |
| 2 | Department | 2016-08-08 07:34:59.113 |

```
-- Populate department code
INSERT INTO LookUp (LookupHeaderID, Code, Description)  VALUES    (2, '1', 'Human Resources');
INSERT INTO LookUp (LookupHeaderID, Code, Description)  VALUES    (2, '2', 'Accounting');
INSERT INTO LookUp (LookupHeaderID, Code, Description)  VALUES    (2, '3', 'Engineering');
```

**-- T-SQL script continued**

```sql
-- Populate country code lookup
INSERT INTO LookUp (LookupHeaderID, Code, Description)
SELECT 1, [CountryRegionCode],[Name]
 FROM [AdventureWorks2012].[Person].[CountryRegion]
ORDER BY CountryRegionCode;
go
```

```sql
-- Check lookup table content
SELECT * FROM  Lookup ORDER  BY LookupHeaderID, Code;
```

Partial display of the Lookup table content.

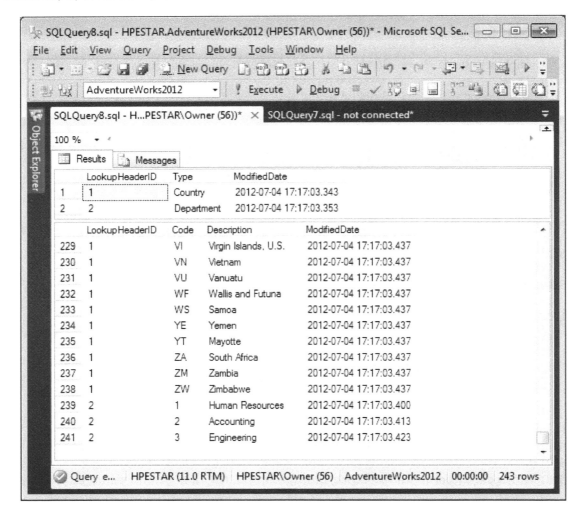

# History Table Design

AdventureWorks2012 EmployeeDepartmentHistory table follows the career of an employee from department to department each with StartDate and EndDate. If EndDate is NULL, that is the employee's current department. For employee ID 250 (BusinessEntityID) the current department is 5. The PRIMARY KEY is composite of BusinessEntityID (employee ID), DepartmentID, ShiftID and StartDate. The first 3 columns in the PRIMARY KEY are FOREIGN KEYs also. BusinessEntityID references (points to) the Employee table, DepartmentID the Department table and ShiftID the Shift table.

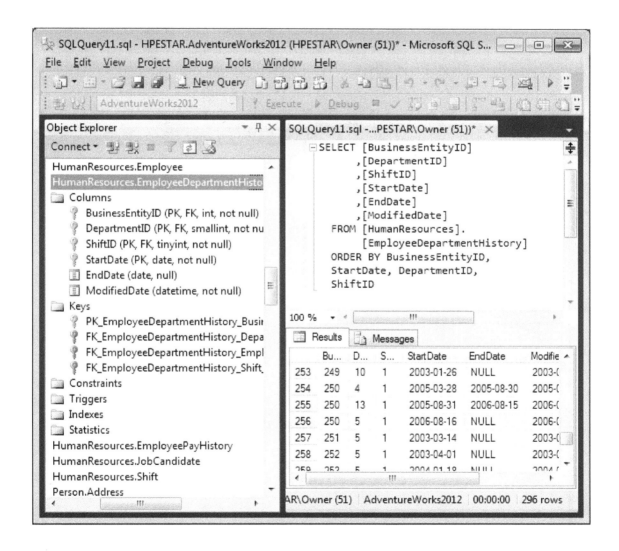

# Implementing One-To-One Relationship

In a one-to-one relationship, a row in the main table can have no more than one matching row in the secondary table, and vice versa. **A one-to-one relationship requires that both of the related columns are primary keys.** One-to-one relationship tables are not very common because most of the time a single table is used. Nonetheless, we might use a one-to-one relationship tables to: Vertically partition a table with many columns; Vertically divide a table to a narrow and wide part for performance reasons - example: email header & email body; Isolate sensitive columns in a table for security reasons; Store information that applies only to a subset of the main table thus avoiding lots of NULLs in the rows. Demonstration to show the one-to-one relationship between Product and ProductInventory tables.

## One-To-One Relationship between publisher & pub_info Tables

The intent of the database designer was to separate the bulk data (logo image, PR description) from the regular size columns which likely are more frequently used as well. The implementation: pub_id in pub_info table is PRIMARY KEY and FOREIGN KEY to publishers pub_id.

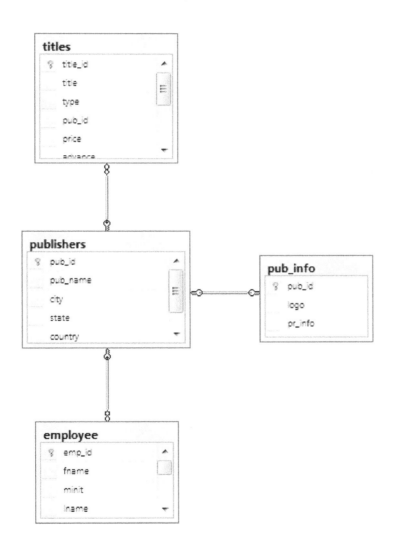

# Tables with Computed Columns

A column can be automatically generated by a formula/expression involving other columns. The generation is "on the fly" when needed. To persist the column the PERSISTED property must be used. That is a requirement for some use such as indexing. The demonstration introduces 2 computed columns into the ProductInventory table.

```
USE tempdb;
GO

CREATE TABLE dbo.Product (
        ProductID int identity(1,1) PRIMARY KEY
        , ProductName nchar(32) NOT NULL UNIQUE
        , Color nvarchar(32)
        , Size varchar(64)
        , ModifiedDate datetime default (CURRENT_TIMESTAMP)
);
GO

-- Table with two computed columns
CREATE TABLE dbo.ProductInventory (
        ProductID int REFERENCES Product(ProductID) PRIMARY KEY
        , QtyOnHand int
        , ReorderPoint int NOT NULL
        , UnitPrice money
        , InventoryCostValue AS QtyOnHand * UnitPrice PERSISTED
        , InventoryCVDEC AS CAST(QtyOnHand * UnitPrice AS DECIMAL(14,0))
        , ModifiedDate datetime default (CURRENT_TIMESTAMP)
);
GO

INSERT Product(ProductName, Color, Size) SELECT 'MusicMobile', 'White', '2" x 3"';
INSERT Product(ProductName, Color, Size) SELECT 'ReaderMobile', 'Black', '5" x 9"';
INSERT Product(ProductName, Color, Size) SELECT 'PhoneMobile', 'Blue', '2 1/2" x 4"';
INSERT Product(ProductName, Color, Size) SELECT 'DELTA laptop', 'Gray', '12" x 16" x 2"';
GO

SELECT * from dbo.Product;
```

| ProductID | ProductName | Color | Size | ModifiedDate |
|-----------|-------------|-------|------|--------------|
| 1 | MusicMobile | White | 2" x 3" | 2016-07-08 10:05:53.943 |
| 2 | ReaderMobile | Black | 5" x 9" | 2016-07-08 10:05:53.947 |
| 3 | PhoneMobile | Blue | 2 1/2" x 4" | 2016-07-08 10:05:53.947 |
| 4 | DELTA laptop | Gray | 12" x 16" x 2" | 2016-07-08 10:05:53.947 |

-- T-SQL script continued

INSERT ProductInventory (ProductID, QtyOnHand, ReorderPoint, UnitPrice) SELECT 1, 105, 30, $99.99;
INSERT ProductInventory (ProductID, QtyOnHand, ReorderPoint, UnitPrice) SELECT 2, 105, 40, $299.99;
INSERT ProductInventory (ProductID, QtyOnHand, ReorderPoint, UnitPrice) SELECT 3, 208, 30, $399.99;
INSERT ProductInventory (ProductID, QtyOnHand, ReorderPoint, UnitPrice) SELECT 4, 103, 30, $599.99;
GO

SELECT * FROM ProductInventory;
GO

| ProductID | QtyOnHand | ReorderPoint | UnitPrice | InventoryCostValue | InventoryCVDEC |
|-----------|-----------|--------------|-----------|--------------------|----------------|
| 1 | 105 | 30 | 99.99 | 10498.95 | 10499 |
| 2 | 105 | 40 | 299.99 | 31498.95 | 31499 |
| 3 | 208 | 30 | 399.99 | 83197.92 | 83198 |
| 4 | 103 | 30 | 599.99 | 61798.97 | 61799 |

Combination query with INNER JOIN and formatting.

```
SELECT          ProductName                                AS [Product Name],
                QtyOnHand                                  AS [Quantity On Hand],
                ReorderPoint                               AS [Reorder Point],
                FORMAT(UnitPrice,'c','en-US')              AS [Unit Price],
                FORMAT(InventoryCostValue, 'c','en-US')    AS [ Inventory Cost Value],
                FORMAT(InventoryCVDEC, 'c','en-US')        AS [Inventory Cost Rounded]
FROM Product P
        INNER JOIN ProductInventory PI
                ON P.ProductID = PI.ProductID
ORDER BY ProductName;
GO
```

| Product Name | Quantity On Hand | Reorder Point | Unit Price | Inventory Cost Value | Inventory Cost Rounded |
|--------------|------------------|---------------|------------|----------------------|------------------------|
| DELTA laptop | 103 | 30 | $599.99 | $61,798.97 | $61,799.00 |
| MusicMobile | 105 | 30 | $99.99 | $10,498.95 | $10,499.00 |
| PhoneMobile | 208 | 30 | $399.99 | $83,197.92 | $83,198.00 |
| ReaderMobile | 105 | 40 | $299.99 | $31,498.95 | $31,499.00 |

-- Cleanup - FOREIGN KEY table must be dropped first
DROP TABLE tempdb.dbo.ProductInventory;
DROP TABLE tempdb.dbo.Product;

# Building the Data Dictionary

The best way to build the data dictionary is the same time when the database objects are created. It can also be done in the final phases of the database development project when changes are rare to the object designs.

## GUI Data Dictionary Maintenance

As an example, right click on a table column name and choose Properties.

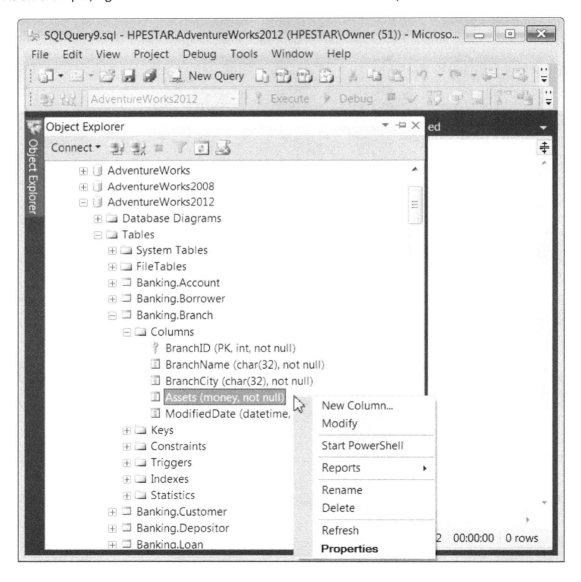

*Extended Properties page can be used for Data Dictionary entry*

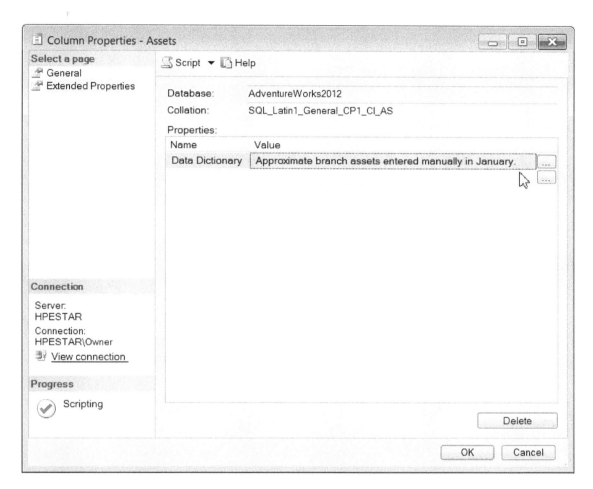

Check the new entry with a query.

```
SELECT *
FROM fn_listextendedproperty (NULL, 'schema', 'Banking', 'table', 'Branch', 'Column', NULL);
GO
```

| objtype | objname | name | value |
|---------|---------|------|-------|
| COLUMN | Assets | Data Dictionary | Approximate branch assets entered manually in January. |

## Data Dictionary Maintenance with T-SQL Scripts

The advantage of using T-SQL scripts for Data Dictionary maintenance is that the script can be saved as a .sql file and rerun when necessary as is or after editing.

```
USE [AdventureWorks2012];
GO


-- Delete Data Dictionary entry
EXEC sys.sp_dropextendedproperty @name=N'Data Dictionary' ,
        @level0type=N'SCHEMA',@level0name=N'Banking',
        @level1type=N'TABLE',@level1name=N'Branch',
        @level2type=N'COLUMN',@level2name=N'Assets';
GO


-- Add Data Dictionary entry
EXEC sys.sp_addextendedproperty @name=N'Data Dictionary',
        @value=N'Approximate branch assets entered manually in January each year.' ,
        @level0type=N'SCHEMA',@level0name=N'Banking', @level1type=N'TABLE',
        @level1name=N'Branch', @level2type=N'COLUMN',@level2name=N'Assets';
GO


-- Check new Data Dictionary entry
SELECT *
FROM fn_listextendedproperty (NULL, 'schema', 'Banking', 'table', 'Branch', 'Column', NULL);
GO
```

| objtype | objname | name | value |
|---------|---------|------|-------|
| COLUMN | Assets | Data Dictionary | Approximate branch assets entered manually in January each year. |

```
-- Data Dictionary entry for BranchName
EXEC sys.sp_addextendedproperty @name=N'Data Dictionary',
        @value=N'Name of the branch. Updated by supervisor only.' ,
        @level0type=N'SCHEMA',@level0name=N'Banking', @level1type=N'TABLE',
        @level1name=N'Branch', @level2type=N'COLUMN',@level2name=N'BranchName';
GO
```

**CHAPTER 8:  Functional Database Design**

## *Updating an Existing Data Dictionary Entry*

```
-- Update Data Dictionary entry
EXEC sys.sp_updateextendedproperty @name=N'Data Dictionary',
@value=N'Approximate branch assets entered in January each year by an automated process.',
@level0type=N'SCHEMA',@level0name=N'Banking',
@level1type=N'TABLE',@level1name=N'Branch',
@level2type=N'COLUMN',@level2name=N'Assets'
GO


SELECT *
FROM fn_listextendedproperty (NULL, 'schema', 'Banking', 'table', 'Branch', 'Column', NULL);
GO
```

| objtype | objname | name | value |
|---|---|---|---|
| COLUMN | Assets | Data Dictionary | Approximate branch assets entered in January each year by an automated process. |

```
-- Data Dictionary entry for BranchCity
EXEC sys.sp_addextendedproperty @name=N'Data Dictionary',
        @value=N'City & State where branch is located.',
        @level0type=N'SCHEMA',@level0name=N'Banking', @level1type=N'TABLE',
        @level1name=N'Branch', @level2type=N'COLUMN',@level2name=N'BranchCity';
GO


-- Listing all Data Dictionary entries for table
SELECT *
FROM fn_listextendedproperty (NULL, 'schema', 'Banking', 'table', 'Branch', 'Column', NULL)
ORDER BY objname;
```

| objtype | objname | name | value |
|---|---|---|---|
| COLUMN | Assets | Data Dictionary | Approximate branch assets entered in January each year by an automated process. |
| COLUMN | BranchCity | Data Dictionary | City & State where branch is located. |
| COLUMN | BranchName | Data Dictionary | Name of the branch. Updated by supervisor only. |

**CHAPTER 8: Functional Database Design**

## Lead Developer as Database Designer

A senior database developer should be able to design a modest business application database. The reason is that he worked with  a number of databases so well-familiar with the concept of 3NF relational database design. Naturally if the lead developer is not familiar with the business, then it is rather difficult, there is a steep learning curve. But then it is difficult also for a professional database designer. Getting a systems analyst on board is the best approach to work with the database designer.

## Database Design Team at Big Budget Projects

Large companies for important projects may setup the following design team:

> ➢ 1-2 database designers
> ➢ 1-3 systems analysts
> ➢ 1-4 subject matter experts

## Hiring Database Design Consultant where Resources  Are Limited

Even a small company or a small project at large company should consider hiring a professional database designer on a consulting basis for a month or so to design the database. A well-designed 3NF database may reduce development from 50 man-months to 35 man-months, thus the payback may start before the project is completed. The payback continues after production deployment due to lower cost of future application software development and database maintenance.

Once this author was consulting in stored procedure development at a small organization which was the fund raiser for a Connecticut seminary. Only one full-time manager/dba/developer, with consultants help. Quite shockingly,  the database  was excellent 3NF design.  Only big-budget places can afford  such a good 3NF design so goes the common wisdom. The manager explained that he hired a consultant expert database designer  for a month. An excellent choice indeed.

### Database System Solution Implementation Hierarchy

Frequently  solutions can be implemented more than one way in a relational database system. For example, the constraint OrderQty > 0 can be implemented as CHECK constraint, stored procedure, trigger and as code in application software.  There are great advantages to implement a solution at the lowest possible level of the following hierarchy.

> ➢ Table design
> ➢ Constraint
> ➢ Stored procedure
> ➢ Trigger
> ➢ Client software

# List All Default Constraints with Definition

T-SQL metadata query to enumerate all column defaults with definition using a system view.

```
SELECT  SCHEMA_NAME(schema_id)                              AS SCHEMA_NAME,
        OBJECT_NAME(PARENT_OBJECT_ID)                       AS TABLE_NAME,
        COL_NAME (PARENT_OBJECT_ID, PARENT_COLUMN_ID)       AS COLUMN_NAME,
        Definition                                          AS DEFAULT_DEFINITION,
        NAME                                                AS DEFAULT_CONSTRAINT_NAME
FROM AdventureWorks2012.SYS.DEFAULT_CONSTRAINTS
ORDER BY 1, 2;  -- column numbers
-- (152 row(s) affected) - Partial results.
```

| SCHEMA_NAME | TABLE_NAME | COLUMN_NAME | DEFAULT_DEFINITION | DEFAULT_CONSTRAINT_NAME |
|---|---|---|---|---|
| dbo | AWBuildVersion | ModifiedDate | (getdate()) | DF_AWBuildVersion_ModifiedDate |
| dbo | ErrorLog | ErrorTime | (getdate()) | DF_ErrorLog_ErrorTime |
| HumanResources | Department | ModifiedDate | (getdate()) | DF_Department_ModifiedDate |
| HumanResources | Employee | SalariedFlag | ((1)) | DF_Employee_SalariedFlag |
| HumanResources | Employee | VacationHours | ((0)) | DF_Employee_VacationHours |
| HumanResources | Employee | SickLeaveHours | ((0)) | DF_Employee_SickLeaveHours |
| HumanResources | Employee | CurrentFlag | ((1)) | DF_Employee_CurrentFlag |
| HumanResources | Employee | rowguid | (newid()) | DF_Employee_rowguid |
| HumanResources | Employee | ModifiedDate | (getdate()) | DF_Employee_ModifiedDate |
| HumanResources | EmployeeDepartmentHistory | ModifiedDate | (getdate()) | DF_EmployeeDepartmentHistory_ModifiedDate |
| HumanResources | EmployeePayHistory | ModifiedDate | (getdate()) | DF_EmployeePayHistory_ModifiedDate |
| HumanResources | JobCandidate | ModifiedDate | (getdate()) | DF_JobCandidate_ModifiedDate |
| HumanResources | Shift | ModifiedDate | (getdate()) | DF_Shift_ModifiedDate |
| Person | Address | rowguid | (newid()) | DF_Address_rowguid |
| Person | Address | ModifiedDate | (getdate()) | DF_Address_ModifiedDate |
| Person | AddressType | rowguid | (newid()) | DF_AddressType_rowguid |
| Person | AddressType | ModifiedDate | (getdate()) | DF_AddressType_ModifiedDate |
| Person | BusinessEntity | rowguid | (newid()) | DF_BusinessEntity_rowguid |
| Person | BusinessEntity | ModifiedDate | (getdate()) | DF_BusinessEntity_ModifiedDate |
| Person | BusinessEntityAddress | rowguid | (newid()) | DF_BusinessEntityAddress_rowguid |
| Person | BusinessEntityAddress | ModifiedDate | (getdate()) | DF_BusinessEntityAddress_ModifiedDate |
| Person | BusinessEntityContact | rowguid | (newid()) | DF_BusinessEntityContact_rowguid |
| Person | BusinessEntityContact | ModifiedDate | (getdate()) | DF_BusinessEntityContact_ModifiedDate |
| Person | ContactType | ModifiedDate | (getdate()) | DF_ContactType_ModifiedDate |
| Person | CountryRegion | ModifiedDate | (getdate()) | DF_CountryRegion_ModifiedDate |
| Person | EmailAddress | rowguid | (newid()) | DF_EmailAddress_rowguid |
| Person | EmailAddress | ModifiedDate | (getdate()) | DF_EmailAddress_ModifiedDate |
| Person | Password | rowguid | (newid()) | DF_Password_rowguid |
| Person | Password | ModifiedDate | (getdate()) | DF_Password_ModifiedDate |
| Person | Person | NameStyle | ((0)) | DF_Person_NameStyle |
| Person | Person | EmailPromotion | ((0)) | DF_Person_EmailPromotion |
| Person | Person | rowguid | (newid()) | DF_Person_rowguid |
| Person | Person | ModifiedDate | (getdate()) | DF_Person_ModifiedDate |
| Person | PersonPhone | ModifiedDate | (getdate()) | DF_PersonPhone_ModifiedDate |
| Person | PhoneNumberType | ModifiedDate | (getdate()) | DF_PhoneNumberType_ModifiedDate |
| Person | StateProvince | IsOnlyStateProvinceFlag | ((1)) | DF_StateProvince_IsOnlyStateProvinceFlag |
| Person | StateProvince | rowguid | (newid()) | DF_StateProvince_rowguid |
| Person | StateProvince | ModifiedDate | (getdate()) | DF_StateProvince_ModifiedDate |

## Partitioning Query via Pure SQL - Ye Olde Way

Add new sequence numbering column for subsets(partition by OrderID) with standard SQL only. Note that the old way is not very efficient, the ROW_NUMBER() OVER PARTITION is better performing.

```
USE Northwind;
SELECT   OD.OrderID,
         SeqNo                                              AS LineItem,
         OD.ProductID,
         UnitPrice,
         Quantity                                           AS Qty,
         CONVERT(NUMERIC(3, 2), Discount)                   AS Discount,
         CONVERT(NUMERIC(12, 2), UnitPrice * Quantity * ( 1.0 - Discount ))   AS LineTotal
FROM  [Order Details] OD
    INNER JOIN (SELECT count(*) SeqNo,   a.OrderID,   a.ProductID
         FROM   [Order Details] A
             INNER JOIN [Order Details] B
                 ON A.ProductID >= B.ProductID    AND A.OrderID = B.OrderID
         GROUP  BY A.OrderID,
                A.ProductID) a
        ON OD.OrderID = a.OrderID
          AND OD.ProductID = a.ProductID
WHERE  OD.OrderID < 10300
ORDER  BY OD.OrderID,  OD.ProductID, SeqNo;
-- (140 row(s) affected) - Partial results.
```

| OrderID | LineItem | ProductID | UnitPrice | Qty | Discount | LineTotal |
|---------|----------|-----------|-----------|-----|----------|-----------|
| 10255 | 1 | 2 | 15.20 | 20 | 0.00 | 304.00 |
| 10255 | 2 | 16 | 13.90 | 35 | 0.00 | 486.50 |
| 10255 | 3 | 36 | 15.20 | 25 | 0.00 | 380.00 |
| 10255 | 4 | 59 | 44.00 | 30 | 0.00 | 1320.00 |
| 10256 | 1 | 53 | 26.20 | 15 | 0.00 | 393.00 |
| 10256 | 2 | 77 | 10.40 | 12 | 0.00 | 124.80 |
| 10257 | 1 | 27 | 35.10 | 25 | 0.00 | 877.50 |
| 10257 | 2 | 39 | 14.40 | 6 | 0.00 | 86.40 |
| 10257 | 3 | 77 | 10.40 | 15 | 0.00 | 156.00 |
| 10258 | 1 | 2 | 15.20 | 50 | 0.20 | 608.00 |
| 10258 | 2 | 5 | 17.00 | 65 | 0.20 | 884.00 |
| 10258 | 3 | 32 | 25.60 | 6 | 0.20 | 122.88 |
| 10259 | 1 | 21 | 8.00 | 10 | 0.00 | 80.00 |
| 10259 | 2 | 37 | 20.80 | 1 | 0.00 | 20.80 |
| 10260 | 1 | 41 | 7.70 | 16 | 0.25 | 92.40 |
| 10260 | 2 | 57 | 15.60 | 50 | 0.00 | 780.00 |
| 10260 | 3 | 62 | 39.40 | 15 | 0.25 | 443.25 |
| 10260 | 4 | 70 | 12.00 | 21 | 0.25 | 189.00 |
| 10261 | 1 | 21 | 8.00 | 20 | 0.00 | 160.00 |
| 10261 | 2 | 35 | 14.40 | 20 | 0.00 | 288.00 |

# CHAPTER 9:  Advanced Database Design Concepts

## FileTable - Integrating Folders with Database

Storing large number of binary files such as images was a challenge until SQL Server 2012: FileTable integrates files in a folder into the database, yet keep them accessible at Windows file system level.  In the past, there were two solutions:

> ➤ Keep only the filenames in the database table.
> ➤ Keep both the filenames and binary file objects ( varbinary(max) ) in the table.

Using the first method, the files were not backed up with the database since they were not part of the database. Applying the second method, the binary objects were in the database, but as a deadweight, since not much can be done with them. FileTable is the best of both worlds: files are backed up / restored with the database, yet they  remain visible at the file system level. So if a new file is dropped (copied) into the folder, it becomes visible to SQL Server instantaneously.  FileTable requires the FILESTREAM feature as shown on the Server Properties dialog box.

CHAPTER 9:  Advanced Database Design Concepts

## The CREATE TABLE statement for a FileTable

```
-- Create FileTable  -- new to SQL Server 2012
CREATE TABLE ImageStore
AS FileTable
  WITH (
     FileTable_Directory = 'ImageStore',
     FileTable_Collate_Filename = database_default
     );
GO
-- (1 row(s) affected)
```

We can determine the FileTable folder name which is visible at the file system level the following way.

```
SELECT DBName=DB_NAME ( database_id ), directory_name
  FROM sys.database_filestream_options
       WHERE directory_name is not null;
GO
```

| DBName | directory_name |
|---|---|
| AdventureWorks2012 | FSDIR |

FileTable directory(path):

\\YOURSERVER\MSSQLSERVER\FSDIR\ImageStore

*The dialog box for database options setup as related to FILESTREAM*

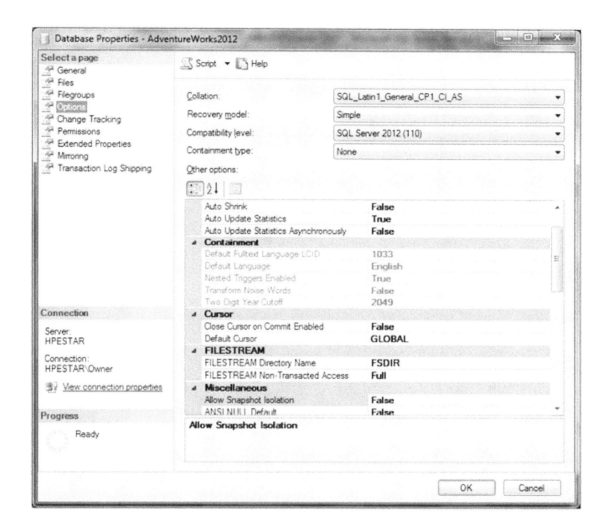

"hpestar" is the name of the SQL Server instance (default instance, same name as the computer).

*The FileTable folder is currently empty.*

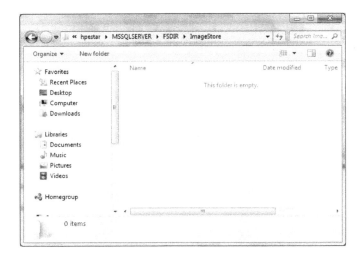

We shall now copy 3 photos in the ImageStore folder using Windows Copy & Paste operation.

**CHAPTER 9: Advanced Database Design Concepts**

*The photos are "visible" from the database side as well.*

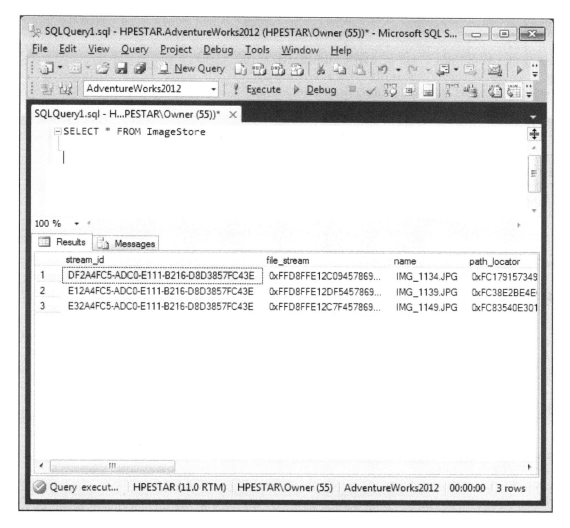

The INSERT, UPDATE and DELETE commands are operational on FileTable, however, a new column cannot be added as demonstrated in the following script:

```
SELECT * FROM ImageStore
GO
UPDATE ImageStore SET name='RollerCoaster.jpg'
WHERE stream_id='E73EA731-AAAA-E111-9078-D8D3857FC43E'
GO
SELECT * FROM ImageStore
```

## Adding Files to FileTable Using T-SQL

There are two T-SQL methods available.

```
-- Adding files from T-SQL - method 1 xp_cmdshell copy
EXEC xp_cmdshell 'copy "C:\photo\000Test\xBermuda.jpg"
"\\HPESTAR\mssqlserver\FSDIR\ImageStore\xBermuda.jpg"'
GO
```

```
-- Adding files from T-SQL - method 2 OPENROWSET
INSERT INTO [dbo].[ImageStore] ([name],[file_stream])
SELECT 'Bermuda9.jpg', * FROM
    OPENROWSET(BULK N'C:\photo\2012\BERMUDA\BERMUDA\IMG_1154.jpg', SINGLE_BLOB)
              AS FileUpload
```

### Deleting Files from FileTable Using T-SQL

```
SELECT * FROM ImageStore
GO
```

```
DELETE ImageStore
WHERE stream_id = '62F55342-ABAA-E111-9078-D8D3857FC43E'
GO
```

```
SELECT * FROM ImageStore
GO
```

```
-- Column(s) cannot be added to a FileTable
ALTER TABLE ImageStore
ADD AddDate smalldatetime NULL
CONSTRAINT AddDateDflt
DEFAULT CURRENT_TIMESTAMP WITH VALUES ;
GO
/* Msg 33422, Level 16, State 1, Line 2
The column 'AddDate' cannot be added to table 'ImageStore' as it is a FileTable.
Adding columns to the fixed schema of a FileTable object is not permitted.
*/
```

```
DROP TABLE ImageStore
GO
```

# Data Compression: Compressed Table

The table compression option has been introduced with SQL Server 2008. Data is compressed inside a database table, and it reduces the size of the table. Performance benefit in addition to space saving: "reads" reduction; queries need to read fewer pages from the disk. Sufficient CPU resources are required for the SQL Server instance to compress and decompress table data, when data is read (SELECT) or written (INSERT, UPDATE, MERGE). Analysis is required to ensure that table compression has no adverse effect on business critical query performance. Data compression may not be available in all editions of SQL Server. In the demonstration, first we create a new table for testing.

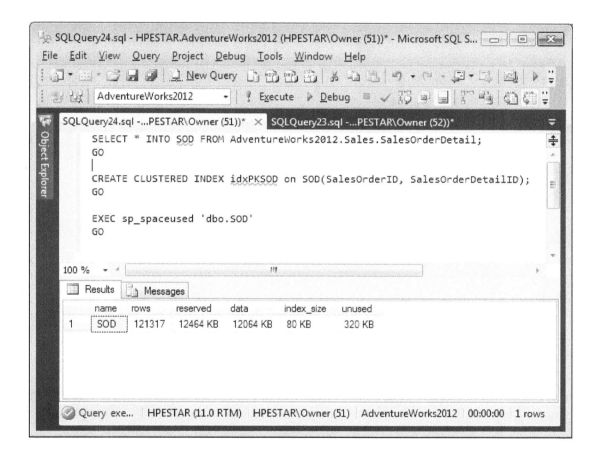

## *Switching to PAGE-LEVEL Compression*

Data storage size decreased from around 12 MB to around 5 MB.

## Testing ROW-LEVEL Compression

We can see the space reduction from 12MB to around 7.5MB.

*Space reduction can be estimated with a system stored procedure.*

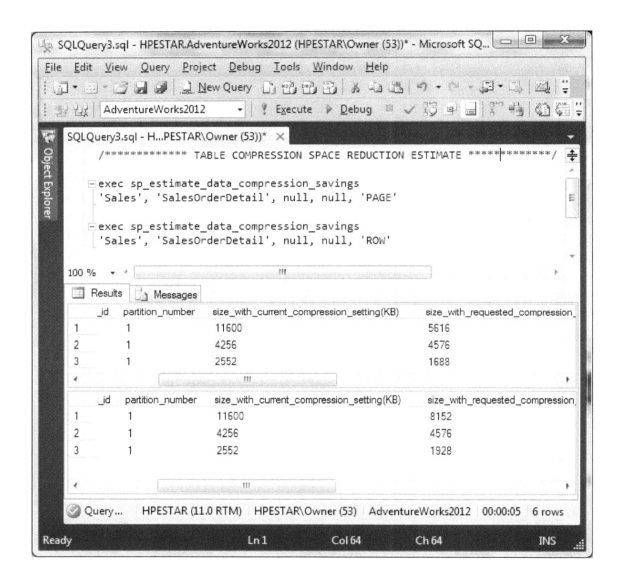

Careful and extensive considerations are required to decide to apply row, page or no compression to a table.

*Query To Check How Many Rows Are Stored In An 8K Page In The Original Non-Compressed Table*

*Query to check the same for the compressed table SOD*

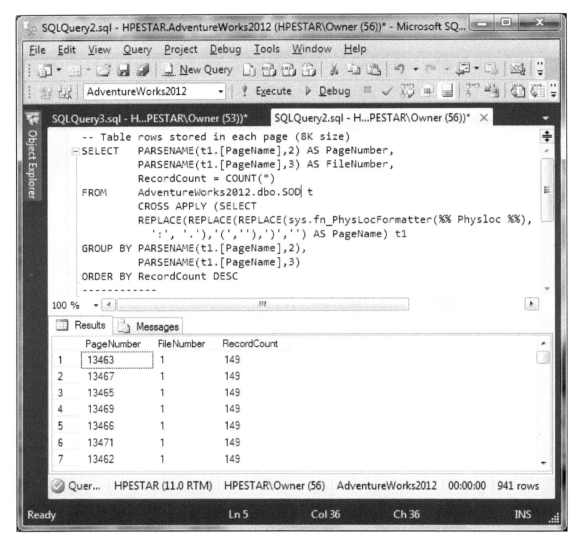

We can see that the best record (rows) count is 149 per page as opposed to 102 when the rows are not compressed.

Since compression and decompression are processing intensive, we are trading CPU load vs. disk load.

Which one to choose?  PAGE compression is the true compression with maximum space saving. Choose PAGE compression for best disk IO reduction. As mentioned earlier careful preparation is required to make sure there are no undesirable side effects.

**CHAPTER 9:  Advanced Database Design Concepts**

## Data Compression: Compressed Index

Index can also be compressed. The following script creates and compresses an index with included columns.

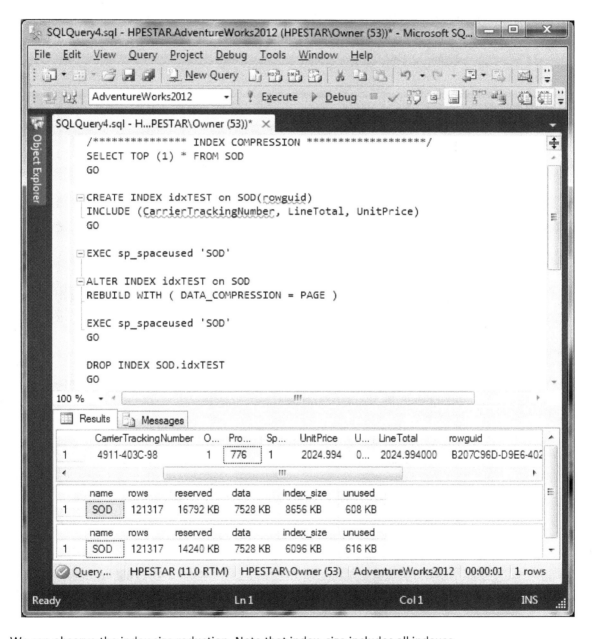

We can observe the index size reduction. Note that index_size includes all indexes.

# The GUI Data Compression Wizard

The wizard can be started with Right Click on the table in SSMS Object Explorer.

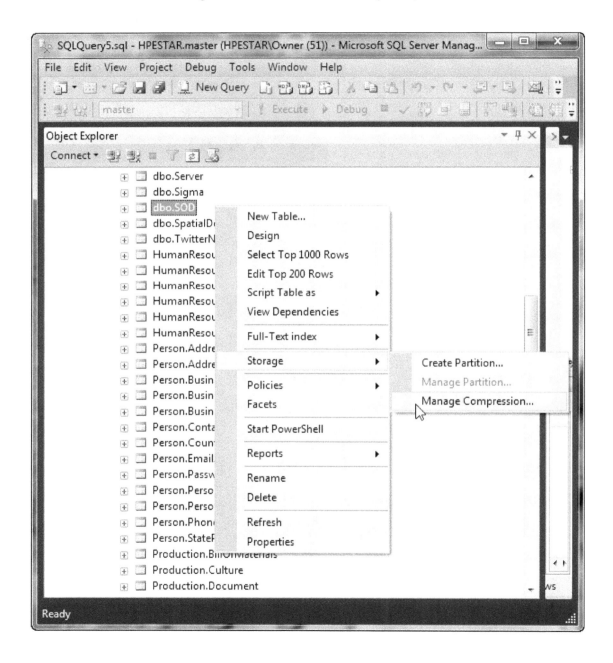

## Space Saving Calculation Wizard Page

The figures include table & indexes total size.

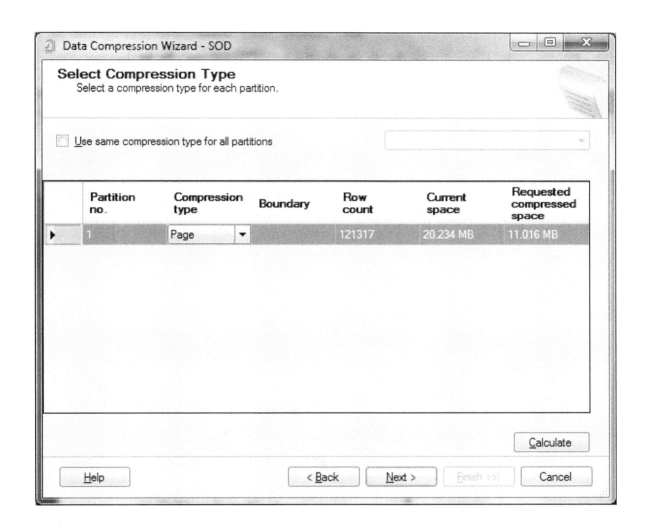

*Output Panel Offers Scripting And Execution Options*

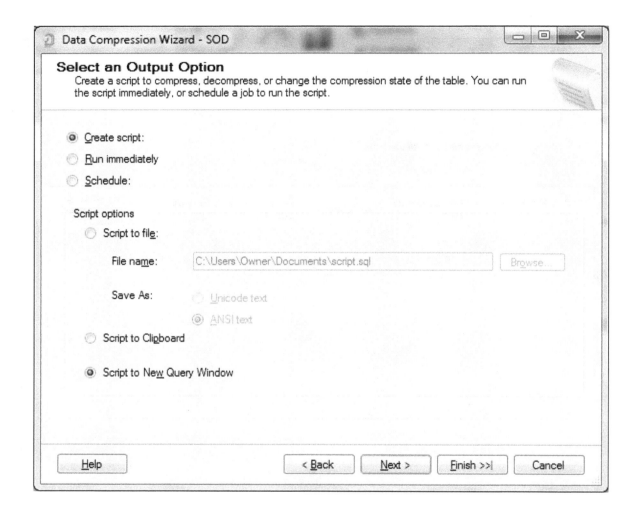

*Testing the generated script with the sp_spaceused system stored procedure*

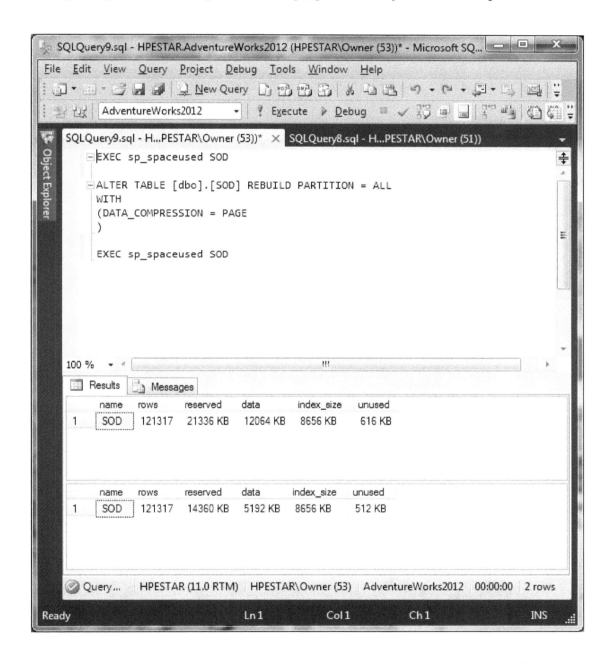

*Indexes Can Be Compressed With The Wizard As Well*

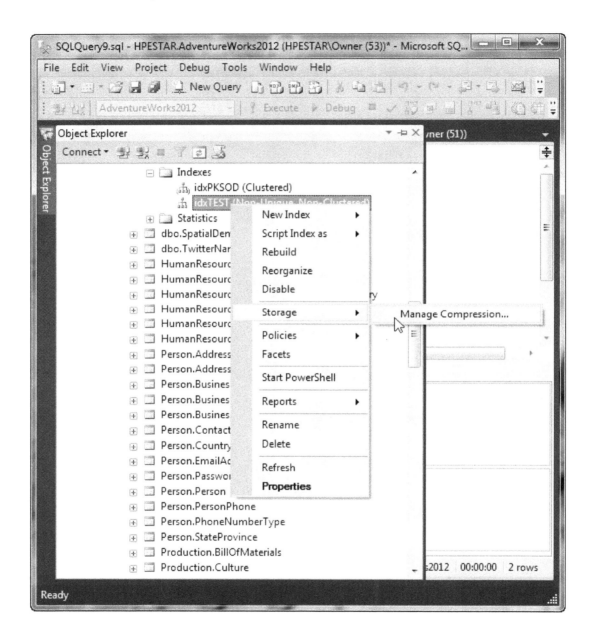

*The generated script follows with measurement before and after index compression.*

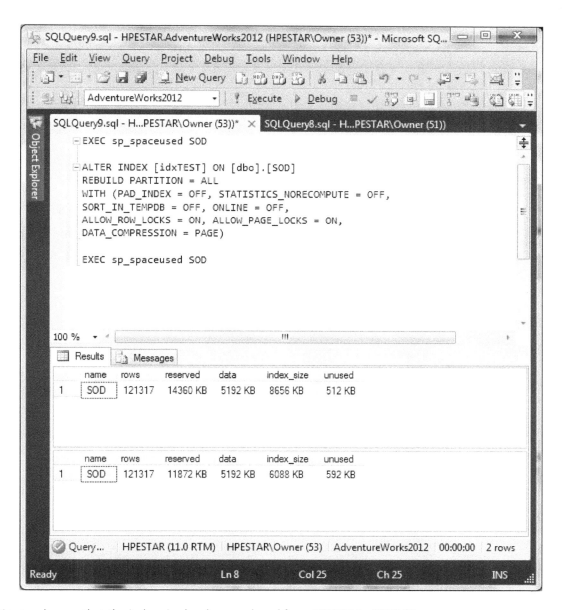

We can observe that the index size has been reduced from 8656KB to 6088 KB.

Articles: Data Compression: Strategy, Capacity Planning and Best Practices (http://msdn.microsoft.com/en-us/library/dd894051(v=sql.100).aspx ); Data Compression (http://msdn.microsoft.com/en-us/library/cc280449.aspx).

# Partitioned Table, Partition Function & Partition Scheme

When data is stored from New York, Chicago, Houston, London and Hong Kong operations in a table, it makes you wonder if the server trips over NYC data when looking for London information. Analogous, 95% of the time in a typical business the last 30 days data may be accessed in a table, yet the dominant storage is for the 5% access of the 5 years prior data. The solution is logical: partition the data according to a usage-based scheme. Partitioning can improve performance, the scalability and manageability of large tables and tables that have varying query access patterns. **Gains with partitioning is not automatic.** Careful design studies are necessary for a successful table partitioning implementation.

In order to carry out a demonstration, first we create a copy of AdventureWorks2012 database from a backup file.

```
/* RESTORE script to create a new copy of AdventureWorks2012
 * Folder  FS1 should exist; FSBeta should not exist; AW12 should exist
 * Folder Backup should exist */
USE [master]
GO
BACKUP DATABASE [AdventureWorks2012] TO
DISK = N'C:\Data\Backup\AW12.bak'
GO
```

```
RESTORE DATABASE [CopyOfAdventureWorks2012]
FROM  DISK = N'C:\Data\Backup\AW12.bak'
WITH  FILE = 1,  MOVE N'FSAlpha' TO N'F:\data\FS1\FSBeta',
MOVE N'AdventureWorks2012_Data' TO N'F:\AW12\xAdventureWorks2012_Data.mdf',
MOVE N'AdventureWorks2012_Log' TO N'F:\AW12\xAdventureWorks2012_log.ldf',
NOUNLOAD,  STATS = 5
GO
```

We will partition a table with SalesOrderDetail subset information. First a partition function is created.

```
USE CopyOfAdventureWorks2012;
GO
```

```
CREATE PARTITION FUNCTION pfSOD (int)
AS RANGE LEFT FOR VALUES (1, 20000, 40000, 60000, 80000, 150000) ;
GO
```

*The next step is to test the partition function to make sure it works as intended.*

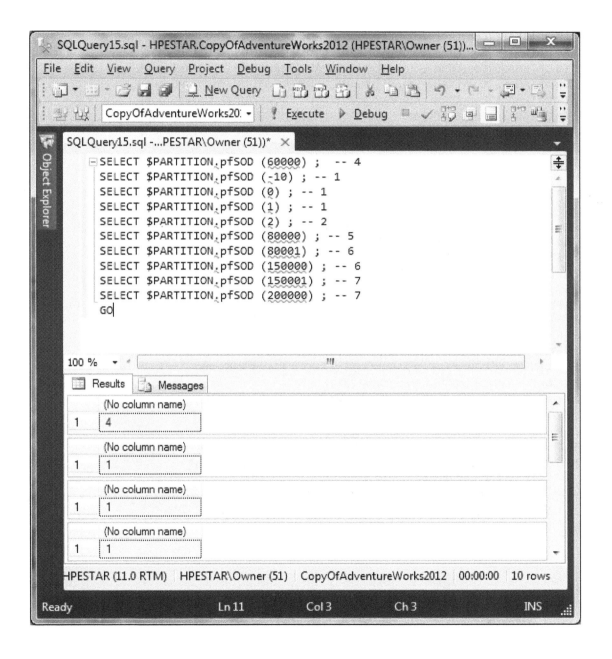

*T-SQL scripts to create FILEGROUPs for the partitions*

```
USE [master]
GO
ALTER DATABASE [CopyOfAdventureWorks2012] ADD FILEGROUP [Test1FileGroup]
ALTER DATABASE [CopyOfAdventureWorks2012] ADD FILEGROUP [Test2FileGroup]
ALTER DATABASE [CopyOfAdventureWorks2012] ADD FILEGROUP [Test3FileGroup]
ALTER DATABASE [CopyOfAdventureWorks2012] ADD FILEGROUP [Test4FileGroup]
ALTER DATABASE [CopyOfAdventureWorks2012] ADD FILEGROUP [Test5FileGroup]
ALTER DATABASE [CopyOfAdventureWorks2012] ADD FILEGROUP [Test6FileGroup]
ALTER DATABASE [CopyOfAdventureWorks2012] ADD FILEGROUP [Test7FileGroup]
GO
USE [master]
GO
ALTER DATABASE [CopyOfAdventureWorks2012]
ADD FILE ( NAME = N'Test1', FILENAME = N'F:\UTIL\Microsoft\sampledatabases\Test1.ndf' ,
SIZE = 3072KB , FILEGROWTH = 1024KB ) TO FILEGROUP [Test1FileGroup]
ALTER DATABASE [CopyOfAdventureWorks2012]
ADD FILE ( NAME = N'Test2', FILENAME = N'F:\UTIL\Microsoft\sampledatabases\Test2.ndf' ,
SIZE = 3072KB , FILEGROWTH = 1024KB ) TO FILEGROUP [Test2FileGroup]
ALTER DATABASE [CopyOfAdventureWorks2012]
ADD FILE ( NAME = N'Test3', FILENAME = N'F:\UTIL\Microsoft\sampledatabases\Test3.ndf' ,
SIZE = 3072KB , FILEGROWTH = 1024KB ) TO FILEGROUP [Test3FileGroup]
ALTER DATABASE [CopyOfAdventureWorks2012]
ADD FILE ( NAME = N'Test4', FILENAME = N'F:\UTIL\Microsoft\sampledatabases\Test4.ndf' ,
SIZE = 3072KB , FILEGROWTH = 1024KB ) TO FILEGROUP [Test4FileGroup]
ALTER DATABASE [CopyOfAdventureWorks2012]
ADD FILE ( NAME = N'Test5', FILENAME = N'F:\UTIL\Microsoft\sampledatabases\Test5.ndf' ,
SIZE = 3072KB , FILEGROWTH = 1024KB ) TO FILEGROUP [Test5FileGroup]
ALTER DATABASE [CopyOfAdventureWorks2012]
ADD FILE ( NAME = N'Test6', FILENAME = N'F:\UTIL\Microsoft\sampledatabases\Test6.ndf' ,
SIZE = 3072KB , FILEGROWTH = 1024KB ) TO FILEGROUP [Test6FileGroup]
ALTER DATABASE [CopyOfAdventureWorks2012]
ADD FILE ( NAME = N'Test7', FILENAME = N'F:\UTIL\Microsoft\sampledatabases\Test7.ndf' ,
SIZE = 3072KB , FILEGROWTH = 1024KB ) TO FILEGROUP [Test7FileGroup]
GO
```

### *T-SQL scripts to create a partition scheme, a partitioned table and populate the new table with INSERT SELECT*

```
USE CopyOfAdventureWorks2012;
GO

CREATE PARTITION SCHEME psSOD
AS PARTITION pfSOD
TO (Test1FileGroup, Test2FileGroup, Test3FileGroup, Test4FileGroup,
Test5FileGroup, Test6FileGroup, Test7FileGroup) ;
GO

CREATE TABLE SODPartitioned   (col1 int, col2 char(30))  ON psSOD (col1) ;
GO

insert SODPartitioned
select    SalesOrderDetailID, 'Unit Price: '+convert(varchar,UnitPrice)
from AdventureWorks2012.Sales.SalesOrderDetail
go

insert SODPartitioned
select SalesOrderDetailID+1,  'Unit Price: '+convert(varchar,UnitPrice+1)
from AdventureWorks2012.Sales.SalesOrderDetail
go

insert SODPartitioned
select SalesOrderDetailID+2,  'Unit Price: '+convert(varchar,UnitPrice+2)
from AdventureWorks2012.Sales.SalesOrderDetail
```

*Query To Check The Data Distribution Within The Partitions*

*A few more counting queries to check entire table and a single partition population*

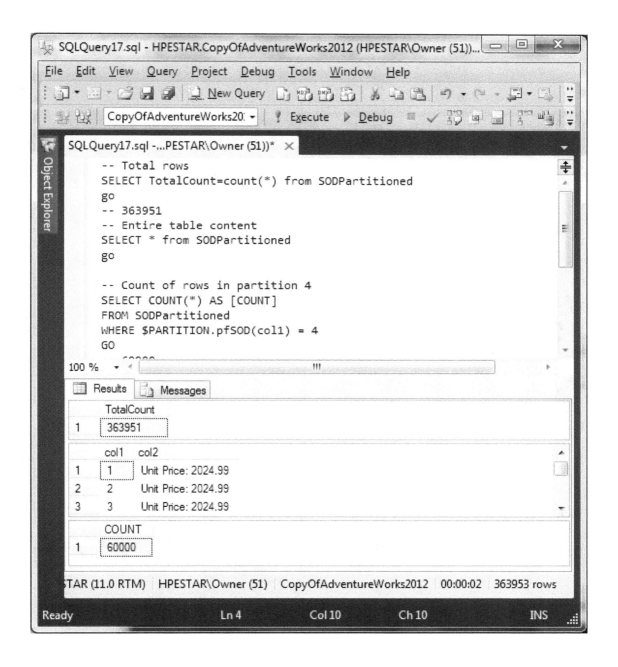

*System views with "partition" prefix contain metadata on partitions.*

*In the following example, we partition for "UK", "US" and other countries.*

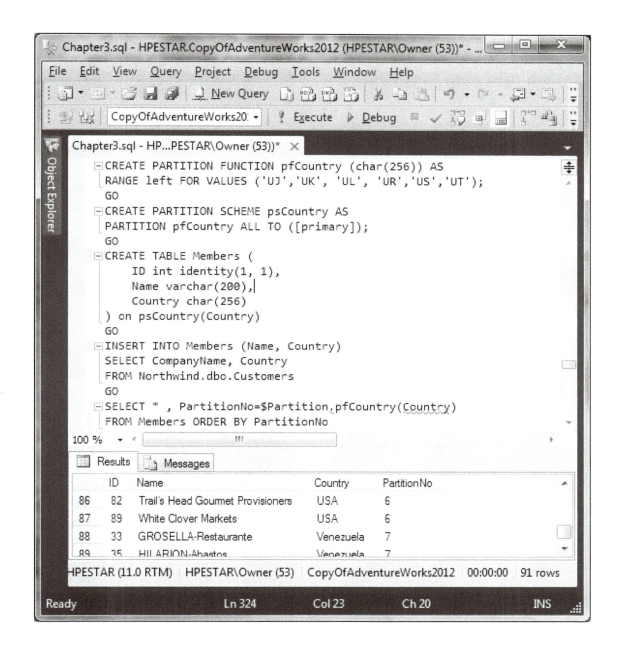

# The GUI Create Partition Wizard

SSMS Object Explorer Create Partition Wizard provides GUI environment for partition design and setup.

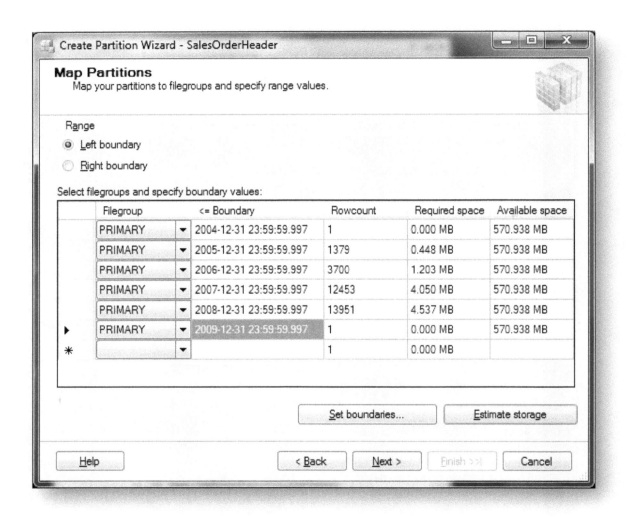

# Columnstore Index for Data Warehouse Performance

Columnstore index for static tables, new to SQL Server 2012, is designed for Data Warehouse performance enhancement. The first script is a timing script for a GROUP BY summary query, and the second script is the creation of the columnstore index.

```
-- Timing before creating Columnstore index (5th timing)
USE AdventureWorksDW2012;
dbcc dropcleanbuffers;
declare @start datetime = getdate()
SELECT SalesTerritoryKey, SUM(ExtendedAmount) AS SalesByTerritory
FROM FactResellerSales    GROUP BY SalesTerritoryKey;
select [Timing]=datediff(millisecond, @Start, getdate());
GO 5
-- 190 msec
```

```
CREATE NONCLUSTERED COLUMNSTORE INDEX [idxColStoreResellerSales]
ON [FactResellerSales]
(
    [ProductKey],
    [OrderDateKey],
    [ShipDateKey],
    [EmployeeKey],
    [PromotionKey],
    [CurrencyKey],
    [SalesTerritoryKey],
    [SalesOrderNumber],
    [SalesOrderLineNumber],
    [OrderQuantity],
    [UnitPrice],
    [ExtendedAmount],
    [UnitPriceDiscountPct],
    [DiscountAmount],
    [ProductStandardCost],
    [TotalProductCost],
    [SalesAmount],
    [TaxAmt],
    [Freight],
    [CarrierTrackingNumber],
    [CustomerPONumber],
    [OrderDate],
    [DueDate],
    [ShipDate]
);
GO
```

CHAPTER 9:  Advanced Database Design Concepts

*Checking the same query after creating the index.*

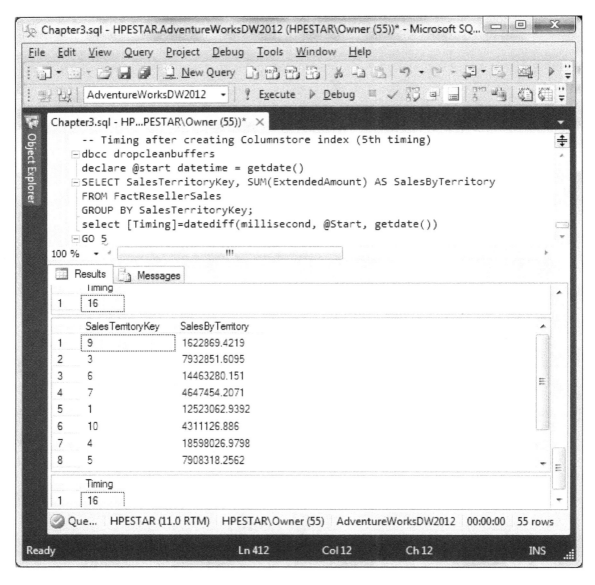

The performance gain on this particular query: from 190 msec to 16 msec. Generally columnstore index leads to significant query performance improvement in Data Warehouse environment.

# Database Design & Programming Standards

Standards have multiple purposes:

> ➤ Increase the productivity of the database developer.
> ➤ Increase the productivity of the project team.
> ➤ Decrease future maintenance cost of the RDBMS system.

Standards are about communications among project team members and among future software engineers who will come in contact with the work done presently by the software project team. Software standards are simple ordinary rules which should be followed. It is like when you turn on the left-turn signal in your car, the driver behind you anticipates you slowing down and making the next left turn. The situation is a little bit different though with software standards: there is no enforcing authority like the state authority in case of traffic rules. Many times argument can break out within the project team: "I like it this way", "it is really stupid to do it that way", "database expert Q says to do it this way in a blog" and so on. The following standards are pretty reasonable, and are based on industry acceptance, albeit not universal acceptance. The project manager has to enlist the support of all of the project team members for successful standards implementation.

Database Design & Programming Standards to aid in optimal usability of SQL Server schema, scripts and stored procedures, user defined functions developed for applications by defining a reasonable, consistent and effective coding style. The identifier segment of the standard will formalize naming conventions. Without standards, database design, function, stored procedure and script development may become sloppy and unreadable, resulting in diminished productivity, usability, reusability, maintainability and extendibility.

## Database Design Standards

Base design is normalized to 3NF or higher. History, log, Data Warehouse and reporting tables, containing second-hand data, need not be normalized. Similar considerations for staging and lookup tables. Each OLTP table has the following layout:

TableNameID (PRIMARY KEY) - commonly int identity(1,1) SURROGATE PRIMARY KEY
TableNameAlphaID (FOREIGN KEY if any)
TableNameBetaID (FOREIGN KEY if any)
natural-key column(s)
non-key columns
row maintenance columns

| | |
|---|---|
| RowGuid | uniqueidentifier |
| IsActive | maintenance flag (bit 0 = not active, 1 = active) |
| CreateDate | maintenance date (datetime if necessary) |
| ModifiedDate | maintenance date (datetime if necessary) |
| ModifiedByUser | last user who modified the record |

CHAPTER 9: Advanced Database Design Concepts

**DATE columns should be DATE type (3 bytes) not DATETIME type (8 bytes) with exception when time is needed for the record such as credit card or online banking transaction.**

Example: Sales.Customer table create with one computed column which has unique index defined.

```
CREATE TABLE Sales.Customer(
        CustomerID int IDENTITY(1,1) PRIMARY KEY,
        PersonID int REFERENCES Person.Person (BusinessEntityID),
        StoreID int REFERENCES Sales.Store (BusinessEntityID),
        TerritoryID int REFERENCES Sales.SalesTerritory (TerritoryID),

        AccountNumber  AS (isnull('AW'+dbo.ufnLeadingZeros(CustomerID),'')) ,

        RowGuid uniqueidentifier ROWGUIDCOL  NOT NULL default (newid()),
        ModifiedDate datetime NOT NULL default (CURRENT_TIMESTAMP));
GO

SELECT TOP 10 *
FROM AdventureWorks.Sales.Customer
ORDER BY AccountNumber;
GO
```

| CustomerID | TerritoryID | AccountNumber | CustomerType | rowguid | ModifiedDate |
|---|---|---|---|---|---|
| 1 | 1 | AW00000001 | S | 3F5AE95E-B87D-4AED-95B4-C3797AFCB74F | 2004-10-13 11:15:07.263 |
| 2 | 1 | AW00000002 | S | E552F657-A9AF-4A7D-A645-C429D6E02491 | 2004-10-13 11:15:07.263 |
| 3 | 4 | AW00000003 | S | 130774B1-DB21-4EF3-98C8-C104BCD6ED6D | 2004-10-13 11:15:07.263 |
| 4 | 4 | AW00000004 | S | FF862851-1DAA-4044-BE7C-3E85583C054D | 2004-10-13 11:15:07.263 |
| 5 | 4 | AW00000005 | S | 83905BDC-6F5E-4F71-B162-C98DA069F38A | 2004-10-13 11:15:07.263 |
| 6 | 4 | AW00000006 | S | 1A92DF88-BFA2-467D-BD54-FCB9E647FDD7 | 2004-10-13 11:15:07.263 |
| 7 | 1 | AW00000007 | S | 03E9273E-B193-448E-9823-FE0C44AEED78 | 2004-10-13 11:15:07.263 |
| 8 | 5 | AW00000008 | S | 801368B1-4323-4BFA-8BEA-5B5B1E4BD4A0 | 2004-10-13 11:15:07.263 |
| 9 | 5 | AW00000009 | S | B900BB7F-23C3-481D-80DA-C49A5BD6F772 | 2004-10-13 11:15:07.263 |
| 10 | 6 | AW00000010 | S | CDB6698D-2FF1-4FBA-8F22-60AD1D11DABD | 2004-10-13 11:15:07.263 |

The ufnLeadingZeros() scalar-valued user-defined function converts the number into a string and pads it with zeros.

```
SELECT [dbo].[ufnLeadingZeros] (999);
GO
-- 00000999
```

CHAPTER 9:  Advanced Database Design Concepts

## Identifiers

CamelCase (Pascal case) naming convention: OrderDetail, ShippingCompany

With prefix example:  vInvoiceHistory (view - Hungarian naming after Charles Simonyi)

Old-style naming example: sales_order_detail

Space usage is not a good idea in identifier: confusing & forces square brackets or double quotation marks use (delimited identifier).

Using spaces example: [sales order detail]

PREFIX ASSIGNMENT

| | |
|---|---|
| Primary Key Clustered | pk |
| Primary Key Nonclustered | pknc |
| Index Clustered | idxc |
| Index Nonclustered | idxnc |
| Foreign Key | fk |
| Unique Constraint | uq |
| Check Constraint | chk |
| Column Default | dflt |
| Synonym | syn |

Passed Parameter  @p  (input/output parameter) or @ - Example: @pStartDate, @StartDate

Local Variable  @  - Example: @WeekOfTransaction

Table                                        usually no prefix; exception large number of tables

| | |
|---|---|
| Reporting table | rpt |
| Log table | log |
| History table | hist or arch |
| Date Warehouse table | dw, dim, fact |
| Common Table Expression | cte |
| View | v or view |
| User Defined Scalar Function | udf or fns or ufn or fn |
| User Defined Table Function | udf or fnt or ufn or fn |
| Stored Procedure | usp, sproc, or none |

**CHAPTER 9:  Advanced Database Design Concepts**

## Principles of T-SQL Identifier Architecture

Each word in the naming must be functional. The first word must be the highest level category  or action indicator.  Examples for stored procedure names:

> uspAccountPayableSummary
> uspInsertAccountPayableTransaction
> uspUpdateStockPrice
> sprocInsertInventoryItem
> sprocAccountReceivableSummary
> AccountReceivableMonthly

Commonly accepted or easily understood abbreviations are allowed.  Examples for business abbreviations usage in view naming:

> vAPSummary
> vAPDetail
> vARSummary
> vARMonthly
> vGLTrialBalance

AdventureWorks2012 long stored procedure and view names.

SELECT name, type FROM sys.objects WHERE LEN(name) > 20 AND type in ('V', 'P') ORDER BY name;

| name | type |
| --- | --- |
| uspGetBillOfMaterials | P |
| uspGetEmployeeManagers | P |
| uspGetManagerEmployees | P |
| uspGetWhereUsedProductID | P |
| uspSearchCandidateResumes | P |
| uspUpdateEmployeeHireInfo | P |
| uspUpdateEmployeeLogin | P |
| uspUpdateEmployeePersonalInfo | P |
| vAdditionalContactInfo | V |
| vEmployeeDepartmentHistory | V |
| vJobCandidateEducation | V |
| vJobCandidateEmployment | V |
| vProductAndDescription | V |
| vProductModelCatalogDescription | V |
| vProductModelInstructions | V |
| vSalesPersonSalesByFiscalYears | V |
| vStateProvinceCountryRegion | V |
| vStoreWithDemographics | V |

**CHAPTER 9:  Advanced Database Design Concepts**

## Stored Procedure Outline

```
use {DatabaseName};
if (objectProperty(object_id('{schema}.{ProcedureName}'),
'IsProcedure') is not null)
    drop procedure {schema}.{ProcedureName}
go

create procedure {schema}.{ProcedureName}
  [{parameter}  {data type}]....
as
/*************************************************************
* PROCEDURE: {ProcedureName}
* PURPOSE: {brief procedure description}
* NOTES: {special set up or requirements, etc.}
* CREATED:  {developer name} {date}
* LAST MODIFIED: {developer name} {date}

* DATE          AUTHOR              DESCRIPTION
-----------------------------------------------------------------
* {date}        {developer} {brief modification description}
*************************************************************/
BEGIN
[declare {variable name} {data type}....
[{set session}] e.g. SET NOCOUNT ON
[{initialize variables}]

{body of procedure - comment only what is not obvious}

return (Value if any)

{error handler}
return (Value if any)
END
 go
```

## User-Defined Function Outline

Similar to stored procedure outline

# How to Create a Database with T-SQL Script

Database can be created by a script (CREATE DATABASE) or in SSMS Object Explorer using GUI. Here is a T-SQL script version.

```
-- SQL CREATE DATABASE
USE master;
GO

-- F:\DB\DATA\ should exist
CREATE DATABASE [Finance] ON  PRIMARY
( NAME = N'Finance_Data',
FILENAME = N'F:\DB\DATA\Finance.mdf' , SIZE = 217152KB ,
MAXSIZE = UNLIMITED, FILEGROWTH = 16384KB )
LOG ON
( NAME = N'Finance_Log',
FILENAME = N'F:\DB\DATA\Finance_1.ldf' ,
SIZE = 67584KB , MAXSIZE = 2048GB , FILEGROWTH = 16384KB )
GO

-- SQL compatibility level 110 is SQL Server 2012
ALTER DATABASE [Finance] SET COMPATIBILITY_LEVEL = 110
GO

USE Finance;
-- SQL select into table create
SELECT * INTO POH
FROM AdventureWorks2012.Purchasing.PurchaseOrderHeader;
GO

 -- SQL select query for 3 random records
SELECT TOP (3) * FROM POH ORDER BY NEWID()
GO
```

| PurchaseOrderID | RevisionNumber | Status | EmployeeID | VendorID |
|---|---|---|---|---|
| 3506 | 1 | 4 | 261 | 1666 |
| 233 | 1 | 4 | 257 | 1578 |
| 84 | 1 | 3 | 261 | 1654 |

**CHAPTER 9:  Advanced Database Design Concepts**

# Adding New Column to a Table with ALTER TABLE

It happens quite often that a table in production for years needs a new column. While adding a new column to a populated table is relatively simple, there is a downside: application software needs to be retested to make sure it still works with the new table. One offending statement is "SELECT * FROM". The application software was programmed, let's say for example, 6 columns, after the addition SELECT * is sending 7 columns which causes error in the application. T-SQL scripts to demonstrate the addition of a new column to a table for sequencing or other purposes.

```
USE AdventureWorks2012;

SELECT NewProductID = ROW_NUMBER()    OVER (   ORDER BY ProductID),
    *
INTO   #Product
FROM   AdventureWorks.Production.Product
GO
-- (504 row(s) affected)
```

```
ALTER TABLE #Product ADD CountryOfOrigin nvarchar(32) not null DEFAULT ('USA');
GO
-- Command(s) completed successfully.
```

```
SELECT         ProductID,
               Name                      AS ProductName,
               ProductNumber,
               ListPrice,
               COALESCE(Color,'')        AS Color,
               CountryOfOrigin
FROM   #Product
ORDER BY ProductName;
GO
```

| ProductID | ProductName | ProductNumber | ListPrice | Color | CountryOfOrigin |
|-----------|-------------|---------------|-----------|-------|-----------------|
| 1 | Adjustable Race | AR-5381 | 0.00 | | USA |
| 879 | All-Purpose Bike Stand | ST-1401 | 159.00 | | USA |
| 712 | AWC Logo Cap | CA-1098 | 8.99 | Multi | USA |
| 3 | BB Ball Bearing | BE-2349 | 0.00 | | USA |
| 2 | Bearing Ball | BA-8327 | 0.00 | | USA |
| 877 | Bike Wash - Dissolver | CL-9009 | 7.95 | | USA |
| 316 | Blade | BL-2036 | 0.00 | | USA |
| 843 | Cable Lock | LO-C100 | 25.00 | | USA |
| 952 | Chain | CH-0234 | 20.24 | Silver | USA |
| 324 | Chain Stays | CS-2812 | 0.00 | | USA |
| 322 | Chainring | CR-7833 | 0.00 | Black | USA |
| 320 | Chainring Bolts | CB-2903 | 0.00 | Silver | USA |

```
-- Cleanup
DROP TABLE #Product
```

## IDENTITY Column in a Table Variable

Using IDENTITY function for row numbering in new column with table variable. Statements must be in one batch, that is the scope of table variable.

```
DECLARE @Product TABLE
(
  ID        INT IDENTITY(1, 1),    -- new column
  ProductID  int,
  ProductName varchar(64),
  ListPrice  money,
  Color     varchar(32)
) ;

INSERT @Product
   (ProductID,
    ProductName,
    ListPrice,
    Color)
SELECT ProductID,
    Name,
    ListPrice,
    Color
FROM   AdventureWorks2012.Production.Product
WHERE  ListPrice > 0
    AND Color IS NOT NULL
ORDER  BY Name;

SELECT TOP(7) *
FROM   @Product
ORDER  BY ID;
GO
```

| ID | ProductID | ProductName | ListPrice | Color |
|----|-----------|-------------|-----------|-------|
| 1 | 712 | AWC Logo Cap | 8.99 | Multi |
| 2 | 952 | Chain | 20.24 | Silver |
| 3 | 866 | Classic Vest, L | 63.50 | Blue |
| 4 | 865 | Classic Vest, M | 63.50 | Blue |
| 5 | 864 | Classic Vest, S | 63.50 | Blue |
| 6 | 948 | Front Brakes | 106.50 | Silver |
| 7 | 945 | Front Derailleur | 91.49 | Silver |

Note: the above "GO" (ending the batch) terminated the scope of @Product table variable.

```
SELECT TOP(7) *  FROM   @Product ;
/* Msg 1087, Level 15, State 2, Line 1     Must declare the table variable "@Product" */
```

**CHAPTER 9:  Advanced Database Design Concepts**

## Partition Data By Country Query

Partition sales data by country and sequence sales staff from best to worst.

NOTE: ROW_NUMBER() only sequencing; to rank use the RANK() function.

```
SELECT CONCAT(LastName,', ', FirstName)              AS SalesPerson,
       CountryRegionName                             AS Country,
       ROW_NUMBER() OVER(
                     PARTITION BY CountryRegionName
                     ORDER BY SalesYTD DESC)         AS 'Row Number',
       FORMAT( SalesYTD, 'c', 'en-US')               AS SalesYTD
INTO  #SalesPersonRank
FROM  AdventureWorks2012.Sales.vSalesPerson
WHERE TerritoryName IS NOT NULL    AND SalesYTD <> 0;


-- Add new column StarRank, which is 1 "*" for each $1,000,000 of sales
ALTER TABLE #SalesPersonRank ADD StarRank varchar(32) NOT NULL DEFAULT ('');
--Command(s) completed successfully.


-- New column empty so far, population follows with UPDATE
UPDATE #SalesPersonRank SET StarRank =
REPLICATE ('*', FLOOR(CONVERT(Money, REPLACE(SalesYTD,',',''))  / 1000000.0));
-- (14 row(s) affected)


SELECT *  FROM  #SalesPersonRank  ORDER  BY Country,    [Row Number];
```

| SalesPerson | Country | Row Number | SalesYTD | StarRank |
|---|---|---|---|---|
| Tsoflias, Lynn | Australia | 1 | $1,421,810.92 | * |
| Saraiva, José | Canada | 1 | $2,604,540.72 | ** |
| Vargas, Garrett | Canada | 2 | $1,453,719.47 | * |
| Varkey Chudukatil, Ranjit | France | 1 | $3,121,616.32 | *** |
| Valdez, Rachel | Germany | 1 | $1,827,066.71 | * |
| Pak, Jae | United Kingdom | 1 | $4,116,871.23 | **** |
| Mitchell, Linda | United States | 1 | $4,251,368.55 | **** |
| Blythe, Michael | United States | 2 | $3,763,178.18 | *** |
| Carson, Jillian | United States | 3 | $3,189,418.37 | *** |
| Ito, Shu | United States | 4 | $2,458,535.62 | ** |
| Reiter, Tsvi | United States | 5 | $2,315,185.61 | ** |
| Mensa-Annan, Tete | United States | 6 | $1,576,562.20 | * |
| Campbell, David | United States | 7 | $1,573,012.94 | * |
| Ansman-Wolfe, Pamela | United States | 8 | $1,352,577.13 | * |

```
DROP TABLE #SalesPersonRank;
```

**CHAPTER 9:  Advanced Database Design Concepts**

## Diagram of Sales.SalesPerson & Related Tables

The sales staff is crucial in any business organization. It is reflected on the following diagram.

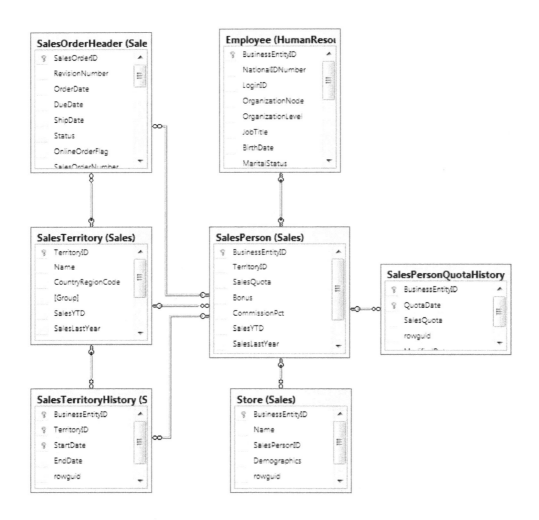

## Adding IDENTITY Column To  Empty Table

Add IDENTITY column to a table for sequential unique numbering (autonumber).

```
USE tempdb;
CREATE TABLE Department
 (
   Name       varchar(32)  UNIQUE,
   GroupName   varchar(256),
   ModifiedDate date default (CURRENT_TIMESTAMP)
 );
GO
-- Command(s) completed successfully.
```

```
-- Add new IDENTITY column
ALTER TABLE Department    ADD DepartmentID smallint IDENTITY(1, 1) PRIMARY KEY;
GO
-- Command(s) completed successfully.
```

```
-- Only one identity column per table
ALTER TABLE Department
 ADD SecondIdentity smallint IDENTITY(1, 1);
GO
/* Msg 2744, Level 16, State 2, Line 1
Multiple identity columns specified for table 'Department'. Only one identity  column per table is allowed.
*/
```

```
INSERT INTO Department ( DepartmentID, Name, Groupname) VALUES (17, 'Student Affairs', 'Executive');
/* Msg 544, Level 16, State 1, Line 1
Cannot insert explicit value for identity column in table 'Department'  when IDENTITY_INSERT is set to
OFF. */
```

## SET IDENTITY INSERT tablename ON

```
-- SQL identity insert enabled
SET IDENTITY_INSERT Department ON;
```

```
INSERT INTO Department ( DepartmentID, Name, Groupname) VALUES (17, 'Student Affairs', 'Executive');
-- (1 row(s) affected)
```

```
-- SQL identity insert disabled (default)
SET IDENTITY_INSERT Department OFF;
GO
```

**CHAPTER 9:  Advanced Database Design Concepts**

## DBCC CHECKIDENT Command

DBCC CHECKIDENT can be used to check and reseed IDENTITY parameters.

```
DBCC CHECKIDENT('Production.Product');
/*Checking identity information: current identity value '999', current column value '999'.
DBCC execution completed. If DBCC printed error messages, contact your system administrator. */


-- SQL reseeding identity column;  reset identity column
DBCC CHECKIDENT ("dbo.Department", RESEED, 999);
/*Checking identity information: current identity value '17'.
DBCC execution completed. If DBCC printed error messages, contact your system administrator. */


INSERT INTO Department (Name, Groupname) VALUES ( 'Alumni Affairs', 'Executive');

SELECT * FROM Department;
```

| Name | GroupName | ModifiedDate | DepartmentID |
|------|-----------|--------------|--------------|
| Student Affairs | Executive | 2016-07-19 | 17 |
| Alumni Affairs | Executive | 2016-07-19 | 1000 |

```
-- Add more records to table with INSERT SELECT
INSERT INTO Department (Name, Groupname)
SELECT Name, GroupName  FROM AdventureWorks2012.HumanResources.Department;

SELECT * FROM Department ORDER BY DepartmentID;
```

| Name | GroupName | ModifiedDate | DepartmentID |
|------|-----------|--------------|--------------|
| Student Affairs | Executive | 2012-07-19 | 17 |
| Alumni Affairs | Executive | 2012-07-19 | 1000 |
| Engineering | Research and Development | 2012-07-19 | 1001 |
| Tool Design | Research and Development | 2012-07-19 | 1002 |
| Sales | Sales and Marketing | 2012-07-19 | 1003 |
| Marketing | Sales and Marketing | 2012-07-19 | 1004 |
| Purchasing | Inventory Management | 2012-07-19 | 1005 |
| Research and Development | Research and Development | 2012-07-19 | 1006 |
| Production | Manufacturing | 2012-07-19 | 1007 |
| Production Control | Manufacturing | 2012-07-19 | 1008 |
| Human Resources | Executive General and Administration | 2012-07-19 | 1009 |
| Finance | Executive General and Administration | 2012-07-19 | 1010 |
| Information Services | Executive General and Administration | 2012-07-19 | 1011 |
| Document Control | Quality Assurance | 2012-07-19 | 1012 |
| Quality Assurance | Quality Assurance | 2012-07-19 | 1013 |
| Facilities and Maintenance | Executive General and Administration | 2012-07-19 | 1014 |
| Shipping and Receiving | Inventory Management | 2012-07-19 | 1015 |
| Executive | Executive General and Administration | 2012-07-19 | 1016 |

```
DROP TABLE tempdb.dbo.Department;
```

CHAPTER 9:  Advanced Database Design Concepts

## ADD Partitioned Sequence Number to Table

Partition table by subcategory (ProductSubcategoryID)  by applying ROW_NUMBER for sequencing within each partition.

```
SELECT ROW_NUMBER()    OVER (  PARTITION BY p.ProductSubcategoryID
                               ORDER BY ProductID)          AS RowID,
       ps.Name                                              AS SubCategory,
       p.Name                                               AS ProductName,
       ProductNumber,
       Color,
       ListPrice
INTO   #ProductsByCategory
FROM   AdventureWorks.Production.Product p
    INNER JOIN AdventureWorks.Production.ProductSubcategory ps
       ON p.ProductSubcategoryID = ps.ProductSubcategoryID ;
GO


-- Add new column for display in currency format
ALTER TABLE #ProductsByCategory ADD Dollar varchar(32) not null DEFAULT ('');
GO
-- Command(s) completed successfully.


-- Populate new column with UPDATE
UPDATE #ProductsByCategory  SET Dollar = FORMAT(ListPrice, 'c', 'en-US');
GO
-- (295 row(s) affected)


SELECT *  FROM  #ProductsByCategory  ORDER BY Subcategory,  RowID;
```

| RowID | SubCategory | ProductName | ProductNumber | Color | ListPrice | Dollar |
|---|---|---|---|---|---|---|
| 1 | Bib-Shorts | Men's Bib-Shorts, S | SB-M891-S | Multi | 89.99 | $89.99 |
| 2 | Bib-Shorts | Men's Bib-Shorts, M | SB-M891-M | Multi | 89.99 | $89.99 |
| 3 | Bib-Shorts | Men's Bib-Shorts, L | SB-M891-L | Multi | 89.99 | $89.99 |
| 1 | Bike Racks | Hitch Rack - 4-Bike | RA-H123 | NULL | 120.00 | $120.00 |
| 1 | Bike Stands | All-Purpose Bike Stand | ST-1401 | NULL | 159.00 | $159.00 |
| 1 | Bottles and Cages | Water Bottle - 30 oz. | WB-H098 | NULL | 4.99 | $4.99 |
| 2 | Bottles and Cages | Mountain Bottle Cage | BC-M005 | NULL | 9.99 | $9.99 |
| 3 | Bottles and Cages | Road Bottle Cage | BC-R205 | NULL | 8.99 | $8.99 |
| 1 | Bottom Brackets | LL Bottom Bracket | BB-7421 | NULL | 53.99 | $53.99 |
| 2 | Bottom Brackets | ML Bottom Bracket | BB-8107 | NULL | 101.24 | $101.24 |
| 3 | Bottom Brackets | HL Bottom Bracket | BB-9108 | NULL | 121.49 | $121.49 |
| 1 | Brakes | Rear Brakes | RB-9231 | Silver | 106.50 | $106.50 |
| 2 | Brakes | Front Brakes | FB-9873 | Silver | 106.50 | $106.50 |
| 1 | Caps | AWC Logo Cap | CA-1098 | Multi | 8.99 | $8.99 |
| 1 | Chains | Chain | CH-0234 | Silver | 20.24 | $20.24 |

```
-- Cleanup
DROP TABLE #ProductsByCategory
```

**CHAPTER 9:  Advanced Database Design Concepts**

## Add ROW_NUMBER & RANK Columns to Table

Add row number and rank number to SELECT INTO table create without partitioning and rank (dense ranking) high price items to low price items.

```
SELECT ROW_NUMBER()
    OVER(
    ORDER BY Name ASC)                      AS ROWID,
    DENSE_RANK()
    OVER(
    ORDER BY ListPrice DESC)                AS RANKID,
    ListPrice                               AS Price,
    *
INTO   tempdb.dbo.RankedProduct
FROM   AdventureWorks2012.Production.Product
ORDER  BY          RANKID,
                   ROWID;
GO
-- (504 row(s) affected)


SELECT * FROM   tempdb.dbo.RankedProduct;
GO
-- (504 row(s) affected) - Partial results.
```

| ROWID | RANKID | Price | ProductID | Name | ProductNumber | MakeFlag | FinishedGoodsFlag | Color |
|---|---|---|---|---|---|---|---|---|
| 376 | 1 | 3578.27 | 750 | Road-150 Red, 44 | BK-R93R-44 | 1 | 1 | Red |
| 377 | 1 | 3578.27 | 751 | Road-150 Red, 48 | BK-R93R-48 | 1 | 1 | Red |
| 378 | 1 | 3578.27 | 752 | Road-150 Red, 52 | BK-R93R-52 | 1 | 1 | Red |
| 379 | 1 | 3578.27 | 753 | Road-150 Red, 56 | BK-R93R-56 | 1 | 1 | Red |
| 380 | 1 | 3578.27 | 749 | Road-150 Red, 62 | BK-R93R-62 | 1 | 1 | Red |
| 332 | 2 | 3399.99 | 771 | Mountain-100 Silver, 38 | BK-M82S-38 | 1 | 1 | Silver |
| 333 | 2 | 3399.99 | 772 | Mountain-100 Silver, 42 | BK-M82S-42 | 1 | 1 | Silver |
| 334 | 2 | 3399.99 | 773 | Mountain-100 Silver, 44 | BK-M82S-44 | 1 | 1 | Silver |
| 335 | 2 | 3399.99 | 774 | Mountain-100 Silver, 48 | BK-M82S-48 | 1 | 1 | Silver |
| 328 | 3 | 3374.99 | 775 | Mountain-100 Black, 38 | BK-M82B-38 | 1 | 1 | Black |
| 329 | 3 | 3374.99 | 776 | Mountain-100 Black, 42 | BK-M82B-42 | 1 | 1 | Black |
| 330 | 3 | 3374.99 | 777 | Mountain-100 Black, 44 | BK-M82B-44 | 1 | 1 | Black |
| 331 | 3 | 3374.99 | 778 | Mountain-100 Black, 48 | BK-M82B-48 | 1 | 1 | Black |
| 381 | 4 | 2443.35 | 793 | Road-250 Black, 44 | BK-R89B-44 | 1 | 1 | Black |
| 382 | 4 | 2443.35 | 794 | Road-250 Black, 48 | BK-R89B-48 | 1 | 1 | Black |
| 383 | 4 | 2443.35 | 795 | Road-250 Black, 52 | BK-R89B-52 | 1 | 1 | Black |
| 384 | 4 | 2443.35 | 796 | Road-250 Black, 58 | BK-R89B-58 | 1 | 1 | Black |
| 385 | 4 | 2443.35 | 789 | Road-250 Red, 44 | BK-R89R-44 | 1 | 1 | Red |
| 386 | 4 | 2443.35 | 790 | Road-250 Red, 48 | BK-R89R-48 | 1 | 1 | Red |
| 387 | 4 | 2443.35 | 791 | Road-250 Red, 52 | BK-R89R-52 | 1 | 1 | Red |

```
DROP TABLE tempdb.dbo.RankedProduct;
GO
```

# CHAPTER 11: JOINing Tables with INNER & OUTER JOINs

## SELECT with INNER JOIN

The SELECT statement is used to retrieve data from table(s). An INNER JOIN is a join in which the values in the columns being joined are compared using a comparison operator. Inner join also known as equi-join when equality condition is applied. Equi-join: PRIMARY KEY (table a) = FOREIGN KEY (table b).

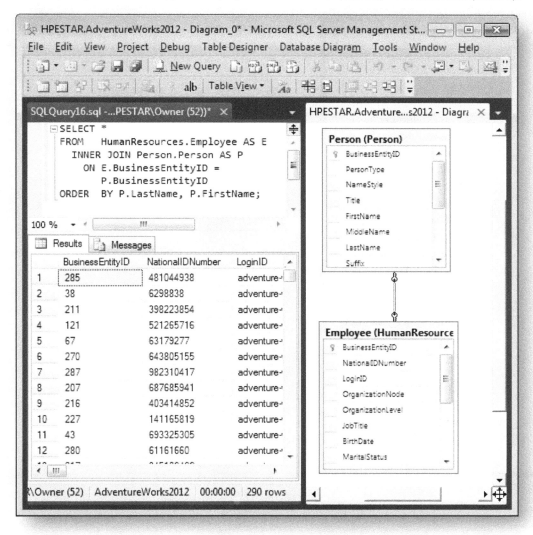

# FOREIGN KEY Constraint as Base for INNER JOIN

The INNER JOIN is based on HumanResources.Employee.BusinessEntityID (PRIMARY KEY) is a FOREIGN KEY to Person.Person.BusinessEntityID.  The Employee table is in one-to-one relationship with a subset of the Person table.

## Diagram of Person.Person and Related Tables

The population of Person.Person includes all employees, contacts, and customers, therefore a key table in the database.

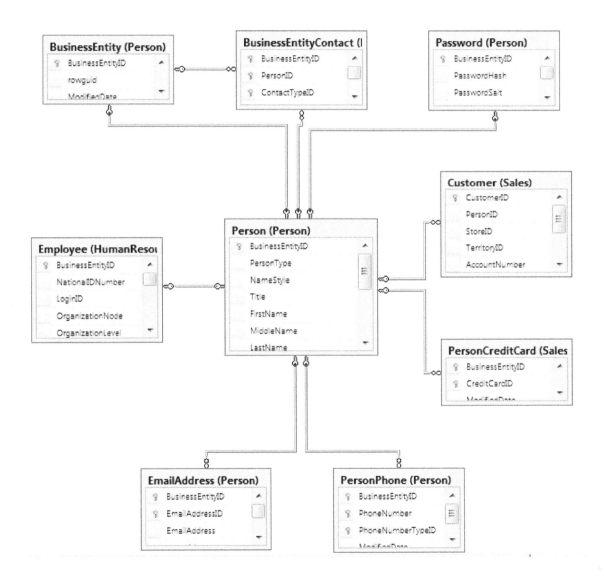

# EQUI-JOIN BETWEEN FOREIGN KEY & PRIMARY KEY

EQUI JOIN means the equality operator is used to match the left and right keys.  The reason for the popularity: the goal of most query is to gather information from related tables records (rows).  Query to demonstrate why  are 3 tables necessary to get a meaningful business report with just a few columns.

```
USE AdventureWorks;
GO


SELECT        CONCAT(LastName, ', ', FirstName)        AS Consumer,
              EmailAddress,
              Phone,
              CU.AccountNumber,
              C.ContactID,
              I.CustomerID
FROM Person.Contact AS C
  INNER JOIN Sales.Individual AS I
    ON C.ContactID = I.ContactID
  INNER JOIN Sales.Customer AS CU
    ON I.CustomerID = CU.CustomerID
WHERE CU.CustomerType = 'I'
ORDER BY LastName, FirstName ;
GO
-- (18484 row(s) affected) - Partial results.
```

| Consumer | EmailAddress | Phone | AccountNumber | ContactID | CustomerID |
|----------|--------------|-------|---------------|-----------|------------|
| Pal, Yolanda | yolanda11@adventure-works.com | 1 (11) 500 555-0110 | AW00023748 | 2837 | 23748 |
| Palit, Punya | punya0@adventure-works.com | 164-555-0118 | AW00017574 | 14759 | 17574 |
| Parker, Adam | adam29@adventure-works.com | 808-555-0157 | AW00018228 | 14771 | 18228 |
| Parker, Alex | alex26@adventure-works.com | 613-555-0123 | AW00029252 | 14783 | 29252 |
| Parker, Alexandra | alexandra50@adventure-works.com | 974-555-0142 | AW00016866 | 8977 | 16866 |
| Parker, Allison | allison30@adventure-works.com | 750-555-0124 | AW00026501 | 9021 | 26501 |
| Parker, Amanda | amanda51@adventure-works.com | 978-555-0167 | AW00018081 | 8985 | 18081 |
| Parker, Amber | amber7@adventure-works.com | 1 (11) 500 555-0198 | AW00023959 | 8999 | 23959 |
| Parker, Andrea | andrea23@adventure-works.com | 612-555-0113 | AW00020091 | 8461 | 20091 |
| Parker, Angel | angel21@adventure-works.com | 815-555-0120 | AW00014273 | 14779 | 14273 |
| Parker, Bailey | bailey28@adventure-works.com | 604-555-0112 | AW00019529 | 9007 | 19529 |
| Parker, Blake | blake44@adventure-works.com | 432-555-0151 | AW00015008 | 3413 | 15008 |
| Parker, Caleb | caleb28@adventure-works.com | 593-555-0116 | AW00026318 | 14760 | 26318 |
| Parker, Carlos | carlos25@adventure-works.com | 937-555-0143 | AW00020676 | 14778 | 20676 |
| Parker, Charles | charles43@adventure-works.com | 266-555-0118 | AW00021267 | 4105 | 21267 |
| Parker, Chloe | chloe5@adventure-works.com | 360-555-0121 | AW00027480 | 8965 | 27480 |
| Parker, Connor | connor28@adventure-works.com | 936-555-0177 | AW00028839 | 14763 | 28839 |
| Parker, Courtney | courtney5@adventure-works.com | 266-555-0176 | AW00017612 | 9002 | 17612 |
| Parker, Dalton | dalton42@adventure-works.com | 535-555-0190 | AW00013064 | 3722 | 13064 |
| Parker, Devin | devin40@adventure-works.com | 897-555-0155 | AW00011684 | 4192 | 11684 |
| Parker, Eduardo | eduardo41@adventure-works.com | 131-555-0192 | AW00012939 | 4269 | 12939 |

# Diagram of Sales.Customer and Related Tables

Customer is the source of revenue for any business. Therefore, proper table design is paramount.

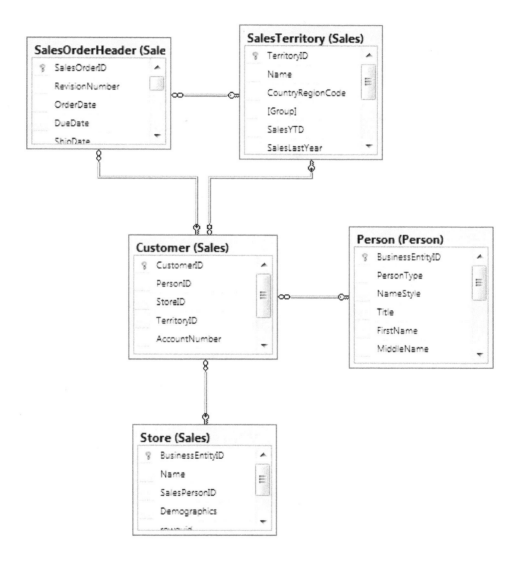

## Extracting All or Partial Data from JOINed Tables

T-SQL scripts to demonstrate how to JOIN two tables and extract all or subset of the information.

```
USE AdventureWorks2012;

-- SELECT all columns from the JOINed tables
SELECT *
FROM   HumanResources.Employee          AS E      -- E is a table alias
    INNER JOIN Person.Person            AS P      -- P is a table alias
        ON E.BusinessEntityID = P.BusinessEntityID
ORDER  BY P.LastName;
-- (290 row(s) affected)  - Partial results.
```

| FirstName | MiddleName | LastName |
|-----------|------------|-----------|
| Syed | E | Abbas |
| Kim | B | Abercrombie |
| Hazem | E | Abolrous |
| Pilar | G | Ackerman |
| Jay | G | Adams |

```
SELECT E.*                      -- SELECT Employee columns from the JOINed tables
FROM   HumanResources.Employee AS E
    INNER JOIN Person.Person AS P    ON E.BusinessEntityID = P.BusinessEntityID
ORDER  BY P.LastName;
-- Partial results.
```

| JobTitle | BirthDate | MaritalStatus | Gender |
|----------|-----------|---------------|--------|
| Pacific Sales Manager | 1969-02-11 | M | M |
| Production Technician - WC60 | 1961-01-14 | M | F |
| Quality Assurance Manager | 1971-11-27 | S | M |
| Shipping and Receiving Supervisor | 1966-10-11 | S | M |

```
-- SELECT Person columns from the JOINed tables
SELECT P.* FROM   HumanResources.Employee AS E
              INNER JOIN Person.Person AS P     ON E.BusinessEntityID = P.BusinessEntityID
ORDER  BY P.LastName;
-- Partial results.
```

| BusinessEntityID | PersonType |
|------------------|------------|
| 285 | SP |
| 38 | EM |
| 211 | EM |

**CHAPTER 11:  JOINing Tables with INNER & OUTER JOINs**

## SELECT All Columns From The Joined Tables Using Table Alias And Wildcard

```
SELECT E.*, P.*
FROM   HumanResources.Employee              AS E      -- E is a table alias
    INNER JOIN Person.Person                AS P      -- P is a table alias
        ON E.BusinessEntityID = P.BusinessEntityID
ORDER  BY P.LastName;
-- Same results as SELECT * FROM


-- Count JOINed rows
SELECT count(*)
FROM   HumanResources.Employee AS E
    INNER JOIN Person.Person AS P
        ON E.BusinessEntityID = P.BusinessEntityID
-- 290


-- Vertically output reduction: eliminate columns from the available pool
SELECT   E.BusinessEntityID               AS EmployeeID,   -- column alias
         E.JobTitle,
         P.FirstName,
         P.LastName
FROM   HumanResources.Employee AS E
    INNER JOIN Person.Person AS P    ON E.BusinessEntityID = P.BusinessEntityID
ORDER  BY P.LastName;
-- (290 row(s) affected) - Partial results.
```

| EmployeeID | JobTitle | FirstName | LastName |
|---|---|---|---|
| 285 | Pacific Sales Manager | Syed | Abbas |
| 38 | Production Technician - WC60 | Kim | Abercrombie |
| 211 | Quality Assurance Manager | Hazem | Abolrous |
| 121 | Shipping and Receiving Supervisor | Pilar | Ackerman |

```
-- Create a new output column from the available pool of columns
SELECT   E.BusinessEntityID                    AS EmployeeID,
         E.JobTitle,
         CONCAT(P.FirstName, ' ', P.LastName)        AS NAME
FROM   HumanResources.Employee AS E
    INNER JOIN Person.Person AS P     ON E.BusinessEntityID = P.BusinessEntityID
ORDER  BY P.LastName;
-- (290 row(s) affected) - Partial results.
```

| EmployeeID | JobTitle | NAME |
|---|---|---|
| 285 | Pacific Sales Manager | Syed Abbas |
| 38 | Production Technician - WC60 | Kim Abercrombie |
| 211 | Quality Assurance Manager | Hazem Abolrous |
| 121 | Shipping and Receiving Supervisor | Pilar Ackerman |

**CHAPTER 11:  JOINing Tables with INNER & OUTER JOINs**

# Table Aliases for Readability

The table alias serves as shorthand for table name to improve the **readability of queries**. It should be as short as possible and as meaningful as possible when we have to use a few letters. The next T-SQL query applies four table aliases: c, soh, sod, p.

```
USE AdventureWorks;
SELECT DISTINCT SalesPerson = CONCAT(c.FirstName,SPACE(1), c.LastName)
FROM   Person.Contact c
    INNER JOIN Sales.SalesOrderHeader soh
    ON soh.SalesPersonId = c.ContactID
    INNER JOIN Sales.SalesOrderDetail sod
    ON soh.SalesOrderId = sod.SalesOrderId
    INNER JOIN Production.Product p
    ON sod.ProductID = p.ProductID    AND p.Name LIKE ('%Touring Frame%');
GO
/*      SalesPerson
        Carla Eldridge
        Carol Elliott
        Gail Erickson  ....*/
```

# Column Aliases for Readability & Presentation

The column alias serves as a meaningful column name either replacing a column name or filling in when there is no column name. In the previous example the = sign was used to establish the column alias. Alternate setting follows applying "AS" (it can be skipped) after the column. If the alias has spaces it has to be included in square brackets like [Bond Sales] or double quotes.

```
USE AdventureWorks;
SELECT DISTINCT  CONCAT(c.FirstName,' ', c.LastName)                 AS SalesPerson
FROM   Person.Contact c
    INNER JOIN Sales.SalesOrderHeader soh
    ON soh.SalesPersonId = c.ContactID
    INNER JOIN Sales.SalesOrderDetail sod
    ON soh.SalesOrderId = sod.SalesOrderId
    INNER JOIN Production.Product p
    ON sod.ProductID = p.ProductID   AND p.Name LIKE ('%Touring Frame%');
-- (17 row(s) affected) - Partial results.
```

| SalesPerson |
| --- |
| Carla Eldridge |
| Carol Elliott |
| Gail Erickson |
| Gary Drury |
| Janeth Esteves |
| Jauna Elson |
| John Emory |

# Derived Table Alias with a List of Column Aliases

Optionally column alias list can be specified for derived tables just like in CTE definition. T-SQL query demonstrates nested derived tables with table-column aliases (P & J).

```
SELECT DISTINCT ProdID, ProdName, ProdPrice, OrderQuantity
FROM    (
                SELECT    ID, ProductName, Price,          -- Derived table columns
                          OrderQty                         -- SOD column
                FROM AdventureWorks2012.Sales.SalesOrderDetail SOD
                  INNER JOIN
                      (SELECT ProductID, Name, ListPrice
                      FROM AdventureWorks2012.Production.Product
                      ) P(ID, ProductName, Price)          -- inner derived table
                  ON SOD.ProductID = P.ID
        ) J (ProdID, ProdName, ProdPrice, OrderQuantity)   -- outer derived table
ORDER BY ProdPrice DESC, ProdName;
-- (2667 row(s) affected) - Partial results.
```

| ProdID | ProdName | ProdPrice | OrderQuantity |
|--------|----------|-----------|---------------|
| 750 | Road-150 Red, 44 | 3578.27 | 3 |
| 750 | Road-150 Red, 44 | 3578.27 | 6 |
| 750 | Road-150 Red, 44 | 3578.27 | 1 |
| 750 | Road-150 Red, 44 | 3578.27 | 4 |
| 750 | Road-150 Red, 44 | 3578.27 | 2 |
| 750 | Road-150 Red, 44 | 3578.27 | 5 |
| 751 | Road-150 Red, 48 | 3578.27 | 6 |
| 751 | Road-150 Red, 48 | 3578.27 | 3 |
| 751 | Road-150 Red, 48 | 3578.27 | 2 |
| 751 | Road-150 Red, 48 | 3578.27 | 5 |
| 751 | Road-150 Red, 48 | 3578.27 | 4 |
| 751 | Road-150 Red, 48 | 3578.27 | 1 |
| 752 | Road-150 Red, 52 | 3578.27 | 5 |
| 752 | Road-150 Red, 52 | 3578.27 | 3 |
| 752 | Road-150 Red, 52 | 3578.27 | 6 |
| 752 | Road-150 Red, 52 | 3578.27 | 1 |
| 752 | Road-150 Red, 52 | 3578.27 | 4 |
| 752 | Road-150 Red, 52 | 3578.27 | 2 |
| 753 | Road-150 Red, 56 | 3578.27 | 6 |
| 753 | Road-150 Red, 56 | 3578.27 | 3 |

# INNER JOIN with Additional Conditions

The ON clause of a JOIN can include additional conditions as the following demonstration shows.  The INNER JOIN is still based on FOREIGN KEY relationship, but only a subset of records (rows) returned due to the additional conditions, or JOIN predicates. The first query returns the distinct set of cases where the Selling Price was below the ListPrice for ProductID 800 which is a yellow road bike. The second query covers the remaining range where the  Selling Price was equal or above the ListPrice

```
USE AdventureWorks2012;
SELECT DISTINCT( P.ProductID ),
        ProductName = P.Name,              -- column alias
        P.ListPrice,
        SOD.UnitPrice AS 'Selling Price'   -- column alias
FROM   Sales.SalesOrderDetail AS SOD       -- table alias
    INNER JOIN  Production.Product AS P     -- table alias
    ON SOD.ProductID = P.ProductID
      AND SOD.UnitPrice < P.ListPrice              -- JOIN predicate
      AND  P.ProductID = 800;                      -- JOIN predicate
```

| ProductID | ProductName | ListPrice | Selling Price |
|---|---|---|---|
| 800 | Road-550-W Yellow, 44 | 1120.49 | 600.2625 |
| 800 | Road-550-W Yellow, 44 | 1120.49 | 672.294 |
| 800 | Road-550-W Yellow, 44 | 1120.49 | 1000.4375 |

```
SELECT DISTINCT( P.ProductID ),
        ProductName = P.Name,
        P.ListPrice,
        SOD.UnitPrice AS 'Selling Price'
FROM   Sales.SalesOrderDetail AS SOD
    INNER JOIN  Production.Product AS P
    ON SOD.ProductID = P.ProductID
      AND SOD.UnitPrice >= P.ListPrice
      AND  P.ProductID BETWEEN 800 AND 900
ORDER BY ProductName;
-- (26 row(s) affected) - Partial results.
```

| ProductID | ProductName | ListPrice | Selling Price |
|---|---|---|---|
| 879 | All-Purpose Bike Stand | 159.00 | 159.00 |
| 877 | Bike Wash - Dissolver | 7.95 | 7.95 |
| 866 | Classic Vest, L | 63.50 | 63.50 |
| 865 | Classic Vest, M | 63.50 | 63.50 |
| 864 | Classic Vest, S | 63.50 | 63.50 |
| 878 | Fender Set - Mountain | 21.98 | 21.98 |
| 860 | Half-Finger Gloves, L | 24.49 | 24.49 |
| 859 | Half-Finger Gloves, M | 24.49 | 24.49 |
| 858 | Half-Finger Gloves, S | 24.49 | 24.49 |
| 876 | Hitch Rack - 4-Bike | 120.00 | 120.00 |

# Counting Rows in JOINs

As the T-SQL script following shows, the basic FOREIGN KEY based JOIN returns 121,317 rows which is all the rows in Sales.SalesOrderDetail table. The additional condition P.ProductID = 800 selects a subset of 495 rows which is then divided between the < and >= conditions.

```
USE AdventureWorks2012;
SELECT Rows = count(*)
FROM   Sales.SalesOrderDetail AS SOD
    INNER JOIN  Production.Product AS P     ON SOD.ProductID = P.ProductID
-- 121317


SELECT Rows = count(*)
FROM   Sales.SalesOrderDetail AS SOD
    INNER JOIN  Production.Product AS P   ON SOD.ProductID = P.ProductID   AND P.ProductID = 800;
-- 495


SELECT Rows = count(*)
FROM   Sales.SalesOrderDetail AS SOD
    INNER JOIN  Production.Product AS P
     ON SOD.ProductID = P.ProductID
       AND SOD.UnitPrice < P.ListPrice
       AND P.ProductID = 800;
-- 285


SELECT Rows = count(*)
FROM   Sales.SalesOrderDetail AS SOD
    INNER JOIN  Production.Product AS P
     ON SOD.ProductID = P.ProductID
       AND SOD.UnitPrice >= P.ListPrice
       AND P.ProductID = 800;
-- 210


SELECT COUNT(P.ProductID)
FROM   Sales.SalesOrderDetail AS SOD
    INNER JOIN  Production.Product AS P
     ON SOD.ProductID = P.ProductID
       AND SOD.UnitPrice >= P.ListPrice
       AND  P.ProductID BETWEEN 800 AND 900;
-- 21085


SELECT COUNT(DISTINCT P.ProductID)
FROM   Sales.SalesOrderDetail AS SOD
    INNER JOIN  Production.Product AS P
     ON SOD.ProductID = P.ProductID   AND SOD.UnitPrice >= P.ListPrice
        AND  P.ProductID BETWEEN 800 AND 900;
```

**CHAPTER 11:  JOINing Tables with INNER & OUTER JOINs**

# INNER JOIN with 3 Tables

T-SQL query to demonstrate JOINing three tables. Due to the application of the FORMAT function, column name is lost. Therefore we have to alias the formatted column with the original column name or something else. Both INNER JOINs are based on FOREIGN KEY relationships. PV.ProductID is an FK to the Production.Product table, and the PV.VendorID is an FK to the Purchasing.Vendor table. The Purchasing.ProductVendor table is a junction table representing many-to-many relationships between products and vendors: a vendor may supply many products (see Beaumont Bikes in results) and a product may be supplied by many vendors (see Chainring in results).

```
USE AdventureWorks;
GO
SELECT          P.ProductNumber,
                P.Name                              AS Product,
                V.Name                              AS Vendor,
                FORMAT (PV.LastReceiptCost, 'c', 'en-US')   AS LastReceiptCost
FROM Production.Product AS P
  INNER JOIN Purchasing.ProductVendor AS PV
        ON P.ProductID = PV.ProductID
  INNER JOIN Purchasing.Vendor AS V
        ON V.VendorID = PV.VendorID
ORDER BY Product;
GO
-- (406 row(s) affected) - Partial results.
```

| ProductNumber | Product | Vendor | LastReceiptCost |
|---|---|---|---|
| AR-5381 | Adjustable Race | Litware, Inc. | $50.26 |
| BA-8327 | Bearing Ball | Wood Fitness | $41.92 |
| CH-0234 | Chain | Varsity Sport Co. | $15.74 |
| CR-7833 | Chainring | Beaumont Bikes | $25.42 |
| CR-7833 | Chainring | Bike Satellite Inc. | $26.37 |
| CR-7833 | Chainring | Training Systems | $28.70 |
| CB-2903 | Chainring Bolts | Beaumont Bikes | $47.47 |
| CB-2903 | Chainring Bolts | Bike Satellite Inc. | $45.37 |
| CB-2903 | Chainring Bolts | Training Systems | $49.64 |
| CN-6137 | Chainring Nut | Beaumont Bikes | $42.80 |
| CN-6137 | Chainring Nut | Bike Satellite Inc. | $40.49 |
| CN-6137 | Chainring Nut | Training Systems | $44.32 |
| RA-7490 | Cone-Shaped Race | Midwest Sport, Inc. | $44.22 |
| CR-9981 | Crown Race | Business Equipment Center | $50.26 |
| RA-2345 | Cup-Shaped Race | Bloomington Multisport | $48.76 |
| DC-8732 | Decal 1 | SUPERSALES INC. | $0.21 |
| DC-9824 | Decal 2 | SUPERSALES INC. | $0.21 |
| LE-6000 | External Lock Washer 1 | Pro Sport Industries | $41.24 |
| LE-6000 | External Lock Washer 1 | Aurora Bike Center | $43.27 |
| LE-6000 | External Lock Washer 1 | Expert Bike Co | $41.17 |

## T-SQL Query To Return All Road Frames Offered For Sale By AdventureWorks Cycles

```
USE AdventureWorks2012;
SELECT          UPPER(PC.Name)        AS Category,   PSC.Name          AS Subcategory,
                P.Name        AS Product,   FORMAT(ListPrice, 'c', 'en-US')    AS ListPrice,
                FORMAT(StandardCost, 'c', 'en-US')                    AS StandardCost
FROM Production.Product AS P
   INNER JOIN Production.ProductSubcategory AS PSC
            ON PSC.ProductSubcategoryID = P.ProductSubcategoryID
   INNER JOIN Production.ProductCategory AS PC
            ON PC.ProductCategoryID = PSC.ProductCategoryID
WHERE PSC.Name like 'Road Frames'  ORDER BY Category, Subcategory, Product;
```

| Category | Subcategory | Product | ListPrice | StandardCost |
|---|---|---|---|---|
| COMPONENTS | Road Frames | HL Road Frame - Black, 44 | $1,431.50 | $868.63 |
| COMPONENTS | Road Frames | HL Road Frame - Black, 48 | $1,431.50 | $868.63 |
| COMPONENTS | Road Frames | HL Road Frame - Black, 52 | $1,431.50 | $868.63 |
| COMPONENTS | Road Frames | HL Road Frame - Black, 58 | $1,431.50 | $1,059.31 |
| COMPONENTS | Road Frames | HL Road Frame - Black, 62 | $1,431.50 | $868.63 |
| COMPONENTS | Road Frames | HL Road Frame - Red, 44 | $1,431.50 | $868.63 |
| COMPONENTS | Road Frames | HL Road Frame - Red, 48 | $1,431.50 | $868.63 |
| COMPONENTS | Road Frames | HL Road Frame - Red, 52 | $1,431.50 | $868.63 |
| COMPONENTS | Road Frames | HL Road Frame - Red, 56 | $1,431.50 | $868.63 |
| COMPONENTS | Road Frames | HL Road Frame - Red, 58 | $1,431.50 | $1,059.31 |
| COMPONENTS | Road Frames | HL Road Frame - Red, 62 | $1,431.50 | $868.63 |
| COMPONENTS | Road Frames | LL Road Frame - Black, 44 | $337.22 | $204.63 |
| COMPONENTS | Road Frames | LL Road Frame - Black, 48 | $337.22 | $204.63 |
| COMPONENTS | Road Frames | LL Road Frame - Black, 52 | $337.22 | $204.63 |
| COMPONENTS | Road Frames | LL Road Frame - Black, 58 | $337.22 | $204.63 |
| COMPONENTS | Road Frames | LL Road Frame - Black, 60 | $337.22 | $204.63 |
| COMPONENTS | Road Frames | LL Road Frame - Black, 62 | $337.22 | $204.63 |
| COMPONENTS | Road Frames | LL Road Frame - Red, 44 | $337.22 | $187.16 |
| COMPONENTS | Road Frames | LL Road Frame - Red, 48 | $337.22 | $187.16 |
| COMPONENTS | Road Frames | LL Road Frame - Red, 52 | $337.22 | $187.16 |
| COMPONENTS | Road Frames | LL Road Frame - Red, 58 | $337.22 | $187.16 |
| COMPONENTS | Road Frames | LL Road Frame - Red, 60 | $337.22 | $187.16 |
| COMPONENTS | Road Frames | LL Road Frame - Red, 62 | $337.22 | $187.16 |
| COMPONENTS | Road Frames | ML Road Frame - Red, 44 | $594.83 | $352.14 |
| COMPONENTS | Road Frames | ML Road Frame - Red, 48 | $594.83 | $352.14 |
| COMPONENTS | Road Frames | ML Road Frame - Red, 52 | $594.83 | $352.14 |
| COMPONENTS | Road Frames | ML Road Frame - Red, 58 | $594.83 | $352.14 |
| COMPONENTS | Road Frames | ML Road Frame - Red, 60 | $594.83 | $352.14 |
| COMPONENTS | Road Frames | ML Road Frame-W - Yellow, 38 | $594.83 | $360.94 |
| COMPONENTS | Road Frames | ML Road Frame-W - Yellow, 40 | $594.83 | $360.94 |
| COMPONENTS | Road Frames | ML Road Frame-W - Yellow, 42 | $594.83 | $360.94 |
| COMPONENTS | Road Frames | ML Road Frame-W - Yellow, 44 | $594.83 | $360.94 |
| COMPONENTS | Road Frames | ML Road Frame-W - Yellow, 48 | $594.83 | $360.94 |

## INNER JOIN with Junction Table

Three tables INNER JOIN includes the titleauthor junction table which represent many-to-many relationship. All JOINs are EQUI-JOINs with FOREIGN KEYs and PRIMARY KEYs.

```
USE pubs;

SELECT          FORMAT(ytd_sales, 'c', 'en-US')                         AS YTDSales,
                CONCAT(au.au_fname, ' ', au.au_lname)                   AS Author,
                FORMAT((ytd_sales * royalty) / 100,'c','en-US')         AS AuthorRev,
                FORMAT((ytd_sales - (ytd_sales * royalty) / 100),'c','en-US')  AS PublisherRev
FROM titles t
        INNER JOIN titleauthor ta
        ON t.title_id = ta.title_id
        INNER JOIN authors au
        ON ta.au_id = au.au_id
ORDER BY        YTDSales DESC,           -- Major sort key
                Author ASC;              -- Minor sort key
GO
```

| YTDSales | Author | AuthorRev | PublisherRev |
|---|---|---|---|
| $8,780.00 | Cheryl Carson | $1,404.00 | $7,376.00 |
| $4,095.00 | Abraham Bennet | $409.00 | $3,686.00 |
| $4,095.00 | Akiko Yokomoto | $409.00 | $3,686.00 |
| $4,095.00 | Ann Dull | $409.00 | $3,686.00 |
| $4,095.00 | Burt Gringlesby | $409.00 | $3,686.00 |
| $4,095.00 | Dean Straight | $409.00 | $3,686.00 |
| $4,095.00 | Marjorie Green | $409.00 | $3,686.00 |
| $4,095.00 | Michael O'Leary | $409.00 | $3,686.00 |
| $4,095.00 | Sheryl Hunter | $409.00 | $3,686.00 |
| $4,072.00 | Johnson White | $407.00 | $3,665.00 |
| $375.00 | Livia Karsen | $37.00 | $338.00 |
| $375.00 | Stearns MacFeather | $37.00 | $338.00 |
| $375.00 | Sylvia Panteley | $37.00 | $338.00 |
| $3,876.00 | Michael O'Leary | $387.00 | $3,489.00 |
| $3,876.00 | Stearns MacFeather | $387.00 | $3,489.00 |
| $3,336.00 | Charlene Locksley | $333.00 | $3,003.00 |
| $22,246.00 | Anne Ringer | $5,339.00 | $16,907.00 |
| $22,246.00 | Michel DeFrance | $5,339.00 | $16,907.00 |
| $2,045.00 | Albert Ringer | $245.00 | $1,800.00 |
| $2,045.00 | Anne Ringer | $245.00 | $1,800.00 |
| $2,032.00 | Innes del Castillo | $243.00 | $1,789.00 |
| $18,722.00 | Marjorie Green | $4,493.00 | $14,229.00 |
| $15,096.00 | Reginald Blotchet-Halls | $2,113.00 | $12,983.00 |
| $111.00 | Albert Ringer | $11.00 | $100.00 |
| NULL | Charlene Locksley | NULL | NULL |

## NON-EQUI JOINs for Data Analytics

We can use not equal operators in JOIN predicates as demonstrated in the next query. The second predicate in the JOIN is less than JOIN.

```
USE AdventureWorks2012;
GO
-- List of "red" products sold at a discount
SELECT DISTINCT        p.ProductNumber,
                       p.Name                              AS ProductName,
                       FORMAT(p.ListPrice,'c','en-US')     AS ListPrice,
                       FORMAT(sod.UnitPrice,'c','en-US')   AS SellPrice
FROM Sales.SalesOrderDetail AS sod
   INNER JOIN Production.Product AS p
        ON sod.ProductID = p.ProductID
        AND sod.UnitPrice < p.ListPrice
WHERE Color = 'Red'
ORDER BY p.ProductNumber;
--(86 row(s) affected) - Partial results.
```

| ProductNumber | ProductName | ListPrice | SellPrice |
|---|---|---|---|
| BK-R50R-44 | Road-650 Red, 44 | $782.99 | $234.90 |
| BK-R50R-44 | Road-650 Red, 44 | $782.99 | $419.46 |
| BK-R50R-44 | Road-650 Red, 44 | $782.99 | $430.64 |
| BK-R50R-44 | Road-650 Red, 44 | $782.99 | $454.13 |
| BK-R50R-44 | Road-650 Red, 44 | $782.99 | $469.79 |
| BK-R50R-44 | Road-650 Red, 44 | $782.99 | $563.75 |
| BK-R50R-44 | Road-650 Red, 44 | $782.99 | $699.10 |
| BK-R50R-48 | Road-650 Red, 48 | $782.99 | $419.46 |
| BK-R50R-48 | Road-650 Red, 48 | $782.99 | $430.64 |
| BK-R50R-48 | Road-650 Red, 48 | $782.99 | $454.13 |
| BK-R50R-48 | Road-650 Red, 48 | $782.99 | $469.79 |
| BK-R50R-48 | Road-650 Red, 48 | $782.99 | $563.75 |

To resolve the duplicate issue which makes DISTINCT usage necessary, we have to include the SalesOrderID column.

```
SELECT                    p.ProductNumber,
                          p.Name                              AS ProductName,
                          FORMAT(p.ListPrice,'c','en-US')     AS ListPrice,
                          FORMAT(sod.UnitPrice,'c','en-US')   AS SellPrice,
                          sod.SalesOrderID
FROM Sales.SalesOrderDetail AS sod
   INNER JOIN Production.Product AS p
         ON sod.ProductID = p.ProductID
         AND sod.UnitPrice < p.ListPrice
WHERE Color = 'Red'   ORDER BY p.ProductNumber;
-- (8408 row(s) affected)
```

## Interchangeability of ON & WHERE Predicates in INNER JOINs

We can freely place the predicates to either the ON clause or the WHERE clause in an INNER JOIN. This is not true for OUTER JOINs such as LEFT JOINs.

```
USE AdventureWorks2012;
-- List of "blue" products sold at a discount
SELECT DISTINCT  p.ProductNumber, p.Name              AS ProductName,
                 FORMAT(p.ListPrice,'c','en-US')       AS ListPrice,
                 FORMAT(sod.UnitPrice,'c','en-US')     AS SellPrice
FROM Sales.SalesOrderDetail AS sod
  INNER JOIN Production.Product AS p
      ON sod.ProductID = p.ProductID
      AND sod.UnitPrice < p.ListPrice
WHERE Color = 'Blue'  ORDER BY p.ProductNumber;
--(57 row(s) affected)


SELECT DISTINCT  p.ProductNumber, p.Name              AS ProductName,
                 FORMAT(p.ListPrice,'c','en-US')       AS ListPrice,
                 FORMAT(sod.UnitPrice,'c','en-US')     AS SellPrice
FROM Sales.SalesOrderDetail AS sod
  INNER JOIN Production.Product AS p
      ON sod.ProductID = p.ProductID
      AND sod.UnitPrice < p.ListPrice
      AND Color = 'Blue'
ORDER BY p.ProductNumber;
--(57 row(s) affected)


SELECT DISTINCT  p.ProductNumber, p.Name              AS ProductName,
                 FORMAT(p.ListPrice,'c','en-US')       AS ListPrice,
                 FORMAT(sod.UnitPrice,'c','en-US')     AS SellPrice
FROM Sales.SalesOrderDetail AS sod
  INNER JOIN Production.Product AS p
  ON sod.ProductID = p.ProductID
WHERE sod.UnitPrice < p.ListPrice   AND Color = 'Blue'  ORDER BY p.ProductNumber;
--(57 row(s) affected)


-- Old-style INNER JOIN with table list and WHERE clause
SELECT DISTINCT  p.ProductNumber, p.Name              AS ProductName,
                 FORMAT(p.ListPrice,'c','en-US')       AS ListPrice,
                 FORMAT(sod.UnitPrice,'c','en-US')     AS SellPrice
FROM Sales.SalesOrderDetail AS sod,  Production.Product AS p
WHERE sod.ProductID = p.ProductID
      AND sod.UnitPrice < p.ListPrice
      AND Color = 'Blue'
ORDER BY p.ProductNumber;       --(57 row(s) affected)
```

**CHAPTER 11:  JOINing Tables with INNER & OUTER JOINs**

# SELF-JOIN for Analytics Within a Table

When a table is JOINed to itself, it is a called a self-join. The purpose of such a JOIN is to examine data relations within the table. The Production.Product table is self-joined to itself on the ProductSubcategoryID FOREIGN KEY(not on a PRIMARY KEY), a many-to-many JOIN.  Subsequently, we made the query "friendlier" by using subcategory names as opposed to ID-s.

```
SELECT DISTINCT  P1.ProductSubcategoryID,
                 P1.ListPrice                    AS ListPrice1,
                 P2.ListPrice                    AS ListPrice2
FROM   Production.Product P1
 INNER JOIN Production.Product P2
  ON P1.ProductSubcategoryID = P2.ProductSubcategoryID
  AND P1.ListPrice < P2.ListPrice
  AND P1.ListPrice < $15
  AND P2.ListPrice < $15;
```

| ProductSubcategoryID | ListPrice1 | ListPrice2 |
|---|---|---|
| 23 | 8.99 | 9.50 |
| 28 | 4.99 | 8.99 |
| 28 | 4.99 | 9.99 |
| 28 | 8.99 | 9.99 |
| 37 | 2.29 | 3.99 |
| 37 | 2.29 | 4.99 |
| 37 | 3.99 | 4.99 |

```
SELECT DISTINCT  PS.Name AS Subcategory,
                 P1.ListPrice     AS ListPrice1,
                 P2.ListPrice     AS ListPrice2
FROM   Production.ProductSubcategory PS
    INNER JOIN Production.Product P1
        ON PS.ProductSubcategoryID = P1.ProductSubcategoryID
    INNER JOIN Production.Product P2
        ON P1.ProductSubcategoryID = P2.ProductSubcategoryID
        AND P1.ListPrice < P2.ListPrice                    -- To prevent duplicate processing
        AND P1.ListPrice < $15
        AND P2.ListPrice < $15;
```

| Subcategory | ListPrice1 | ListPrice2 |
|---|---|---|
| Bottles and Cages | 4.99 | 8.99 |
| Bottles and Cages | 4.99 | 9.99 |
| Bottles and Cages | 8.99 | 9.99 |
| Socks | 8.99 | 9.50 |
| Tires and Tubes | 2.29 | 3.99 |
| Tires and Tubes | 2.29 | 4.99 |
| Tires and Tubes | 3.99 | 4.99 |

## T-SQL SELF-JOIN Query Lists The Competing Suppliers For Each Product Purchased From Vendor

Since the ProductID in the ProductVendor table is part of a composite PRIMARY KEY,  we can conclude that it is a many-to-many JOIN.

```
SELECT DISTINCT
            Vendor = V.[Name],
            P1.BusinessEntityID,
            Product = P.[Name],
            P1.ProductID
FROM   Production.Product P
    INNER JOIN Purchasing.ProductVendor P1
        ON P.ProductID = P1.ProductID
    INNER JOIN Purchasing.Vendor V
        ON P1.BusinessEntityID = V.BusinessEntityID
    INNER JOIN Purchasing.ProductVendor P2
        ON P1.ProductID = P2.ProductID
WHERE  P1.BusinessEntityID <> P2.BusinessEntityID
ORDER  BY Product, Vendor
-- (347 row(s) affected) - Partial results.
```

| Vendor | BusinessEntityID | Product | ProductID |
|---|---|---|---|
| Beaumont Bikes | 1602 | Chainring | 322 |
| Bike Satellite Inc. | 1604 | Chainring | 322 |
| Training Systems | 1514 | Chainring | 322 |
| Beaumont Bikes | 1602 | Chainring Bolts | 320 |
| Bike Satellite Inc. | 1604 | Chainring Bolts | 320 |
| Training Systems | 1514 | Chainring Bolts | 320 |
| Beaumont Bikes | 1602 | Chainring Nut | 321 |
| Bike Satellite Inc. | 1604 | Chainring Nut | 321 |
| Training Systems | 1514 | Chainring Nut | 321 |
| Aurora Bike Center | 1616 | External Lock Washer 1 | 409 |
| Expert Bike Co | 1672 | External Lock Washer 1 | 409 |
| Pro Sport Industries | 1686 | External Lock Washer 1 | 409 |
| Aurora Bike Center | 1616 | External Lock Washer 2 | 411 |
| Pro Sport Industries | 1686 | External Lock Washer 2 | 411 |
| Aurora Bike Center | 1616 | External Lock Washer 3 | 403 |
| Expert Bike Co | 1672 | External Lock Washer 3 | 403 |
| Pro Sport Industries | 1686 | External Lock Washer 3 | 403 |
| Aurora Bike Center | 1616 | External Lock Washer 4 | 404 |
| Expert Bike Co | 1672 | External Lock Washer 4 | 404 |
| Pro Sport Industries | 1686 | External Lock Washer 4 | 404 |
| Aurora Bike Center | 1616 | External Lock Washer 5 | 406 |
| Expert Bike Co | 1672 | External Lock Washer 5 | 406 |
| Pro Sport Industries | 1686 | External Lock Washer 5 | 406 |
| Aurora Bike Center | 1616 | External Lock Washer 6 | 408 |
| Expert Bike Co | 1672 | External Lock Washer 6 | 408 |

## Applying SELF-JOIN for Numbering Result Lines

T-SQL script to demonstrate how SELF-JOIN can be used for numbering lines in query results. Note that in these days we would use **ROW_NUMBER()** function which has been introduced with SQL Server 2005.

```
USE Northwind ;
GO


SELECT   OD.OrderID,
                SeqNo                                   AS LineItem,
                OD.ProductID,
                FORMAT(UnitPrice,'c','en-US')           AS UnitPrice,
                Quantity,
                FORMAT(Discount, 'p')                   AS Discount
FROM    [Order Details] OD
  INNER JOIN (SELECT   count(* ) AS SeqNo,
                a.OrderID,
                a.ProductID
        FROM    [Order Details] A
              INNER JOIN [Order Details] B
              ON A.ProductID >= B.ProductID              -- Prevent duplicates
              AND A.OrderID = B.OrderID
        GROUP BY A.OrderID,   A.ProductID) a
      ON OD.OrderID = a.OrderID
      AND OD.ProductID = a.ProductID
WHERE   OD.OrderID < 10400
ORDER BY        OD.OrderID,
                LineItem
-- (405 row(s) affected) - Partial results.
```

| Vendor | AddressLine1 | AddressLine2 | City | State | Country |
|---|---|---|---|---|---|
| A. Datum Corporation | 2596 Big Canyon Road | | New York | New York | United States |
| Advanced Bicycles | 7995 Edwards Ave. | | Lynnwood | Washington | United States |
| Allenson Cycles | 4659 Montoya | | Altadena | California | United States |
| American Bicycles and Wheels | 1667 Warren Street | | West Covina | California | United States |
| American Bikes | 7179 Montana | | Torrance | California | United States |
| Anderson's Custom Bikes | 9 Guadalupe Dr. | | Burbank | California | United States |
| Aurora Bike Center | 65 Park Glen Court | | Port Orchard | Washington | United States |
| Australia Bike Retailer | 28 San Marino Ct. | | Bellingham | Washington | United States |
| Beaumont Bikes | 2472 Alexander Place | | West Covina | Idaho | United States |
| Bergeron Off-Roads | 9830 May Way | | Mill Valley | Montana | United States |
| Bicycle Specialists | 1286 Cincerto Circle | | Lake Oswego | Oregon | United States |
| Bike Satellite Inc. | 2141 Delaware Ct. | | Downey | Tennessee | United States |
| Bloomington Multisport | 218 Fall Creek Road | | West Covina | California | United States |
| Burnett Road Warriors | 5807 Churchill Dr. | | Corvallis | Oregon | United States |
| Business Equipment Center | 6061 St. Paul Way | | Everett | Montana | United States |
| Capital Road Cycles | 628 Muir Road | | Los Angeles | California | United States |
| Carlson Specialties | 2313 B Southampton Rd | | Missoula | Montana | United States |
| Chicago City Saddles | 3 Gehringer Drive | | Daly City | California | United States |
| Chicago Rent-All | 15 Pear Dr. | | Newport Beach | California | United States |
| Circuit Cycles | 1 Mt. Dell Drive | | Portland | Oregon | United States |

# INNER JOIN with 5 Tables

It takes accessing five tables to get the vendor name & address information in AdventureWorks. In fact this is the main complaint against 3NF relational database design: too many JOINs required to extract data. True, but the benefits of 3NF design are overwhelming. A way to overcome the "too many JOINs" issue is creating views which are pre-canned SELECT queries.

```
USE AdventureWorks;
GO

SELECT V.Name               AS Vendor,
    A.AddressLine1,
    isnull(A.AddressLine2, '')      AS AddressLine2,
    A.City,
    SP.Name                 AS State,
    CR.Name             AS Country
FROM   Purchasing.Vendor AS V
    INNER JOIN Purchasing.VendorAddress AS VA
        ON VA.VendorID = V.VendorID
    INNER JOIN Person.Address AS A
        ON A.AddressID = VA.AddressID
    INNER JOIN Person.StateProvince AS SP
        ON SP.StateProvinceID = A.StateProvinceID
    INNER JOIN Person.CountryRegion AS CR
        ON CR.CountryRegionCode = SP.CountryRegionCode
ORDER  BY Vendor;
GO
-- (104 row(s) affected) - Partial results.
```

| Vendor | AddressLine1 | AddressLine2 | City | State | Country |
|---|---|---|---|---|---|
| A. Datum Corporation | 2596 Big Canyon Road | | New York | New York | United States |
| Advanced Bicycles | 7995 Edwards Ave. | | Lynnwood | Washington | United States |
| Allenson Cycles | 4659 Montoya | | Altadena | California | United States |
| American Bicycles and Wheels | 1667 Warren Street | | West Covina | California | United States |
| American Bikes | 7179 Montana | | Torrance | California | United States |
| Anderson's Custom Bikes | 9 Guadalupe Dr. | | Burbank | California | United States |
| Aurora Bike Center | 65 Park Glen Court | | Port Orchard | Washington | United States |
| Australia Bike Retailer | 28 San Marino Ct. | | Bellingham | Washington | United States |
| Beaumont Bikes | 2472 Alexander Place | | West Covina | Idaho | United States |
| Bergeron Off-Roads | 9830 May Way | | Mill Valley | Montana | United States |
| Bicycle Specialists | 1286 Cincerto Circle | | Lake Oswego | Oregon | United States |
| Bike Satellite Inc. | 2141 Delaware Ct. | | Downey | Tennessee | United States |

# Creating View as Workaround for "Too Many JOINs"

It is so simple to create a view, that sinful if not done for queries which are used again and again.

```
-- No implicit ORDER BY can be included in a view - no trick around it either
CREATE VIEW vVendorAddress  AS
SELECT V.Name                    AS Vendor,
    A.AddressLine1,
    isnull(A.AddressLine2, '')        AS AddressLine2,
    A.City,
    SP.Name                    AS State,
    CR.Name            AS Country
FROM   Purchasing.Vendor AS V
    INNER JOIN Purchasing.VendorAddress AS VA        ON VA.VendorID = V.VendorID
    INNER JOIN Person.Address AS A            ON A.AddressID = VA.AddressID
    INNER JOIN Person.StateProvince AS SP        ON SP.StateProvinceID = A.StateProvinceID
    INNER JOIN Person.CountryRegion AS CR        ON CR.CountryRegionCode =
SP.CountryRegionCode
ORDER  BY Vendor;
GO
/* Msg 1033, Level 15, State 1, Procedure vVendorAddress, Line 18
The ORDER BY clause is invalid in views, inline functions, derived tables, subqueries, and common table
expressions, unless TOP, OFFSET or FOR XML is also specified.  */
```

```
CREATE VIEW vVendorAddress  AS
SELECT V.Name                    AS Vendor,
    A.AddressLine1,
    isnull(A.AddressLine2, '')        AS AddressLine2,
    A.City,
    SP.Name                    AS State,
    CR.Name            AS Country
FROM   Purchasing.Vendor AS V
    INNER JOIN Purchasing.VendorAddress AS VA        ON VA.VendorID = V.VendorID
    INNER JOIN Person.Address AS A            ON A.AddressID = VA.AddressID
    INNER JOIN Person.StateProvince AS SP        ON SP.StateProvinceID = A.StateProvinceID
    INNER JOIN Person.CountryRegion AS CR        ON CR.CountryRegionCode =
SP.CountryRegionCode
GO
```

```
SELECT TOP 5 * FROM vVendorAddress ORDER BY Vendor;
```

| Vendor | AddressLine1 | AddressLine2 | City | State | Country |
|---|---|---|---|---|---|
| A. Datum Corporation | 2596 Big Canyon Road | | New York | New York | United States |
| Advanced Bicycles | 7995 Edwards Ave. | | Lynnwood | Washington | United States |
| Allenson Cycles | 4659 Montoya | | Altadena | California | United States |
| American Bicycles and Wheels | 1667 Warren Street | | West Covina | California | United States |
| American Bikes | 7179 Montana | | Torrance | California | United States |

**CHAPTER 11:  JOINing Tables with INNER & OUTER JOINs**

## Non-Key INNER JOIN for Analytics

So far we have seen INNER JOINs based on FOREIGN KEY to PRIMARY equality relationships. The next
INNER JOIN is based on the equality of the first 5 letters of last names.  It is also a SELF-JOIN. In addition to
the last name part equality, two more conditions are reducing the result set. The < condition is intended
to reduce duplicates and the first letter of last name is 'S' limits the query results further.  This is a many-
to-many JOIN.

```
USE AdventureWorks2012;

SELECT  DISTINCT
    CONCAT( A.FirstName, space(1), A.LastName)      AS Person,
    CONCAT( B.FirstName, space(1), B.LastName)      AS LastNameNeighbor
FROM   Person.Person A
    INNER JOIN  Person.Person B
      ON LEFT(A.LastName, 5) = LEFT(B.LastName, 5)
        AND A.LastName < B.LastName
        AND LEFT(A.LastName, 1) = 'S'
ORDER  BY        Person,
                 LastNameNeighbor;
-- (169 row(s) affected) - Partial results.
```

| Person | LastNameNeighbor |
| --- | --- |
| Abigail Smith | Lorrin Smith-Bates |
| Adriana Smith | Lorrin Smith-Bates |
| Alexander Smith | Lorrin Smith-Bates |
| Alexandra Smith | Lorrin Smith-Bates |
| Alexis Smith | Lorrin Smith-Bates |
| Allen Smith | Lorrin Smith-Bates |
| Alyssa Smith | Lorrin Smith-Bates |
| Andre Smith | Lorrin Smith-Bates |
| Andrew Smith | Lorrin Smith-Bates |
| Arthur Smith | Lorrin Smith-Bates |
| Ashley Smith | Lorrin Smith-Bates |
| Austin Smith | Lorrin Smith-Bates |
| Barry Srini | Sethu Srinivasan |
| Ben Smith | Lorrin Smith-Bates |
| Benjamin Smith | Lorrin Smith-Bates |
| Beth Srini | Sethu Srinivasan |
| Brandon Smith | Lorrin Smith-Bates |
| Brandy Srini | Sethu Srinivasan |
| Brett Srini | Sethu Srinivasan |
| Brianna Smith | Lorrin Smith-Bates |

## JOINing Tables without Relationship for Combinatorics

While it is not commonly done, SQL Server will execute such a JOIN as demonstrated by the next T-SQL query. Note this is only a demo, there is no business meaning to it unless the combinatorial results are useful for some application.

```
USE Northwind;
-- Cross database JOIN query
SELECT   P.ProductID,
         P.ProductName            AS NorthwindProduct,
         PP.Name                  AS AWProduct
FROM dbo.Products P
         INNER JOIN AdventureWorks2008.Production.Product PP      ON P.ProductID = PP.ProductID
ORDER BY P.ProductID;
```

| ProductID | NorthwindProduct | AWProduct |
|---|---|---|
| 1 | Chai | Adjustable Race |
| 2 | Chang | Bearing Ball |
| 3 | Aniseed Syrup | BB Ball Bearing |
| 4 | Chef Anton's Cajun Seasoning | Headset Ball Bearings |

## Cartesian Product

When all rows in one table combined with all rows of another table it is called a Cartesian product. The cardinality of such a JOIN is (Table 1 Rows) x (Table 2 Rows).

```
-- Old-fashioned no JOIN predicate 2-table query - Cardinality 4x4 = 16
SELECT Category1 = A.Name, Category2 = B.Name
FROM Production.ProductCategory A, Production.ProductCategory B ORDER BY Category1, Category2;
```

```
-- Equivalent CROSS JOIN
SELECT Category1 = A.Name, Category2 = B.Name
FROM Production.ProductCategory A  CROSS JOIN Production.ProductCategory B
ORDER BY Category1, Category2;
```

| Category1 | Category2 |
|---|---|
| Accessories | Accessories |
| Accessories | Bikes |
| Accessories | Clothing |
| Accessories | Components |
| Bikes | Accessories |
| Bikes | Bikes |
| Bikes | Clothing |
| Bikes | Components |
| Clothing | Accessories |
| Clothing | Bikes |
| Clothing | Clothing |
| Clothing | Components |
| Components | Accessories |
| Components | Bikes |
| Components | Clothing |
| Components | Components |

**CHAPTER 11: JOINing Tables with INNER & OUTER JOINs**

# SQL OUTER JOIN for Inclusion of Unmatched Rows

We have seen that INNER JOINs return rows only when there is at least one row from both tables that satisfies the join condition or conditions such as FOREIGN KEY matching the referenced PRIMARY KEY. Inner join queries do not return the rows that do not meet the ON condition  with a row from the other table.

OUTER JOINs, however, return all rows from  one  or both  tables in the JOIN.  All rows are returned from the left table in a LEFT OUTER JOIN (including non-matching rows), and all rows are returned from the right table  in a RIGHT OUTER JOIN.  All rows from both tables are returned in a FULL OUTER JOIN.  LEFT OUTER JOIN is totally equivalent to RIGHT OUTER JOIN.  LEFT OUTER JOIN is mostly used  by programmers in countries where the writing is left to right. **RIGHT OUTER JOIN is typically used by developers in countries where the writing is right to left**.  **The non-matching rows in an OUTER JOIN are returned with NULL value fields**, therefore, they can be distinquished from the matching rows with a null test.

The following are synonyms:

LEFT JOIN - LEFT OUTER JOIN

RIGHT JOIN - RIGHT OUTER JOIN

FULL JOIN  - FULL OUTER JOIN

The legacy syntax for outer joins *= (left join) or =* (right join) is not supported anymore.

T-SQL example script lists products (left table) even if they are not being sold such as assembly parts.

```
USE AdventureWorks2012;

SELECT        P.Name,        SOD.SalesOrderID,
              CASE    WHEN SalesOrderID is null THEN 'Non-matching'
                      ELSE 'Matching' END            AS JoinInfo
FROM   Production.Product P
    LEFT OUTER JOIN Sales.SalesOrderDetail SOD     ON P.ProductID = SOD.ProductID
ORDER  BY P.Name;
-- (121555 row(s) affected)  - Partial results.
```

| Name | SalesOrderID | JoinInfo |
|---|---|---|
| Adjustable Race | NULL | Non-matching |
| All-Purpose Bike Stand | 51179 | Matching |
| All-Purpose Bike Stand | 51488 | Matching |
| All-Purpose Bike Stand | 51520 | Matching |
| All-Purpose Bike Stand | 51558 | Matching |
| All-Purpose Bike Stand | 51882 | Matching |
| All-Purpose Bike Stand | 51903 | Matching |
| All-Purpose Bike Stand | 51970 | Matching |
| All-Purpose Bike Stand | 52010 | Matching |
| All-Purpose Bike Stand | 52032 | Matching |

# LEFT JOIN: Include Unmatched Rows from Left Table

In the LEFT JOIN example, the Vendor table is LEFT JOINed to the PurchaseOrderHeader table to find out which vendors did not supply anything. The LEFT JOIN is based on FOREIGN KEY relationship.

```
USE AdventureWorks2012;

SELECT Vendor = V.Name
FROM   Purchasing.Vendor V
     LEFT JOIN Purchasing.PurchaseOrderHeader POH
      ON V.BusinessEntityID = POH.VendorID
WHERE  POH.VendorID IS NULL              -- Test if POH columns are null
ORDER by Vendor;
-- (18 row(s) affected) - Partial results.
```

| Vendor |
| --- |
| A. Datum Corporation |
| Cycling Master |
| Electronic Bike Co. |
| GMA Ski & Bike |
| Holiday Skate & Cycle |
| Illinois Trek & Clothing |

T-SQL query to check which pedal  products for sale were reviewed and which ones not.

```
SELECT   p.Name          AS ProductName,
         ProductNumber,
         pr.ProductReviewID,
         pr.ReviewerName,
         pr.Rating
FROM Production.Product p
   LEFT JOIN Production.ProductReview pr
     ON p.ProductID = pr.ProductID
WHERE p.ProductSubcategoryID is not null   AND p.Name like '%pedal%'  ORDER BY ProductNumber;
-- (8 row(s) affected)
```

| ProductName | ProductNumber | ProductReviewID | ReviewerName | Rating |
| --- | --- | --- | --- | --- |
| LL Mountain Pedal | PD-M282 | NULL | NULL | NULL |
| ML Mountain Pedal | PD-M340 | NULL | NULL | NULL |
| HL Mountain Pedal | PD-M562 | 2 | David | 4 |
| HL Mountain Pedal | PD-M562 | 3 | Jill | 2 |
| LL Road Pedal | PD-R347 | NULL | NULL | NULL |
| ML Road Pedal | PD-R563 | NULL | NULL | NULL |
| HL Road Pedal | PD-R853 | NULL | NULL | NULL |
| Touring Pedal | PD-T852 | NULL | NULL | NULL |

CHAPTER II:  JOINing Tables with INNER & OUTER JOINs

## RIGHT JOIN - Same as LEFT with Tables Switched

The  RIGHT JOIN is totally equivalent, including performance, to the corresponding LEFT JOIN.

```
USE AdventureWorks2012;

SELECT Vendor = V.Name
FROM   Purchasing.PurchaseOrderHeader POH
    RIGHT JOIN Purchasing.Vendor V
      ON V.BusinessEntityID = POH.VendorID
WHERE  POH.VendorID IS NULL
ORDER by Vendor;
-- (18 row(s) affected) - Partial results.
```

| Vendor |
| --- |
| A. Datum Corporation |
| Cycling Master |
| Electronic Bike Co. |
| GMA Ski & Bike |
| Holiday Skate & Cycle |

T-SQL RIGHT JOIN examples progress toward a query to provide users with a good report.

```
USE AdventureWorks2012;

SELECT ST.Name AS  Territory,
    SP.BusinessEntityID
FROM   Sales.SalesTerritory ST
    RIGHT OUTER JOIN Sales.SalesPerson SP
      ON ST.TerritoryID = SP.TerritoryID;
-- (17 row(s) affected)

SELECT   isnull(ST.Name, ' ')                       AS Territory,
        SP.BusinessEntityID,
        CONCAT (C.FirstName, ' ', C.LastName)       AS Name
FROM   Sales.SalesTerritory ST
    RIGHT OUTER JOIN Sales.SalesPerson SP
    ON ST.TerritoryID = SP.TerritoryID
    INNER JOIN Person.Person C
    ON SP.BusinessEntityID = C.BusinessEntityID;
-- (17 row(s) affected)
```

## Add a WHERE condition filter on Sales.SalesPerson  SalesYTD column

The NULLs indicate the no match rows in the RIGHT OUTER JOIN.

```
SELECT   ST.CountryRegionCode,
         ST.Name                                    AS Territory,
         SP.BusinessEntityID                        AS EmployeeID,
         CONCAT(C.FirstName, ' ', C.LastName )      AS Name
FROM   Sales.SalesTerritory ST
    RIGHT OUTER JOIN Sales.SalesPerson SP
    ON ST.TerritoryID = SP.TerritoryID
    INNER JOIN Person.Person C
    ON SP.BusinessEntityID = C.BusinessEntityID
WHERE SP.SalesYTD > 1000.0
ORDER BY         CountryRegionCode,
                Territory;
GO
-- (17 row(s) affected)
```

| CountryRegionCode | Territory | EmployeeID | Name |
|---|---|---|---|
| NULL | NULL | 274 | Stephen Jiang |
| NULL | NULL | 285 | Syed Abbas |
| NULL | NULL | 287 | Amy Alberts |
| AU | Australia | 286 | Lynn Tsoflias |
| CA | Canada | 278 | Garrett Vargas |
| CA | Canada | 282 | José Saraiva |
| DE | Germany | 288 | Rachel Valdez |
| FR | France | 290 | Ranjit Varkey Chudukatil |
| GB | United Kingdom | 289 | Jae Pak |
| US | Central | 277 | Jillian Carson |
| US | Northeast | 275 | Michael Blythe |
| US | Northwest | 283 | David Campbell |
| US | Northwest | 284 | Tete Mensa-Annan |
| US | Northwest | 280 | Pamela Ansman-Wolfe |
| US | Southeast | 279 | Tsvi Reiter |
| US | Southwest | 276 | Linda Mitchell |
| US | Southwest | 281 | Shu Ito |

## Cardinality of OUTER JOINs

The number of rows returned in an OUTER JOIN is equal to the matching rows plus the non-matching rows from either or both tables. **To identify the non-matching rows (the ones with the NULLs) in an outer join we have to choose a not-nullable column like the PRIMARY KEY column.**

T-SQL script demonstrates the cardinality involved with a LEFT JOIN.

```
USE AdventureWorks2012;

-- Rows in LEFT JOIN
SELECT Rows = count(*)
FROM   Production.Product P
    LEFT OUTER JOIN Sales.SalesOrderDetail SOD
        ON P.ProductID = SOD.ProductID
-- 121555

-- Rows in right table
SELECT Rows = count(*)
FROM Sales.SalesOrderDetail
-- 121317

-- Non-matching rows in left table
SELECT Rows = count(*)
FROM   Production.Product P
    LEFT OUTER JOIN Sales.SalesOrderDetail SOD
        ON P.ProductID = SOD.ProductID
WHERE SalesOrderID is NULL
-- 238

-- Right table rows + non-matching left table rows = rows returned by left join
SELECT 121317 + 238
-- 121555
```

Since the count queries are single valued, we can do the following summation.

```
SELECT (SELECT Rows = count(*)  FROM Sales.SalesOrderDetail )
+
(SELECT Rows = count(*)
FROM   Production.Product P
    LEFT OUTER JOIN Sales.SalesOrderDetail SOD
        ON P.ProductID = SOD.ProductID
WHERE SalesOrderID is NULL);
GO
-- 121555
```

**CHAPTER 11: JOINing Tables with INNER & OUTER JOINs**

# LEFT JOIN & RIGHT JOIN on the Same Table

LEFT JOIN & RIGHT JOIN can be combined on the same table to keep all rows from that table even if they don't match the other two tables. The Production.Product table has a FOREIGN KEY referencing the ProductSubcategory table and another FOREIGN KEY referencing the UnitMeasure table.

# FULL JOIN to Include All Unmatched Rows

The operation FULL JOIN combines LEFT JOIN and RIGHT JOIN, therefore it does not matter which is the left table or right table, it is a fully symmetrical set operation. T-SQL script demonstrates FULL OUTER JOIN.

```
USE tempdb;
-- Create tables for demo
SELECT distinct Color INTO Color
FROM AdventureWorks2012.Production.Product
WHERE Color is not null;
GO

SELECT ID=IDENTITY(int, 1, 1), * INTO NormalColor
FROM Color;
SELECT ID=IDENTITY(int, 1, 1), Color=CONCAT('Light', Color)  INTO LightColor
FROM Color;

DELETE NormalColor WHERE Color = 'Red';

DELETE LightColor WHERE Color = 'LightBlue';

-- Demo tables ready - full join query
SELECT   NormalColor      = n.Color,
         LightColor       = l.Color
FROM   NormalColor n      FULL OUTER JOIN LightColor l     ON n.ID = l.ID
ORDER BY NormalColor;
```

| NormalColor | LightColor |
|---|---|
| NULL | LightRed |
| Black | LightBlack |
| Blue | NULL |
| Grey | LightGrey |
| Multi | LightMulti |
| Silver | LightSilver |
| Silver/Black | LightSilver/Black |
| White | LightWhite |
| Yellow | LightYellow |

```
DROP TABLE  tempdb.dbo.Color;  DROP TABLE tempdb.dbo.NormalColor;
DROP TABLE tempdb.dbo.LightColor;
GO
```

**CHAPTER 11:  JOINing Tables with INNER & OUTER JOINs**

# CROSS JOIN for Cartesian Product

A CROSS JOIN with no connecting columns for joining produces a Cartesian product: combines all rows of the left table with all rows of the right tables. If the left table has x rows and the right table y rows, the CROSS JOIN is going to have x*y rows. That is called Cartesian explosion as it happens sometimes unintentionally in database development. In fact, a huge CROSS JOIN can bring SQL Server "to its knees", overwhelming CPU and disk resources. On the same note, no matter how powerful is the hardware platform, a bad runaway query can make SQL Server unresponsive to normal queries from other connections.  T-SQL script to demonstrate CROSS JOIN.

```
USE AdventureWorks2012;

-- Cardinality of CROSS JOIN
SELECT count(*) from HumanResources.Employee;          -- 290
SELECT count(*) from HumanResources.Department;         -- 16
SELECT 16 * 290;                                        -- 4640


SELECT          E.BusinessEntityID          AS EMPLOYEEID,
                D.Name                       AS DEPARTMENT
FROM   HumanResources.Employee E   CROSS JOIN HumanResources.Department D
ORDER  BY       EMPLOYEEID,       DEPARTMENT;
-- (4640 row(s) affected) - Partial results.
```

| EMPLOYEEID | DEPARTMENT |
|---|---|
| 1 | Production Control |
| 1 | Purchasing |
| 1 | Quality Assurance |
| 1 | Research and Development |
| 1 | Sales |
| 1 | Shipping and Receiving |
| 1 | Tool Design |
| 2 | Document Control |
| 2 | Engineering |
| 2 | Executive |
| 2 | Facilities and Maintenance |
| 2 | Finance |
| 2 | Human Resources |
| 2 | Information Services |
| 2 | Marketing |
| 2 | Production |

# CROSS JOIN Generated Multiplication Table

A CROSS JOIN can be used to create combinatorical results. In the next example, a multiplication table is created using a CROSS JOIN which is also a SELF-JOIN. CTE stands for Common Table Expression, which can be used as a table in SELECT and other queries. The master database spt_values table is used to get a sequence of numbers. The ".." in the table reference means: use the default schema which is "dbo".

```
; WITH cteNumber                        -- cte for numbers 1 to 10
    AS (SELECT NUMBER
      FROM   master..spt_values
      WHERE  TYPE = 'P'
          AND NUMBER BETWEEN 1 AND 10)
SELECT MULTIPLICATION=CONCAT( ltrim(str(B.NUMBER)) , ' * '
          , ltrim(str(A.NUMBER)) , ' = '
          , ltrim(str(A.NUMBER * B.NUMBER)) )
FROM   cteNumber A   CROSS JOIN cteNumber B;
-- (100 row(s) affected) - Partial results.
```

| MULTIPLICATION |
| --- |
| 1 * 1 = 1 |
| 1 * 2 = 2 |
| 1 * 3 = 3 |
| 1 * 4 = 4 |
| 1 * 5 = 5 |
| 1 * 6 = 6 |
| 1 * 7 = 7 |
| 1 * 8 = 8 |
| 1 * 9 = 9 |
| 1 * 10 = 10 |
| 2 * 1 = 2 |
| 2 * 2 = 4 |
| 2 * 3 = 6 |
| 2 * 4 = 8 |
| 2 * 5 = 10 |
| 2 * 6 = 12 |
| 2 * 7 = 14 |
| 2 * 8 = 16 |
| 2 * 9 = 18 |
| 2 * 10 = 20 |
| 3 * 1 = 3 |
| 3 * 2 = 6 |
| 3 * 3 = 9 |
| 3 * 4 = 12 |
| 3 * 5 = 15 |

# INNER JOIN with 7 Tables

 T-SQL query lists AdventureWorks Cycles retail (web) customers with  total purchase amount and order dates. The name & address displays multiple times if a customer did multiple purchases. Generally, that is undesirable, and requires end-user report design considerations how to resolve it. The sorting uses Sales.SalesOrderHeader OrderDate which is datetime data type, instead of the mdy format string report date. mdy string format dates do not sort in chronological order.

```
USE AdventureWorks;
GO


SELECT CONCAT(C.LastName, ', ', C.FirstName)          AS CustomerName,
        A.City,
        SP.Name                                       AS State,
        CR.Name                                       AS Country,
        A.PostalCode,
        FORMAT(SOH.TotalDue, 'c','en-US')             AS SalesAmount,
        FORMAT(SOH.OrderDate,'d')                     AS OrderDate
FROM Person.Contact AS C
   INNER JOIN Sales.Individual AS I
         ON C.ContactID = I.ContactID
   INNER JOIN Sales.CustomerAddress AS CA
         ON CA.CustomerID = I.CustomerID
   INNER JOIN Person.Address AS A
         ON A.AddressID = CA.AddressID
   INNER JOIN Person.StateProvince SP
         ON SP.StateProvinceID = A.StateProvinceID
   INNER JOIN Person.CountryRegion CR
         ON CR.CountryRegionCode = SP.CountryRegionCode
   INNER JOIN Sales.SalesOrderHeader SOH
         ON C.ContactID = SOH.CustomerID
ORDER BY CustomerName, soh.OrderDate ;
-- (16493 row(s) affected)  - Partial results.
```

| CustomerName | City | State | Country | PostalCode | SalesAmount | OrderDate |
|---|---|---|---|---|---|---|
| Adams, Aaron | Downey | California | United States | 90241 | $734.70 | 3/4/2004 |
| Adams, Adam | Newport Beach | California | United States | 92625 | $2,566.12 | 4/16/2004 |
| Adams, Alex | Lake Oswego | Oregon | United States | 97034 | $2,410.63 | 3/18/2003 |
| Adams, Alex | Lake Oswego | Oregon | United States | 97034 | $1,293.38 | 12/9/2003 |
| Adams, Alex | Lake Oswego | Oregon | United States | 97034 | $2,643.12 | 2/1/2004 |
| Adams, Angel | Burlingame | California | United States | 94010 | $865.20 | 5/24/2003 |
| Adams, Angel | Burlingame | California | United States | 94010 | $2,597.81 | 3/1/2004 |
| Adams, Carlos | Langford | British Columbia | Canada | V9 | $44.18 | 6/28/2004 |
| Adams, Connor | Westminster | British Columbia | Canada | V3L 1H4 | $183.74 | 4/14/2004 |
| Adams, Elijah | Seattle | Washington | United States | 98104 | $8.04 | 11/2/2003 |

# INNER JOIN with GROUP BY Subquery

We have to make the GROUP BY subquery into a derived table first. Subsequently, we can apply it just like any other table in a query.

```
USE AdventureWorks2012;
GO

SELECT  Subcategory = Name,
        Color,
        ColorCount,
        AvgListPrice
FROM   (
        SELECT ProductSubcategoryID,                    -- grouping column
        Color = COALESCE(Color, 'N/A'),                 -- grouping column with transformation
        ColorCount = COUNT(*),                          -- aggregate function
        AvgListPrice = AVG(COALESCE(ListPrice, 0.0))    -- aggregate function
        FROM   AdventureWorks2008.Production.Product
        GROUP  BY       ProductSubcategoryID,
                        Color) x                        -- derived table (subquery)
    INNER JOIN Production.ProductSubcategory psc
        ON psc.ProductSubcategoryID = x.ProductSubcategoryID
ORDER  BY Subcategory,
        Color;
GO
-- (48 row(s) affected) - Partial results.
```

| Subcategory | Color | ColorCount | AvgListPrice |
|-------------|-------|------------|--------------|
| Bib-Shorts | Multi | 3 | 89.990000 |
| Bike Racks | N/A | 1 | 120.000000 |
| Bike Stands | N/A | 1 | 159.000000 |
| Bottles and Cages | N/A | 3 | 7.990000 |
| Bottom Brackets | N/A | 3 | 92.240000 |
| Brakes | Silver | 2 | 106.500000 |
| Caps | Multi | 1 | 8.990000 |
| Chains | Silver | 1 | 20.240000 |
| Cleaners | N/A | 1 | 7.950000 |
| Cranksets | Black | 3 | 278.990000 |
| Derailleurs | Silver | 2 | 106.475000 |
| Fenders | N/A | 1 | 21.980000 |

# Making Queries Readable & Results Presentable

A database developer has to make a query readable for productivity gain in development and ease of maintenance. At the same time the results must be readable to the user. The next query with results demonstrates how to achieve both objectives.

```
USE AdventureWorks2012;
GO

SELECT   PC.Name                                   AS Category,
         PSC.Name                                  AS Subcategory,
         PM.Name                                   AS Model,
         P.Name                                    AS ProductName,
         FORMAT(ListPrice,'c','en-US')             AS Price
FROM Production.Product AS P
    INNER JOIN Production.ProductModel AS PM
        ON PM.ProductModelID = P.ProductModelID
    INNER JOIN Production.ProductSubcategory AS PSC
        ON PSC.ProductSubcategoryID = P.ProductSubcategoryID
    INNER JOIN Production.ProductCategory AS PC
        ON PC.ProductCategoryID = PSC.ProductCategoryID
ORDER BY Category, Subcategory, ProductName;
-- (295 row(s) affected) - Partial results.
```

The confusing 4 "Name" columns are clarified by well-chosen column aliases. The meaningful column aliases are used in the ORDER BY clause even though not required. To help the user, the list price is currency formatted.

| Category | Subcategory | Model | ProductName | Price |
|----------|-------------|-------|-------------|-------|
| Accessories | Bike Racks | Hitch Rack - 4-Bike | Hitch Rack - 4-Bike | $120.00 |
| Accessories | Bike Stands | All-Purpose Bike Stand | All-Purpose Bike Stand | $159.00 |
| Accessories | Bottles and Cages | Mountain Bottle Cage | Mountain Bottle Cage | $9.99 |
| Accessories | Bottles and Cages | Road Bottle Cage | Road Bottle Cage | $8.99 |
| Accessories | Bottles and Cages | Water Bottle | Water Bottle - 30 oz. | $4.99 |
| Accessories | Cleaners | Bike Wash | Bike Wash - Dissolver | $7.95 |
| Accessories | Fenders | Fender Set - Mountain | Fender Set - Mountain | $21.98 |
| Accessories | Helmets | Sport-100 | Sport-100 Helmet, Black | $34.99 |
| Accessories | Helmets | Sport-100 | Sport-100 Helmet, Blue | $34.99 |
| Accessories | Helmets | Sport-100 | Sport-100 Helmet, Red | $34.99 |

## A 12 Tables JOIN Query

The next query JOINs 11 tables, some of the tables occur more than once in the query.

```
USE AdventureWorks;

DECLARE @Year  int,
        @Month int

SET @Year    = 2004;
SET @Month   = 1;

SELECT SOH.SalesOrderNumber              AS SON,
   SOH.PurchaseOrderNumber               AS PO,
   S.Name                                AS Store,
   CONVERT(VARCHAR, SOH.OrderDate, 110)  AS OrderDate,
   CONVERT(VARCHAR, SOH.ShipDate, 110)   AS ShipDate,
   FORMAT(TotalDue,'c','en-US')          AS [Total Due],
   CONCAT(C.FirstName,' ',C.LastName)    AS SalesStaff,
   SM.Name                               AS ShpngMethod,
   BA.AddressLine1                       AS BlngAddress1,
   Isnull(BA.AddressLine2, '')           AS BlngAddress2,
   BA.City                               AS BlngCity,
   BSP.Name                              AS BlngStateProvince,
   BA.PostalCode                         AS BlngPostalCode,
   BCR.Name                              AS BlngCountryRegion,
   SA.AddressLine1                       AS ShpngAddress1,
   Isnull(SA.AddressLine2, '')           AS ShpngAddress2,
   SA.City                               AS ShpngCity,
   SSP.Name                              AS ShpngStateProvince,
   SA.PostalCode                         AS ShpngPostalCode,
   SCR.Name                              AS ShpngCountryRegion,
   CONCAT(CC.FirstName,' ',CC.LastName)  AS CustomerContact,
   CC.Phone                              AS CustomerPhone,
   SOH.AccountNumber
FROM   Person.Address SA
    INNER JOIN Person.StateProvince SSP
        ON SA.StateProvinceID = SSP.StateProvinceID
    INNER JOIN Person.CountryRegion SCR
        ON SSP.CountryRegionCode = SCR.CountryRegionCode
    INNER JOIN Sales.SalesOrderHeader SOH
        INNER JOIN Person.Contact CC
            ON SOH.ContactID = CC.ContactID
        INNER JOIN Person.Address BA
            INNER JOIN Person.StateProvince BSP
                ON BA.StateProvinceID = BSP.StateProvinceID
            INNER JOIN Person.CountryRegion BCR
```

```
-- T-SQL query continued

                    ON BSP.CountryRegionCode =
                    BCR.CountryRegionCode
                ON SOH.BillToAddressID = BA.AddressID
            ON SA.AddressID = SOH.ShipToAddressID
        INNER JOIN Person.Contact C
            INNER JOIN HumanResources.Employee E
                ON C.ContactID = E.ContactID
            ON SOH.SalesPersonID = E.EmployeeID
        INNER JOIN Purchasing.ShipMethod SM
            ON SOH.ShipMethodID = SM.ShipMethodID
        INNER JOIN Sales.Store S
            ON SOH.CustomerID = S.CustomerID
    WHERE  SOH.OrderDate >= datefromparts(@Year, @month, 1)
        AND  SOH.OrderDate < dateadd(mm,1,datefromparts(@Year, @month, 1))
    ORDER  BY Store,  OrderDate DESC;
    -- (96 row(s) affected) - Partial results.
```

| SON | PO | Store | OrderDate | ShipDate | Total Due | SalesStaff | ShpngMethod | BlngAddress1 |
|---|---|---|---|---|---|---|---|---|
| SO61257 | PO3741176337 | Activity Center | 01-01-2004 | 01-08-2004 | $12,764.08 | Tsvi Reiter | CARGO TRANSPORT 5 | Factory Stores Of America |
| SO61256 | PO1421187796 | All Cycle Shop | 01-01-2004 | 01-08-2004 | $201.08 | Tete Mensa-Annan | CARGO TRANSPORT 5 | 25111 228th St Sw |
| SO61251 | PO6380165323 | All Seasons Sports Supply | 01-01-2004 | 01-08-2004 | $2,863.30 | Michael Blythe | CARGO TRANSPORT 5 | Ohms Road |
| SO61263 | PO5452121402 | Amalgamated Parts Shop | 01-01-2004 | 01-08-2004 | $39,103.04 | Rachel Valdez | CARGO TRANSPORT 5 | Brunnenstr 422 |
| SO61227 | PO10730172247 | Area Bike Accessories | 01-01-2004 | 01-08-2004 | $75,916.89 | Shu Ito | CARGO TRANSPORT 5 | 6900 Sisk Road |
| SO61187 | PO13978135025 | Basic Bike Company | 01-01-2004 | 01-08-2004 | $72.92 | David Campbell | CARGO TRANSPORT 5 | 15 East Main |
| SO61190 | PO12441157171 | Best Cycle Store | 01-01-2004 | 01-08-2004 | $49,337.61 | Rachel Valdez | CARGO TRANSPORT 5 | Berliner Platz 45 |
| SO61221 | PO15399128383 | Best o' Bikes | 01-01-2004 | 01-08-2004 | $5,872.73 | Michael Blythe | CARGO TRANSPORT 5 | 250880 Baur Blvd |
| SO61173 | PO522171689 | Better Bike Shop | 01-01-2004 | 01-08-2004 | $38,511.29 | Tsvi Reiter | CARGO TRANSPORT 5 | 42525 Austell Road |
| SO61254 | PO4872176154 | Bicycle Exporters | 01-01-2004 | 01-08-2004 | $10,665.06 | Rachel Valdez | CARGO TRANSPORT 5 | Hellweg 4934 |
| SO61243 | PO7859152962 | Bike Dealers Association | 01-01-2004 | 01-08-2004 | $18,976.48 | Shu Ito | CARGO TRANSPORT 5 | 9952 E. Lohman Ave. |
| SO61250 | PO4930183869 | Bikes for Kids and Adults | 01-01-2004 | 01-08-2004 | $3,852.87 | Jae Pak | CARGO TRANSPORT 5 | 9900 Ronson Drive |
| SO61209 | PO11484136165 | Casual Bicycle Store | 01-01-2004 | 01-08-2004 | $37,314.33 | Jillian Carson | CARGO TRANSPORT 5 | Westside Plaza |
| SO61204 | PO15312134209 | Citywide Service and Repair | 01-01-2004 | 01-08-2004 | $29,797.18 | Jae Pak | CARGO TRANSPORT 5 | Box 99354 300 Union Street |
| SO61192 | PO10092119585 | Classic Cycle Store | 01-01-2004 | 01-08-2004 | $3,691.57 | Jillian Carson | CARGO TRANSPORT 5 | 630 Oldgate Lane |

## Order of Tables or Predicates Does Not Matter

A frequent question: does the order of tables matter in a JOIN? Should I put BETWEEN predicate before LIKE predicate? Valid syntax variations do not matter. The database engine translates the query to an internal form prior to creating an execution plan. Thus the different variations get translated to the same internal form. The only way we have some control over the database engine if we rewrite a single statement complex query to a multi-statements script.

### *Nondeterministic CTE*

CTE is evaluated for every reference, therefore it may return different results if certain functions are used such as newid(), thus yielding a nondeterministic CTE.

```
;WITH CTE AS (SELECT Random = NEWID()),
CTE1 AS (SELECT * FROM CTE),
CTE2 AS (SELECT * FROM CTE),
CTE3 AS (SELECT * FROM CTE),
CTE4 AS (SELECT * FROM CTE),
CTE5 AS (SELECT * FROM CTE)
SELECT * FROM CTE1
UNION ALL
SELECT * FROM CTE2
UNION ALL
SELECT * FROM CTE3
UNION ALL
SELECT * FROM CTE4
UNION ALL
SELECT * FROM CTE5
UNION ALL
SELECT * FROM CTE
UNION ALL
SELECT * FROM CTE
UNION ALL
SELECT * FROM CTE;
```

```
Random
08D45FE2-52C6-4E15-83A3-0B2F27837887
D6A094E6-0C8A-43E4-B6C4-8821F6EE8E73
281A5852-3D9A-4F2A-99FA-F60EE28FD2E0
C327ED19-5C03-4D9B-A8E8-6ACABAA08F1C
80DDE508-A6AA-4F2B-AB2F-CEEF7EC5E163
5F611B03-46F4-4EED-A8E0-76020527899D
FF8DAE17-65F6-4D80-8AF5-29EBAEBD2FEB
CF342DC9-4CF9-46FD-87F0-3213106C447D
```

**CHAPTER 11: JOINing Tables with INNER & OUTER JOINs**

# The CROSS APPLY Operator

The APPLY (CROSS APPLY & OUTER APPLY) operators were introduced with SQL Server 2005. The CROSS APPLY operator merges rows from tables (or views) with rows from table-valued function, a form of JOIN.

```
USE AdventureWorks2012;
SELECT
        q.last_execution_time              AS LastRun,
        t.TEXT                             AS QueryText,
        q.sql_handle                       AS SQLHandle
FROM    sys.dm_exec_query_stats AS q                      -- system view
             CROSS APPLY
             sys.dm_exec_sql_text(q.sql_handle) AS t      -- table-valued system function
WHERE LEFT(t.TEXT,8)='SELECT *'  ORDER BY LastRun DESC;
```

| LastRun | QueryText |
|---------|-----------|
| 2016-08-01 14:46:12.537 | SELECT * FROM Sales.SalesOrderHeader |
| 2016-08-01 14:44:54.257 | SELECT * FROM Production.Product |
| 2016-08-01 13:29:25.213 | SELECT * FROM sys.dm_os_wait_stats |
| 2016-08-01 09:36:57.980 | select *  from sys.sysforeignkeys s |
| 2016-08-01 09:36:39.077 | select *  from sysforeignkeys s |

```
-- Return the top N purchase order by amount - inline table-valued function
CREATE FUNCTION dbo.ufnGetTopNPurchases(@VendorID AS INT, @N AS INT)
RETURNS TABLE  AS
RETURN
 SELECT TOP ( @N ) *   FROM Purchasing.PurchaseOrderHeader
 WHERE VendorID = @VendorID    ORDER BY TotalDue DESC;
GO
-- Command(s) completed successfully.
```

```
-- List the top 5 highest purchases from vendors
SELECT  V.VendorID,
        P.PurchaseOrderID,
        FORMAT(P.TotalDue, 'c','en-US')    AS TotalDue
FROM    Purchasing.Vendor AS V  CROSS APPLY  dbo.ufnGetTopNPurchases(V.VendorID, 5) AS P
ORDER BY  V.VendorID, TotalDue DESC
-- (395 row(s) affected) - Partial results.
```

| VendorID | PurchaseOrderID | TotalDue |
|----------|-----------------|----------|
| 74 | 325 | $1,654.75 |
| 74 | 1727 | $855.22 |
| 74 | 2517 | $855.22 |
| 74 | 3307 | $855.22 |
| 74 | 167 | $785.61 |

CHAPTER 11:  JOINing Tables with INNER & OUTER JOINs

## Using CROSS APPLY with Columns Specified Table Alias

A regular table alias would result in error in the following delimited string list query. Table alias with column(s) specifications "o(list)" works, the table alias is "o", it has one column "list".

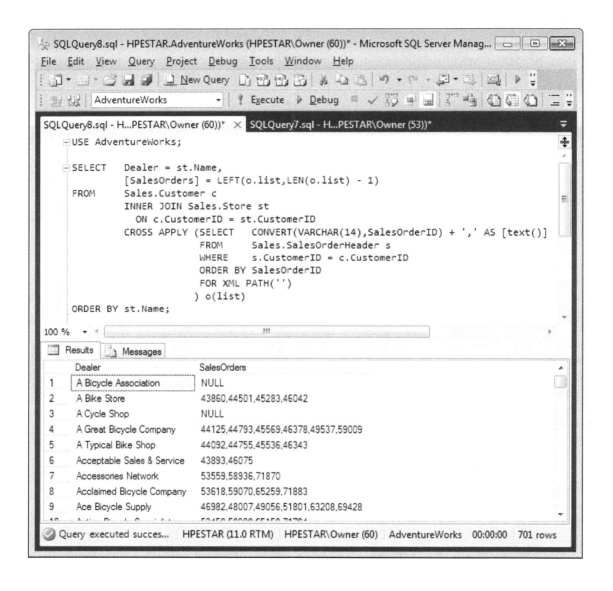

# CHAPTER 12: Basic SELECT Statement Syntax & Examples

## Simple SELECT Statement Variations

SELECT is the most famous statement in the SQL language. It is used to query tables, and generate reports for users. Although SQL Server Reporting Services and other 3rd party packages available for reporting purposes, frequently reports are generated straight from the database with SELECT queries. The next query returns all rows, all columns sorted on DepartmentID.

USE AdventureWorks2012;

SELECT * FROM   HumanResources.Department  ORDER BY DepartmentID;
-- (16 row(s) affected)

| DepartmentID | Name | GroupName | ModifiedDate |
|---|---|---|---|
| 1 | Engineering | Research and Development | 1998-06-01 00:00:00.000 |
| 2 | Tool Design | Research and Development | 1998-06-01 00:00:00.000 |
| 3 | Sales | Sales and Marketing | 1998-06-01 00:00:00.000 |
| 4 | Marketing | Sales and Marketing | 1998-06-01 00:00:00.000 |
| 5 | Purchasing | Inventory Management | 1998-06-01 00:00:00.000 |
| 6 | Research and Development | Research and Development | 1998-06-01 00:00:00.000 |
| 7 | Production | Manufacturing | 1998-06-01 00:00:00.000 |
| 8 | Production Control | Manufacturing | 1998-06-01 00:00:00.000 |
| 9 | Human Resources | Executive General and Administration | 1998-06-01 00:00:00.000 |
| 10 | Finance | Executive General and Administration | 1998-06-01 00:00:00.000 |
| 11 | Information Services | Executive General and Administration | 1998-06-01 00:00:00.000 |
| 12 | Document Control | Quality Assurance | 1998-06-01 00:00:00.000 |
| 13 | Quality Assurance | Quality Assurance | 1998-06-01 00:00:00.000 |
| 14 | Facilities and Maintenance | Executive General and Administration | 1998-06-01 00:00:00.000 |
| 15 | Shipping and Receiving | Inventory Management | 1998-06-01 00:00:00.000 |
| 16 | Executive | Executive General and Administration | 1998-06-01 00:00:00.000 |

Since the time part of ModifiedDate is not being used, and that makes business sense, we can format it just as date.

SELECT TOP (3) DepartmentID, Name, GroupName, CONVERT(DATE, ModifiedDate) AS ModifiedDate
FROM   HumanResources.Department  ORDER BY DepartmentID;
-- (16 row(s) affected)

| DepartmentID | Name | GroupName | ModifiedDate |
|---|---|---|---|
| 1 | Engineering | Research and Development | 1998-06-01 |
| 2 | Tool Design | Research and Development | 1998-06-01 |
| 3 | Sales | Sales and Marketing | 1998-06-01 |

## *SELECT query with sort on EnglishProductName in DESCending order*
**ASCending sort is the default.**

USE AdventureWorksDW2012
GO


SELECT　*
FROM　　DimProduct
ORDER BY EnglishProductName DESC
GO
-- (606 row(s) affected) - Partial results.

| EnglishProductName | SpanishProductName | FrenchProductName | StandardCost |
|---|---|---|---|
| Women's Tights, S | Mallas para mujer, P | Collants pour femmes, taille S | 30.9334 |
| Women's Tights, M | Mallas para mujer, M | Collants pour femmes, taille M | 30.9334 |
| Women's Tights, L | Mallas para mujer, G | Collants pour femmes, taille L | 30.9334 |
| Women's Mountain Shorts, S | | | 26.1763 |
| Women's Mountain Shorts, M | | | 26.1763 |
| Women's Mountain Shorts, L | | | 26.1763 |
| Water Bottle - 30 oz. | | | 1.8663 |
| Touring-Panniers, Large | Cesta de paseo, grande | Sacoches de vélo de randonnée, grande capacité | 51.5625 |
| Touring-3000 Yellow, 62 | Paseo: 3000, amarilla, 62 | Vélo de randonnée 3000 jaune, 62 | 461.4448 |
| Touring-3000 Yellow, 58 | Paseo: 3000, amarilla, 58 | Vélo de randonnée 3000 jaune, 58 | 461.4448 |


The next query sorts on the SpanishProductName column in ascending order.

SELECT　*
FROM　　DimProduct
ORDER BY SpanishProductName ASC
GO
-- (606 row(s) affected) - Partial results.

| EnglishProductName | SpanishProductName |
|---|---|
| HL Crankset | Bielas GA |
| LL Crankset | Bielas GB |
| ML Crankset | Bielas GM |
| Mountain Pump | Bomba de montaña |
| Cable Lock | Cable antirrobo |
| Chain | Cadena |
| Mountain Bike Socks, | Calcetines para bicicleta de montaña, G |

Sorting on FrenchProductName, if empty, use EnglishProductName.

SELECT　* FROM　　DimProduct ORDER BY FrenchProductName, EnglishProductName;
GO

# Using the TOP Clause in SELECT Queries

The TOP clause limits the number of rows returned as specified in the TOP expression according the sorted order if any. In the following query, the sorting is based on a major key (LastName) and a minor key (FirstName).

```
USE AdventureWorks2012
GO


SELECT   TOP 100 *
FROM     Person.Person ORDER BY LastName, FirstName
-- (100 row(s) affected) - Partial results.
```

| BusinessEntityID | PersonType | Title | FirstName | LastName | EmailPromotion |
|---|---|---|---|---|---|
| 285 | SP | Mr. | Syed | Abbas | 0 |
| 293 | SC | Ms. | Catherine | Abel | 1 |
| 295 | SC | Ms. | Kim | Abercrombie | 0 |
| 2170 | GC | NULL | Kim | Abercrombie | 2 |
| 38 | EM | NULL | Kim | Abercrombie | 2 |
| 211 | EM | NULL | Hazem | Abolrous | 0 |
| 2357 | GC | NULL | Sam | Abolrous | 1 |
| 297 | SC | Sr. | Humberto | Acevedo | 2 |
| 291 | SC | Mr. | Gustavo | Achong | 2 |
| 299 | SC | Sra. | Pilar | Ackerman | 0 |

The total population of the Person.Person table is 19,972 rows.

```
SELECT  * FROM    Person.Person ORDER BY LastName, FirstName
-- (19972 row(s) affected)
```

We can also count the rows applying the COUNT function.

```
SELECT   RowsCount = count(*)  FROM    Person.Person
-- 19972
```

When counting, it is safe to count the PRIMARY KEY (ProductID) values.

```
SELECT   RowsCount = count(ProductID)   FROM    Production.Product;
-- 504
```

```
SELECT   RowsCount = count(Color)   FROM    Production.Product;     -- 256
```

**CHAPTER 12:  Basic SELECT Statement Syntax & Examples**

## Using the WHERE Clause in SELECT Queries

The WHERE clause filters the rows to be returned according the one or more predicates. The next T-SQL scripts demonstrate simple WHERE clause predicates, including multiple WHERE conditions.

```
-- Last name starts with S
SELECT *
FROM    Person.Person
WHERE    LEFT(LastName,1) = 'S'
ORDER BY LastName;
-- (2130 row(s) affected)
```

```
-- First name is Shelly
SELECT  *
FROM    Person.Person
WHERE    FirstName = 'Shelly'
ORDER BY LastName;
-- (1 row(s) affected)
```

```
-- First name is John
SELECT  *
FROM    Person.Person
WHERE    FirstName = 'John'
ORDER BY LastName;
-- (58 row(s) affected)
```

```
-- First name John, last name starts with S - Multiple WHERE conditions
SELECT  *
FROM    Person.Person
WHERE    FirstName = 'John'
    AND LEFT(LastName,1) = 'S'
ORDER BY LastName ;
-- (2 row(s) affected)
```

```
-- Last name starts with S OR first name starts with J
SELECT  *
FROM    Person.Person
WHERE    LEFT(FirstName,1) = 'J'   OR LEFT(LastName,1) = 'S'
ORDER BY LastName;
-- (4371 row(s) affected)
```

```
-- Last name starts with S AND first name starts with J
SELECT *
FROM    Person.Person  WHERE   LEFT(FirstName,1) = 'J'   AND LEFT(LastName,1) = 'S'
ORDER BY LastName;
-- (221 row(s) affected)
```

# Using Literals in SELECT Queries

Literals or constants are used commonly in T-SQL queries, also as defaults for columns, local variables, and parameters. The format of a literal depends on the data type of the value it represents. The database engine may perform implicit conversion to match data types. Explicit conversion of literals can be achieved with the CONVERT or CAST functions. T-SQL scripts demonstrate literal use in WHERE clause predicates.

```
USE AdventureWorks2012;
-- Integer literal  in WHERE clause predicate
SELECT * FROM Production.Product
WHERE ProductID = 800;
-- (1 row(s) affected)
```

```
-- String literal in WHERE clause predicate
SELECT * FROM Production.Product WHERE Color = 'Blue';
-- (26 row(s) affected)
```

```
USE AdventureWorksDW2012;
-- UNICODE (2 bytes per character) string literal
SELECT * FROM DimProduct
WHERE SpanishProductName = N'Jersey clásico de manga corta, G';
-- (1 row(s) affected)
```

```
-- UNICODE string literal
SELECT * FROM DimProduct
WHERE FrenchProductName = N'Roue arrière de vélo de randonnée';
-- (1 row(s) affected)
```

```
USE AdventureWorks2012;
-- Money literal in WHERE clause predicate
SELECT * FROM Production.Product
WHERE ListPrice > = $2000.0;
-- (35 row(s) affected)
```

```
-- Floating point literal with implicit conversion to MONEY
SELECT * FROM Production.Product  WHERE ListPrice > = 2.000E+3;
-- (35 row(s) affected)
```

```
-- Hex (binary) literal
SELECT * FROM Production.Product  WHERE rowguid >= 0x23D89CEE9F444F3EB28963DE6BA2B737
-- (302 row(s) affected)
```

```
-- The rest of the 504 products
SELECT * FROM Production.Product  WHERE rowguid < 0x23D89CEE9F444F3EB28963DE6BA2B737
-- (202 row(s) affected)
```

**CHAPTER 12:  Basic SELECT Statement Syntax & Examples**

# Date & Time Literals in SELECT Queries

Date and time literals appear to come from an infinite pool. Every country has tens of string date & time variations. Despite the many external string representation, **date, datetime, datetime, time, smalldatetime** and other temporal data types have unique, well-defined representation within the database engine.

ymd date literal format is the cleanest. There is eternal confusion about the North American mdy string date format and the European dmy string date format. The date and time format with "T" separator (last one) is the ISO date time format literal.  ANSI Date literal - YYYYMMDD - the best choice since it work in any country.

| CONVERT or CAST Date Time Literal | Result |
|---|---|
| SELECT [Date] =    CAST('20160228' AS date) | 2016-02-28 |
| SELECT [Datetime] = CAST('20160228' AS datetime) | 2016-02-28 00:00:00.000 |
| SELECT [SmallDatetime] = CAST('20160228' AS smalldatetime) | 2016-02-28 00:00:00 |
| SELECT [Datetime] = CONVERT(datetime,'2016-02-28') | 2016-02-28 00:00:00.000 |
| SELECT [Datetime2] = CONVERT(datetime2,'2016-02-28') | 2016-02-28 00:00:00.0000000 |
| SELECT [Datetime] = CONVERT(datetime, '20160228') | 2016-02-28 00:00:00.000 |
| SELECT [Datetime2] = CONVERT(datetime2,'20160228') | 2016-02-28 00:00:00.0000000 |
| SELECT [Datetime] = CAST('Mar 15, 2016' AS datetime) | 2016-03-15 00:00:00.000 |
| SELECT [Datetime2] = CAST('Mar 15, 2016' AS datetime2) | 2016-03-15 00:00:00.0000000 |
| SELECT [Date] = CAST('Mar 15, 2016' AS date) | 2016-03-15 |
| SELECT CAST('16:40:31' AS datetime) | 1900-01-01 16:40:31.000 |
| SELECT CAST('16:40:31' AS time) | 16:40:31.0000000 |
| SELECT [Datetime] = CAST('Mar 15, 2016 12:07:34.444' AS datetime) | 2016-03-15 12:07:34.443 |
| SELECT [Datetime2] = CAST('Mar 15, 2016 12:07:34.4445555' AS datetime2) | 2016-03-15 12:07:34.4445555 |
| SELECT [Datetime] = CAST('2016-03-15T12:07:34.513' AS datetime) | 2016-03-15 12:07:34.513 |

# ymd, dmy & mdy String Date Format Literals

Date and time string literals are the least understood part of the T-SQL language by database developers. It is a constant source of confusion and frustration, in addition huge economic cost of lost programmer's productivity. ymd, dmy & mdy are the main string date formats. Some countries use ydm format. Setting dateformat overrides the implicit setting by language.

The basic principles:

> ➢ **There is only one DATETIME data type internal format**, independent where SQL Server is operated: New York, London, Amsterdam, Berlin, Moscow, Hong Kong, Singapore, Tokyo, Melbourne or Rio de Janeiro.
> ➢ There are hundreds of national string date & time formats which have nothing to do with SQL Server.
> ➢ String date must be properly converted to DATETIME format.

```
SET DATEFORMAT ymd
SELECT convert(datetime,'16/05/08')          -- 2016-05-08 00:00:00.000


-- Setting DATEFORMAT to UK-Style (European)
SET DATEFORMAT dmy
SELECT convert(datetime,'20/05/16')          -- 2016-05-20 00:00:00.000


-- Setting DATEFORMAT to US-Style
SET DATEFORMAT mdy
SELECT convert(datetime,'05/20/16')          -- 2016-05-20 00:00:00.000
SELECT convert(datetime,'05/20/2016')        -- 2016-05-20 00:00:00.000
```
Interestingly we can achieve the same implicit conversion action by setting language.

```
-- Setting DATEFORMAT ymd  via language
SET LANGUAGE Japanese;  SELECT convert(datetime,'16/05/08') ;        -- 2016-05-08
00:00:00.000


-- Setting DATEFORMAT to UK-Style (European) via language
SET LANGUAGE British;  SELECT convert(datetime,'20/05/16');          -- 2016-05-20
00:00:00.000
SELECT convert(datetime,'05/20/16');
/* Msg 242, Level 16, State 3, Line 3
The conversion of a varchar data type to a datetime data type resulted in an out-of-range value.  */


-- Setting DATEFORMAT to US-Style via language
SET LANGUAGE English;  SELECT convert(datetime,'05/20/16');        -- 2016-05-20 00:00:00.000
SELECT convert(datetime,'05/20/2016');          -- 2016-05-20 00:00:00.000
SELECT convert(datetime,'20/05/2016');  /* Msg 242, Level 16, State 3, Line 4
The conversion of a varchar data type to a datetime data type resulted in an out-of-range value.  */
```

**CHAPTER 12:  Basic SELECT Statement Syntax & Examples**

# Setting DATEFIRST with Literal

DATEFIRST indicates the first day of the week which may vary by country, culture or business. The next T-SQL script demonstrates how it can be set by integer literal 1-7. It overrides the implicit setting by language. @@DATEFIRST is a system (SQL Server database engine) variable.

```
SET DATEFIRST 7 -- Sunday as first day of the week
SELECT DATEPART(dw, '20160315');                    -- 3
SELECT DATENAME(dw, '20160315');                    -- Tuesday
SELECT @@DATEFIRST                                  -- 7


SET DATEFIRST 1 -- Monday as first day of the week
SELECT DATEPART(dw, '20160315');                    -- 2
SELECT DATENAME(dw, '20160315');                    -- Tuesday
SELECT @@DATEFIRST                                  -- 1
```

# Language Setting - SET LANGUAGE

DATEFIRST is tied to the language setting, just the like the date format (ymd, dmy, or mdy).

```
SET LANGUAGE us_english
SELECT DATEPART(dw, '20160315');                    -- 3
SELECT DATENAME(dw, '20160315');                    -- Tuesday
SELECT @@DATEFIRST                                  -- 7


SET LANGUAGE german
SELECT DATEPART(dw, '20160315');                    -- 2
SELECT DATENAME(dw, '20160315');                    -- Dienstag
SELECT @@DATEFIRST                                  -- 1


SET LANGUAGE british
SELECT DATEPART(dw, '20160315');                    -- 2
SELECT DATENAME(dw, '20160315');                    -- Tuesday
SELECT @@DATEFIRST                                  -- 1


SET LANGUAGE hungarian
SELECT DATEPART(dw, '20160315');                    -- 2
SELECT DATENAME(dw, '20160315');                    -- kedd
SELECT @@DATEFIRST                                  -- 1


SET LANGUAGE spanish
SELECT DATEPART(dw, '20160315');                    -- 2
SELECT DATENAME(dw, '20160315');                    -- Martes
SELECT @@DATEFIRST                                  -- 1
```

# The sys.syslanguages System View

The syslanguages table contains not only language related information, but date related settings as well.

```
SELECT  langid,
        dateformat,
        datefirst,
        name                            AS native_language,
        alias                           AS english,
        left(shortmonths, 15)           AS shortmonths,
         left(days,15)                  AS days
FROM AdventureWorks2012.sys.syslanguages
ORDER BY langid;
-- (34 row(s) affected)  -  Partial results.
```

| langid | dateformat | datefirst | native_language | english | shortmonths | days |
|--------|-----------|-----------|-----------------|---------|-------------|------|
| 0 | mdy | 7 | us_english | English | Jan,Feb,Mar,Apr | Monday,Tuesday, |
| 1 | dmy | 1 | Deutsch | German | Jan,Feb,Mär,Apr | Montag,Dienstag |
| 2 | dmy | 1 | Français | French | janv,févr,mars, | lundi,mardi,mer |
| 3 | ymd | 7 | 日本語 | Japanese | 01,02,03,04,05, | 月曜日,火曜日,水曜日,木曜日 |
| 4 | dmy | 1 | Dansk | Danish | jan,feb,mar,apr | mandag,tirsdag, |
| 5 | dmy | 1 | Español | Spanish | Ene,Feb,Mar,Abr | Lunes,Martes,Mi |
| 6 | dmy | 1 | Italiano | Italian | gen,feb,mar,apr | lunedì,martedì, |
| 7 | dmy | 1 | Nederlands | Dutch | jan,feb,mrt,apr | maandag,dinsdag |
| 8 | dmy | 1 | Norsk | Norwegian | jan,feb,mar,apr | mandag,tirsdag, |
| 9 | dmy | 7 | Português | Portuguese | jan,fev,mar,abr | segunda-feira,t |
| 10 | dmy | 1 | Suomi | Finnish | tammi,helmi,maa | maanantai,tiist |
| 11 | ymd | 1 | Svenska | Swedish | jan,feb,mar,apr | måndag,tisdag,o |
| 12 | dmy | 1 | čeština | Czech | I,II,III,IV,V,V | pondělí,úterý,s |
| 13 | ymd | 1 | magyar | Hungarian | jan,febr,márc,á | hétfő,kedd,szer |
| 14 | dmy | 1 | polski | Polish | I,II,III,IV,V,V | poniedziałek,wt |
| 15 | dmy | 1 | română | Romanian | Ian,Feb,Mar,Apr | luni,marţi,mier |
| 16 | ymd | 1 | hrvatski | Croatian | sij,vel,ožu,tra | ponedjeljak,uto |
| 17 | dmy | 1 | slovenčina | Slovak | I,II,III,IV,V,V | pondelok,utorok |
| 18 | dmy | 1 | slovenski | Slovenian | jan,feb,mar,apr | ponedeljek,tore |
| 19 | dmy | 1 | ελληνικά | Greek | Ιαν,Φεβ,Μαρ,Απρ | Δευτέρα,Τρίτη,Τ |
| 20 | dmy | 1 | български | Bulgarian | януари,февруари | понеделник,втор |
| 21 | dmy | 1 | русский | Russian | янв,фев,мар,апр | понедельник,вто |
| 22 | dmy | 1 | Türkçe | Turkish | Oca,Şub,Mar,Nis | Pazartesi,Salı, |
| 23 | dmy | 1 | British | British English | Jan,Feb,Mar,Apr | Monday,Tuesday, |
| 24 | dmy | 1 | eesti | Estonian | jaan,veebr,märt | esmaspäev,teisi |
| 25 | ymd | 1 | latviešu | Latvian | jan,feb,mar,apr | pirmdiena,otrdi |
| 26 | ymd | 1 | lietuvių | Lithuanian | sau,vas,kov,bal | pirmadienis,ant |
| 27 | dmy | 7 | Português (Brasil) | Brazilian | Jan,Fev,Mar,Abr | Segunda-Feira,T |
| 28 | ymd | 7 | 繁體中文 | Traditional Chinese | 01,02,03,04,05, | 星期一,星期二,星期三,星期四 |
| 29 | ymd | 7 | 한국어 | Korean | 01,02,03,04,05, | 월요일,화요일,수요일,목요일 |
| 30 | ymd | 7 | 简体中文 | Simplified Chinese | 01,02,03,04,05, | 星期一,星期二,星期三,星期 |
| 31 | dmy | 1 | Arabic | Arabic | Jan,Feb,Mar,Apr | Monday,Tuesday, |
| 32 | dmy | 7 | ไทย | Thai | ม.ค.,ก.พ.,มี.ค. | จันทร์,อังคาร,พ |
| 33 | dmy | 1 | norsk (bokmål) | Bokmål | jan,feb,mar,apr | mandag,tirsdag, |

# DBCC USEROPTIONS

The DBCC USEROPTIONS command displays some of the connection (session) settings. As we have seen these settings play an important part on how date literals are interpreted by the system such as dateformat.

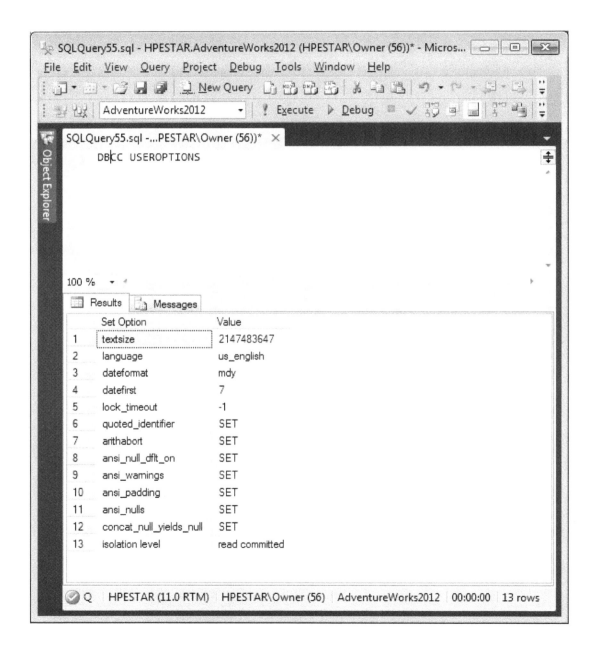

# Easy SELECT Queries for Fun & Learning

T-SQL scripts to demonstrate simple, easy-to-read SELECT query variations. Important note: alias column names cannot be reused in successive computed columns by expressions or anywhere else in the query except the ORDER BY clause.

```
-- Datetime range with string literal date
SELECT  *  FROM    Person.Person
WHERE   ModifiedDate <= '2002-08-09 00:00:00.000'  ORDER BY LastName;
-- (38 row(s) affected)
```

---

NOTE

The string literal above looks like datetime, but it is not. It is only a string literal. The database engine will try to convert it to datetime data type at runtime (implicit conversion), and if successful the query will be executed.

The syntax of the following query is OK, however, it will fail at execution time.

```
SELECT  *  FROM    Person.Person  WHERE    ModifiedDate <= 'New York City'  ORDER BY LastName;
/* Msg 241, Level 16, State 1, Line 1 Conversion failed when converting date and/or time from character
string. */
```

---

```
-- Complimentary (remaining) datetime range specified again with string literal
SELECT * FROM    Person.Person  WHERE    ModifiedDate > '2002-08-09 00:00:00.000'  ORDER BY
LastName;
-- (19934 row(s) affected)
```

```
-- Total rows in Person.Person
SELECT ( 38 + 19934 ) AS TotalRows;
-- 19972
```

```
SELECT count(* ) FROM   Person.Person -- 19972
```

```
SELECT TableRows = count(* ),  Calc = 38 + 19934  FROM   Person.Person;  -- 19972      19972
```

```
-- Get prefix left of comma or entire string if there is no comma present
SELECT TOP 4                                                                   ProductNumber,
       LEFT(Name, COALESCE(NULLIF(CHARINDEX(',',Name)-1,-1),LEN(Name)))        AS NamePrefix,
       Name                                                                    AS ProductName
FROM AdventureWorks2012.Production.Product   WHERE CHARINDEX(',',Name) > 0
ORDER BY ProductName;
```

| ProductNumber | NamePrefix | ProductName |
| --- | --- | --- |
| VE-C304-L | Classic Vest | Classic Vest, L |
| VE-C304-M | Classic Vest | Classic Vest, M |
| VE-C304-S | Classic Vest | Classic Vest, S |
| GL-F110-L | Full-Finger Gloves | Full-Finger Gloves, L |

**CHAPTER 12:  Basic SELECT Statement Syntax & Examples**

*NULL refers to no information available. Note: "=" and "!=" operators are not used with NULL; "IS" or "IS NOT" operators are applicable.*

```
SELECT *
FROM    Person.Person
WHERE   AdditionalContactInfo IS NOT NULL
ORDER BY LastName;
-- (10 row(s) affected)
```

```
SELECT *
FROM    Person.Person
WHERE   AdditionalContactInfo IS NULL
ORDER BY LastName;
-- (19962 row(s) affected)
```

```
SELECT   DISTINCT FirstName
FROM    Person.Person
ORDER BY FirstName;
-- (1018 row(s) affected)
```

```
-- Summary revenue by product, interesting sort
USE AdventureWorks2012;
GO
SELECT   TOP 10 p.Name                                          AS ProductName,
       FORMAT(SUM(((OrderQty * UnitPrice) * (1.0 - UnitPriceDiscount))),'c','en-US') AS SubTotal
FROM Production.Product AS p
INNER JOIN Sales.SalesOrderDetail AS sod
ON p.ProductID = sod.ProductID
GROUP BY p.Name
ORDER BY REVERSE(p.Name);
```

| ProductName | SubTotal |
| --- | --- |
| Water Bottle - 30 oz. | $28,654.16 |
| Hydration Pack - 70 oz. | $105,826.42 |
| LL Mountain Frame - Black, 40 | $1,198.99 |
| ML Mountain Frame - Black, 40 | $14,229.41 |
| Mountain-300 Black, 40 | $501,648.88 |
| Mountain-500 Black, 40 | $101,734.12 |
| LL Mountain Frame - Silver, 40 | $69,934.28 |
| ML Mountain Frame-W - Silver, 40 | $195,826.39 |
| Mountain-500 Silver, 40 | $145,089.43 |
| Mountain-400-W Silver, 40 | $323,703.82 |

*DISTINCT & GROUP BY operations are generally "expensive".*

SELECT   DISTINCT LastName FROM     Person.Person ORDER BY LastName;  -- (1206 row(s) affected)

```
-- LastName popularity descending
SELECT LastName,     Frequency = count(* )
FROM     Person.Person
GROUP BY LastName
ORDER BY Frequency DESC;
```

| LastName | Frequency |
|----------|-----------|
| Diaz | 211 |
| Hernandez | 188 |
| Sanchez | 175 |
| Martinez | 173 |
| Torres | 172 |
| Martin | 171 |
| Perez | 170 |
| Gonzalez | 169 |
| Lopez | 168 |
| Rodriguez | 166 |

```
-- Sort on column not in SELECT list - Note: demo only, confusing to end user
SELECT   LastName
FROM     Person.Person
ORDER BY FirstName;
-- (19972 row(s) affected)
```

```
-- Sort on column not in SELECT list
SELECT   Name = CONCAT(LastName, ', ', FirstName )
FROM     Person.Person
ORDER BY LastName;
-- (19972 row(s) affected)
```

```
-- Sort on column alias
SELECT   Name = CONCAT(LastName, ', ', FirstName )
FROM     Person.Person
ORDER BY Name;
-- (19972 row(s) affected)
```

```
SELECT   CONCAT(LastName, ', ', FirstName ) AS FullName
FROM     Person.Person
WHERE    LastName >= 'K'  ORDER BY LastName;
-- (12057 row(s) affected)
```

**CHAPTER 12:  Basic SELECT Statement Syntax & Examples**

### *The NULLIF Function Actually Creates A NULL*

```
SELECT   CONCAT(LastName, ', ', FirstName )  AS FullName
FROM     Person.Person  WHERE    LastName < 'K'  ORDER BY LastName;
-- (7915 row(s) affected)


-- Cardinality check
SELECT Difference= ((count(*)) - (12057 + 7915)) FROM  Person.Person; -- 0


-- Using the NULLIF function in counting
-- Count of all list prices - no NULLs in column
SELECT COUNT(ListPrice) FROM   AdventureWorks2012.Production.Product
-- 504


-- Counts only when ListPrice != 0 - does not count NULLs (ListPrice = 0.0)
SELECT COUNT(NULLIF(ListPrice,0.0)) FROM   AdventureWorks2012.Production.Product
-- 304


SELECT COUNT(ListPrice)  FROM   AdventureWorks2012.Production.Product  WHERE ListPrice = 0;
-- 200
```

## Cardinality of DISTINCT & GROUP BY Clauses

The cardinality of DISTINCT and the cardinality of GROUP BY are the same with the same column(s).

```
-- FirstName by popularity descending
SELECT FirstName,
        Freq = count(* )
FROM     Person.Person
GROUP BY FirstName
ORDER BY Freq DESC;
-- (1018 row(s) affected)
```

| FirstName | Freq |
|-----------|------|
| Richard   | 103  |
| Katherine | 99   |
| Marcus    | 97   |
| James     | 97   |
| Jennifer  | 96   |
| Dalton    | 93   |
| Lucas     | 93   |
| Alexandra | 93   |
| Morgan    | 92   |
| Seth      | 92   |

```
SELECT   DISTINCT FirstName  FROM     Person.Person  ORDER BY FirstName;
-- (1018 row(s) affected)
```

## Column Alias Can only Be Used in ORDER BY

Column aliases cannot be used in other computed columns (expressions), neither in the WHERE clause or GROUP BY clause.

```
SELECT  TableRows = count(* ),
        Calculated = 38 + 19934,
        Difference = (count(*) - 38 - 19934)
FROM   Person.Person;
```

| TableRows | Calculated | Difference |
|-----------|-----------|-----------|
| 19972 | 19972 | 0 |

### Workaround for Column Alias Use Restriction

There is a simple workaround for recycling column aliases in other clauses than just the ORDER BY: make the query into a derived table (x) and include it in an outer query. Similarly, CTEs can be used instead of derived tables.

```
-- Derived table workaround
SELECT TableRows, Calculated, Difference = TableRows - Calculated
FROM (
        SELECT  TableRows = count(* ),    Calculated = 38 + 19934,
        FROM   Person.Person
        ) x ;  -- Derived table
GO
```

| TableRows | Calculated | Difference |
|-----------|-----------|-----------|
| 19972 | 19972 | 0 |

```
-- CTE workaround
;WITH CTE AS (
        SELECT  TableRows = count(* ),    Calculated = 38 + 19934
        FROM   Person.Person)
-- Outer query
SELECT TableRows, Calculated, Difference = TableRows - Calculated
FROM CTE;
```

| TableRows | Calculated | Difference |
|-----------|-----------|-----------|
| 19972 | 19972 | 0 |

*CHAPTER 12: Basic SELECT Statement Syntax & Examples*

## When the Clock Strikes Midnight: datetime Behaviour

This is one of the most troublesome issues in T-SQL programming: the predicate YYYYMMDD (date string literal) = DatetimeColumn does not include the entire day, only records with time at midnight: 00:00:00.000 .

```
-- Note: only midnight 2003-08-09 included
-- Even a second after midnight is not included like 2003-08-09 00:00:01.000
SELECT   *
FROM     Person.Person
WHERE    ModifiedDate BETWEEN '2002-08-09 00:00:00.000'
             AND '2003-08-09 00:00:00.000'
ORDER BY LastName;
GO
-- (396 row(s) affected)
```

```
-- Entire day of 2003-08-09 included
-- The count same as before because no records after midnight 2003-08-09
SELECT   *
FROM     Person.Person
WHERE      ModifiedDate >= '2002-08-09 00:00:00.000'
     AND ModifiedDate < '2003-08-10 00:00:00.000'
ORDER BY LastName;
GO
-- (396 row(s) affected)
```

CHAPTER 12: Basic SELECT Statement Syntax & Examples

## LEFT(), RIGHT() & SUBSTRING() String Functions

```
SELECT   FirstCharOfFirstName = LEFT(FirstName,1),          -- column alias
         FirstCharOfLastName  = LEFT(LastName,1),           -- column alias
         LastCharOfLastName   = RIGHT(LastName,1),          -- column alias
         FullName = CONCAT(FirstName, SPACE(1), LastName) , -- column alias
         *                                                  -- wild card, all columns
FROM     Person.Person
WHERE    SUBSTRING(FirstName,1,1) = 'J'
    AND SUBSTRING (LastName,1,1) = 'S'
    AND (RIGHT(LastName,1) = 'H' OR RIGHT(LastName,1) = 'Z')
ORDER BY LastName;
-- (59 row(s) affected) - Partial result.
```

| FirstCharOfFirstName | FirstCharOfLastName | LastCharOfLastName | FullName | BusinessEntityID |
|---|---|---|---|---|
| J | S | z | Jacqueline Sanchez | 8975 |
| J | S | z | Jada Sanchez | 9499 |
| J | S | z | Jade Sanchez | 9528 |
| J | S | z | Janelle Sanchez | 18590 |
| J | S | z | Jared Sanchez | 15266 |
| J | S | z | Jarrod Sanchez | 2948 |
| J | S | z | Jay Sanchez | 10298 |
| J | S | z | Jennifer Sanchez | 20440 |
| J | S | z | Jeremiah Sanchez | 15292 |
| J | S | z | Jermaine Sanchez | 8040 |

```
-- Sort on first column
SELECT BusinessEntityID, JobTitle, SUBSTRING(JobTitle, 5, 7)  AS MiddleOfJobTitle
FROM   HumanResources.Employee
WHERE  BirthDate <= '1960/12/31'    -- date literal (constant)
ORDER BY 1;
-- (27 row(s) affected) - Partial results.
```

| BusinessEntityID | JobTitle | MiddleOfJobTitle |
|---|---|---|
| 5 | Design Engineer | gn Engi |
| 6 | Design Engineer | gn Engi |
| 12 | Tool Designer | Design |
| 15 | Design Engineer | gn Engi |
| 23 | Marketing Specialist | eting S |
| 27 | Production Supervisor - WC60 | uction |

```
-- String functions usage in formatting
DECLARE @SSN char(9) = '123456789';
SELECT SSN=CONCAT(LEFT(@SSN,3),'-', SUBSTRING(@SSN,4,2),'-', RIGHT(@SSN,4));
-- 123-45-6789
```

**CHAPTER 12:  Basic SELECT Statement Syntax & Examples**

*ASCII value range is 0-127.  Extended ASCII: 128-255. Size is 8-bit, one  byte.*

```
SELECT TOP 5    ProductNumber,
                SUBSTRING(ProductNumber,9,1)          AS MiddleSubstring,
                ASCII(SUBSTRING(ProductNumber,9,1))   AS ASCIIValue
FROM AdventureWorks2008.Production.Product
WHERE LEN(ProductNumber) > 8
ORDER BY Name;                          - OK syntax, but does not make sense
```

| ProductNumber | MiddleSubstring | ASCIIValue |
|---------------|-----------------|------------|
| VE-C304-L     | L               | 76         |
| VE-C304-M     | M               | 77         |
| VE-C304-S     | S               | 83         |
| GL-F110-L     | L               | 76         |
| GL-F110-M     | M               | 77         |

---

NOTE
Table columns and columns by expressions (computed) can be  mixed in a query at will.

---

```
-- Computed (expressions) & table columns
SELECT FirstCharOfFirstName = LEFT(FirstName,1),        -- string expression
       FirstCharOfLastName  = LEFT(LastName,1),          -- string expression
       FullName = CONCAT(LastName, ', ', FirstName ),    -- string expression
       SquareOfID = SQUARE(BusinessEntityID),            -- math expression
       *                                                 -- wild card, all table columns
FROM    Person.Person
WHERE   LEFT(FirstName,1) = 'J'
    AND LEFT(LastName,2) = 'Sm'
ORDER BY FullName;
-- (14 row(s) affected)  - Partial results.
```

| FirstCharOfFirstName | FirstCharOfLastName | FullName | SquareOfID | BusinessEntityID |
|----------------------|---------------------|----------|------------|------------------|
| J | S | Smith, Jacob | 348680929 | 18673 |
| J | S | Smith, James | 308986084 | 17578 |
| J | S | Smith, Jasmine | 129572689 | 11383 |
| J | S | Smith, Jeff | 3139984 | 1772 |
| J | S | Smith, Jennifer | 122699929 | 11077 |
| J | S | Smith, Jeremiah | 20511841 | 4529 |
| J | S | Smith, Jessica | 145829776 | 12076 |
| J | S | Smith, John | 332041284 | 18222 |
| J | S | Smith, Jonathan | 312228900 | 17670 |
| J | S | Smith, Jose | 300710281 | 17341 |
| J | S | Smith, Joseph | 357474649 | 18907 |
| J | S | Smith, Joshua | 351825049 | 18757 |
| J | S | Smith, Julia | 121616784 | 11028 |
| J | S | Smith, Justin | 324900625 | 18025 |

# Transact-SQL Reserved Keywords

List of reserved keywords in SQL Server 2012 Transact-SQL. Keywords can only be used as delimited identifiers such as [Inner] or "Order".

| | | |
|---|---|---|
| ADD | EXTERNAL | PROCEDURE |
| ALL | FETCH | PUBLIC |
| ALTER | FILE | RAISERROR |
| AND | FILLFACTOR | READ |
| ANY | FOR | READTEXT |
| AS | FOREIGN | RECONFIGURE |
| ASC | FREETEXT | REFERENCES |
| AUTHORIZATION | FREETEXTTABLE | REPLICATION |
| BACKUP | FROM | RESTORE |
| BEGIN | FULL | RESTRICT |
| BETWEEN | FUNCTION | RETURN |
| BREAK | GOTO | REVERT |
| BROWSE | GRANT | REVOKE |
| BULK | GROUP | RIGHT |
| BY | HAVING | ROLLBACK |
| CASCADE | HOLDLOCK | ROWCOUNT |
| CASE | IDENTITY | ROWGUIDCOL |
| CHECK | IDENTITY_INSERT | RULE |
| CHECKPOINT | IDENTITYCOL | SAVE |
| CLOSE | IF | SCHEMA |
| CLUSTERED | IN | SECURITYAUDIT |
| COALESCE | INDEX | SELECT |
| COLLATE | INNER | SEMANTICKEYPHRASETABLE |
| COLUMN | INSERT | SEMANTICSIMILARITYDETAILSTABLE |
| COMMIT | INTERSECT | SEMANTICSIMILARITYTABLE |
| COMPUTE | INTO | SESSION_USER |
| CONSTRAINT | IS | SET |
| CONTAINS | JOIN | SETUSER |
| CONTAINSTABLE | KEY | SHUTDOWN |
| CONTINUE | KILL | SOME |
| CONVERT | LEFT | STATISTICS |
| CREATE | LIKE | SYSTEM_USER |
| CROSS | LINENO | TABLE |
| CURRENT | LOAD | TABLESAMPLE |
| CURRENT_DATE | MERGE | TEXTSIZE |
| CURRENT_TIME | NATIONAL | THEN |
| CURRENT_TIMESTAMP | NOCHECK | TO |
| CURRENT_USER | NONCLUSTERED | TOP |
| CURSOR | NOT | TRAN |
| DATABASE | NULL | TRANSACTION |
| DBCC | NULLIF | TRIGGER |
| DEALLOCATE | OF | TRUNCATE |
| DECLARE | OFF | TRY_CONVERT |
| DEFAULT | OFFSETS | TSEQUAL |
| DELETE | ON | UNION |
| DENY | OPEN | UNIQUE |
| DESC | OPENDATASOURCE | UNPIVOT |
| DISK | OPENQUERY | UPDATE |
| DISTINCT | OPENROWSET | UPDATETEXT |
| DISTRIBUTED | OPENXML | USE |
| DOUBLE | OPTION | USER |
| DROP | OR | VALUES |
| DUMP | ORDER | VARYING |
| ELSE | OUTER | VIEW |
| END | OVER | WAITFOR |
| ERRLVL | PERCENT | WHEN |
| ESCAPE | PIVOT | WHERE |
| EXCEPT | PLAN | WHILE |
| EXEC | PRECISION | WITH |
| EXECUTE | PRIMARY | WITHIN GROUP |
| EXISTS | PRINT | WRITETEXT |
| EXIT | PROC | |

## Case Sensitive Sort with Latin1_General_CS_AI

For case sensitive sort on a column with case insensitive collation, we have use a case sensitive (CS) collation such as Latin1_General_CS_AI.

```
-- CASE INSENSITIVE sort using default collation
SELECT lname FROM
        (SELECT TOP 5 UPPER (LastName) AS lname FROM Person.Person ORDER BY FirstName) x
UNION ALL   SELECT lname FROM
        (SELECT TOP 5 LOWER (LastName) AS lname FROM Person.Person ORDER BY FirstName) y
ORDER BY lname;
-- ADAMS, adams, alexander, ALEXANDER, leonetti, LEONETTI, WRIGHT, WRIGHT, wright, wright


-- CASE SENSITIVE sort using %CS% collation
SELECT lname FROM ( SELECT lname FROM
  (SELECT TOP 5 UPPER (LastName) AS lname FROM Person.Person ORDER BY FirstName) x
  UNION ALL  SELECT lname FROM
  (SELECT TOP 5 LOWER (LastName) AS lname FROM Person.Person ORDER BY FirstName) y  ) z
ORDER BY lname COLLATE Latin1_General_CS_AI;
-- adams,ADAMS,alexander,ALEXANDER,leonetti,LEONETTI,wright,wright,WRIGHT,WRIGHT
```

**CHAPTER 12:  Basic SELECT Statement Syntax & Examples**

# The ORDER BY Clause for Sorting Query Results

The ORDER BY clause is located at the very end of the query. In fact the sorting itself takes place after the query executed and generated **an unordered result set**. Although frequently, especially for small sets, the results appear to be sorted, **only an ORDER BY clause can guarantee proper sorting**. INSERT, UPDATE, DELETE & MERGE statement do not support sorting, **the database engine performs all set operations unordered**. T-SQL scripts demonstrate the many variations of the ORDER BY clause.

```
USE AdventureWorks2012;
GO


-- A column can be used for sorting even though not explicitly used in the SELECT list
SELECT *
FROM   Production.Product
ORDER  BY Name ASC;
GO


-- Sort on the second column, whatever it may be
SELECT *
FROM   Production.Product
ORDER  BY 2 DESC;
GO


-- ASCending is the default sort order, it is not necessary to use
SELECT  Name AS ProductName,
        *
FROM   Production.Product
ORDER  BY ProductName ASC;
GO


SELECT  TOP (10) Name AS ProductName,           *
FROM   Production.Product  ORDER  BY 1 ASC;
```

| ProductName | ProductID | Name | ProductNumber | MakeFlag | FinishedGoodsFlag | Color | SafetyStockLevel |
|---|---|---|---|---|---|---|---|
| Adjustable Race | 1 | Adjustable Race | AR-5381 | 0 | 0 | NULL | 1000 |
| All-Purpose Bike Stand | 879 | All-Purpose Bike Stand | ST-1401 | 0 | 1 | NULL | 4 |
| AWC Logo Cap | 712 | AWC Logo Cap | CA-1098 | 0 | 1 | Multi | 4 |
| BB Ball Bearing | 3 | BB Ball Bearing | BE-2349 | 1 | 0 | NULL | 800 |
| Bearing Ball | 2 | Bearing Ball | BA-8327 | 0 | 0 | NULL | 1000 |
| Bike Wash - Dissolver | 877 | Bike Wash - Dissolver | CL-9009 | 0 | 1 | NULL | 4 |
| Blade | 316 | Blade | BL-2036 | 1 | 0 | NULL | 800 |
| Cable Lock | 843 | Cable Lock | LO-C100 | 0 | 1 | NULL | 4 |
| Chain | 952 | Chain | CH-0234 | 0 | 1 | Silver | 500 |
| Chain Stays | 324 | Chain Stays | CS-2812 | 1 | 0 | NULL | 1000 |

## Using Column Alias in the ORDER BY Clause

Column alias can be used in an ORDER BY clause. In fact, it should be used to make the query more readable.

```
-- ProductName is a column alias, it can only be used in the ORDER BY clause, not anywhere before
SELECT ProductName = Name, *
FROM Production.Product
WHERE ProductName like '%glove%'
ORDER BY ProductName ASC ;
GO
/* ERROR
Msg 207, Level 16, State 1, Line 3
Invalid column name 'ProductName'.
*/
```

```
-- The TOP clause uses the ORDER BY sorting to select the 5 rows
SELECT TOP (5) ProductName = Name, *
FROM Production.Product
WHERE Name like '%glove%'
ORDER BY ProductName ASC ;
```

| ProductName | ProductID | Name | ProductNumber | MakeFlag | FinishedGoodsFlag | Color | SafetyStockLevel |
|---|---|---|---|---|---|---|---|
| Full-Finger Gloves, L | 863 | Full-Finger Gloves, L | GL-F110-L | 0 | 1 | Black | 4 |
| Full-Finger Gloves, M | 862 | Full-Finger Gloves, M | GL-F110-M | 0 | 1 | Black | 4 |
| Full-Finger Gloves, S | 861 | Full-Finger Gloves, S | GL-F110-S | 0 | 1 | Black | 4 |
| Half-Finger Gloves, L | 860 | Half-Finger Gloves, L | GL-H102-L | 0 | 1 | Black | 4 |
| Half-Finger Gloves, M | 859 | Half-Finger Gloves, M | GL-H102-M | 0 | 1 | Black | 4 |

```
-- Descending sort on name which is string data type
SELECT TOP (10) ProductName = Name, *
FROM Production.Product
WHERE Name like '%road%'
ORDER BY ProductName DESC ;
```
.

| ProductName | ProductID | Name | ProductNumber | MakeFlag | FinishedGoodsFlag | Color | SafetyStockLevel |
|---|---|---|---|---|---|---|---|
| Road-750 Black, 58 | 977 | Road-750 Black, 58 | BK-R19B-58 | 1 | 1 | Black | 100 |
| Road-750 Black, 52 | 999 | Road-750 Black, 52 | BK-R19B-52 | 1 | 1 | Black | 100 |
| Road-750 Black, 48 | 998 | Road-750 Black, 48 | BK-R19B-48 | 1 | 1 | Black | 100 |
| Road-750 Black, 44 | 997 | Road-750 Black, 44 | BK-R19B-44 | 1 | 1 | Black | 100 |
| Road-650 Red, 62 | 761 | Road-650 Red, 62 | BK-R50R-62 | 1 | 1 | Red | 100 |
| Road-650 Red, 60 | 760 | Road-650 Red, 60 | BK-R50R-60 | 1 | 1 | Red | 100 |
| Road-650 Red, 58 | 759 | Road-650 Red, 58 | BK-R50R-58 | 1 | 1 | Red | 100 |
| Road-650 Red, 52 | 764 | Road-650 Red, 52 | BK-R50R-52 | 1 | 1 | Red | 100 |
| Road-650 Red, 48 | 763 | Road-650 Red, 48 | BK-R50R-48 | 1 | 1 | Red | 100 |
| Road-650 Red, 44 | 762 | Road-650 Red, 44 | BK-R50R-44 | 1 | 1 | Red | 100 |

## Using Table Alias in the ORDER BY Clause
Unlike the column alias, table alias can be used anywhere in the query within the scope of the alias.

```
-- Using table alias in ORDER BY
SELECT P.*
FROM   Production.Product P
ORDER  BY P.Name ASC;
GO
```

| ProductID | Name | ProductNumber | MakeFlag | FinishedGoodsFlag | Color | SafetyStockLevel |
|---|---|---|---|---|---|---|
| 958 | Touring-3000 Blue, 54 | BK-T18U-54 | 1 | 1 | Blue | 100 |
| 959 | Touring-3000 Blue, 58 | BK-T18U-58 | 1 | 1 | Blue | 100 |
| 960 | Touring-3000 Blue, 62 | BK-T18U-62 | 1 | 1 | Blue | 100 |
| 961 | Touring-3000 Yellow, 44 | BK-T18Y-44 | 1 | 1 | Yellow | 100 |
| 962 | Touring-3000 Yellow, 50 | BK-T18Y-50 | 1 | 1 | Yellow | 100 |
| 963 | Touring-3000 Yellow, 54 | BK-T18Y-54 | 1 | 1 | Yellow | 100 |
| 964 | Touring-3000 Yellow, 58 | BK-T18Y-58 | 1 | 1 | Yellow | 100 |
| 965 | Touring-3000 Yellow, 62 | BK-T18Y-62 | 1 | 1 | Yellow | 100 |
| 842 | Touring-Panniers, Large | PA-T100 | 0 | 1 | Grey | 4 |
| 870 | Water Bottle - 30 oz. | WB-H098 | 0 | 1 | NULL | 4 |
| 869 | Women's Mountain Shorts, L | SH-W890-L | 0 | 1 | Black | 4 |
| 868 | Women's Mountain Shorts, M | SH-W890-M | 0 | 1 | Black | 4 |
| 867 | Women's Mountain Shorts, S | SH-W890-S | 0 | 1 | Black | 4 |
| 854 | Women's Tights, L | TG-W091-L | 0 | 1 | Black | 4 |
| 853 | Women's Tights, M | TG-W091-M | 0 | 1 | Black | 4 |
| 852 | Women's Tights, S | TG-W091-S | 0 | 1 | Black | 4 |

```
-- Specific column list instead of all (*)
SELECT   Name,
         ProductNumber,
         ListPrice AS PRICE
FROM   Production.Product  P
ORDER  BY P.Name ASC;
GO
```

```
SELECT           Name,
                 ProductNumber,
                 ListPrice AS PRICE
FROM   Production.Product  P
ORDER  BY P.ListPrice DESC;
```

```
-- Equivalent to above with column alias usage
SELECT           Name,
                 ProductNumber,
                 ListPrice AS PRICE
FROM   Production.Product  P ORDER  BY PRICE DESC;
```

**CHAPTER 12:  Basic SELECT Statement Syntax & Examples**

## Easy ORDER BY Queries for Exercises

T-SQL scripts demonstrate easily readable queries with sorted result sets.

```
USE pubs ;
GO
```

```
SELECT TYPE,  AvgPrice=FORMAT(AVG(price) , 'c', 'en-US')
FROM  titles WHERE  royalty = 10 GROUP  BY TYPE ORDER  BY TYPE ;
```

| TYPE | AvgPrice |
|------|----------|
| business | $17.31 |
| popular_comp | $20.00 |
| psychology | $14.14 |
| trad_cook | $17.97 |

```
SELECT          type = type,
                AvgPrice = FORMAT(AVG(price),'c', 'en-US')
FROM   titles
WHERE  royalty = 10
GROUP  BY type
ORDER  BY AvgPrice;
```

| type | AvgPrice |
|------|----------|
| psychology | $14.14 |
| business | $17.31 |
| trad_cook | $17.97 |
| popular_comp | $20.00 |

```
SELECT  type                            AS [type],
        FORMAT(AVG(price),'c', 'en-US')     AS AvgPrice
FROM   titles  GROUP  BY [type] ORDER  BY [type] desc;
```

| type | AvgPrice |
|------|----------|
| UNDECIDED | NULL |
| trad_cook | $15.96 |
| psychology | $13.50 |
| popular_comp | $21.48 |
| mod_cook | $11.49 |
| business | $13.73 |

## Eliminate NULL in result with COALESCE or ISNULL functions

```
SELECT [type] = type,
        AvgPrice = COALESCE(FORMAT(AVG(price),'c', 'en-US') ,'')
FROM  titles  GROUP  BY [type]  ORDER  BY [type] desc;
```

| type | AvgPrice |
|------|----------|
| UNDECIDED | |
| trad_cook | $15.96 |
| psychology | $13.50 |
| popular_comp | $21.48 |
| mod_cook | $11.49 |
| business | $13.73 |

```
SELECT           pub_name                              Publisher,
                 FORMAT(AVG(price),'c', 'en-US')    AvgPrice
FROM   titles
    INNER JOIN publishers
    ON  titles.pub_id = publishers.pub_id
GROUP  BY pub_name
ORDER  BY pub_name;
```

| Publisher | AvgPrice |
|-----------|----------|
| Algodata Infosystems | $18.98 |
| Binnet & Hardley | $15.41 |
| New Moon Books | $9.78 |

```
SELECT TOP(3) * FROM   titles ORDER  BY title;
```

| title_id | title | type | pub_id | price | advance | royalty | ytd_sales | notes | pubdate |
|----------|-------|------|--------|-------|---------|---------|-----------|-------|---------|
| PC1035 | But Is It User Friendly? | popular_comp | 1389 | 22.95 | 7000.00 | 16 | 8780 | A survey of software for the naive user, focusing on the 'friendliness' of each. | 1991-06-30 00:00:00.000 |
| PS1372 | Computer Phobic AND Non-Phobic Individuals: Behavior Variations | psychology | 0877 | 21.59 | 7000.00 | 10 | 375 | A must for the specialist, this book examines the difference between those who hate and fear computers and those who don't. | 1991-10-21 00:00:00.000 |
| BU1111 | Cooking with Computers: Surreptitious Balance Sheets | business | 1389 | 11.95 | 5000.00 | 10 | 3876 | Helpful hints on how to use your electronic resources to the best advantage. | 1991-06-09 00:00:00.000 |

```
SELECT TOP(3) * FROM   publishers  ORDER  BY pub_name;
```

| pub_id | pub_name | city | state | country |
|--------|----------|------|-------|---------|
| 1389 | Algodata Infosystems | Berkeley | CA | USA |
| 0877 | Binnet & Hardley | Washington | DC | USA |
| 1622 | Five Lakes Publishing | Chicago | IL | USA |

## *Sorting Products by Attributes*

```
USE Northwind;
GO

SELECT          UnitsInStock,
                ProductID,
                ProductName,
                QuantityPerUnit,
                FORMAT( UnitPrice, 'c', 'en-US')          AS UnitPrice  -- Column alias is same as
column
FROM   Northwind.dbo.Products WHERE  UnitsInStock BETWEEN 15 AND 25  ORDER  BY UnitsInStock;
```

| UnitsInStock | ProductID | ProductName | QuantityPerUnit | UnitPrice |
|---|---|---|---|---|
| 15 | 7 | Uncle Bob's Organic Dried Pears | 12 - 1 lb pkgs. | $30.00 |
| 15 | 26 | Gumbär Gummibärchen | 100 - 250 g bags | $31.23 |
| 15 | 48 | Chocolade | 10 pkgs. | $12.75 |
| 15 | 70 | Outback Lager | 24 - 355 ml bottles | $15.00 |
| 17 | 38 | Côte de Blaye | 12 - 75 cl bottles | $263.50 |
| 17 | 43 | Ipoh Coffee | 16 - 500 g tins | $46.00 |
| 17 | 62 | Tarte au sucre | 48 pies | $49.30 |
| 17 | 2 | Chang | 24 - 12 oz bottles | $19.00 |
| 19 | 60 | Camembert Pierrot | 15 - 300 g rounds | $34.00 |
| 20 | 24 | Guaraná Fantástica | 12 - 355 ml cans | $4.50 |
| 20 | 35 | Steeleye Stout | 24 - 12 oz bottles | $18.00 |
| 20 | 51 | Manjimup Dried Apples | 50 - 300 g pkgs. | $53.00 |
| 21 | 54 | Tourtière | 16 pies | $7.45 |
| 21 | 56 | Gnocchi di nonna Alice | 24 - 250 g pkgs. | $38.00 |
| 22 | 11 | Queso Cabrales | 1 kg pkg. | $21.00 |
| 22 | 64 | Wimmers gute Semmelknödel | 20 bags x 4 pieces | $33.25 |
| 24 | 13 | Konbu | 2 kg box | $6.00 |
| 24 | 63 | Vegie-spread | 15 - 625 g jars | $43.90 |
| 25 | 19 | Teatime Chocolate Biscuits | 10 boxes x 12 pieces | $9.20 |

```
-- A second key is necessary for unique ordering
SELECT   TOP(8)   UnitsInStock,
                ProductID,
                ProductName,
                QuantityPerUnit,
                FORMAT( UnitPrice, 'c', 'en-US') AS UnitPrice
FROM   Northwind.dbo.Products
WHERE  UnitsInStock BETWEEN 15 AND 25 ORDER  BY UnitsInStock, ProductName;
```

| UnitsInStock | ProductID | ProductName | QuantityPerUnit | UnitPrice |
|---|---|---|---|---|
| 15 | 48 | Chocolade | 10 pkgs. | $12.75 |
| 15 | 26 | Gumbär Gummibärchen | 100 - 250 g bags | $31.23 |
| 15 | 70 | Outback Lager | 24 - 355 ml bottles | $15.00 |
| 15 | 7 | Uncle Bob's Organic Dried Pears | 12 - 1 lb pkgs. | $30.00 |
| 17 | 2 | Chang | 24 - 12 oz bottles | $19.00 |
| 17 | 38 | Côte de Blaye | 12 - 75 cl bottles | $263.50 |
| 17 | 43 | Ipoh Coffee | 16 - 500 g tins | $46.00 |
| 17 | 62 | Tarte au sucre | 48 pies | $49.30 |

*Changing WHERE condition changes the cardinality of result set*

```
SELECT          UnitsInStock,
                ProductID,
                ProductName,
                QuantityPerUnit,
                FORMAT( UnitPrice, 'c', 'en-US')          AS UnitPrice
FROM   Northwind.dbo.Products
WHERE  UnitsInStock = 15 or UnitsInStock = 25  -- same as UnitsInStock IN (15, 25)
ORDER  BY UnitsInStock, ProductName;
```

| UnitsInStock | ProductID | ProductName | QuantityPerUnit | UnitPrice |
|---|---|---|---|---|
| 15 | 48 | Chocolade | 10 pkgs. | $12.75 |
| 15 | 26 | Gumbär Gummibärchen | 100 - 250 g bags | $31.23 |
| 15 | 70 | Outback Lager | 24 - 355 ml bottles | $15.00 |
| 15 | 7 | Uncle Bob's Organic Dried Pears | 12 - 1 lb pkgs. | $30.00 |
| 25 | 19 | Teatime Chocolate Biscuits | 10 boxes x 12 pieces | $9.20 |

```
SELECT  TOP(7)  UnitsInStock,
                ProductID,
                ProductName,
                QuantityPerUnit,
                FORMAT( UnitPrice, 'c', 'en-US')          AS UnitPrice
FROM   Northwind.dbo.Products  ORDER  BY UnitsInStock DESC, ProductName ASC;
```

| UnitsInStock | ProductID | ProductName | QuantityPerUnit | UnitPrice |
|---|---|---|---|---|
| 125 | 75 | Rhönbräu Klosterbier | 24 - 0.5 l bottles | $7.75 |
| 123 | 40 | Boston Crab Meat | 24 - 4 oz tins | $18.40 |
| 120 | 6 | Grandma's Boysenberry Spread | 12 - 8 oz jars | $25.00 |
| 115 | 55 | Pâté chinois | 24 boxes x 2 pies | $24.00 |
| 113 | 61 | Sirop d'érable | 24 - 500 ml bottles | $28.50 |
| 112 | 33 | Geitost | 500 g | $2.50 |
| 112 | 36 | Inlagd Sill | 24 - 250 g  jars | $19.00 |

```
SELECT  TOP(5)  UnitsInStock, ProductID, ProductName,       QuantityPerUnit,
                FORMAT( UnitPrice, 'c', 'en-US') AS UnitPrice
FROM   Northwind.dbo.Products
WHERE  UnitsInStock > 15  AND UnitsInStock < 25  ORDER  BY UnitsInStock DESC, ProductName ASC;
```

| UnitsInStock | ProductID | ProductName | QuantityPerUnit | UnitPrice |
|---|---|---|---|---|
| 24 | 13 | Konbu | 2 kg box | $6.00 |
| 24 | 63 | Vegie-spread | 15 - 625 g jars | $43.90 |
| 22 | 11 | Queso Cabrales | 1 kg pkg. | $21.00 |
| 22 | 64 | Wimmers gute Semmelknödel | 20 bags x 4 pieces | $33.25 |
| 21 | 56 | Gnocchi di nonna Alice | 24 - 250 g pkgs. | $38.00 |

**CHAPTER 12:  Basic SELECT Statement Syntax & Examples**

## *The "Tricky" BETWEEN & NOT BETWEEN Operators*
**They are very English-like, but results should be verified to make sure they work as intended.**

```
SELECT  TOP(5)  UnitsInStock, ProductID, ProductName,      QuantityPerUnit,
                FORMAT( UnitPrice, 'c', 'en-US') AS UnitPrice
FROM  Northwind.dbo.Products
WHERE  UnitsInStock BETWEEN 15 AND 25  ORDER  BY UnitsInStock DESC, ProductName ASC;
```

| UnitsInStock | ProductID | ProductName | QuantityPerUnit | UnitPrice |
|---|---|---|---|---|
| 25 | 19 | Teatime Chocolate Biscuits | 10 boxes x 12 pieces | $9.20 |
| 24 | 13 | Konbu | 2 kg box | $6.00 |
| 24 | 63 | Vegie-spread | 15 - 625 g jars | $43.90 |
| 22 | 11 | Queso Cabrales | 1 kg pkg. | $21.00 |
| 22 | 64 | Wimmers gute Semmelknödel | 20 bags x 4 pieces | $33.25 |

```
SELECT  TOP(5)  UnitsInStock, ProductID, ProductName,      QuantityPerUnit,
                FORMAT( UnitPrice, 'c', 'en-US') AS UnitPrice
FROM  Northwind.dbo.Products
WHERE  UnitsInStock NOT BETWEEN 15 AND 25
ORDER  BY UnitsInStock DESC, ProductName ASC;
```

| UnitsInStock | ProductID | ProductName | QuantityPerUnit | UnitPrice |
|---|---|---|---|---|
| 125 | 75 | Rhönbräu Klosterbier | 24 - 0.5 l bottles | $7.75 |
| 123 | 40 | Boston Crab Meat | 24 - 4 oz tins | $18.40 |
| 120 | 6 | Grandma's Boysenberry Spread | 12 - 8 oz jars | $25.00 |
| 115 | 55 | Pâté chinois | 24 boxes x 2 pies | $24.00 |
| 113 | 61 | Sirop d'érable | 24 - 500 ml bottles | $28.50 |

```
SELECT          Orders.OrderID,
                Shippers.*
FROM  Shippers
    INNER JOIN Orders
    ON ( Shippers.ShipperID = Orders.ShipVia )
ORDER  BY Orders.OrderID;
GO
-- (830 row(s) affected) - Partial results.
```

| OrderID | ShipperID | CompanyName | Phone |
|---|---|---|---|
| 10248 | 3 | Federal Shipping | (503) 555-9931 |
| 10249 | 1 | Speedy Express | (503) 555-9831 |
| 10250 | 2 | United Package | (503) 555-3199 |
| 10251 | 1 | Speedy Express | (503) 555-9831 |
| 10252 | 2 | United Package | (503) 555-3199 |
| 10253 | 2 | United Package | (503) 555-3199 |

*A second key is frequently required in sorting exception is PRIMARY KEY column.*

```
SELECT   OrderID,
         ProductID,
         FORMAT( UnitPrice, 'c', 'en-US')        AS UnitPrice,
         Quantity,
         Discount
FROM   [Order Details]  ORDER  BY OrderID ASC, ProductID ASC;
-- (2155 row(s) affected) - Partial results.
```

| OrderID | ProductID | UnitPrice | Quantity | Discount |
|---------|-----------|-----------|----------|----------|
| 10248 | 11 | $14.00 | 12 | 0 |
| 10248 | 42 | $9.80 | 10 | 0 |
| 10248 | 72 | $34.80 | 5 | 0 |
| 10249 | 14 | $18.60 | 9 | 0 |
| 10249 | 51 | $42.40 | 40 | 0 |
| 10250 | 41 | $7.70 | 10 | 0 |
| 10250 | 51 | $42.40 | 35 | 0.15 |
| 10250 | 65 | $16.80 | 15 | 0.15 |

```
-- Sort keys are different from expression column EmployeeName
SELECT   CONCAT(LastName,', ', FirstName)  AS EmployeeName ,
         Title, City, Country
FROM   Northwind.dbo.Employees ORDER  BY LastName,  FirstName ASC;
```

| EmployeeName | Title | City | Country |
|--------------|-------|------|---------|
| Buchanan, Steven | Sales Manager | London | UK |
| Callahan, Laura | Inside Sales Coordinator | Seattle | USA |
| Davolio, Nancy | Sales Representative | Seattle | USA |
| Dodsworth, Anne | Sales Representative | London | UK |
| Fuller, Andrew | Vice President, Sales | Tacoma | USA |
| King, Robert | Sales Representative | London | UK |
| Leverling, Janet | Sales Representative | Kirkland | USA |
| Peacock, Margaret | Sales Representative | Redmond | USA |
| Suyama, Michael | Sales Representative | London | UK |

```
-- Equivalent sort
SELECT TOP(3)    CONCAT(LastName,', ', FirstName) AS EmployeeName ,    Title, City, Country
FROM   Northwind.dbo.Employees  ORDER  BY EmployeeName ASC;
```

| EmployeeName | Title | City | Country |
|--------------|-------|------|---------|
| Buchanan, Steven | Sales Manager | London | UK |
| Callahan, Laura | Inside Sales Coordinator | Seattle | USA |
| Davolio, Nancy | Sales Representative | Seattle | USA |

## Using Multiple Keys in the ORDER BY Clause

If a single sort key does not result in unique ordering, multiple keys can be used. In the next example the Price (major) key is based on a column which is not unique. If we add Name as a second (minor) key, unique ordering will be guaranteed since Name is a unique column, it has a unique index and not null.  It's worth noting if Name would allow nulls, we would need a third key for unique ordering.

```
-- Single key sort
SELECT    P.Name,
          P.ProductNumber,
          P.ListPrice              AS PRICE
FROM   Production.Product  P
WHERE  P.ProductLine = 'R'   AND P.DaysToManufacture < 4    ORDER  BY  P. ListPrice DESC;
```

| Name | ProductNumber | PRICE |
|------|---------------|-------|
| HL Road Frame - Black, 58 | FR-R92B-58 | 1431.50 |
| HL Road Frame - Red, 58 | FR-R92R-58 | 1431.50 |
| HL Road Frame - Red, 62 | FR-R92R-62 | 1431.50 |
| HL Road Frame - Red, 44 | FR-R92R-44 | 1431.50 |
| HL Road Frame - Red, 48 | FR-R92R-48 | 1431.50 |
| HL Road Frame - Red, 52 | FR-R92R-52 | 1431.50 |
| HL Road Frame - Red, 56 | FR-R92R-56 | 1431.50 |
| HL Road Frame - Black, 62 | FR-R92B-62 | 1431.50 |
| HL Road Frame - Black, 44 | FR-R92B-44 | 1431.50 |
| HL Road Frame - Black, 48 | FR-R92B-48 | 1431.50 |
| HL Road Frame - Black, 52 | FR-R92B-52 | 1431.50 |
| ML Road Frame-W - Yellow, 40 | FR-R72Y-40 | 594.83 |

```
-- Double key sort - PRICE is the major key, Name is the minor key
SELECT    P.Name,
          P.ProductNumber,
          P.ListPrice              AS PRICE
FROM   Production.Product  P
WHERE  P.ProductLine = 'R'   AND P.DaysToManufacture < 4  ORDER  BY  PRICE DESC, Name;
```

| Name | ProductNumber | PRICE |
|------|---------------|-------|
| HL Road Frame - Black, 44 | FR-R92B-44 | 1431.50 |
| HL Road Frame - Black, 48 | FR-R92B-48 | 1431.50 |
| HL Road Frame - Black, 52 | FR-R92B-52 | 1431.50 |
| HL Road Frame - Black, 58 | FR-R92B-58 | 1431.50 |
| HL Road Frame - Black, 62 | FR-R92B-62 | 1431.50 |
| HL Road Frame - Red, 44 | FR-R92R-44 | 1431.50 |
| HL Road Frame - Red, 48 | FR-R92R-48 | 1431.50 |
| HL Road Frame - Red, 52 | FR-R92R-52 | 1431.50 |
| HL Road Frame - Red, 56 | FR-R92R-56 | 1431.50 |
| HL Road Frame - Red, 58 | FR-R92R-58 | 1431.50 |
| HL Road Frame - Red, 62 | FR-R92R-62 | 1431.50 |
| ML Road Frame - Red, 44 | FR-R72R-44 | 594.83 |

## ORDER BY in Complex Queries

An ORDER BY can be in a complex query and/or ORDER BY can be complex itself.  T-SQL scripts demonstrate complex ORDER BY usage.

```
-- We cannot tell just by query inspection if the second key is sufficient for unique ordering or not
-- If we inspect the result set it becomes obvious that we need a third key at least (SalesOrderID unsorted)
SELECT   ProductName          = P.Name,
         NonDiscountSales      = ( OrderQty * UnitPrice ),
         Discounts             = ( ( OrderQty * UnitPrice ) * UnitPriceDiscount ) ,
         SalesOrderID
FROM   Production.Product P
   INNER JOIN Sales.SalesOrderDetail SOD
      ON P.ProductID = SOD.ProductID
ORDER  BY        ProductName DESC,
                 NonDiscountSales DESC;
GO
```

| ProductName | NonDiscountSales | Discounts | SalesOrderID |
|---|---|---|---|
| Women's Tights, S | 1049.86 | 104.986 | 47355 |
| Women's Tights, S | 824.89 | 41.2445 | 46987 |
| Women's Tights, S | 783.6455 | 39.1823 | 47400 |
| Women's Tights, S | 742.401 | 37.1201 | 50206 |
| Women's Tights, S | 701.1565 | 35.0578 | 46993 |
| Women's Tights, S | 701.1565 | 35.0578 | 46671 |
| Women's Tights, S | 701.1565 | 35.0578 | 50688 |
| Women's Tights, S | 701.1565 | 35.0578 | 49481 |
| Women's Tights, S | 659.912 | 32.9956 | 48295 |
| Women's Tights, S | 659.912 | 32.9956 | 46967 |
| Women's Tights, S | 618.6675 | 30.9334 | 46652 |
| Women's Tights, S | 608.9188 | 12.1784 | 46672 |
| Women's Tights, S | 608.9188 | 12.1784 | 47365 |
| Women's Tights, S | 565.4246 | 11.3085 | 47004 |
| Women's Tights, S | 565.4246 | 11.3085 | 50663 |

> NOTE
> Even though SELECT DISTINCT results may appear to be sorted, **only ORDER BY clause can guarantee sort**. This holds true for any kind of SELECT statement, simple or complex.

```
SELECT DISTINCT JobTitle   FROM   HumanResources.Employee ;

SELECT DISTINCT JobTitle   FROM   HumanResources.Employee ORDER  BY JobTitle;
```

**CHAPTER 12:  Basic SELECT Statement Syntax & Examples**

## ORDER BY with ROW_NUMBER()

T-SQL queries demonstrate sorting with not matching and matching ROW_NUMBER() sequence number.

```
SELECT
  ROW_NUMBER()  OVER( PARTITION BY CountryRegionName  ORDER BY SalesYTD ASC) AS SeqNo,
  CountryRegionName AS Country,  FirstName, LastName,  JobTitle,
  FORMAT(SalesYTD, 'c', 'en-US') AS SalesYTD,
  FORMAT(SalesLastYear, 'c', 'en-US') AS SalesLastYear
FROM  Sales.vSalesPerson          ORDER  BY JobTitle,   SalesYTD DESC;
```

| SeqNo | Country | FirstName | LastName | JobTitle | SalesYTD | SalesLastYear |
|---|---|---|---|---|---|---|
| 2 | United States | Amy | Alberts | European Sales Manager | $519,905.93 | $0.00 |
| 3 | United States | Stephen | Jiang | North American Sales Manager | $559,697.56 | $0.00 |
| 1 | United States | Syed | Abbas | Pacific Sales Manager | $172,524.45 | $0.00 |
| 11 | United States | Linda | Mitchell | Sales Representative | $4,251,368.55 | $1,439,156.03 |
| 1 | United Kingdom | Jae | Pak | Sales Representative | $4,116,871.23 | $1,635,823.40 |
| 10 | United States | Michael | Blythe | Sales Representative | $3,763,178.18 | $1,750,406.48 |
| 9 | United States | Jillian | Carson | Sales Representative | $3,189,418.37 | $1,997,186.20 |
| 1 | France | Ranjit | Varkey Chudukatil | Sales Representative | $3,121,616.32 | $2,396,539.76 |
| 2 | Canada | José | Saraiva | Sales Representative | $2,604,540.72 | $2,038,234.65 |
| 8 | United States | Shu | Ito | Sales Representative | $2,458,535.62 | $2,073,506.00 |
| 7 | United States | Tsvi | Reiter | Sales Representative | $2,315,185.61 | $1,849,640.94 |
| 1 | Germany | Rachel | Valdez | Sales Representative | $1,827,066.71 | $1,307,949.79 |
| 6 | United States | Tete | Mensa-Annan | Sales Representative | $1,576,562.20 | $0.00 |
| 5 | United States | David | Campbell | Sales Representative | $1,573,012.94 | $1,371,635.32 |
| 1 | Canada | Garrett | Vargas | Sales Representative | $1,453,719.47 | $1,620,276.90 |
| 1 | Australia | Lynn | Tsoflias | Sales Representative | $1,421,810.92 | $2,278,548.98 |
| 4 | United States | Pamela | Ansman-Wolfe | Sales Representative | $1,352,577.13 | $1,927,059.18 |

```
-- ROW_NUMBER() ORDER BY in synch with sort ORDER BY
SELECT  ROW_NUMBER()  OVER( ORDER BY JobTitle, SalesYTD DESC) AS SeqNo,
    CountryRegionName AS Country,  FirstName, LastName,  JobTitle,
    FORMAT(SalesYTD, 'c', 'en-US') AS SalesYTD, FORMAT(SalesLastYear, 'c', 'en-US') AS SalesLastYear
FROM  Sales.vSalesPerson  ORDER  BY        SeqNo;
```

| SeqNo | Country | FirstName | LastName | JobTitle | SalesYTD | SalesLastYear |
|---|---|---|---|---|---|---|
| 1 | United States | Amy | Alberts | European Sales Manager | $519,905.93 | $0.00 |
| 2 | United States | Stephen | Jiang | North American Sales Manager | $559,697.56 | $0.00 |
| 3 | United States | Syed | Abbas | Pacific Sales Manager | $172,524.45 | $0.00 |
| 4 | United States | Linda | Mitchell | Sales Representative | $4,251,368.55 | $1,439,156.03 |
| 5 | United Kingdom | Jae | Pak | Sales Representative | $4,116,871.23 | $1,635,823.40 |
| 6 | United States | Michael | Blythe | Sales Representative | $3,763,178.18 | $1,750,406.48 |
| 7 | United States | Jillian | Carson | Sales Representative | $3,189,418.37 | $1,997,186.20 |
| 8 | France | Ranjit | Varkey Chudukatil | Sales Representative | $3,121,616.32 | $2,396,539.76 |
| 9 | Canada | José | Saraiva | Sales Representative | $2,604,540.72 | $2,038,234.65 |
| 10 | United States | Shu | Ito | Sales Representative | $2,458,535.62 | $2,073,506.00 |
| 11 | United States | Tsvi | Reiter | Sales Representative | $2,315,185.61 | $1,849,640.94 |
| 12 | Germany | Rachel | Valdez | Sales Representative | $1,827,066.71 | $1,307,949.79 |
| 13 | United States | Tete | Mensa-Annan | Sales Representative | $1,576,562.20 | $0.00 |
| 14 | United States | David | Campbell | Sales Representative | $1,573,012.94 | $1,371,635.32 |
| 15 | Canada | Garrett | Vargas | Sales Representative | $1,453,719.47 | $1,620,276.90 |
| 16 | Australia | Lynn | Tsoflias | Sales Representative | $1,421,810.92 | $2,278,548.98 |
| 17 | United States | Pamela | Ansman-Wolfe | Sales Representative | $1,352,577.13 | $1,927,059.18 |

## ORDER BY Clause with CASE Conditional Expression

Sort  by LastName, MiddleName if exists else FirstName,  and FirstName in case MiddleName is used.

USE AdventureWorks;

```
SELECT          FirstName,
                COALESCE(MiddleName, '')          AS MName,  -- ISNULL can also be used
                LastName,
                AddressLine1,
                COALESCE(AddressLine2, '')         AS Addr2,
                City,
                SP.Name                           AS [State],
                CR.Name                           AS Country,
                I.CustomerID
FROM   Person.Contact AS C
   INNER JOIN Sales.Individual AS I
      ON C.ContactID = I.ContactID
   INNER JOIN Sales.CustomerAddress AS CA
      ON CA.CustomerID = I.CustomerID
   INNER JOIN Person.[Address] AS A
      ON A.AddressID = CA.AddressID
   INNER JOIN Person.StateProvince SP
      ON SP.StateProvinceID = A.StateProvinceID
   INNER JOIN Person.CountryRegion CR
      ON CR.CountryRegionCode = SP.CountryRegionCode
ORDER  BY LastName,
      CASE
      WHEN MiddleName != '' THEN MiddleName
      ELSE FirstName
      END,
      FirstName;
-- (18508 row(s) affected) -Partial results.
```

| FirstName | MName | LastName | AddressLine1 | Addr2 | City | State | Country | CustomerID |
|-----------|-------|----------|--------------|-------|------|-------|---------|------------|
| Chloe | A | Adams | 3001 N. 48th Street | | Marysville | Washington | United States | 19410 |
| Eduardo | A | Adams | 4283 Meaham Drive | | San Diego | California | United States | 25292 |
| Kaitlyn | A | Adams | 3815 Berry Dr. | | Westminster | British Columbia | Canada | 11869 |
| Mackenzie | A | Adams | 9639 Ida Drive | | Langford | British Columbia | Canada | 14640 |
| Sara | A | Adams | 7503 Hill Drive | | Milwaukie | Oregon | United States | 16986 |
| Adam | | Adams | 9381 Bayside Way | | Newport Beach | California | United States | 13323 |
| Amber | | Adams | 9720 Morning Glory Dr. | | Brisbane | Queensland | Australia | 26746 |
| Angel | | Adams | 9556 Lyman Rd. | | Burlingame | California | United States | 18504 |
| Aaron | B | Adams | 4116 Stanbridge Ct. | | Downey | California | United States | 28866 |
| Noah | B | Adams | 6738 Wallace Dr. | | El Cajon | California | United States | 16977 |
| Bailey | | Adams | 1817 Adobe Drive | | Kirkland | Washington | United States | 13280 |
| Ben | | Adams | 1534 Land Ave | | Bremerton | Washington | United States | 28678 |
| Alex | C | Adams | 237 Bellwood Dr. | | Lake Oswego | Oregon | United States | 21139 |
| Courtney | C | Adams | 6089 Santa Fe Dr. | | Torrance | California | United States | 18075 |
| Ian | C | Adams | 7963 Elk Dr | #4 | Versailles | Yveline | France | 29422 |

## *Special Sorting, Like United States On Top Of The Country Pop-Up List*
**It requires CASE or IIF conditional expression.**

```
-- Major sort key is Color if not null, else product name
-- Minor sort on ProductNumber
SELECT ProductID,
    ProductNumber,
    Name AS ProductName,
    FORMAT(ListPrice, 'c', 'en-US')  AS ListPrice,
    Color
FROM   Production.Product
WHERE  Name LIKE ( '%Road%' )
ORDER  BY        CASE
                    WHEN Color IS NULL THEN Name
                    ELSE Color
                 END,
                 ProductNumber DESC;
-- (103 row(s) affected) - Partial results.
```

| ProductID | ProductNumber | ProductName | ListPrice | Color |
|---|---|---|---|---|
| 768 | BK-R50B-44 | Road-650 Black, 44 | $782.99 | Black |
| 977 | BK-R19B-58 | Road-750 Black, 58 | $539.99 | Black |
| 999 | BK-R19B-52 | Road-750 Black, 52 | $539.99 | Black |
| 998 | BK-R19B-48 | Road-750 Black, 48 | $539.99 | Black |
| 997 | BK-R19B-44 | Road-750 Black, 44 | $539.99 | Black |
| 813 | HB-R956 | HL Road Handlebars | $120.27 | NULL |
| 512 | RM-R800 | HL Road Rim | $0.00 | NULL |
| 519 | SA-R522 | HL Road Seat Assembly | $196.92 | NULL |
| 913 | SE-R995 | HL Road Seat/Saddle | $52.64 | NULL |
| 933 | TI-R982 | HL Road Tire | $32.60 | NULL |
| 811 | HB-R504 | LL Road Handlebars | $44.54 | NULL |
| 510 | RM-R436 | LL Road Rim | $0.00 | NULL |
| 517 | SA-R127 | LL Road Seat Assembly | $133.34 | NULL |
| 911 | SE-R581 | LL Road Seat/Saddle | $27.12 | NULL |
| 931 | TI-R092 | LL Road Tire | $21.49 | NULL |
| 812 | HB-R720 | ML Road Handlebars | $61.92 | NULL |
| 511 | RM-R600 | ML Road Rim | $0.00 | NULL |
| 518 | SA-R430 | ML Road Seat Assembly | $147.14 | NULL |
| 912 | SE-R908 | ML Road Seat/Saddle | $39.14 | NULL |
| 932 | TI-R628 | ML Road Tire | $24.99 | NULL |
| 717 | FR-R92R-62 | HL Road Frame - Red, 62 | $1,431.50 | Red |
| 706 | FR-R92R-58 | HL Road Frame - Red, 58 | $1,431.50 | Red |
| 721 | FR-R92R-56 | HL Road Frame - Red, 56 | $1,431.50 | Red |

*T-SQL queries demonstrate complex sorting with the CASE expression usage.*
**CASE expression returns a SINGLE SCALAR VALUE of the same data type.**

```
SELECT  SellStartDate,
        SellEndDate,
        *
FROM    Production.Product
WHERE   Name LIKE ( '%mountain%' )
ORDER  BY CASE
                WHEN SellEndDate IS NULL THEN SellStartDate
                ELSE SellEndDate
          END DESC, Name;
GO
-- (94 row(s) affected) -Partial results.
```

| SellStartDate | SellEndDate | ProductID | Name | ProductNumber |
|---|---|---|---|---|
| 2007-07-01 00:00:00.000 | NULL | 986 | Mountain-500 Silver, 44 | BK-M18S-44 |
| 2007-07-01 00:00:00.000 | NULL | 987 | Mountain-500 Silver, 48 | BK-M18S-48 |
| 2007-07-01 00:00:00.000 | NULL | 988 | Mountain-500 Silver, 52 | BK-M18S-52 |
| 2007-07-01 00:00:00.000 | NULL | 869 | Women's Mountain Shorts, L | SH-W890-L |
| 2007-07-01 00:00:00.000 | NULL | 868 | Women's Mountain Shorts, M | SH-W890-M |
| 2007-07-01 00:00:00.000 | NULL | 867 | Women's Mountain Shorts, S | SH-W890-S |
| 2006-07-01 00:00:00.000 | 2007-06-30 00:00:00.000 | 817 | HL Mountain Front Wheel | FW-M928 |
| 2006-07-01 00:00:00.000 | 2007-06-30 00:00:00.000 | 825 | HL Mountain Rear Wheel | RW-M928 |
| 2006-07-01 00:00:00.000 | 2007-06-30 00:00:00.000 | 815 | LL Mountain Front Wheel | FW-M423 |
| 2006-07-01 00:00:00.000 | 2007-06-30 00:00:00.000 | 823 | LL Mountain Rear Wheel | RW-M423 |
| 2006-07-01 00:00:00.000 | 2007-06-30 00:00:00.000 | 814 | ML Mountain Frame - Black, 38 | FR-M63B-38 |
| 2006-07-01 00:00:00.000 | 2007-06-30 00:00:00.000 | 830 | ML Mountain Frame - Black, 40 | FR-M63B-40 |

```
-- 2 keys descending sort
SELECT          PRODUCTNAME  = P.Name,
                SALETOTAL        = ( OrderQty * UnitPrice ),
                NETSALETOTAL  = ( ( OrderQty - RejectedQty ) * UnitPrice )
FROM   Production.Product P
    INNER JOIN Purchasing.PurchaseOrderDetail SOD
        ON P.ProductID = SOD.ProductID
ORDER  BY PRODUCTNAME  DESC,  SALETOTAL DESC;

-- Column alias sorting of GROUP BY aggregation results
SELECT [YEAR]=YEAR(OrderDate), Orders = COUNT(*)
FROM AdventureWorks2012.Sales.SalesOrderHeader
GROUP BY YEAR(OrderDate)  ORDER BY [YEAR];
```

| YEAR | Orders |
|---|---|
| 2005 | 1379 |
| 2006 | 3692 |
| 2007 | 12443 |
| 2008 | 13951 |

**CHAPTER 12:  Basic SELECT Statement Syntax & Examples**

## ORDER BY Clause with IIF Conditional Function

Sort  by LastName, MiddleName if exists else FirstName,  and FirstName in case MiddleName is used.

USE AdventureWorks;

```
SELECT          FirstName,
                COALESCE(MiddleName, '')          AS MName,  -- ISNULL can also be used
                LastName,
                AddressLine1,
                COALESCE(AddressLine2, '')        AS Addr2,
                City,
                SP.Name                           AS [State],
                CR.Name                           AS Country,
                I.CustomerID
FROM   Person.Contact AS C
    INNER JOIN Sales.Individual AS I
        ON C.ContactID = I.ContactID
    INNER JOIN Sales.CustomerAddress AS CA
        ON CA.CustomerID = I.CustomerID
    INNER JOIN Person.[Address] AS A
        ON A.AddressID = CA.AddressID
    INNER JOIN Person.StateProvince SP
        ON SP.StateProvinceID = A.StateProvinceID
    INNER JOIN Person.CountryRegion CR
        ON CR.CountryRegionCode = SP.CountryRegionCode
ORDER  BY       LastName,
                IIF( MiddleName != '', MiddleName, FirstName),
                FirstName;
```
-- (18508 row(s) affected) -Partial results.

| FirstName | MName | LastName | AddressLine1 | Addr2 | City | State | Country | CustomerID |
|---|---|---|---|---|---|---|---|---|
| Chloe | A | Adams | 3001 N. 48th Street | | Marysville | Washington | United States | 19410 |
| Eduardo | A | Adams | 4283 Meaham Drive | | San Diego | California | United States | 25292 |
| Kaitlyn | A | Adams | 3815 Berry Dr. | | Westminster | British Columbia | Canada | 11869 |
| Mackenzie | A | Adams | 9639 Ida Drive | | Langford | British Columbia | Canada | 14640 |
| Sara | A | Adams | 7503 Hill Drive | | Milwaukie | Oregon | United States | 16986 |
| Adam | | Adams | 9381 Bayside Way | | Newport Beach | California | United States | 13323 |
| Amber | | Adams | 9720 Morning Glory Dr. | | Brisbane | Queensland | Australia | 26746 |
| Angel | | Adams | 9556 Lyman Rd. | | Burlingame | California | United States | 18504 |
| Aaron | B | Adams | 4116 Stanbridge Ct. | | Downey | California | United States | 28866 |
| Noah | B | Adams | 6738 Wallace Dr. | | El Cajon | California | United States | 16977 |
| Bailey | | Adams | 1817 Adobe Drive | | Kirkland | Washington | United States | 13280 |
| Ben | | Adams | 1534 Land Ave | | Bremerton | Washington | United States | 28678 |
| Alex | C | Adams | 237 Bellwood Dr. | | Lake Oswego | Oregon | United States | 21139 |
| Courtney | C | Adams | 6089 Santa Fe Dr. | | Torrance | California | United States | 18075 |
| Ian | C | Adams | 7963 Elk Dr | #4 | Versailles | Yveline | France | 29422 |

## ORDER BY Clause with the RANK() Function

T-SQL query demonstrates the combination of CASE expression and RANK() function in an ORDER BY clause. Note that while such a complex sort is technically impressive, ultimately it has to make sense to the user, the Business Intelligence consumer.

```
-- SQL complex sorting
USE AdventureWorks;

SELECT          ContactID,
                FirstName,
                LastName,
                COALESCE(Title, '')  AS Title
FROM   Person.Contact
WHERE  LEFT(FirstName, 1) = 'M'
ORDER  BY CASE
                WHEN LEFT(LastName, 1) = 'A' THEN RANK()
                            OVER( ORDER BY CONCAT(FirstName, SPACE(1), LastName))
                WHEN LEFT(LastName, 1) = 'M' THEN RANK()
                             OVER( ORDER BY CONCAT(LastName,', ', FirstName), Title)
                WHEN LEFT(LastName, 1) = 'U' THEN RANK()
                             OVER( ORDER BY CONCAT(LastName,', ', FirstName)  DESC)
                ELSE RANK()
                             OVER( ORDER BY LastName ASC, FirstName DESC)
        END;
```

| ContactID | FirstName | LastName | Title |
|-----------|-----------|-----------|-------|
| 9500 | Mackenzie | Adams | |
| 10144 | Mackenzie | Allen | |
| 10128 | Madeline | Allen | |
| 11708 | Madison | Alexander | |
| 11527 | Madison | Anderson | |
| 19872 | Morgan | Bailey | |
| 8059 | Michelle | Bailey | |
| 8080 | Melissa | Bailey | |
| 18291 | Megan | Bailey | |
| 8070 | Mariah | Bailey | |
| 2432 | Maria | Bailey | |
| 14378 | Marcus | Bailey | |
| 8063 | Makayla | Bailey | |
| 8032 | Mackenzie | Bailey | |
| 9521 | Morgan | Baker | |
| 3320 | Miguel | Baker | |
| 15437 | Mason | Baker | |
| 9546 | Mary | Baker | |
| 1082 | Mary | Baker | |
| 9539 | Maria | Baker | |

## ORDER BY Clause with Custom Mapped Sort Sequence

Typically we rely on alphabets or numbers for sorting. What if, for example, we don't want United States way down on a website drop-down menu, rather than on the top with Canada and United Kingdom just above "lucky" Australia?  We have to do custom mapping for such a sort in the ORDER BY clause.

```
USE AdventureWorks;
GO

SELECT          AddressLine1,
                City,
                SP.StateProvinceCode              AS State,
                PostalCode,
                CR.Name                           AS  Country
FROM   Person.[Address] A
    INNER JOIN Person.StateProvince SP            ON A.StateProvinceID = SP.StateProvinceID
    INNER JOIN Person.CountryRegion CR            ON SP.CountryRegionCode = CR.CountryRegionCode
ORDER  BY (     CASE
                    WHEN CR.Name = 'United States' THEN 0
                    WHEN CR.Name = 'Canada' THEN 1
                    WHEN CR.Name = 'United Kingdom' THEN 2
                    ELSE 3
                END ),
                Country,
                City
                AddressLine1;
-- (19614 row(s) affected) - Partial results.
```

| AddressLine1 | City | State | PostalCode | Country |
|---|---|---|---|---|
| 9355 Armstrong Road | York | ENG | YO15 | United Kingdom |
| 939 Vista Del Diablo | York | ENG | YO15 | United Kingdom |
| 9458 Flame Drive | York | ENG | YO15 | United Kingdom |
| 9557 Steven Circle | York | ENG | YO3 4TN | United Kingdom |
| 9589 Rae Anne Dr | York | ENG | YO3 4TN | United Kingdom |
| 9643 Willow Pass Road | York | ENG | YO15 | United Kingdom |
| 9700 Terra Grand | York | ENG | YO24 1GF | United Kingdom |
| 9790 Deer Creek Lane | York | ENG | YO24 1GF | United Kingdom |
| 9896 Ida Ave | York | ENG | YO24 1GF | United Kingdom |
| 9903 Mt. Washington Way | York | ENG | YO24 1GF | United Kingdom |
| 9907 Via Appia | York | ENG | YO3 4TN | United Kingdom |
| P. O. Box 5413 | York | ENG | YO24 1GF | United Kingdom |
| 2565-175 Mitchell Road | Alexandria | NSW | 2015 | Australia |
| Level 59 | Alexandria | NSW | 2015 | Australia |
| 1058 Kirker Pass Road | Bendigo | VIC | 3550 | Australia |
| 1153 Loma Linda | Bendigo | VIC | 3550 | Australia |
| 1218 Trasher Road | Bendigo | VIC | 3550 | Australia |
| 1277 Argenta Dr. | Bendigo | VIC | 3550 | Australia |
| 1286 Cincerto Circle | Bendigo | VIC | 3550 | Australia |
| 1589 Mt. Tamalpais Place | Bendigo | VIC | 3550 | Australia |
| 1688 Sudan Loop | Bendigo | VIC | 3550 | Australia |
| 1729 Panorama Drive | Bendigo | VIC | 3550 | Australia |

## ORDER BY Clause with Custom Alphanumeric Sort Sequence

A frequent requirement is custom sorting on alphanumeric field (column). The next T-SQL query demonstrates special alphanumeric sorting.

```
USE AdventureWorks;

SELECT AddressLine1,
            isnull(AddressLine2, '')    AS Addressline2,
            City,
            SP.StateProvinceCode    AS State,
            PostalCode,
            CR.Name            AS Country
FROM   Person.[Address] A
    INNER JOIN Person.StateProvince SP
    ON A.StateProvinceID = SP.StateProvinceID
    INNER JOIN Person.CountryRegion CR
    ON SP.CountryRegionCode = CR.CountryRegionCode
ORDER  BY (     CASE
                    WHEN Ascii([AddressLine1]) BETWEEN 65 AND 90 THEN 0 -- Upper case alpha
                    WHEN Ascii([AddressLine1]) BETWEEN 48 AND 57 THEN 1 -- Digits
                    ELSE 2
                END ),
            AddressLine1,
            City;
-- (19614 row(s) affected) - Partial results.
```

| AddressLine1 | Addressline2 | City | State | PostalCode | Country |
|---|---|---|---|---|---|
| Zur Lindung 46 | | Leipzig | NW | 04139 | Germany |
| Zur Lindung 6 | | Saarlouis | SL | 66740 | Germany |
| Zur Lindung 6 | | Solingen | NW | 42651 | Germany |
| Zur Lindung 609 | | Sulzbach Taunus | SL | 66272 | Germany |
| Zur Lindung 7 | | Berlin | HE | 14129 | Germany |
| Zur Lindung 7 | | Neunkirchen | SL | 66578 | Germany |
| Zur Lindung 764 | | Paderborn | HH | 33041 | Germany |
| Zur Lindung 78 | | Berlin | HH | 10791 | Germany |
| Zur Lindung 787 | | München | NW | 80074 | Germany |
| 00, rue Saint-Lazare | | Dunkerque | 59 | 59140 | France |
| 02, place de Fontenoy | | Verrieres Le Buisson | 91 | 91370 | France |
| 035, boulevard du Montparnasse | | Verrieres Le Buisson | 91 | 91370 | France |
| 081, boulevard du Montparnasse | | Saint-Denis | 93 | 93400 | France |
| 081, boulevard du Montparnasse | | Seattle | WA | 98104 | United States |
| 084, boulevard du Montparnasse | | Les Ulis | 91 | 91940 | France |
| 1 Corporate Center Drive | | Miami | FL | 33127 | United States |
| 1 Mt. Dell Drive | | Portland | OR | 97205 | United States |
| 1 Smiling Tree Court | Space 55 | Los Angeles | CA | 90012 | United States |
| 1, allée des Princes | | Courbevoie | 92 | 92400 | France |

*T-SQL Script Demonstrates Unusual Sorting Techniques*

```
/***************************************************
*   SORTING ON THE LAST WORD OF A STRING
***************************************************/
USE tempdb;

-- SELECT INTO table create sorted on BusinessEntityID
SELECT BusinessEntityID,
        FULLNAME = CONCAT(FirstName , SPACE(1), LastName )
INTO   People
FROM   AdventureWorks2012.Person.Person
ORDER  BY BusinessEntityID

SELECT TOP 2 * FROM   People;
```

| BusinessEntityID | FULLNAME |
|---|---|
| 285 | Syed Abbas |
| 293 | Catherine Abel |

```
-- Sorting on the Last Name given the Full Name string
SELECT *
FROM   People
ORDER  BY REVERSE(LEFT(REVERSE(FullName), charindex(' ', REVERSE(FullName) + ' '  ) - 1)),
        FullName ;
GO
-- (19972 row(s) affected) - Partial results.
```

| BusinessEntityID | FULLNAME |
|---|---|
| 285 | Syed Abbas |
| 293 | Catherine Abel |
| 295 | Kim Abercrombie |
| 2170 | Kim Abercrombie |
| 38 | Kim Abercrombie |
| 211 | Hazem Abolrous |

```
DROP TABLE People
GO
```

# Date & Time Conversion To / From String

While there are only a few internal representation of date and time, string representations are many, even not deterministic since they may change from one country to another such as weekday and month names.   T-SQL scripts demonstrate the myriad of date and time conversion possibilities.

## The CONVERT() Function with Style Number Parameter

```
-- String source  format: mon dd yyyy hh:mmAM (or PM)
-- 100 is the style number parameter for CONVERT
SELECT [Date&Time] = convert(datetime, 'Oct 23 2020 11:01AM', 100)
```

| Date&Time |
|---|
| 2020-10-23 11:01:00.000 |

```
-- Default without style number
SELECT convert(datetime, 'Oct 23 2020 11:01AM')              -- 2020-10-23 11:01:00.000
```

```
-- Without century (yy) string date conversion with style number 0
-- Input format: mon dd yy hh:mmAM (or PM)
SELECT [Date&Time] = convert(datetime, 'Oct 23 20 11:01AM', 0)
```

| Date&Time |
|---|
| 2020-10-23 11:01:00.000 |

```
-- Default without style number
SELECT convert(datetime, 'Oct 23 20 11:01AM')               -- 2020-10-23
11:01:00.000
```

Convert string date & time to datetime (8-bytes internal representation)  data type.

```
SELECT convert(datetime, '10/23/2016', 101)        -- mm/dd/yyyy

SELECT convert(datetime, '2016.10.23', 102)        -- yyyy.mm.dd ANSI date with century

SELECT convert(datetime, '23/10/2016', 103)        -- dd/mm/yyyy

SELECT convert(datetime, '23.10.2016', 104)-- dd.mm.yyyy

SELECT convert(datetime, '23-10-2016', 105)        -- dd-mm-yyyy

-- mon (month) types are nondeterministic conversions, dependent on language setting.
SELECT convert(datetime, '23 OCT 2016', 106)       -- dd mon yyyy
```

**CHAPTER 12:  Basic SELECT Statement Syntax & Examples**

## String Datetime Formats With "Mon" Are Nondeterministic, Language Dependent

SELECT [Date&Time] = convert(datetime, 'Oct 23, 2016', 107)  -- mon dd, yyyy

    Date&Time
    2016-10-23 00:00:00.000

SELECT [Date&Time ]=convert(datetime, '20:10:44', 108)          -- hh:mm:ss

    Date&Time
    1900-01-01 20:10:44.000

SELECT [Date&Time ]=convert(datetime, 'Oct 23 2016 11:02:44:013AM', 109) --  mon dd yyyy hh:mm:ss:mmmAM (or PM)

    Date&Time
    2016-10-23 11:02:44.013

SELECT convert(datetime, '10-23-2016', 110)                    -- mm-dd-yyyy
SELECT convert(datetime, '2016/10/23', 111)                    -- yyyy/mm/dd

**-- YYYYMMDD ISO date format works at any language setting - international standard**
SELECT [Date&Time ]=convert(datetime, '20161023')

    Date&Time
    2016-10-23 00:00:00.000

SELECT [Date&Time ]=convert(datetime, '20161023', 112)     -- ISO yyyymmdd

    Date&Time
    2016-10-23 00:00:00.000

SELECT [Date&Time ]=convert(datetime, '23 Oct 2016 11:02:07:577', 113)  -- dd mon yyyy hh:mm:ss:mmm

    Date&Time
    2016-10-23 11:02:07.577

SELECT [Date&Time ]=convert(datetime, '20:10:25:300', 114)             -- hh:mm:ss:mmm(24h)

    Date&Time
    1900-01-01 20:10:25.300

SELECT [Date&Time ]=convert(datetime, '2016-10-23 20:44:11', 120)    -- yyyy-mm-dd hh:mm:ss(24h)
    Date&Time
    2016-10-23 20:44:11.000

**CHAPTER 12:  Basic SELECT Statement Syntax & Examples**

### *Style 126 Is ISO 8601 Format: International Standard; Works With Any Language Setting*

```
SELECT [Date&Time ]=convert(datetime, '2018-10-23T18:52:47.513', 126) -- yyyy-mm-
ddThh:mm:ss(.mmm)
```

> Date&Time
> 2018-10-23 18:52:47.513

```
SELECT [Date&Time ]=convert(datetime, '2016-10-23 20:44:11.500', 121)        -- yyyy-mm-dd
hh:mm:ss.mmm
```

> Date&Time
> 2016-10-23 20:44:11.500

```
-- Islamic / Hijri date conversion

SELECT CONVERT(nvarchar(32), convert(datetime,'2016-10-23'), 130);
-- 22 محرم 1438 12:00:00:000AM

SELECT [Date&Time ]=convert(datetime, N'23 شوال  1441  6:52:47:513PM', 130)
```

> Date&Time
> 2020-06-14 18:52:47.513

```
SELECT [Date&Time ]=convert(datetime, '23/10/1441  6:52:47:513PM',   131)
```

> Date&Time
> 2020-06-14 18:52:47.513

```
-- Convert DDMMYYYY format to datetime with intermediate conversion using STUFF().

SELECT STUFF(STUFF('31012016',3,0,'-'),6,0,'-');
-- 31-01-2016

SELECT [Date&Time ]=convert(datetime, STUFF(STUFF('31012016',3,0,'-'),6,0,'-'), 105)
```

> Date&Time
> 2016-01-31 00:00:00.000

```
-- Equivalent
SELECT STUFF(STUFF('31012016',3,0,'/'),6,0,'/');   -- 31/01/2016
SELECT [Date&Time ]=convert(datetime, STUFF(STUFF('31012016',3,0,'/'),6,0,'/'), 103)
```

## String to Datetime Conversion Without Century

String to datetime conversion without century - some exceptions.   Nondeterministic means language setting dependent such as Mar/Mär/mars/márc .

SELECT [Date&Time ]=convert(datetime, 'Oct 23 16 11:02:44AM')        -- Default

Date&Time
2016-10-23 11:02:44.000

| | | |
|---|---|---|
| SELECT convert(datetime, '10/23/16', 1) | mm/dd/yy | U.S. |
| SELECT convert(datetime, '16.10.23', 2) | yy.mm.dd | ANSI |
| SELECT convert(datetime, '23/10/16', 3) | dd/mm/yy | UK/FR |
| SELECT convert(datetime, '23.10.16', 4) | dd.mm.yy | German |
| SELECT convert(datetime, '23-10-16', 5) | dd-mm-yy | Italian |
| SELECT convert(datetime, '23 OCT 16', 6) | dd mon yy | non-det. |
| SELECT convert(datetime, 'Oct 23, 16', 7) | mon dd, yy | non-det. |
| SELECT convert(datetime, '20:10:44', 8) | hh:mm:ss | |
| SELECT convert(datetime, 'Oct 23 16 11:02:44:013AM', 9) | Default with msec | |
| SELECT convert(datetime, '10-23-16', 10) | mm-dd-yy | U.S. |
| SELECT convert(datetime, '16/10/23', 11) | yy/mm/dd | Japan |
| SELECT convert(datetime, '161023', 12) | yymmdd | ISO |
| SELECT convert(datetime, '23 Oct 16 11:02:07:577', 13) | dd mon yy hh:mm:ss:mmm EU dflt | |
| SELECT convert(datetime, '20:10:25:300', 14) | hh:mm:ss:mmm(24h) | |
| SELECT convert(datetime, '2016-10-23 20:44:11',20) | yyyy-mm-dd hh:mm:ss(24h) ODBC can. | |
| SELECT convert(datetime, '2016-10-23 20:44:11.500', 21) | yyyy-mm-dd hh:mm:ss.mmm ODBC | |

## Combine Date & Time String into Datetime

```
DECLARE @DateTimeValue varchar(32), @DateValue char(8), @TimeValue char(6)
 SELECT @DateValue = '20200718',            @TimeValue = '211920'
SELECT          @DateTimeValue =
                CONCAT(
                convert(varchar, convert(datetime, @DateValue), 111),
                ' ', substring(@TimeValue, 1, 2) , ':', substring(@TimeValue, 3, 2) , ':',
substring(@TimeValue, 5, 2)  )

SELECT  DateInput = @DateValue, TimeInput = @TimeValue,  DateTimeOutput = @DateTimeValue;
GO
```

| DateInput | TimeInput | DateTimeOutput |
|-----------|-----------|----------------------|
| 20200718  | 211920    | 2020/07/18 21:19:20  |

```
SELECT DATETIMEFROMPARTS (2020, 07, 1, 21, 01, 20, 700)              -- New in SQL Server 2012
```

## Date and Time Internal Storage Format

DATETIME 8 bytes internal storage structure:

- ➢ 1st 4 bytes:        number of days after the base date 1900-01-01
- ➢ 2nd 4 bytes:        number of clock-ticks (3.33 milliseconds) since midnight

```
SELECT CONVERT(binary(8), CURRENT_TIMESTAMP);
```

| Hex |
|-----|
| 0x0000A09C00F23CE1 |

DATE 3 bytes internal storage structure:

- ➢ 3 bytes integer:   number of days after the first date 0001-01-01
- ➢ Note: hex byte order reversed

SMALLDATETIME 4 bytes internal storage structure

- ➢ 1st 2 bytes:        number of days after the base date 1900-01-01
- ➢ 2nd 2 bytes:        number of minutes since midnight

```
SELECT Hex=CONVERT(binary(4), convert(smalldatetime, getdate()));
```

| Hex |
|-----|
| 0xA09C0375 |

**CHAPTER 12:  Basic SELECT Statement Syntax & Examples**

## Date & Time Operations Using System Operators & Functions

```
-- Conversion from hex (binary) to datetime value
DECLARE @dtHex binary(8)= 0x00009966002d3344;  DECLARE @dt datetime = @dtHex;
SELECT @dt;   -- 2007-07-09 02:44:34.147
```

```
-- SQL convert seconds to HH:MM:SS -
DECLARE  @Seconds INT;  SET @Seconds = 20000 ;
SELECT HH = @Seconds / 3600, MM = (@Seconds%3600) / 60, SS = (@Seconds%60) ;
```

| HH | MM | SS |
|----|----|----|
| 5  | 33 | 20 |

## Extract Date Only from DATETIME Data Type

```
DECLARE @Now datetime = CURRENT_TIMESTAMP -- getdate()

SELECT  DateAndTime       = @Now      -- Date portion and Time portion
        ,DateString               = REPLACE(LEFT(CONVERT (varchar, @Now, 112),10),' ','-')
        ,[Date]                   = CONVERT(DATE, @Now)  -- SQL Server 2008 and on - date part
        ,Midnight1                = dateadd(day, datediff(day,0, @Now), 0)
        ,Midnight2                = CONVERT(DATETIME,CONVERT(int, @Now))
        ,Midnight3                = CONVERT(DATETIME,CONVERT(BIGINT,@Now) &
(POWER(Convert(bigint,2),32)-1));
```

| DateAndTime | DateString | Date | Midnight1 | Midnight2 | Midnight3 |
|---|---|---|---|---|---|
| 2020-07-28 15:01:51.960 | 20200728 | 2020-07-28 | 2020-07-28 00:00:00.000 | 2020-07-29 00:00:00.000 | 2020-07-29 00:00:00.000 |

```
-- Compare today with database dates
SELECT         TOP (10)  OrderDate = CONVERT(date, OrderDate),
               Today = CONVERT(date, getdate()),
               DeltaDays = DATEDIFF(DD, OrderDate, getdate())
FROM AdventureWorks2012.Sales.SalesOrderHeader  ORDER BY NEWID(); -- random sort
```

| OrderDate | Today | DeltaDays |
|---|---|---|
| 2008-01-15 | 2012-08-10 | 1669 |
| 2006-07-14 | 2012-08-10 | 2219 |
| 2008-07-05 | 2012-08-10 | 1497 |
| 2008-03-01 | 2012-08-10 | 1623 |
| 2007-10-01 | 2012-08-10 | 1775 |
| 2007-01-15 | 2012-08-10 | 2034 |
| 2008-05-27 | 2012-08-10 | 1536 |
| 2008-04-18 | 2012-08-10 | 1575 |
| 2008-04-25 | 2012-08-10 | 1568 |
| 2006-12-17 | 2012-08-10 | 2063 |

## String Date Formats Without Time

```
-- String date format yyyy/mm/dd from datetime
SELECT CONVERT(VARCHAR(10), GETDATE(), 111) AS [YYYY/MM/DD] ;
```

> YYYY/MM/DD
> 2012/07/28

```
SELECT CONVERT(VARCHAR(10), GETDATE(), 112) AS [YYYYMMDD];
```

> YYYYMMDD
> 20120728

```
SELECT REPLACE(CONVERT(VARCHAR(10), GETDATE(), 111),'/',' ') AS [YYYY MM DD];
```

> YYYY MM DD
> 2020 07 28

```
-- Converting to special (non-standard) date formats: DD-MMM-YY
SELECT UPPER(REPLACE(CONVERT(VARCHAR,GETDATE(),6),' ','-')) AS CustomDate;
```

> CustomDate
> 28-JUL-20

```
-- SQL convert date string to datetime - time set to 00:00:00.000 or 12:00AM

PRINT CONVERT(datetime,'07-10-2020',110) ;        -- Jul 10 2020 12:00AM
PRINT CONVERT(datetime,'2020/07/10',111) ;        -- Jul 10 2020 12:00AM
PRINT CONVERT(datetime,'20200710',  112);         -- Jul 10 2020 12:00AM
GO
```

```
-- SQL Server cast string to date / datetime
DECLARE @DateValue char(8) = '20200718'

SELECT [Date] = CAST (@DateValue AS datetime);
GO
```

> Date
> 2020-07-18 00:00:00.000

### String date to string date conversion with nested CONVERT

```
SELECT CONVERT(varchar, CONVERT(datetime, '20140508'), 100) AS StringDate;
GO
```

> StringDate
> May  8 2014 12:00AM

```
-- T-SQL convert date to integer

DECLARE @Date datetime;  SET @Date = getdate();
SELECT DateAsInteger = CAST (CONVERT(varchar,@Date,112) as INT);
GO
```

> DateAsInteger
> 20120728

```
-- SQL Server convert integer to datetime

DECLARE @iDate int = 20151225;
SELECT IntegerToDatetime = CAST(convert(varchar,@iDate) as datetime)
GO
```

> IntegerToDatetime
> 2015-12-25 00:00:00.000

```
-- Alternates: date-only datetime values

SELECT [DATE-ONLY]=CONVERT(DATETIME, FLOOR(CONVERT(FLOAT, GETDATE())));

SELECT [DATE-ONLY]=CONVERT(DATETIME, FLOOR(CONVERT(MONEY, GETDATE())));

SELECT [DATE-ONLY]=CONVERT(DATETIME, CONVERT(DATE, GETDATE()));

-- CAST string to datetime

-- String date preparation, length is 10 characters
SELECT CONVERT(varchar, GETDATE(), 101), LEN (CONVERT(varchar, GETDATE(), 101))
--        07/28/2018        10

SELECT [DATE-ONLY]=CAST(CONVERT(varchar, GETDATE(), 101) AS DATETIME);
```

> DATE-ONLY
> 2018-07-28 00:00:00.000

**CHAPTER 12:  Basic SELECT Statement Syntax & Examples**

## DATEADD() and DATEDIFF() Functions

```
-- T-SQL strip time from date
SELECT getdate() AS [DateTime], dateadd(dd, datediff(dd, 0, getdate()), 0) [DateOnly];
```

| DateTime | DateOnly |
|---|---|
| 2012-07-28 17:24:07.300 | 2012-07-28 00:00:00.000 |

```
-- First day of current month
SELECT dateadd(month, datediff(month, 0, getdate()), 0)  AS FirstDayOfCurrentMonth;
SELECT dateadd(dd,1, EOMONTH(getdate(),-1)); -- New to SQL Server 2012
```

| FirstDayOfCurrentMonth |
|---|
| 2020-07-01 00:00:00.000 |

```
-- 15th day of current month
SELECT dateadd(day,14,dateadd(month, datediff(month,0,getdate()),0)) AS MiddleOfCurrentMonth;
SELECT dateadd(dd,15, EOMONTH(getdate(),-1)); -- New to SQL Server 2012
```

| MiddleOfCurrentMonth |
|---|
| 2012-07-15 00:00:00.000 |

```
-- First Monday of current month

SELECT   dateadd(day, (9-datepart(weekday,
         dateadd(month, datediff(month, 0, getdate()), 0)))%7,
         dateadd(month, datediff(month, 0, getdate()), 0))  AS [First Monday Of Current Month];
GO
```

| First Monday Of Current Month |
|---|
| 2012-07-02 00:00:00.000 |

```
-- Next Monday calculation from the reference date which was a Monday
DECLARE @Now datetime = GETDATE();
DECLARE @NextMonday datetime = dateadd(dd, ((datediff(dd, '19000101', @Now)
          / 7) * 7) + 7, '19000101');
SELECT [Now]=@Now, [Next Monday]=@NextMonday;
GO
```

| Now | Next Monday |
|---|---|
| 2012-07-28 17:35:29.657 | 2012-07-30 00:00:00.000 |

**CHAPTER 12: Basic SELECT Statement Syntax & Examples**

## Last Date & First Date Calculations

-- Last Friday of current month

SELECT   dateadd(day, -7+(6-datepart(weekday,

        dateadd(month, datediff(month, 0, getdate())+1, 0)))%7,

        dateadd(month, datediff(month, 0, getdate())+1, 0)) ;

-- First day of next month

SELECT dateadd(month, datediff(month, 0, getdate())+1, 0) ;

-- 15th of next month

SELECT dateadd(day,14, dateadd(month, datediff(month, 0, getdate())+1, 0));

-- First Monday of next month

SELECT   dateadd(day, (9-datepart(weekday,
        dateadd(month, datediff(month, 0, getdate())+1, 0)))%7,
        dateadd(month, datediff(month, 0, getdate())+1, 0));


-- Next 12 months start & end - EOMONTH is new to SQL Server 2012
SELECT TOP 12
        DATEADD(DD,1, EOMONTH(getdate(),number-1))     AS Start,
        EOMONTH(getdate(),number)                      AS [End]
FROM master.dbo.spt_values   -- get integer sequence
WHERE type='P'  ORDER BY number;

| Start | End |
|---|---|
| 2016-08-01 | 2016-08-31 |
| 2016-09-01 | 2016-09-30 |
| 2016-10-01 | 2016-10-31 |
| 2016-11-01 | 2016-11-30 |
| 2016-12-01 | 2016-12-31 |
| 2017-01-01 | 2017-01-31 |
| 2017-02-01 | 2017-02-28 |
| 2017-03-01 | 2017-03-31 |
| 2017-04-01 | 2017-04-30 |
| 2017-05-01 | 2017-05-31 |
| 2017-06-01 | 2017-06-30 |
| 2017-07-01 | 2017-07-31 |

## BETWEEN Operator for Date Range

Date time range SELECT using the using >= and < operators. Count Sales Orders for date range 2007 OCT-NOV.

```
DECLARE  @StartDate DATETIME,  @EndDate DATETIME
SET @StartDate = convert(DATETIME,'10/01/2007',101)
SET @EndDate   = convert(DATETIME,'11/30/2007',101)
SELECT @StartDate, @EndDate
-- 2007-10-01 00:00:00.000  2007-11-30 00:00:00.000
SELECT dateadd(DAY,1,@EndDate),    dateadd(ms,-3,dateadd(DAY,1,@EndDate))
-- 2007-12-01 00:00:00.000  2007-11-30 23:59:59.997

SELECT [Sales Orders for 2007 OCT-NOV] = COUNT(* )
FROM   AdventureWorks2012.Sales.SalesOrderHeader
WHERE  OrderDate >= @StartDate AND OrderDate < dateadd(DAY,1,@EndDate)
```

| Sales Orders for 2007 OCT-NOV |
| --- |
| 3668 |

Equivalent date range query using BETWEEN comparison. It requires a bit of trick programming. 23.59.59.997 is the last available time in a day.

```
SELECT [Sales Orders for 2007 OCT-NOV] = COUNT(* )
FROM   AdventureWorks2012.Sales.SalesOrderHeader
WHERE  OrderDate BETWEEN @StartDate AND dateadd(ms,-3, dateadd(DAY, 1, @EndDate))
```

| Sales Orders for 2007 OCT-NOV |
| --- |
| 3668 |

The BETWEEN operator can be used with string dates as well. Note: anything after midnight on  2004-02-10 is not included.

```
USE AdventureWorks;
SELECT POs=COUNT(*) FROM Purchasing.PurchaseOrderHeader
WHERE OrderDate BETWEEN '20040201' AND '20040210'
```

| POs |
| --- |
| 108 |

**CHAPTER 12:  Basic SELECT Statement Syntax & Examples**

*BETWEEN Dates Without Time: Entire 2004-02-10 Day Included This Fashion*

```
SELECT POs=COUNT(*) FROM Purchasing.PurchaseOrderHeader
WHERE datediff(dd,0,OrderDate)
       BETWEEN datediff(dd,0,'20040201 12:11:39') AND datediff(dd,0,'20040210 14:33:19')
```

| POs |
|-----|
| 108 |

The datetime range BETWEEN is equivalent to >=...AND....<= operators.

```
SELECT POs=COUNT(*) FROM Purchasing.PurchaseOrderHeader
WHERE OrderDate  BETWEEN '2004-02-01 00:00:00.000' AND '2004-02-10  00:00:00.000'
```

| POs |
|-----|
| 108 |

Orders with datetime OrderDate-s  of

| '2004-02-10  00:00:01.000' | 1 second after midnight (start of day at 12:00AM) |
|----------------------------|---------------------------------------------------|
| '2004-02-10  00:01:00.000' | 1 minute after midnight                           |
| '2004-02-10  01:00:00.000' | 1 hour after midnight                             |
| '2004-02-10  23:00:00.000' | 23 hours after midnight                           |

would  not included in the preceding two queries.  Only datetime OrderDate of '2004-02-10 00:00:00.000'  would be included. That would be OK if the time part is not used. But even in that case and order can be entered accidentally with a time part, that would throw off the count.

To include the entire day of 2004-02-10, move the day up by one and use the < operator:

```
SELECT POs=COUNT(*) FROM Purchasing.PurchaseOrderHeader
WHERE OrderDate >= '20040201' AND OrderDate < '20040211';
```

| POs |
|-----|
| 108 |

The reason we cannot detect a difference is due to lack of data passed midnight on 2004-02-11.

```
SELECT  [PurchaseOrderID], [RevisionNumber], [Status],
        [EmployeeID], [VendorID], [ShipMethodID], [OrderDate]
FROM [AdventureWorks].[Purchasing].[PurchaseOrderHeader] WHERE PurchaseOrderID = 1665;
```

| PurchaseOrderID | RevisionNumber | Status | EmployeeID | VendorID | ShipMethodID | OrderDate |
|-----------------|----------------|--------|------------|----------|--------------|-----------|
| 1665            | 0              | 4      | 261        | 43       | 5            | 2004-02-10 00:00:00.000 |

**CHAPTER 12:  Basic SELECT Statement Syntax & Examples**

### *Advance the datetime one second from midnight, the BETWEEN datetime query is not going to count it*

```
UPDATE [AdventureWorks].[Purchasing].[PurchaseOrderHeader]
      SET OrderDate = '2004-02-10 00:00:01.000'
WHERE PurchaseOrderID = 1665;
-- (1 row(s) affected)
```

This is the current value for OrderDate datetime.

| PurchaseOrderID | RevisionNumber | Status | EmployeeID | VendorID | ShipMethodID | OrderDate |
|---|---|---|---|---|---|---|
| 1665 | 0 | 4 | 261 | 43 | 5 | 2004-02-10 00:00:01.000 |

The following queries are not going to count this passed midnight record any more.

```
SELECT POs=COUNT(*) FROM Purchasing.PurchaseOrderHeader
WHERE OrderDate BETWEEN '2004-02-01 00:00:00.000' AND '2004-02-10  00:00:00.000'
```

| POs |
|---|
| 107 |

```
USE AdventureWorks; SELECT POs=COUNT(*) FROM Purchasing.PurchaseOrderHeader
WHERE OrderDate BETWEEN '20040201' AND '20040210'
```

| POs |
|---|
| 107 |

While the query we designed specifically for a case like this will count it correctly.

```
SELECT POs=COUNT(*) FROM Purchasing.PurchaseOrderHeader
WHERE OrderDate >= '20040201' AND OrderDate < '20040211'
```

| POs |
|---|
| 108 |

We restore the data to its original value.

```
UPDATE [AdventureWorks].[Purchasing].[PurchaseOrderHeader]
      SET OrderDate = '2004-02-10 00:00:00.000'
WHERE PurchaseOrderID = 1665;     -- (1 row(s) affected)
```

### CHAPTER 12:  Basic SELECT Statement Syntax & Examples

## Date Validation Function ISDATE()

```
DECLARE @StringDate varchar(32);
SET @StringDate = '2011-03-15 18:50';
IF EXISTS( SELECT * WHERE ISDATE(@StringDate) = 1)
  PRINT 'VALID DATE: ' + @StringDate
ELSE
  PRINT 'INVALID DATE: ' + @StringDate;
```

```
     VALID DATE: 2011-03-15 18:50
```

```
DECLARE @StringDate varchar(32) ;
SET @StringDate = '20112-03-15 18:50';
IF EXISTS( SELECT * WHERE ISDATE(@StringDate) = 1)
  PRINT 'VALID DATE: ' + @StringDate
ELSE  PRINT 'INVALID DATE: ' + @StringDate;
GO
```

```
     INVALID DATE: 20112-03-15 18:50
```

### *First and Last Day of Date Periods*

Calculating date periods markers is a very important task in T-SQL programming, especially related to reporting queries.

```
DECLARE @Date DATE = '20161023';  SELECT ReferenceDate  = @Date;

SELECT FirstDayOfYear  = CONVERT(DATE, dateadd(yy, datediff(yy,0, @Date),0));

SELECT LastDayOfYear  = CONVERT(DATE, dateadd(yy, datediff(yy,0, @Date)+1,-1));

SELECT FDofSemester = CONVERT(DATE, dateadd(qq,((datediff(qq,0,@Date)/2)*2),0));

SELECT LastDayOfSemester  = CONVERT(DATE, dateadd(qq,((datediff(qq,0,@Date)/2)*2)+2,-1));

SELECT FirstDayOfQuarter  = CONVERT(DATE, dateadd(qq, datediff(qq,0, @Date),0));

SELECT LastDayOfQuarter = CONVERT(DATE, dateadd(qq, datediff(qq,0,@Date)+1,-1));
```

| LastDayOfQuarter |
|------------------|
| 2016-12-31       |

**CHAPTER 12:  Basic SELECT Statement Syntax & Examples**

## The brand-new EOMonth() function simplifies month end formulas

SELECT LastDayOfMonth = EOMonth (@Date);  -- New in SQL Server 2012

SELECT FirstDayOfMonth = CONVERT(DATE, dateadd(mm, datediff(mm,0, @Date),0));

SELECT LastDayOfMonth  = CONVERT(DATE, dateadd(mm, datediff(mm,0, @Date)+1,-1));

SELECT FirstDayOfWeek  = CONVERT(DATE, dateadd(wk, datediff(wk,0, @Date),0));

SELECT LastDayOfWeek   = CONVERT(DATE, dateadd(wk, datediff(wk,0, @Date)+1,-1));
GO

## Month Sequence Generator

Sometimes date based data may have gaps missing months. For reporting purposes we may want to include all months from start date to end date. To do that we have to generate a continuous sequence of months, and use it to fill in the gaps. Calendar table can also be used for such a task.

```
DECLARE @Date date = '2000-01-01'
SELECT MonthStart=dateadd(MM, number, @Date)
FROM  master.dbo.spt_values
WHERE type='P' AND  dateadd(MM, number, @Date) <= CURRENT_TIMESTAMP
ORDER BY MonthStart;
-- (151 row(s) affected) - Partial results.
```

| MonthStart |
| --- |
| 2000-01-01 |
| 2000-02-01 |
| 2000-03-01 |
| 2000-04-01 |
| 2000-05-01 |
| 2000-06-01 |
| 2000-07-01 |
| 2000-08-01 |
| 2000-09-01 |
| 2000-10-01 |
| 2000-11-01 |
| 2000-12-01 |
| 2001-01-01 |
| 2001-02-01 |
| 2001-03-01 |
| 2001-04-01 |

## Selected U.S. & International Date Styles

The U.S. date style is m/d/y.

```
DECLARE @DateTimeValue varchar(32) = '10/23/2016';

SELECT StringDate=@DateTimeValue, [SSMS-Style] = CONVERT(datetime, @DatetimeValue);

SELECT @DateTimeValue = '10/23/2016 23:01:05';

SELECT StringDate = @DateTimeValue, [SSMS-Style] = CONVERT(datetime, @DatetimeValue);
GO
```

| StringDate | SSMS-Style |
|---|---|
| 10/23/2016 | 2016-10-23 00:00:00.000 |

| StringDate | SSMS-Style |
|---|---|
| 10/23/2016 23:01:05 | 2016-10-23 23:01:05.000 |

The UK or British/French style is dmy.

```
DECLARE @DateTimeValue varchar(32) = '23/10/16 23:01:05';

SELECT StringDate = @DateTimeValue, [SSMS-Style] = CONVERT(datetime, @DatetimeValue, 3);

SELECT @DateTimeValue = '23/10/2016 04:01 PM';

SELECT StringDate = @DateTimeValue, [SSMS-Style] = CONVERT(datetime, @DatetimeValue, 103);
GO
```

## The German style is dmy as well with a new twist to it: period instead of slash.

```
DECLARE @DateTimeValue varchar(32)  = '23.10.16 23:01:05';
SELECT StringDate = @DateTimeValue, [SSMS -Style] = CONVERT(datetime, @DatetimeValue, 4);
SELECT @DateTimeValue = '23.10.2016 04:01 PM';
SELECT StringDate = @DateTimeValue, [SSMS -Style] = CONVERT(datetime, @DatetimeValue, 104);
GO
```

```
-- Nondeterministic month name (mon)
SET LANGUAGE Spanish; SELECT CONVERT(varchar, getdate(), 100);        -- Ago 10 2018  4:43PM
SET LANGUAGE Turkish; SELECT CONVERT(varchar, getdate(), 100);        -- Agu 10 2018  4:44PM
SET LANGUAGE Polish; SELECT CONVERT(varchar, getdate(), 100);         -- VIII 10 2018  4:46PM
SET LANGUAGE Hungarian; SELECT CONVERT(varchar, getdate(), 100);      -- aug 10 2018  4:46PM
SET LANGUAGE Russian; SELECT CONVERT(nvarchar, getdate(), 100);       -- авг 10 2018  4:47PM
```

## The DATEPART() Function to Decompose a Date

The DATEPART() function returns a part of a date.

```
DECLARE @dt datetime = getdate();
SELECT DATEPART(YEAR, @dt)          AS YYYY,
       DATEPART(MONTH, @dt)         AS MM,
       DATEPART(DAY, @dt)           AS DD;
```

| YYYY | MM | DD |
|------|----|----|
| 2016 | 7  | 29 |

```
SELECT * FROM Northwind.dbo.Orders
WHERE DATEPART(YEAR, OrderDate)          = '1996' AND
      DATEPART(MONTH,OrderDate)          = '07'   AND
      DATEPART(DAY, OrderDate)           = '10'
```

```
/*OrderID     CustomerID      EmployeeID      OrderDate       RequiredDate      ShippedDate
    ShipVia Freight ShipName          Shipaddress       ShipCity ShipRegion       ShipPostalCode
    ShipCountry
10253   HANAR  3         1996-07-10 00:00:00.000  1996-07-24 00:00:00.000  1996-07-16 00:00:00.000
        2         58.17    Hanari Carnes     Rua do Paço, 67  Rio de Janeiro   RJ        05454-876
        Brazil  */
```

Alternate syntax for DATEPART.

```
SELECT * FROM Northwind.dbo.Orders
WHERE       YEAR(OrderDate)     = 1996      AND
            MONTH(OrderDate)   = 07       AND
            DAY(OrderDate)      = 10
GO
```

```
-- Additional datepart parameters including Julian date
DECLARE @dt datetime = getdate();
SELECT DATEPART(DAY, @dt)               AS DD,
       DATEPART(WEEKDAY, @dt)           AS WD,
       DATEPART(DAYOFYEAR, @dt)         AS JulianDate,
       DATEPART(WEEK, @dt)              AS Week,
       DATEPART(ISO_WEEK, @dt)          AS ISOWeek,
       DATEPART(HOUR, @dt)              AS HH;
```

| DD | WD | JulianDate | Week | ISOWeek | HH |
|----|----|-----------|------|---------|----|
| 10 | 5  | 223       | 33   | 32      | 17 |

## The DATENAME() Function to Get Date Part Names

The DATENAME() function can be used to find out the words for months and weekdays.

```
SELECT DayName=DATENAME(weekday, OrderDate), SalesPerWeekDay = COUNT(*)
FROM AdventureWorks2008.Sales.SalesOrderHeader
GROUP BY DATENAME(weekday, OrderDate), DATEPART(weekday,OrderDate)
ORDER BY DATEPART(weekday,OrderDate);
```

| DayName | SalesPerWeekDay |
|---|---|
| Sunday | 4482 |
| Monday | 4591 |
| Tuesday | 4346 |
| Wednesday | 4244 |
| Thursday | 4483 |
| Friday | 4444 |
| Saturday | 4875 |

### *DATENAME application for month names*

```
SELECT MonthName=DATENAME(month, OrderDate), SalesPerMonth = COUNT(*)
FROM AdventureWorks2008.Sales.SalesOrderHeader
GROUP BY DATENAME(month, OrderDate), MONTH(OrderDate) ORDER BY MONTH(OrderDate);
```

| MonthName | SalesPerMonth |
|---|---|
| January | 2483 |
| February | 2686 |
| March | 2750 |
| April | 2740 |
| May | 3154 |
| June | 3079 |
| July | 2094 |
| August | 2411 |
| September | 2298 |
| October | 2282 |
| November | 2474 |
| December | 3014 |

```
SELECT DATENAME(MM,dateadd(MM,7,-1))  -- July  - Month name from month number
```

## Extract Date from Text with PATINDEX Pattern Matching

```
USE tempdb;
go

CREATE TABLE InsiderTransaction (
    InsiderTransactionID int identity primary key,
    TradeDate datetime,
    TradeMsg varchar(256),
    ModifiedDate datetime default (getdate())  );

-- Populate table with dummy data
INSERT InsiderTransaction (TradeMsg)
VALUES ('INSIDER TRAN QABC Hammer, Bruce D. CSO 09-02-08 Buy 2,000 6.10');
INSERT InsiderTransaction (TradeMsg)
VALUES ('INSIDER TRAN QABC Schmidt, Steven CFO 08-25-08 Buy 2,500 6.70') ;
INSERT InsiderTransaction (TradeMsg)
VALUES ('INSIDER TRAN QABC  Hammer, Bruce D. CSO  08-20-08 Buy 3,000 8.59');
INSERT InsiderTransaction (TradeMsg)
VALUES ('INSIDER TRAN QABC Walters,  Jeff CTO 08-15-08  Sell 5,648 8.49');
INSERT InsiderTransaction (TradeMsg)
VALUES  ('INSIDER TRAN  QABC  Walters, Jeff CTO   08-15-08 Option Exercise 5,648 2.15');
INSERT InsiderTransaction (TradeMsg)
VALUES('INSIDER TRAN QABC Hammer, Bruce D. CSO 07-31-08  Buy 5,000 8.05');
INSERT InsiderTransaction (TradeMsg)
VALUES('INSIDER TRAN QABC Lennot, Mark  Director  08-31-07 Buy 1,500 9.97');
INSERT InsiderTransaction (TradeMsg)
VALUES('INSIDER TRAN QABC  O''Neal, Linda COO  08-01-08 Sell 5,000 6.50');
```

Pattern match for MM-DD-YY using the PATINDEX string function  to extract dates from stock trade message text.

```
SELECT  InsiderTransactionID ,      substring(TradeMsg,
        patindex('%[01][0-9]-[0123][0-9]-[0-9][0-9]%', TradeMsg),8) AS TradeDate
FROM InsiderTransaction  WHERE  patindex('%[01][0-9]-[0123][0-9]-[0-9][0-9]%', TradeMsg) > 0;
```

| InsiderTransactionID | TradeDate |
|---|---|
| 1 | 09-02-08 |
| 2 | 08-25-08 |
| 3 | 08-20-08 |
| 4 | 08-15-08 |
| 5 | 08-15-08 |
| 6 | 07-31-08 |
| 7 | 08-31-07 |
| 8 | 08-01-08 |

*CHAPTER 12:  Basic SELECT Statement Syntax & Examples*

## *Valid Ranges for Date & Time Data Types*

> ➢ DATE (3 bytes) date range:

> ➢ January 1, 1  through December 31, 9999 A.D.

> ➢ SMALLDATETIME (4 bytes) date range:

> ➢ January 1, 1900 through June 6, 2079

> ➢ DATETIME (8 bytes) date range:

> ➢ January 1, 1753 through December 31, 9999

> ➢ DATETIME2 (6-8 bytes) date range:

> ➢ January 1, 1 A.D. through December 31, 9999 A.D.

Smalldatetime has limited range. The statement below will give a date range error.

```
SELECT CONVERT(smalldatetime, '2110-01-01')
/* Msg 242, Level 16, State 3, Line 1
The conversion of a varchar data type to a smalldatetime data type
resulted in an out-of-range value. */
```

```
-- Date Columbus discovers America
SELECT CONVERT(datetime, '14921012');
/* Msg 242, Level 16, State 3, Line 2
The conversion of a varchar data type to a datetime data type resulted in an out-of-range value. */
```

```
SELECT CONVERT(datetime2, '14921012');   -- 1492-10-10 00:00:00.0000000
```

```
SELECT CONVERT(date, '14921012');                -- 1492-10-12
```

**CHAPTER 12:  Basic SELECT Statement Syntax & Examples**

## Last Week Calculations

```
-- SQL last Friday - Implied string to datetime conversions in dateadd & datediff
DECLARE @BaseFriday CHAR(8), @LastFriday datetime, @LastMonday datetime;
SET @BaseFriday = '19000105';
SELECT  @LastFriday = dateadd(dd,
        (datediff (dd, @BaseFriday, CURRENT_TIMESTAMP) / 7) * 7, @BaseFriday) ;
SELECT [Last Friday] = @LastFriday ;
```

| Last Friday |
| --- |
| 2012-07-27 00:00:00.000 |

```
-- Last Monday (last week's Monday)
SELECT  @LastMonday=dateadd(dd,  (datediff (dd, @BaseFriday,
        CURRENT_TIMESTAMP) / 7) * 7 - 4, @BaseFriday)
SELECT [Last Monday]= @LastMonday;
```

| Last Monday |
| --- |
| 2012-07-23 00:00:00.000 |

```
-- Last week - SUN - SAT
SELECT          [Last Week] = CONCAT(CONVERT(varchar,dateadd(day, -1, @LastMonday), 101), ' - ',
                CONVERT(varchar, dateadd(day, 1,  @LastFriday), 101))
```

| Last Week |
| --- |
| 07/22/2012 - 07/28/2012 |

```
-- Next 10 weeks including this one; SUN - SAT
SELECT  TOP 10  [ Week] = CONCAT(CONVERT(varchar,dateadd(day, -1+number*7, @LastMonday), 101),
        ' - ',    CONVERT(varchar, dateadd(day, 1+number*7,  @LastFriday), 101))
FROM master.dbo.spt_values  WHERE type = 'P';
GO
```

| Week |
| --- |
| 08/05/2012 - 08/11/2012 |
| 08/12/2012 - 08/18/2012 |
| 08/19/2012 - 08/25/2012 |
| 08/26/2012 - 09/01/2012 |
| 09/02/2012 - 09/08/2012 |
| 09/09/2012 - 09/15/2012 |
| 09/16/2012 - 09/22/2012 |
| 09/23/2012 - 09/29/2012 |
| 09/30/2012 - 10/06/2012 |
| 10/07/2012 - 10/13/2012 |

## Specific Day Calculations

```
-- First day of current month
SELECT dateadd(month, datediff(month, 0, getdate()), 0);


 -- 15th day of current month
SELECT dateadd(day,14,dateadd(month,datediff(month,0,getdate()),0));


-- First Monday of current month
SELECT   dateadd(day, (9-datepart(weekday,
        dateadd(month, datediff(month, 0, getdate()), 0)))%7,
        dateadd(month, datediff(month, 0, getdate()), 0)) ;


-- Next Monday calculation from the reference date which was a Monday
DECLARE @Now datetime = GETDATE();
DECLARE @NextMonday datetime = dateadd(dd, ((datediff(dd, '19000101', @Now)  / 7) * 7) + 7,
'19000101');
SELECT [Now]=@Now, [Next Monday]=@NextMonday;


-- Last Friday of current month
SELECT   dateadd(day, -7+(6-datepart(weekday,
        dateadd(month, datediff(month, 0, getdate())+1, 0)))%7,
        dateadd(month, datediff(month, 0, getdate())+1, 0)) ;


-- First day of next month
SELECT dateadd(month, datediff(month, 0, getdate())+1, 0);


-- 15th of next month
SELECT dateadd(day,14, dateadd(month, datediff(month, 0, getdate())+1, 0));


-- First Monday of next month
SELECT   dateadd(day, (9-datepart(weekday,
        dateadd(month, datediff(month, 0, getdate())+1, 0)))%7,
         dateadd(month, datediff(month, 0, getdate())+1, 0))  AS NextMonthMonday;
```

| NextMonthMonday |
| --- |
| 2012-08-06 00:00:00.000 |

# CHAPTER 13: Subqueries in SELECT Statements

## Subqueries

Subquery ("inner query") is query within a query which is called the "outer query".

When a subquery involves columns form the outer query, it is called correlated subquery.

When a subquery has a table alias, it is called a derived table.

With SQL Server 2005 a new kind of subquery was introduced: Common Table Expression (CTE). A query can have one or more CTEs. If they are related, they are called nested CTEs. CTEs support recursion.

Correlated subquery is used to retrieve the last freight cost for the customer.

```
-- Correlated subquery - it has reference to an outer query column: A.CustomerID
USE Northwind;

SELECT  A.CustomerID,
      FORMAT(MIN(A.OrderDate), 'd')                    AS FirstOrder,
      FORMAT(MAX(A.OrderDate), 'd')                    AS LastOrder,
      FORMAT( (SELECT  TOP 1 B.Freight
               FROM    Orders B
               WHERE   B.CustomerID = A.CustomerID
               ORDER BY OrderDate DESC),'c','en-US')   AS LastFreight
FROM    Orders A
GROUP BY A.CustomerID ORDER BY A.CustomerID;
-- (89 row(s) affected) - Partial results.
```

| CustomerID | FirstOrder | LastOrder | LastFreight |
|---|---|---|---|
| ALFKI | 8/25/1997 | 4/9/1998 | $1.21 |
| ANATR | 9/18/1996 | 3/4/1998 | $39.92 |
| ANTON | 11/27/1996 | 1/28/1998 | $58.43 |
| AROUT | 11/15/1996 | 4/10/1998 | $33.80 |
| BERGS | 8/12/1996 | 3/4/1998 | $151.52 |
| BLAUS | 4/9/1997 | 4/29/1998 | $31.14 |
| BLONP | 7/25/1996 | 1/12/1998 | $7.09 |
| BOLID | 10/10/1996 | 3/24/1998 | $16.16 |
| BONAP | 10/16/1996 | 5/6/1998 | $38.28 |
| BOTTM | 12/20/1996 | 4/24/1998 | $24.12 |
| BSBEV | 8/26/1996 | 4/14/1998 | $123.83 |
| CACTU | 4/29/1997 | 4/28/1998 | $0.33 |

## Non-Correlated Subqueries

In the next query, the inner query is not linked to the outer query at all (no outer column is used in the inner query). The implication is that the inner query can be executed by itself. The inner query needs to return a single value in this instance due to the ">=" operator. If it were to return multiple values, error would result.

```
-- Non-correlated subquery
SELECT          Name,
                FORMAT(ListPrice, 'c','en-US')           AS ListPrice,
                ProductNumber,
                FORMAT(StandardCost, 'c','en-US')        AS StandardCost
FROM AdventureWorks2012.Production.Product
WHERE ListPrice >=
                  (SELECT ListPrice
                   FROM AdventureWorks.Production.Product
                   WHERE Name = 'Road-250 Black, 48' )

ORDER BY ListPrice DESC, Name;
GO
```

| Name | ListPrice | ProductNumber | StandardCost |
|------|-----------|---------------|--------------|
| Road-150 Red, 44 | $3,578.27 | BK-R93R-44 | $2,171.29 |
| Road-150 Red, 48 | $3,578.27 | BK-R93R-48 | $2,171.29 |
| Road-150 Red, 52 | $3,578.27 | BK-R93R-52 | $2,171.29 |
| Road-150 Red, 56 | $3,578.27 | BK-R93R-56 | $2,171.29 |
| Road-150 Red, 62 | $3,578.27 | BK-R93R-62 | $2,171.29 |
| Mountain-100 Silver, 38 | $3,399.99 | BK-M82S-38 | $1,912.15 |
| Mountain-100 Silver, 42 | $3,399.99 | BK-M82S-42 | $1,912.15 |
| Mountain-100 Silver, 44 | $3,399.99 | BK-M82S-44 | $1,912.15 |
| Mountain-100 Silver, 48 | $3,399.99 | BK-M82S-48 | $1,912.15 |
| Mountain-100 Black, 38 | $3,374.99 | BK-M82B-38 | $1,898.09 |
| Mountain-100 Black, 42 | $3,374.99 | BK-M82B-42 | $1,898.09 |
| Mountain-100 Black, 44 | $3,374.99 | BK-M82B-44 | $1,898.09 |
| Mountain-100 Black, 48 | $3,374.99 | BK-M82B-48 | $1,898.09 |
| Road-250 Black, 44 | $2,443.35 | BK-R89B-44 | $1,554.95 |
| Road-250 Black, 48 | $2,443.35 | BK-R89B-48 | $1,554.95 |
| Road-250 Black, 52 | $2,443.35 | BK-R89B-52 | $1,554.95 |
| Road-250 Black, 58 | $2,443.35 | BK-R89B-58 | $1,554.95 |
| Road-250 Red, 44 | $2,443.35 | BK-R89R-44 | $1,518.79 |
| Road-250 Red, 48 | $2,443.35 | BK-R89R-48 | $1,518.79 |
| Road-250 Red, 52 | $2,443.35 | BK-R89R-52 | $1,518.79 |
| Road-250 Red, 58 | $2,443.35 | BK-R89R-58 | $1,554.95 |

## Subquery returned more than 1 value Error

The following query fails. The reason: the ">=" requires a single value on the right side. The subquery returns 46 values.

```
-- Non-correlated subquery
SELECT          Name,
                FORMAT(ListPrice, 'c','en-US')              AS ListPrice,
                ProductNumber,
                FORMAT(StandardCost, 'c','en-US')           AS StandardCost
FROM AdventureWorks2012.Production.Product
WHERE ListPrice >=
  (SELECT ListPrice
   FROM AdventureWorks.Production.Product
   WHERE Name LIKE 'Road%' )
ORDER BY ListPrice DESC, Name;
GO
/*
Msg 512, Level 16, State 1, Line 3
Subquery returned more than 1 value. This is not permitted when the subquery follows =, !=, <, <= , >, >=
or when the subquery is used as an expression. */
```

If we change the WHERE clause predicate operator from ">=" to "IN" then the query will execute correctly since the IN operator works with a set of values on the right side.

```
-- Non-correlated subquery
SELECT   Name,
         FORMAT(ListPrice, 'c','en-US')              AS ListPrice,
         ProductNumber,
         FORMAT(StandardCost, 'c','en-US')           AS StandardCost
FROM AdventureWorks2012.Production.Product
WHERE ListPrice IN
         (SELECT ListPrice
          FROM AdventureWorks.Production.Product  WHERE Name LIKE 'Road%' )
ORDER BY ListPrice DESC, Name;
-- (253 row(s) affected)  -- Partial results.
```

| Name | ListPrice | ProductNumber | StandardCost |
|------|-----------|---------------|--------------|
| AWC Logo Cap | $8.99 | CA-1098 | $6.92 |
| Racing Socks, L | $8.99 | SO-R809-L | $3.36 |
| Racing Socks, M | $8.99 | SO-R809-M | $3.36 |
| Road Bottle Cage | $8.99 | BC-R205 | $3.36 |
| Road-650 Black, 44 | $782.99 | BK-R50B-44 | $486.71 |
| Road-650 Black, 48 | $782.99 | BK-R50B-48 | $486.71 |
| Road-650 Black, 52 | $782.99 | BK-R50B-52 | $486.71 |

## Correlated Subqueries

In a correlated subquery there is a reference to an outer query column. In other words, the subquery by itself cannot be executed due to the correlation. In the next query, the inner query references soh.SalesOrderID column from the outer query in the WHERE clause predicate which is like an EQUI-JOIN.

```
SELECT          soh.SalesOrderID,
                FORMAT (soh.OrderDate, 'yyyy-MM-dd')                    AS OrderDate,

                ( SELECT FORMAT(MAX(sod.UnitPrice),'c','en-US')
                  FROM   AdventureWorks2012.Sales.SalesOrderDetail      AS sod
                  WHERE  soh.SalesOrderID = sod.SalesOrderID )          AS MaxUnitPrice,

                FORMAT(TotalDue, 'c', 'en-US')                          AS TotalDue
FROM    AdventureWorks2012.Sales.SalesOrderHeader AS soh
ORDER BY MaxUnitPrice DESC, SalesOrderID;
-- (31465 row(s) affected) - Partial results.
```

| SalesOrderID | OrderDate | MaxUnitPrice | TotalDue |
|---|---|---|---|
| 51087 | 2007-07-01 | $953.63 | $2,721.27 |
| 51099 | 2007-07-01 | $953.63 | $5,276.64 |
| 51119 | 2007-07-01 | $953.63 | $2,040.14 |
| 51173 | 2007-07-01 | $953.63 | $1,457.54 |
| 51701 | 2007-08-01 | $953.63 | $2,634.93 |
| 51798 | 2007-08-01 | $953.63 | $907.09 |
| 51805 | 2007-08-01 | $953.63 | $907.09 |
| 51808 | 2007-08-01 | $953.63 | $1,827.45 |
| 51861 | 2007-08-01 | $953.63 | $11,762.43 |
| 53489 | 2007-09-01 | $953.63 | $1,814.18 |

The next query with correlated subquery list sales staff with 0.015 commission rate.

```
SELECT CONCAT(p.LastName,', ', p.FirstName) AS SalesPerson, e.BusinessEntityID AS EmployeeID
FROM AdventureWorks2012.Person.Person AS p
            INNER JOIN AdventureWorks2012.HumanResources.Employee AS e
            ON e.BusinessEntityID = p.BusinessEntityID
WHERE 0.015 IN  (SELECT CommissionPct   FROM AdventureWorks2012.Sales.SalesPerson sp
            WHERE e.BusinessEntityID = sp.BusinessEntityID)  ORDER BY SalesPerson;
```

| SalesPerson | EmployeeID |
|---|---|
| Carson, Jillian | 277 |
| Mitchell, Linda | 276 |
| Saraiva, José | 282 |

**CHAPTER 13:  Subqueries in SELECT Statements**

## Correlated Subqueries with Same Table

In a correlated subquery, we can use a table from the outer query. In such a case table alias usage is required. In the next query with correlated subquery which lists same part suppliers, the Purchasing.ProductVendor table is referenced by both the outer query and inner query, therefore table alias is required.

```
SELECT          p.Name                    AS ProductName,
                v.Name                    AS Vendor,
                pv1.BusinessEntityID      AS VendorID
FROM AdventureWorks2012.Purchasing.ProductVendor pv1
   INNER JOIN AdventureWorks2012.Production.Product p
     ON p.ProductID = pv1.ProductID
   INNER JOIN AdventureWorks2012.Purchasing.Vendor v
     ON v.BusinessEntityID = pv1.BusinessEntityID
WHERE pv1.ProductID IN

   (SELECT pv2.ProductID
    FROM AdventureWorks2012.Purchasing.ProductVendor pv2
    WHERE pv1.BusinessEntityID <> pv2.BusinessEntityID)

ORDER  BY ProductName, Vendor;
-- (347 row(s) affected) - Partial results.
```

| ProductName | Vendor | VendorID |
|---|---|---|
| Internal Lock Washer 7 | Aurora Bike Center | 1616 |
| Internal Lock Washer 7 | Pro Sport Industries | 1686 |
| Internal Lock Washer 8 | Aurora Bike Center | 1616 |
| Internal Lock Washer 8 | Pro Sport Industries | 1686 |
| Internal Lock Washer 9 | Aurora Bike Center | 1616 |
| Internal Lock Washer 9 | Pro Sport Industries | 1686 |
| LL Crankarm | Proseware, Inc. | 1678 |
| LL Crankarm | Vision Cycles, Inc. | 1578 |
| LL Grip Tape | Gardner Touring Cycles | 1516 |
| LL Grip Tape | National Bike Association | 1572 |
| LL Mountain Pedal | Crowley Sport | 1658 |
| LL Mountain Pedal | Greenwood Athletic Company | 1506 |
| LL Mountain Rim | Comfort Road Bicycles | 1530 |
| LL Mountain Rim | Competition Bike Training Systems | 1624 |
| LL Mountain Seat/Saddle | Chicago City Saddles | 1696 |
| LL Mountain Seat/Saddle | First Rate Bicycles | 1570 |
| LL Mountain Tire | Sport Fan Co. | 1632 |
| LL Mountain Tire | Vista Road Bikes | 1538 |
| LL Nipple | Lindell | 1592 |
| LL Nipple | Northern Bike Travel | 1662 |
| LL Road Pedal | Jackson Authority | 1680 |
| LL Road Pedal | Mitchell Sports | 1586 |
| LL Road Rim | Electronic Bike Repair & Supplies | 1646 |
| LL Road Rim | International Bicycles | 1526 |

## CROSS APPLY with Correlated Subquery

The CROSS APPLY operator can connect tables with correlated subqueries as demonstrated following, INNER JOIN would not work in this case.

```
USE AdventureWorks;
DECLARE        @Year  INT,
               @Month INT;
SET @Year      = 2003;
SET @Month     = 2;

SELECT   s.Name                                        AS Customer,
         FORMAT(SalesAmount.OrderTotal,'c','en-US')    AS [Total Sales]
FROM    Sales.Customer AS c
    INNER JOIN Sales.Store AS s
      ON s.CustomerID = c.CustomerID
    CROSS APPLY
            (        SELECT   soh.CustomerId,
                             Sum(sod.LineTotal)        AS OrderTotal
                   FROM    Sales.SalesOrderHeader AS soh
              INNER JOIN Sales.SalesOrderDetail AS sod
                     ON sod.SalesOrderId = soh.SalesOrderId
                  WHERE soh.CustomerId = c.CustomerId
              AND OrderDate > = DATEFROMPARTS(@Year, @Month, 1)
              AND OrderDate <  DATEADD(mm, 1, DATEFROMPARTS(@Year, @Month, 1))
                  GROUP BY soh.CustomerId)             AS SalesAmount
ORDER BY Customer;
-- (132 row(s) affected) - Partial results.
```

| Customer | Total Sales |
|---|---|
| Ace Bicycle Supply | $647.99 |
| Affordable Sports Equipment | $50,953.32 |
| Alpine Ski House | $939.59 |
| Basic Sports Equipment | $159.56 |
| Bicycle Lines Distributors | $22,243.33 |
| Big-Time Bike Store | $20,078.26 |
| Bike Boutique | $20,038.36 |
| Bike Experts | $25,503.15 |
| Bike Products and Accessories | $404.87 |
| Bikes and Motorbikes | $17,060.91 |
| Black Bicycle Company | $1,242.85 |
| Bold Bike Accessories | $141.62 |
| Brakes and Gears | $66,265.33 |
| Brightwork Company | $7,736.05 |
| Catalog Store | $17,259.86 |

# Derived Tables: SELECT from SELECT

A non-correlated subquery can be made into a derived table by enclosing it in parenthesis and assigning a table alias, such as "CAT" in the following example. It can then be used like a regular table for example in JOINs.

```
USE Northwind;

SELECT   c.CategoryName  AS Category,
         p.ProductName,   p.UnitPrice,   CAT.NoOfProducts
FROM    Categories c
    INNER JOIN Products p
     ON c.CategoryID = p.CategoryID
    INNER JOIN
                    (SELECT   c.CategoryID,
                              NoOfProducts = count(* )
                     FROM    Categories c
                      INNER JOIN Products p1
                            ON c.CategoryID = p1.CategoryID
                     GROUP BY c.CategoryID)                       AS CAT

     ON c.CategoryID = CAT.CategoryID
ORDER BY Category;
-- (77 row(s) affected)  - Partial results.
```

| Category | ProductName | UnitPrice |
|----------|-------------|-----------|
| Dairy Products | Raclette Courdavault | 55.00 |
| Dairy Products | Camembert Pierrot | 34.00 |
| Dairy Products | Gudbrandsdalsost | 36.00 |
| Dairy Products | Flotemysost | 21.50 |
| Dairy Products | Mozzarella di Giovanni | 34.80 |
| Grains/Cereals | Gustaf's Knäckebröd | 21.00 |
| Grains/Cereals | Tunnbröd | 9.00 |
| Grains/Cereals | Singaporean Hokkien Fried Mee | 14.00 |
| Grains/Cereals | Filo Mix | 7.00 |
| Grains/Cereals | Gnocchi di nonna Alice | 38.00 |
| Grains/Cereals | Ravioli Angelo | 19.50 |

Results from the subquery (derived table).

| CategoryID | NoOfProducts |
|------------|--------------|
| 1 | 12 |
| 2 | 12 |
| 3 | 13 |
| 4 | 10 |
| 5 | 7 |
| 6 | 6 |
| 7 | 5 |
| 8 | 12 |

**CHAPTER 13:  Subqueries in SELECT Statements**

# The UNION & UNION ALL Set Operators

UNION (distinct, duplicates eliminated) and UNION ALL (duplicates allowed) merge two or more sets of data into one set.  Important points to remember about UNION:

> ➤ First SELECT column list establishes column names and data types; if INTO used it goes here
> ➤ Subsequent SELECTs must match the column structure; column names can be any; NULL if no data
> ➤ ORDER BY goes at the very end with the last SELECT

T-SQL UNION query merges data from different countries into a single result set.

```
USE NorthWind;
SELECT  ContactName,
        CompanyName,
        City,
        Country,
        Phone
FROM   Customers
WHERE  Country IN ( 'USA', 'Canada' )
-- (16 row(s) affected)
UNION
SELECT  ContactName,
        CompanyName          AS Company,
        City,    Country,
        Phone                AS Telephone
FROM   Customers
WHERE  Country IN ( 'Germany', 'France' )
-- (22 row(s) affected)
UNION
SELECT  ContactName          AS Contact,
        CompanyName,   City,   Country,
        Phone                AS Telephone
FROM   Customers
WHERE  Country IN ( 'Brazil', 'Spain' )
-- (14 row(s) affected)
ORDER  BY CompanyName,
    ContactName ASC;
-- (52 row(s) affected)  - Partial results.
```

| ContactName | CompanyName | City | Country | Phone |
|---|---|---|---|---|
| Maria Anders | Alfreds Futterkiste | Berlin | Germany | 030-0074321 |
| Hanna Moos | Blauer See Delikatessen | Mannheim | Germany | 0621-08460 |
| Frédérique Citeaux | Blondesddsl père et fils | Strasbourg | France | 88.60.15.31 |
| Martín Sommer | Bólido Comidas preparadas | Madrid | Spain | (91) 555 22 82 |

**CHAPTER 13:  *Subqueries in SELECT Statements***

# CTE: Common Table Expression for Structured Coding

Common Table Expression is new in SQL Server 2005. It is similar to derived tables in one aspect with a difference: it is defined at the very beginning of a the query, above the main(outer) query. In addition, CTEs can be nested and defined as recursive.

```
USE AdventureWorks;

WITH CTE(ManagerID, StaffCount)
AS
(
    SELECT ManagerID, COUNT(*)
    FROM HumanResources.Employee AS e
    GROUP BY ManagerID
)

SELECT          CONCAT(LEFT(FirstName,1), '. ', LastName)          AS Manager,
                e.Title, StaffCount
FROM CTE s
        INNER JOIN HumanResources.Employee e
    ON s.ManagerID = e.EmployeeID
        INNER JOIN Person.Contact c
    ON c.ContactID = e.ContactID
ORDER BY Manager;
-- (47 row(s) affected) - Partial results.
```

| Manager | Title | StaffCount |
|---|---|---|
| A. Alberts | European Sales Manager | 3 |
| A. Hill | Production Supervisor - WC10 | 7 |
| A. Wright | Master Scheduler | 4 |
| B. Diaz | Production Supervisor - WC40 | 12 |
| B. Welcker | Vice President of Sales | 3 |
| C. Kleinerman | Maintenance Supervisor | 4 |
| C. Petculescu | Production Supervisor - WC10 | 5 |
| C. Randall | Production Supervisor - WC30 | 6 |
| D. Bradley | Marketing Manager | 8 |
| D. Hamilton | Production Supervisor - WC40 | 6 |
| D. Liu | Accounts Manager | 7 |
| D. Miller | Research and Development Manager | 3 |
| E. Gubbels | Production Supervisor - WC20 | 10 |
| G. Altman | Facilities Manager | 2 |
| H. Abolrous | Quality Assurance Manager | 2 |

## Multiple CTEs Query

A query can have multiple CTEs, they can even be nested (CTE has reference to previous CTE). The two CTEs in the following query are first name and last name frequencies.

```
USE AdventureWorks2012;

WITH cteLastNameFreq

    AS (SELECT      LastName        AS [LastNames],
                    count(* )       AS [LNFrequency]
        FROM    Person.Person
        GROUP BY LastName),

    cteFirstNameFreq
    AS (SELECT      FirstName       AS [FirstNames],
                    count(* )       AS [FNFrequency]
        FROM    Person.Person
        GROUP BY FirstName)

SELECT   CONCAT(rtrim(FirstName), ' ', rtrim(LastName))      AS [Name],
                    isnull(Title,'')                         AS [Title] ,
                    f.FNFrequency,
                    l.LNFrequency
FROM    Person.Person c
    INNER JOIN cteFirstNameFreq AS f
    ON c.FirstName = f.FirstNames
    INNER JOIN cteLastNameFreq AS l
    ON c.LastName = l.LastNames
WHERE   LastName LIKE 'P%' ORDER BY [Name];
-- (1187 row(s) affected) - Partial results;
```

| Name | Title | FNFrequency | LNFrequency |
|------|-------|-------------|-------------|
| Aaron Patterson | | 56 | 117 |
| Aaron Perez | | 56 | 170 |
| Aaron Perry | | 56 | 122 |
| Aaron Phillips | | 56 | 80 |
| Aaron Powell | | 56 | 116 |
| Abby Patel | | 19 | 86 |
| Abby Perez | | 19 | 170 |
| Abigail Patterson | | 76 | 117 |
| Abigail Patterson | | 76 | 117 |
| Abigail Perry | | 76 | 122 |
| Abigail Peterson | | 76 | 92 |
| Abigail Powell | | 76 | 116 |

## Testing Common Table Expressions

A CTE can be tested independently of the main query if it does not have nesting (reference to a previous CTE). The following screen snapshot displays the execution of the first CTE SELECT query.

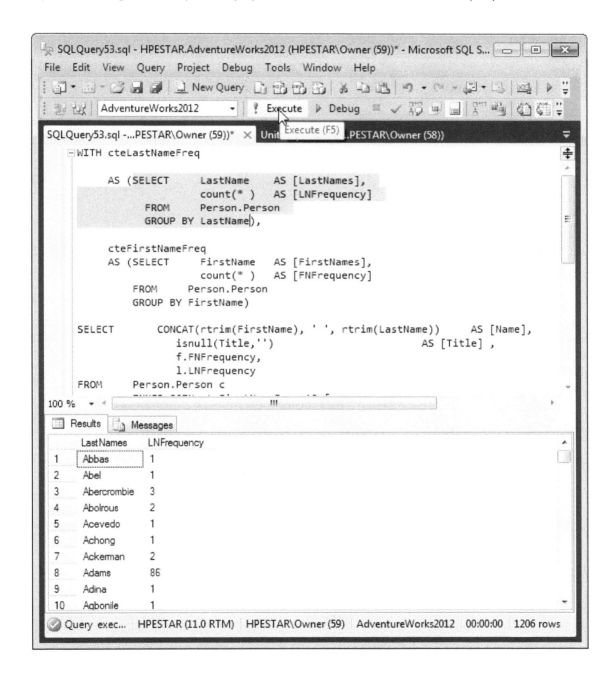

## Nested CTEs Queries

CTEs can be nested by reference to a previous CTE like a table.

```
;WITH CTE1
   AS (SELECT 1 AS NUMBER
      UNION ALL
      SELECT 1),
   CTE2
   AS (SELECT 1 AS NUMBER
      FROM   CTE1 x,
          CTE1 y),
   CTE3
   AS (SELECT 1 AS NUMBER
      FROM   CTE2 x,
          CTE2 y),
   CTE4
   AS (SELECT 1 AS NUMBER
      FROM   CTE3 x,
          CTE3 y),
   CTE8BIT
   AS (SELECT ROW_NUMBER()
          OVER(ORDER BY NUMBER) AS INTSequence
      FROM   CTE4)
SELECT *
FROM   CTE8BIT
ORDER BY INTSequence;
-- (256 row(s) affected) - Partial results.
```

| INTSequence |
| --- |
| 241 |
| 242 |
| 243 |
| 244 |
| 245 |
| 246 |
| 247 |
| 248 |
| 249 |
| 250 |
| 251 |
| 252 |
| 253 |
| 254 |
| 255 |
| 256 |

**CHAPTER 13:  Subqueries in SELECT Statements**

### CTE nesting:  *cteLastSalary has a nested reference to cteLastSalaryChange*

```
USE AdventureWorks2012;

WITH cteLastSalaryChange
    AS (SELECT      BusinessEntityID          AS EmployeeID,
                    Max(RateChangeDate)              AS ChangeDate
      FROM    HumanResources.EmployeePayHistory      GROUP BY BusinessEntityID),

    cteLastSalary
    AS (SELECT      eph.BusinessEntityID              AS EmployeeID,      Rate
      FROM   HumanResources.EmployeePayHistory eph
          INNER JOIN cteLastSalaryChange lsc
            ON lsc.EmployeeID = eph.BusinessEntityID
              AND lsc.ChangeDate = eph.RateChangeDate)

-- SELECT * FROM cteLastSalary  -- for testing & debugging

SELECT TOP 1 FORMAT( Rate, 'c', 'en-US') AS SecondHighestPayRate
FROM    (SELECT   TOP 2 Rate     FROM    cteLastSalary     ORDER BY Rate DESC) a    -- Derived table
ORDER BY Rate ASC;
```

| SecondHighestPayRate |
|---|
| $84.13 |

## Testing Nested CTEs

Nested CTEs can be tested independently of the main query the following way.

```
USE AdventureWorks2012;
WITH cteLastSalaryChange
    AS (SELECT      BusinessEntityID          AS EmployeeID,
                    Max(RateChangeDate)              AS ChangeDate
      FROM    HumanResources.EmployeePayHistory
      GROUP BY BusinessEntityID),
    cteLastSalary
    AS (SELECT      eph.BusinessEntityID              AS EmployeeID,
                    Rate
      FROM   HumanResources.EmployeePayHistory eph
          INNER JOIN cteLastSalaryChange lsc
            ON lsc.EmployeeID = eph.BusinessEntityID
              AND lsc.ChangeDate = eph.RateChangeDate)
SELECT * FROM cteLastSalary  -- for testing & debugging
```

**CHAPTER 13:  Subqueries in SELECT Statements**

*In Query Editor, uncomment the testing line, select (highlight) the top part of the query and execute it*

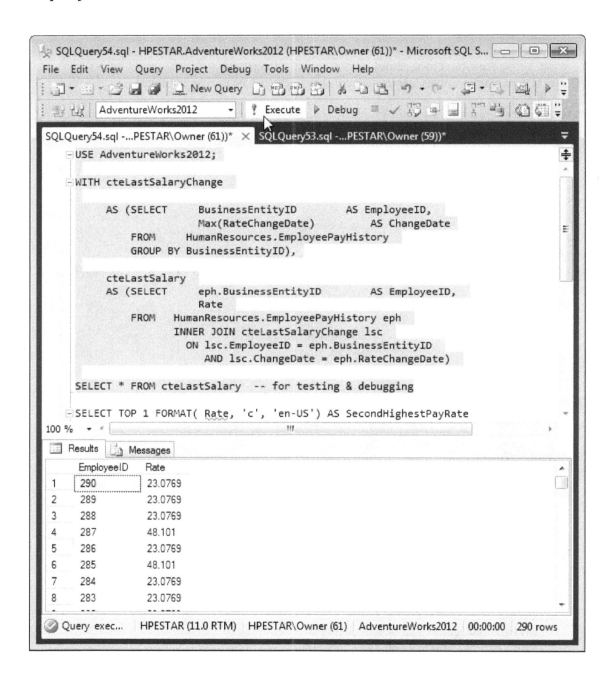

## Recursive CTEs for Tree Hierarchy Processing

Recursive CTEs are one of the most exciting new features introduced with SQL Server 2005. They allow tree processing, such as organizational charts or bill of materials parts assembly, as well as generating sets of data without tables. The following recursive CTE generates 1 million integers all by itself. The query execution time is 10 seconds as it can be seen in the lower right.

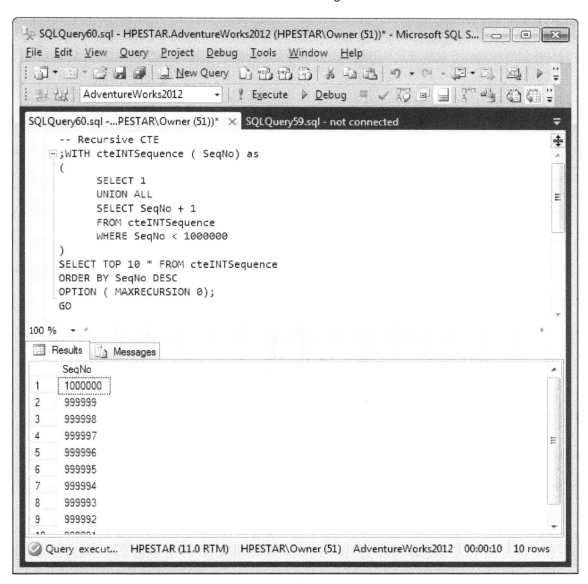

## Recursive Generation of Date & Month Sequences

Date sequence can be generated without a calendar table (Note: generally it is helpful to have a calendar table in the database) using recursive CTE.

```
DECLARE @StartDate date = '20160701', @Range smallint = 1000;

WITH cteSEQ ( SeqNo) as
(
    SELECT 0                                -- Anchor member
    UNION ALL                               -- Assemble set
    SELECT SeqNo + 1                        -- Recursive member
    FROM cteSEQ
    WHERE SeqNo < @Range
)
SELECT TOP 10 [DATE]=DATEADD(day, SeqNo, @StartDate)
FROM cteSEQ
OPTION ( MAXRECURSION 0);
GO
```

| DATE |
| --- |
| 2016-07-01 |
| 2016-07-02 |
| 2016-07-03 |
| 2016-07-04 |
| 2016-07-05 |
| 2016-07-06 |
| 2016-07-07 |
| 2016-07-08 |
| 2016-07-09 |
| 2016-07-10 |

```
-- Month sequence generation
DECLARE @StartDate date = '20160701', @Range smallint = 100;
WITH cteSEQ ( SeqNo) as
(
    SELECT 0                                -- Anchor member
    UNION ALL                               -- Assemble set
    SELECT SeqNo + 1                        -- Recursive member
    FROM cteSEQ
    WHERE SeqNo < @Range
)
SELECT TOP 3 [DATE]=DATEADD(month, SeqNo, @StartDate)
FROM cteSEQ  OPTION ( MAXRECURSION 0);
```

## Generate Month Names in Different Languages

The following query can be used to generate month names in any of the SQL Server 2012 supported languages.

```
SET language Spanish;  -- Se cambió la configuración de idioma a Español.
;WITH CTE AS
(   SELECT    1 MonthNo, CONVERT(DATE, '19000101') MonthFirst
    UNION ALL
    SELECT    MonthNo+1, DATEADD(Month, 1, MonthFirst)
    FROM  CTE
    WHERE Month(MonthFirst) < 12    )
SELECT  MonthNo AS MonthNumber,  DATENAME(MONTH, MonthFirst) AS MonthName
FROM  CTE
ORDER BY MonthNo;
SET language English; -- Changed language setting to us_english.
```

```
SET language Hungarian;  -- Nyelvi beállítás átállítva a következőre: magyar.
;WITH CTE AS
(   SELECT    1 MonthNo, CONVERT(DATE, '19000101') MonthFirst
    UNION ALL
    SELECT    MonthNo+1, DATEADD(Month, 1, MonthFirst)
    FROM  CTE
    WHERE Month(MonthFirst) < 12    )
SELECT  MonthNo AS MonthNumber,  DATENAME(MONTH, MonthFirst) AS MonthName
FROM  CTE
ORDER BY MonthNo;
SET language English; -- Changed language setting to us_english.
```

| MonthNumber | MonthName | MonthNumber | MonthName |
|---|---|---|---|
| 1 | Enero | 1 | január |
| 2 | Febrero | 2 | február |
| 3 | Marzo | 3 | március |
| 4 | Abril | 4 | április |
| 5 | Mayo | 5 | május |
| 6 | Junio | 6 | június |
| 7 | Julio | 7 | július |
| 8 | Agosto | 8 | augusztus |
| 9 | Septiembre | 9 | szeptember |
| 10 | Octubre | 10 | október |
| 11 | Noviembre | 11 | november |
| 12 | Diciembre | 12 | december |

## Graphical Organizational Chart of AdventureWorks Cycles

T-SQL recursive CTE query generates the entire company chart of AdventureWorks Cycles. The anchor term is Ken Sanchez CEO with ManagerID as NULL. Everybody else in the company has a ManagerID which is not NULL.

```
USE AdventureWorks;

WITH cteEmployeeTree
   AS (SELECT      Root.EmployeeName,  Root.ManagerName,
                   Root.EmployeeId, Root.ManagerId,
                   CONVERT(VARCHAR(MAX),Root.PathSequence) AS PathLabel
      FROM   (SELECT EmployeeName = CONCAT(c.FirstName, SPACE(1), c.LastName),
                  ManagerName = convert(VARCHAR(128),''),
                  e.EmployeeId,
                  e.ManagerId,
                  char(64 + ROW_NUMBER() OVER(ORDER BY e.EmployeeId)) AS PathSequence
            FROM   HumanResources.Employee e
            INNER JOIN Person.Contact c
            ON e.ContactID = c.ContactID
         WHERE  e.ManagerId IS NULL) Root          -- Anchor/root term (above)
   UNION ALL                                       -- Build a set
   SELECT      Branch.EmployeeName,                -- Recursive term (below)
               Branch.ManagerName,
               Branch.EmployeeId, Branch.ManagerId,
               PathLabel = Branch.PathLabel + CONVERT(VARCHAR(MAX),  Branch.PathSequence)
      FROM   (SELECT EmployeeName = CONCAT(c.FirstName, SPACE(1), c.LastName),
               ManagerName = CONVERT(VARCHAR(128),CONCAT(cm.FirstName, SPACE(1), cm.LastName)),
                  e.EmployeeId,
                  e.ManagerId,
                  cte.PathLabel,
                  PathSequence = char(64 + ROW_NUMBER() OVER(ORDER BY e.EmployeeId))
            FROM   cteEmployeeTree cte
               INNER JOIN HumanResources.Employee e
               ON e.ManagerId = cte.EmployeeId
               INNER JOIN Person.Contact c
               ON e.ContactID = c.ContactID
               INNER JOIN HumanResources.Employee em
               ON em.EmployeeID = e.ManagerID
               INNER JOIN Person.Contact cm
               ON em.ContactID = cm.ContactID) Branch)
-- Outer / main query
SELECT   CONCAT(REPLICATE(CHAR(9), LEN(PathLabel)-1),   -- tabs for indenting
            EmployeeName) AS EmployeeName
FROM    cteEmployeeTree  ORDER BY PathLabel;
```

*The resulting organizational chart was generated by Word as tabs (CHAR(9) )
were converted to table columns.*

| EmployeeName | | | | |
|---|---|---|---|---|
| Ken Sánchez | | | | |
| | David Bradley | | | |
| | | Kevin Brown | | |
| | | Sariya Harnpadoungsataya | | |
| | | Mary Gibson | | |
| | | Jill Williams | | |
| | | Terry Eminhizer | | |
| | | Wanida Benshoof | | |
| | | John Wood | | |
| | | Mary Dempsey | | |
| | Terri Duffy | | | |
| | | Roberto Tamburello | | |
| | | | Rob Walters | |
| | | | Gail Erickson | |
| | | | Jossef Goldberg | |
| | | | Dylan Miller | |
| | | | | Diane Margheim |
| | | | | Gigi Matthew |
| | | | | Michael Raheem |
| | | | Ovidiu Cracium | |
| | | | | Thierry D'Hers |
| | | | | Janice Galvin |
| | | | Michael Sullivan | |
| | | | Sharon Salavaria | |
| | Jean Trenary | | | |
| | | Janaina Bueno | | |
| | | Dan Bacon | | |
| | | François Ajenstat | | |
| | | Dan Wilson | | |
| | | Ramesh Meyyappan | | |
| | | Stephanie Conroy | | |
| | | | Ashvini Sharma | |
| | | | Peter Connelly | |
| | | Karen Berg | | |
| | Laura Norman | | | |
| | | Paula Barreto de Mattos | | |
| | | | Willis Johnson | |
| | | | Mindy Martin | |
| | | | Vidur Luthra | |
| | | | Hao Chen | |
| | | | Grant Culbertson | |

**CHAPTER 13:  Subqueries in SELECT Statements**

| | | | | |
|---|---|---|---|---|
| | | Wendy Kahn | | |
| | | | Sheela Word | |
| | | | | Mikael Sandberg |
| | | | | Arvind Rao |
| | | | | Linda Meisner |
| | | | | Fukiko Ogisu |
| | | | | Gordon Hee |
| | | | | Frank Pellow |
| | | | | Eric Kurjan |
| | | | | Erin Hagens |
| | | | | Ben Miller |
| | | | | Annette Hill |
| | | | | Reinout Hillmann |
| | | David Barber | | |
| | | David Liu | | |
| | | | Deborah Poe | |
| | | | Candy Spoon | |
| | | | Bryan Walton | |
| | | | Dragan Tomic | |
| | | | Barbara Moreland | |
| | | | Janet Sheperdigian | |
| | | | Mike Seamans | |
| | James Hamilton | | | |
| | | Peter Krebs | | |
| | | | JoLynn Dobney | |
| | | | | Simon Rapier |
| | | | | James Kramer |
| | | | | Nancy Anderson |
| | | | | Bryan Baker |
| | | | | Eugene Kogan |
| | | | | Thomas Michaels |
| | | | Taylor Maxwell | |
| | | | | Kendall Keil |
| | | | | Bob Hohman |
| | | | | Pete Male |
| | | | | Diane Tibbott |
| | | | | Denise Smith |
| | | | | Frank Miller |
| | | | Jo Brown | |
| | | | | Guy Gilbert |
| | | | | Annik Stahl |
| | | | | Rebecca Laszlo |
| | | | | Margie Shoop |
| | | | | Mark McArthur |
| | | | | Britta Simon |
| | | | | Brandon Heidepriem |
| | | | | Jose Lugo |
| | | | | Suchitra Mohan |

**CHAPTER 13: Subqueries in SELECT Statements**

| | | | | Chris Okelberry |
|---|---|---|---|---|
| | | | | Kim Abercrombie |
| | | | | Ed Dudenhoefer |
| | | | John Campbell | |
| | | | | David Ortiz |
| | | | | Steve Masters |
| | | | | Jay Adams |
| | | | | Charles Fitzgerald |
| | | | | Karan Khanna |
| | | | | Maciej Dusza |
| | | | | Michael Zwilling |
| | | | | Randy Reeves |
| | | | Zheng Mu | |
| | | | | Ebru Ersan |
| | | | | Mary Baker |
| | | | | Kevin Homer |
| | | | | Christopher Hill |
| | | | | John Kane |
| | | | Jinghao Liu | |
| | | | | Alice Ciccu |
| | | | | Jun Cao |
| | | | | Suroor Fatima |
| | | | | Linda Moschell |
| | | | | John Evans |
| | | | | Mindaugas Krapauskas |
| | | | | Angela Barbariol |
| | | | | Michael Patten |
| | | | | Don Hall |
| | | | | Chad Niswonger |
| | | | | Michael Entin |
| | | | | Kitti Lertpiriyasuwat |
| | | | Reuben D'sa | |
| | | | | Ryan Cornelsen |
| | | | | Brian Goldstein |
| | | | | Mihail Frintu |
| | | | | Sandeep Kaliyath |
| | | | | Eric Brown |
| | | | | Frank Martinez |
| | | | | Patrick Cook |
| | | | | Jack Creasey |
| | | | Cristian Petculescu | |
| | | | | Betsy Stadick |
| | | | | Kimberly Zimmerman |
| | | | | Patrick Wedge |
| | | | | Danielle Tiedt |
| | | | | Tom Vande Velde |
| | | | Kok-Ho Loh | |
| | | | | Russell Hunter |
| | | | | Jim Scardelis |

CHAPTER 13: Subqueries in SELECT Statements

| | | | | |
|---|---|---|---|---|
| | | | | Nuan Yu |
| | | | | Lolan Song |
| | | | | Houman Pournasseh |
| | | | | Mandar Samant |
| | | | | Sameer Tejani |
| | | | | Elizabeth Keyser |
| | | | Pilar Ackerman | |
| | | | | Susan Eaton |
| | | | | Vamsi Kuppa |
| | | | | Kim Ralls |
| | | | | Matthias Berndt |
| | | | | Jimmy Bischoff |
| | | | David Hamilton | |
| | | | | Paul Komosinski |
| | | | | Gary Yukish |
| | | | | Michael Rothkugel |
| | | | | Rob Caron |
| | | | | Baris Cetinok |
| | | | | Nicole Holliday |
| | | | Eric Gubbels | |
| | | | | Ivo Salmre |
| | | | | Paul Singh |
| | | | | Samantha Smith |
| | | | | Anibal Sousa |
| | | | | Sylvester Valdez |
| | | | | Hung-Fu Ting |
| | | | | Prasanna Samarawickrama |
| | | | | Min Su |
| | | | | Krishna Sunkammurali |
| | | | | Olinda Turner |
| | | | Jeff Hay | |
| | | | | Kirk Koenigsbauer |
| | | | | Laura Steele |
| | | | | Chris Preston |
| | | | | Alex Nayberg |
| | | | | Andrew Cencini |
| | | | Cynthia Randall | |
| | | | | Jian Shuo Wang |
| | | | | Sandra Reátegui Alayo |
| | | | | Jason Watters |
| | | | | Andy Ruth |
| | | | | Rostislav Shabalin |
| | | | | Michael Vanderhyde |
| | | | Yuhong Li | |
| | | | | Hanying Feng |
| | | | | Raymond Sam |
| | | | | Fadi Fakhouri |
| | | | | Lane Sacksteder |

| | | | | |
|---|---|---|---|---|
| | | | | Linda Randall |
| | | | | Terrence Earls |
| | | | | Shelley Dyck |
| | | | Shane Kim | |
| | | | | Yvonne McKay |
| | | | | Douglas Hite |
| | | | | Janeth Esteves |
| | | | | Robert Rounthwaite |
| | | | | Lionel Penuchot |
| | | | Michael Ray | |
| | | | | Steven Selikoff |
| | | | | Carole Poland |
| | | | | Bjorn Rettig |
| | | | | Michiko Osada |
| | | | | Carol Philips |
| | | | | Merav Netz |
| | | | Katie McAskill-White | |
| | | | | Michael Hines |
| | | | | Nitin Mirchandani |
| | | | | Barbara Decker |
| | | | | John Chen |
| | | | | Stefen Hesse |
| | | | Jack Richins | |
| | | | | David Johnson |
| | | | | Garrett Young |
| | | | | Susan Metters |
| | | | | George Li |
| | | | | David Yalovsky |
| | | | | Marc Ingle |
| | | | | Eugene Zabokritski |
| | | | | Benjamin Martin |
| | | | | Reed Koch |
| | | | | David Lawrence |
| | | | | Russell King |
| | | | | John Frum |
| | | | | Jan Miksovsky |
| | | | Andrew Hill | |
| | | | | Ruth Ellerbrock |
| | | | | Barry Johnson |
| | | | | Sidney Higa |
| | | | | Jeffrey Ford |
| | | | | Doris Hartwig |
| | | | | Diane Glimp |
| | | | | Bonnie Kearney |
| | | | Lori Kane | |
| | | | | Stuart Munson |
| | | | | Greg Alderson |
| | | | | Scott Gode |

**CHAPTER 13: Subqueries in SELECT Statements**

| | | | |
|---|---|---|---|
| | | | Kathie Flood |
| | | | Belinda Newman |
| | | Brenda Diaz | |
| | | | Alejandro McGuel |
| | | | Fred Northup |
| | | | Kevin Liu |
| | | | Shammi Mohamed |
| | | | Rajesh Patel |
| | | | Lorraine Nay |
| | | | Paula Nartker |
| | | | Frank Lee |
| | | | Brian Lloyd |
| | | | Tawana Nusbaum |
| | | | Ken Myer |
| | | | Gabe Mares |
| | A. Scott Wright | | |
| | | William Vong | |
| | | Sairaj Uddin | |
| | | Alan Brewer | |
| | | Brian LaMee | |
| | Hazem Abolrous | | |
| | | Peng Wu | |
| | | | Sean Alexander |
| | | | Mark Harrington |
| | | | Andreas Berglund |
| | | | Sootha Charncherngkha |
| | | Zainal Arifin | |
| | | | Tengiz Kharatishvili |
| | | | Sean Chai |
| | | | Karen Berge |
| | | | Chris Norred |
| | Gary Altman | | |
| | | Christian Kleinerman | |
| | | | Pat Coleman |
| | | | Lori Penor |
| | | | Stuart Macrae |
| | | | Jo Berry |
| | | Magnus Hedlund | |
| Brian Welcker | | | |
| | Stephen Jiang | | |
| | | Michael Blythe | |
| | | Linda Mitchell | |
| | | Jillian Carson | |
| | | Garrett Vargas | |
| | | Tsvi Reiter | |
| | | Pamela Ansman-Wolfe | |

**CHAPTER 13:  Subqueries in SELECT Statements**

| | | Shu Ito |
| --- | --- | --- |
| | | José Saraiva |
| | | David Campbell |
| | | Tete Mensa-Annan |
| | Amy Alberts | |
| | | Jae Pak |
| | | Ranjit Varkey Chudukatil |
| | | Rachel Valdez |
| | Syed Abbas | |
| | | Lynn Tsoflias |

CHAPTER 13:  Subqueries in SELECT Statements

## Graphical Bill of Materials for Mountain-100 Silver, 44 Bike

T-SQL query will generate bill of materials (assembly) listing for Mountain-100 Silver, 44  mountain bike.
The AdventureWorks2012 database image for Mountain-100 Silver, 44 in Production.ProductPhoto table.

```
USE AdventureWorks2012;
DECLARE          @StartProductID int        = 773,             -- Mountain-100 Silver, 44
                 @CheckDate datetime        = '20080201';

  WITH cteBOM(ProductAssemblyID, ComponentID, ComponentName,  RecursionLevel)
  AS (
    SELECT b.ProductAssemblyID, b.ComponentID, p.Name,  0
         FROM Production.BillOfMaterials b
         INNER JOIN Production.Product p
          ON b.ComponentID = p.ProductID
      WHERE       b.ProductAssemblyID = @StartProductID
                  AND @CheckDate >= b.StartDate
                  AND @CheckDate <= ISNULL(b.EndDate, @CheckDate)            -- Anchor/root member
(above)
      UNION ALL                                                             -- Build a set
      SELECT      b.ProductAssemblyID, b.ComponentID, p.Name,     -- Recursive member (below)
                  RecursionLevel + 1
      FROM cteBOM c
        INNER JOIN Production.BillOfMaterials b
        ON b.ProductAssemblyID = c.ComponentID
        INNER JOIN Production.Product p
        ON b.ComponentID = p.ProductID
      WHERE       @CheckDate >= b.StartDate          AND @CheckDate <= ISNULL(b.EndDate, @CheckDate)
)
-- Outer/main query
  SELECT CONCAT(REPLICATE(CHAR(9), RecursionLevel),  -- Generate indents with tab character
                (SELECT Name FROM Production.Product WHERE ProductID=ProductAssemblyID)) AS PartName,
                ComponentName
      FROM cteBOM    GROUP BY  RecursionLevel,ProductAssemblyID,ComponentName
  ORDER BY      RecursionLevel, ProductAssemblyID,ComponentName    OPTION (MAXRECURSION 10);
-- (87 row(s) affected)
```

**CHAPTER 13:  *Subqueries in SELECT Statements***

*The resulting graphical bill of materials for the mountain bike.*

| PartName | ComponentName | | |
|---|---|---|---|
| Mountain-100 Silver, 44 | Chain | | |
| Mountain-100 Silver, 44 | Front Brakes | | |
| Mountain-100 Silver, 44 | Front Derailleur | | |
| Mountain-100 Silver, 44 | HL Bottom Bracket | | |
| Mountain-100 Silver, 44 | HL Crankset | | |
| Mountain-100 Silver, 44 | HL Headset | | |
| Mountain-100 Silver, 44 | HL Mountain Frame - Silver, 44 | | |
| Mountain-100 Silver, 44 | HL Mountain Front Wheel | | |
| Mountain-100 Silver, 44 | HL Mountain Handlebars | | |
| Mountain-100 Silver, 44 | HL Mountain Pedal | | |
| Mountain-100 Silver, 44 | HL Mountain Rear Wheel | | |
| Mountain-100 Silver, 44 | HL Mountain Seat Assembly | | |
| Mountain-100 Silver, 44 | Rear Brakes | | |
| Mountain-100 Silver, 44 | Rear Derailleur | | |
| | HL Mountain Seat Assembly | HL Mountain Seat/Saddle | |
| | HL Mountain Seat Assembly | Pinch Bolt | |
| | HL Mountain Seat Assembly | Seat Lug | |
| | HL Mountain Seat Assembly | Seat Post | |
| | HL Mountain Frame - Silver, 44 | Chain Stays | |
| | HL Mountain Frame - Silver, 44 | Decal 1 | |
| | HL Mountain Frame - Silver, 44 | Decal 2 | |
| | HL Mountain Frame - Silver, 44 | Down Tube | |
| | HL Mountain Frame - Silver, 44 | Head Tube | |
| | HL Mountain Frame - Silver, 44 | HL Fork | |
| | HL Mountain Frame - Silver, 44 | Paint - Silver | |

**CHAPTER 13: Subqueries in SELECT Statements**

| | | |
|---|---|---|
| HL Mountain Frame - Silver, 44 | Seat Stays | |
| HL Mountain Frame - Silver, 44 | Seat Tube | |
| HL Mountain Frame - Silver, 44 | Top Tube | |
| HL Headset | Adjustable Race | |
| HL Headset | Crown Race | |
| HL Headset | Headset Ball Bearings | |
| HL Headset | Keyed Washer | |
| HL Headset | Lock Nut 19 | |
| HL Headset | Lower Head Race | |
| HL Mountain Handlebars | Handlebar Tube | |
| HL Mountain Handlebars | HL Grip Tape | |
| HL Mountain Handlebars | Mountain End Caps | |
| HL Mountain Handlebars | Stem | |
| HL Mountain Front Wheel | HL Hub | |
| HL Mountain Front Wheel | HL Mountain Rim | |
| HL Mountain Front Wheel | HL Mountain Tire | |
| HL Mountain Front Wheel | HL Nipple | |
| HL Mountain Front Wheel | Mountain Tire Tube | |
| HL Mountain Front Wheel | Reflector | |
| HL Mountain Front Wheel | Spokes | |
| HL Mountain Rear Wheel | HL Hub | |
| HL Mountain Rear Wheel | HL Mountain Rim | |
| HL Mountain Rear Wheel | HL Mountain Tire | |
| HL Mountain Rear Wheel | HL Nipple | |
| HL Mountain Rear Wheel | Mountain Tire Tube | |
| HL Mountain Rear Wheel | Reflector | |
| HL Mountain Rear Wheel | Spokes | |
| Rear Derailleur | Guide Pulley | |
| Rear Derailleur | Rear Derailleur Cage | |
| Rear Derailleur | Tension Pulley | |
| Front Derailleur | Front Derailleur Cage | |
| Front Derailleur | Front Derailleur Linkage | |
| HL Crankset | Chainring | |
| HL Crankset | Chainring Bolts | |
| HL Crankset | Chainring Nut | |
| HL Crankset | Freewheel | |
| HL Crankset | HL Crankarm | |
| HL Bottom Bracket | BB Ball Bearing | |
| HL Bottom Bracket | HL Shell | |
| | BB Ball Bearing | Bearing Ball |
| | BB Ball Bearing | Cone-Shaped Race |
| | BB Ball Bearing | Cup-Shaped Race |
| | BB Ball Bearing | Lock Ring |
| | Chain Stays | Metal Sheet 5 |
| | Down Tube | Metal Sheet 3 |

**CHAPTER 13: Subqueries in SELECT Statements**

| | | Mountain End Caps | Metal Sheet 2 | |
| | | Handlebar Tube | Metal Sheet 6 | |
| | | Head Tube | Metal Sheet 4 | |
| | | HL Hub | HL Shell | |
| | | HL Hub | HL Spindle/Axle | |
| | | Stem | Metal Bar 1 | |
| | | Seat Stays | Metal Sheet 7 | |
| | | Seat Tube | Metal Bar 2 | |
| | | Top Tube | Metal Sheet 2 | |
| | | HL Fork | Blade | |
| | | HL Fork | Fork Crown | |
| | | HL Fork | Fork End | |
| | | HL Fork | Steerer | |
| | | | Blade | Metal Sheet 5 |
| | | | Fork End | Metal Sheet 2 |
| | | | Fork Crown | Metal Sheet 5 |
| | | | Steerer | Metal Sheet 6 |

CHAPTER 13: Subqueries in SELECT Statements

# PIVOT Operator to Transform Rows Into Columns

The PIVOT operator, new to SQL Server 2005, can be used to create pivot table also called cross tabulation (crosstab).  The data to be PIVOTed is generated by a CTE.

```
USE AdventureWorks2012;
;WITH CTE    AS (SELECT   YEAR            = YEAR(orderDate),
                          QUARTER         = DatePart(qq,OrderDate),
                          Sales           = Sum(TotalDue)
       FROM    Sales.SalesOrderHeader   GROUP BY YEAR(OrderDate), DatePart(qq,OrderDate))
SELECT * FROM CTE;
```

| YEAR | QUARTER | Sales |
|------|---------|-------|
| 2007 | 4 | 14886562.6775 |
| 2006 | 3 | 11555907.1472 |
| 2007 | 1 | 7492396.3224 |
| 2007 | 2 | 9379298.7027 |
| 2006 | 1 | 6562121.6796 |
| 2006 | 4 | 9397824.1785 |
| 2008 | 3 | 56178.9223 |
| 2007 | 3 | 15413231.8434 |
| 2005 | 3 | 5203127.8807 |
| 2008 | 1 | 12744940.3554 |
| 2005 | 4 | 7490122.7457 |
| 2008 | 2 | 16087078.2305 |
| 2006 | 2 | 6947995.43 |

The PIVOT operator takes the data from the CTE source, aggregates it and transforms it to columns.

```
;WITH CTE    AS (SELECT   YEAR            = YEAR(orderDate),
                          QUARTER         = DatePart(qq,OrderDate),
                          Sales           = Sum(TotalDue)
       FROM    Sales.SalesOrderHeader   GROUP BY YEAR(OrderDate), DatePart(qq,OrderDate)   )
SELECT    YEAR
              ,FORMAT ([1], 'c','en-US') AS Q1
              ,FORMAT ([2], 'c','en-US') AS Q2
              ,FORMAT ([3], 'c','en-US') AS Q3
              ,FORMAT ([4], 'c','en-US') AS Q4
FROM    (SELECT * FROM CTE) AS PivotInput
    PIVOT    (SUM(Sales)   FOR QUARTER IN ( [1],[2],[3],[4] ) ) AS PivotOutput  ORDER BY YEAR;
```

| YEAR | Q1 | Q2 | Q3 | Q4 |
|------|-----|-----|-----|-----|
| 2005 | NULL | NULL | $5,203,127.88 | $7,490,122.75 |
| 2006 | $6,562,121.68 | $6,947,995.43 | $11,555,907.15 | $9,397,824.18 |
| 2007 | $7,492,396.32 | $9,379,298.70 | $15,413,231.84 | $14,886,562.68 |
| 2008 | $12,744,940.36 | $16,087,078.23 | $56,178.92 | NULL |

**CHAPTER 13:  Subqueries in SELECT Statements**

# UNPIVOT Crosstab View Results

The vSalesPersonSalesByFiscalYears view is a crosstab listing of sales person (rows) and sales by year (columns). The UNPIVOT operation transforms the year columns into rows.

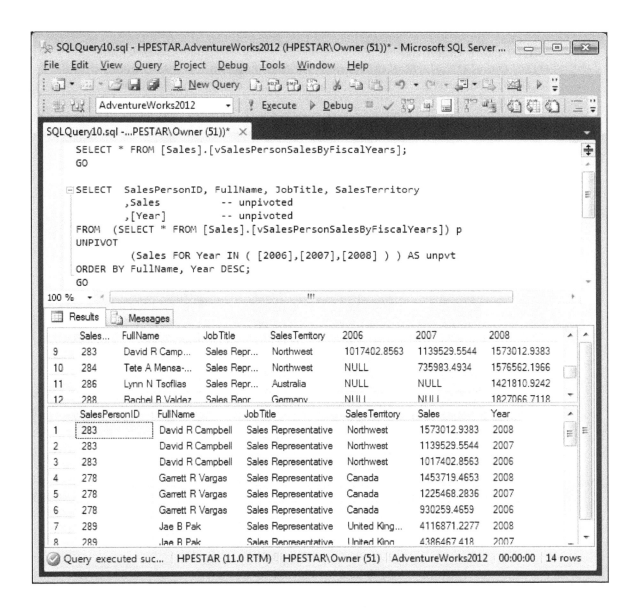

# Using  Subquery in Column List of SELECT

A subquery can be used in the column list of a SELECT statement.

```
USE Northwind;
GO
;WITH CTE AS
( SELECT ShipCity,
         CONVERT(DATE, OrderDate)                                    AS OrderDate,
         (SELECT CONVERT(DATE, MAX(OrderDate))   FROM dbo.Orders)    AS CurrentOrderDate,
         DATEDIFF(dd,OrderDate,(SELECT MAX(OrderDate) FROM dbo.Orders)) AS DeltaDays,
         ROW_NUMBER() OVER (PARTITION BY ShipCity
                          ORDER BY OrderDate DESC)                   AS RN
 FROM dbo.Orders
)
SELECT TOP 20 ShipCity, OrderDate, CurrentOrderDate, DeltaDays
FROM CTE
WHERE RN=1
ORDER BY DeltaDays DESC;
```

| ShipCity | OrderDate | CurrentOrderDate | DeltaDays |
|---|---|---|---|
| Walla Walla | 1997-05-22 | 1998-05-06 | 349 |
| Elgin | 1997-09-08 | 1998-05-06 | 240 |
| Montréal | 1997-10-30 | 1998-05-06 | 188 |
| Reims | 1997-11-12 | 1998-05-06 | 175 |
| Caracas | 1997-12-18 | 1998-05-06 | 139 |
| Lille | 1997-12-22 | 1998-05-06 | 135 |
| Vancouver | 1998-01-01 | 1998-05-06 | 125 |
| Kirkland | 1998-01-08 | 1998-05-06 | 118 |
| Strasbourg | 1998-01-12 | 1998-05-06 | 114 |
| Lyon | 1998-01-23 | 1998-05-06 | 103 |
| San Francisco | 1998-02-12 | 1998-05-06 | 83 |
| Luleå | 1998-03-04 | 1998-05-06 | 63 |
| Barcelona | 1998-03-05 | 1998-05-06 | 62 |
| Cowes | 1998-03-06 | 1998-05-06 | 61 |
| Resende | 1998-03-09 | 1998-05-06 | 58 |
| Leipzig | 1998-03-12 | 1998-05-06 | 55 |
| Bergamo | 1998-03-16 | 1998-05-06 | 51 |
| Münster | 1998-03-23 | 1998-05-06 | 44 |
| Nantes | 1998-03-24 | 1998-05-06 | 43 |
| Versailles | 1998-03-24 | 1998-05-06 | 43 |

# CHAPTER 14:  SELECT INTO Table Creation & Population

## Simple SELECT INTO Statement Variations

SELECT INTO is an easy way to create a table for ad-hoc purposes in database development and administration. **An added benefit is minimal logging, therefore good performance**. INSERT SELECT is logged, although with special setup  minimal logging can be achieved in some cases.

```
-- Create and populate copy of the product table in tempdb
SELECT *
INTO   tempdb.dbo.Product
FROM   AdventureWorks2012.Production.Product;
-- (504 row(s) affected)

SELECT TableRows = count(*)  FROM tempdb.dbo.Product;  -- 504
```

```
-- Copy all persons into new table with last name starting with 'A'
SELECT   BusinessEntityID                 AS ID,
         CONCAT(FirstName, ' ', LastName)  AS FullName,
         PersonType
INTO   ListA
FROM   AdventureWorks2012.Person.Person
WHERE  LEFT(LastName, 1) = 'A'
ORDER BY LastName, FirstName;
-- (911 row(s) affected)

SELECT TOP (10) ID, FullName, PersonType FROM ListA ORDER BY ID;
```

| ID | FullName | PersonType |
|----|----------|------------|
| 38 | Kim Abercrombie | EM |
| 43 | Nancy Anderson | EM |
| 67 | Jay Adams | EM |
| 121 | Pilar Ackerman | EM |
| 207 | Greg Alderson | EM |
| 211 | Hazem Abolrous | EM |
| 216 | Sean Alexander | EM |
| 217 | Zainal Arifin | EM |
| 227 | Gary Altman | EM |
| 270 | François Ajenstat | EM |

```
USE AdventureWorks2012;

-- Create a copy of table in a different schema, same name
-- The WHERE clause predicate with >=, < comparison is better performing than the YEAR function
SELECT *
INTO   dbo.SalesOrderHeader
FROM   Sales.SalesOrderHeader
WHERE  OrderDate >= '20080101' AND OrderDate < '20090101';  -- YEAR(OrderDate)=2008
-- (13951 row(s) affected)


-- Create a table without population
SELECT TOP (0)    SalesOrderID,
          OrderDate
INTO   SOH
FROM   Sales.SalesOrderHeader;
-- (0 row(s) affected)


-- SELECT INTO cannot be used to target an existing table
SELECT * INTO   SOH FROM   Sales.SalesOrderHeader;
/* Msg 2714, Level 16, State 6, Line 1
There is already an object named 'SOH' in the database.  */
```

| NOTE |
| --- |
| IDENTITY column is automatically populated. Direct insert into IDENTITY column requires using of SET IDENTITY_INSERT. |

```
INSERT SOH (SalesOrderID, OrderDate)
SELECT SalesOrderID, OrderDate
FROM   Sales.SalesOrderHeader ORDER BY SalesOrderID;
GO
/* ERROR due to SalesOrderID in SOH inherited the IDENTITY property.
Msg 544, Level 16, State 1, Line 1
Cannot insert explicit value for identity column in table 'SOH' when IDENTITY_INSERT is set to OFF.  */


-- Turn on forced IDENTITY insert
SET IDENTITY_INSERT dbo.SOH ON;
GO


INSERT SOH(SalesOrderID, OrderDate)
SELECT SalesOrderID, OrderDate
FROM   Sales.SalesOrderHeader ORDER BY SalesOrderID;
GO
-- (31465 row(s) affected)


SET IDENTITY_INSERT dbo.SOH OFF;
```

**CHAPTER 14:  SELECT INTO Table Creation & Population**

```
-- Filter on date
SELECT *
INTO   SOH1
FROM   Sales.SalesOrderHeader
WHERE  OrderDate >= '20080101' AND OrderDate < '20090101';
-- (13951 row(s) affected)


-- Descending sort for population
SELECT *
INTO   SOH2
FROM   Sales.SalesOrderHeader
ORDER  BY SalesOrderID DESC
-- (31465 row(s) affected)


-- 3 columns only
SELECT   SalesOrderID,
         OrderDate,
         SubTotal
INTO   SOH3
FROM   Sales.SalesOrderHeader;
-- (31465 row(s) affected)


-- SELECT INTO with GROUP BY query source
SELECT   [Year]=YEAR(OrderDate),
         Orders=COUNT(*)
INTO   SOH4
FROM   Sales.SalesOrderHeader
GROUP  BY YEAR(OrderDate)
-- (4 row(s) affected)


SELECT * FROM SOH4 ORDER BY Year DESC;
```

| Year | Orders |
|------|--------|
| 2008 | 13951 |
| 2007 | 12443 |
| 2006 | 3692 |
| 2005 | 1379 |

```
-- All source columns, and a new populated datetime column
SELECT   *,
         [CreateDate]=getdate()
INTO   SOH5
FROM   Sales.SalesOrderHeader ;
-- (31465 row(s) affected)
```

**CHAPTER 14:  SELECT INTO Table Creation & Population**

```
-- SELECT INTO temporary table
SELECT TotalOrders = COUNT(*)
INTO   #TotalOrders
FROM   Sales.SalesOrderHeader ;
-- (1 row(s) affected)
```

```
SELECT * FROM #TotalOrders;
```

| TotalOrders |
|---|
| 31465 |

```
-- Empty table create with one NULL row
SELECT   Name=CONVERT(VARCHAR(45), NULL),
         Age=CONVERT(INT, NULL)
INTO   tempdb.dbo.Person;
```

```
INSERT tempdb.dbo.Person (Name, Age)
SELECT 'Roger Bond', 45;
-- (1 row(s) affected)
```

```
SELECT * FROM tempdb.dbo.Person;
```

| Name | Age |
|---|---|
| NULL | NULL |
| Roger Bond | 45 |

```
DELETE tempdb.dbo.Person WHERE Name is NULL;
-- (1 row(s) affected)
```

```
SELECT * FROM tempdb.dbo.Person;
```

| Name | Age |
|---|---|
| Roger Bond | 45 |

```
-- Create gaps in ID sequence; increment by 2:  2, 4, 6, 8 instead of 1, 2, 3, 4
SELECT   2 * [BusinessEntityID]              AS BusinessEntityID
         ,[PhoneNumber]
         ,[PhoneNumberTypeID]
         ,[ModifiedDate]
 INTO dbo.Phone
 FROM [AdventureWorks2012].[Person].[PersonPhone] pp    ORDER BY pp.BusinessEntityID;
-- (19972 row(s) affected)
```

**CHAPTER 14:  SELECT INTO Table Creation & Population**

```
-- Populate with 100 random rows
SELECT TOP (100) *
INTO   POH
FROM   Purchasing.PurchaseOrderHeader
ORDER  BY NEWID();
-- (100 row(s) affected)
```

```
SELECT        PurchaseOrderID,
              CONVERT(date, OrderDate)       AS OrderDate,
              FORMAT(SubTotal, 'c', 'en-US')  AS SubTotal
FROM POH;
```

| PurchaseOrderID | OrderDate | SubTotal |
|---|---|---|
| 3553 | 2008-08-03 | $9,948.33 |
| 1637 | 2008-02-07 | $25,531.28 |
| 2796 | 2008-05-31 | $97.97 |
| 684 | 2007-09-26 | $270.81 |
| 3478 | 2008-07-28 | $28,072.28 |
| 1904 | 2008-03-09 | $43,878.45 |
| 755 | 2007-10-01 | $50,860.43 |
| 2660 | 2008-05-19 | $944.37 |
| 2787 | 2008-05-31 | $34,644.23 |
| 601 | 2007-09-19 | $146.29 |

```
-- SELECT INTO with data transformation
SELECT    CultureID
      ,UPPER(Name)                          AS Name
      ,CONVERT(date,ModifiedDate)           AS ModifiedDate
INTO dbo.Culture
FROM [AdventureWorks2012].[Production].[Culture]
ORDER BY CultureID;
-- (8 row(s) affected)
```

```
SELECT * FROM dbo.Culture WHERE CultureID != '' ORDER BY CultureID;  -- exclude empty ID
```

| CultureID | Name | ModifiedDate |
|---|---|---|
| ar | ARABIC | 2002-06-01 |
| en | ENGLISH | 2002-06-01 |
| es | SPANISH | 2002-06-01 |
| fr | FRENCH | 2002-06-01 |
| he | HEBREW | 2002-06-01 |
| th | THAI | 2002-06-01 |
| zh-cht | CHINESE | 2002-06-01 |

**CHAPTER 14: SELECT INTO Table Creation & Population**

## SELECT INTO with IDENTITY Column

The column data types are inherited in SELECT INTO table create. The IDENTITY property is also inherited in a SELECT INTO unless it is prevented with special coding. No other constraint is inherited.

```
-- IDENTITY property of ProductID is inherited
SELECT TOP (0) ProductID, ProductNumber, ListPrice, Color
INTO tempdb.dbo.Product
FROM AdventureWorks2012.Production.Product;
-- (0 row(s) affected)
```

```
INSERT tempdb.dbo.Product (ProductID, ProductNumber, ListPrice, Color)
SELECT 20001, 'FERRARI007RED', $400000, 'Red';
GO
/* Msg 544, Level 16, State 1, Line 1
Cannot insert explicit value for identity column in table 'Product'
when IDENTITY_INSERT is set to OFF. */
```

```
-- The following is one way to check for IDENTITY property
USE tempdb;
EXEC sp_help 'dbo.Product';
```

| Identity | Seed | Increment | Not For Replication |
|----------|------|-----------|---------------------|
| ProductID | 1 | 1 | 0 |

```
USE AdventureWorks2012;
```

```
DROP TABLE tempdb.dbo.Product;
GO
```

```
-- The following construct will prevent IDENTITY inheritance
SELECT TOP (0)    CAST(ProductID AS INT) AS ProductID,  -- Cast/Convert the identity column
                 ProductNumber,
                 ListPrice,
                 Color
INTO tempdb.dbo.Product  FROM AdventureWorks2012.Production.Product;
-- (0 row(s) affected)
```

```
INSERT tempdb.dbo.Product (ProductID, ProductNumber, ListPrice, Color)
SELECT 20001, 'FERRARI007RED', $400000, 'Firehouse Red';
GO
```

```
SELECT * FROM tempdb.dbo.Product;
```

| ProductID | ProductNumber | ListPrice | Color |
|-----------|---------------|-----------|-------|
| 20001 | FERRARI007RED | 400000.00 | Firehouse Red |

**CHAPTER 14:  SELECT INTO Table Creation & Population**

# SELECT INTO From Multiple-Table Queries

SELECT INTO works with any query with some restrictions such as XML data type columns cannot be included.

```
SELECT   JobCandidateID
        ,BusinessEntityID
        ,Resume
        ,ModifiedDate
 INTO dbo.Resume
 FROM AdventureWorks2012.HumanResources.JobCandidate;
/* ERROR Msg 458, Level 16, State 0, Line 2
Cannot create the SELECT INTO target table "dbo.Resume" because the xml column "Resume"
is typed with a schema collection "HRResumeSchemaCollection" from database "AdventureWorks2012".
Xml columns cannot refer to schemata across databases. */


-- SELECT INTO from joined tables
 SELECT           soh.SalesOrderID,
                  OrderDate,
                  OrderQty,
                  ProductID
INTO   SalesOrder
FROM   Sales.SalesOrderHeader soh
     INNER JOIN Sales.SalesOrderDetail sod     ON soh.SalesOrderID = sod.SalesOrderID ;
-- (121317 row(s) affected)
```

SELECT TOP(5) * FROM SalesOrder ORDER BY SalesOrderID DESC;

| SalesOrderID | OrderDate | OrderQty | ProductID |
|---|---|---|---|
| 75123 | 2008-07-31 00:00:00.000 | 1 | 878 |
| 75123 | 2008-07-31 00:00:00.000 | 1 | 879 |
| 75123 | 2008-07-31 00:00:00.000 | 1 | 712 |
| 75122 | 2008-07-31 00:00:00.000 | 1 | 878 |
| 75122 | 2008-07-31 00:00:00.000 | 1 | 712 |

-- Check column types - partial results
EXEC sp_help SalesOrder;

| Column_name | Type | Computed | Length | Prec | Scale |
|---|---|---|---|---|---|
| SalesOrderID | int | no | 4 | 10 | 0 |
| OrderDate | datetime | no | 8 | | |
| OrderQty | smallint | no | 2 | 5 | 0 |
| ProductID | int | no | 4 | 10 | 0 |

**CHAPTER 14:  SELECT INTO Table Creation & Population**

## SELECT INTO with Sorted Table Population

We can create ordering in a new temporary table by using the IDENTITY function. **There is no guarantee though that the IDENTITY sequence will be the same as the ORDER BY clause specifications**. Unique identity values on the other hand are guaranteed.

```
SELECT  ID=IDENTITY(int, 1, 1),
        ProductNumber,
        ProductID=CAST(ProductID AS INT),
        ListPrice,
        COALESCE(Color, 'N/A') AS Color
INTO    #Product
FROM    Production.Product WHERE  ListPrice > 0.0 ORDER BY ProductNumber;
GO
-- (304 row(s) affected)

SELECT TOP 10 * FROM #Product  ORDER BY ID;
```

| ID | ProductNumber | ProductID | ListPrice | Color |
|----|---------------|-----------|-----------|-------|
| 1  | BB-7421       | 994       | 53.99     | N/A   |
| 2  | BB-8107       | 995       | 101.24    | N/A   |
| 3  | BB-9108       | 996       | 121.49    | N/A   |
| 4  | BC-M005       | 871       | 9.99      | N/A   |
| 5  | BC-R205       | 872       | 8.99      | N/A   |
| 6  | BK-M18B-40    | 989       | 539.99    | Black |
| 7  | BK-M18B-42    | 990       | 539.99    | Black |
| 8  | BK-M18B-44    | 991       | 539.99    | Black |
| 9  | BK-M18B-48    | 992       | 539.99    | Black |
| 10 | BK-M18B-52    | 993       | 539.99    | Black |

```
-- Permanent table create
SELECT * INTO ProductByProdNo FROM #Product ORDER BY ID;
GO -- (304 row(s) affected)

SELECT TOP (6) * FROM ProductByProdNo ORDER BY ID;
```

| ID | ProductNumber | ProductID | ListPrice | Color |
|----|---------------|-----------|-----------|-------|
| 1  | BB-7421       | 994       | 53.99     | N/A   |
| 2  | BB-8107       | 995       | 101.24    | N/A   |
| 3  | BB-9108       | 996       | 121.49    | N/A   |
| 4  | BC-M005       | 871       | 9.99      | N/A   |
| 5  | BC-R205       | 872       | 8.99      | N/A   |
| 6  | BK-M18B-40    | 989       | 539.99    | Black |

**CHAPTER 14:  SELECT INTO Table Creation & Population**

# SELECT INTO with Random Population

We can create a random population by sorting with the NEWID() function.

```
USE tempdb;

SELECT TOP(5)    ID            = ContactID,
                 FullName      = CONCAT(FirstName, ' ', LastName),
                 Email         = EmailAddress
INTO  dbo.Person
FROM  AdventureWorks.Person.Contact
WHERE  EmailPromotion = 2
ORDER  BY NEWID();
-- (5 row(s) affected)

SELECT *  FROM  dbo.Person;
GO
```

| ID | FullName | Email |
|---|---|---|
| 1075 | Diane Glimp | diane0@adventure-works.com |
| 15739 | Jesse Mitchell | jesse36@adventure-works.com |
| 5405 | Jose Patterson | jose33@adventure-works.com |
| 1029 | Wanida Benshoof | wanida0@adventure-works.com |
| 8634 | Andrea Collins | andrea26@adventure-works.com |

```
-- Rerun the script again after dropping the table
DROP TABLE tempdb.dbo.Person;
GO
-- Command(s) completed successfully.

SELECT TOP(5) ID        = ContactID,
       FullName         = CONCAT(FirstName, ' ', LastName),
       Email            = EmailAddress
INTO  dbo.Person
FROM  AdventureWorks.Person.Contact
WHERE  EmailPromotion = 2 ORDER  BY NEWID();

SELECT * FROM  dbo.Person;
```

| ID | FullName | Email |
|---|---|---|
| 9984 | Sydney Clark | sydney81@adventure-works.com |
| 15448 | Denise Raman | denise13@adventure-works.com |
| 12442 | Carson Jenkins | carson5@adventure-works.com |
| 1082 | Mary Baker | mary1@adventure-works.com |
| 18728 | Emma Kelly | emma46@adventure-works.com |

## Combining SELECT INTO with INSERT SELECT

First we create an empty table with identity property using SELECT INTO, then we populate it with INSERT SELECT.

```
-- Following will fail - only one IDENTITY column per table
SELECT TOP (0)    IDENTITY(int, 1, 1)                AS ID,
        ProductID,
        Name                              AS ProductName,
        ListPrice,
        COALESCE(Color, 'N/A')            AS Color
INTO  #Product  FROM  Production.Product;
GO
/* ERROR Msg 8108, Level 16, State 1, Line 1
Cannot add identity column, using the SELECT INTO statement, to table '#Product',
which already has column 'ProductID' that inherits the identity property.  */
```

```
SELECT TOP (0)    IDENTITY(int, 1, 1)        AS ID,
        CAST(ProductID AS INT)        AS ProductID, -- IDENTITY will not be inherited
        Name                          AS ProductName,
        ListPrice,
        COALESCE(Color, 'N/A')        AS Color
INTO  #Product  FROM  Production.Product;
GO
-- (0 row(s) affected)
```

```
DECLARE @Rows tinyint = 5;
INSERT INTO #Product    (ProductID, ProductName,  ListPrice,  Color)
SELECT TOP (@Rows)        ProductID,
                Name,
                ListPrice,
                Color
FROM  Production.Product
WHERE  ListPrice > 0.0    AND Color IS NOT NULL  ORDER BY ListPrice DESC;
-- (5 row(s) affected)
```

```
SELECT * FROM  #Product;
```

| ID | ProductID | ProductName | ListPrice | Color |
|----|-----------|-------------|-----------|-------|
| 1 | 749 | Road-150 Red, 62 | 3578.27 | Red |
| 2 | 750 | Road-150 Red, 44 | 3578.27 | Red |
| 3 | 751 | Road-150 Red, 48 | 3578.27 | Red |
| 4 | 752 | Road-150 Red, 52 | 3578.27 | Red |
| 5 | 753 | Road-150 Red, 56 | 3578.27 | Red |

## Copy Table into Different Database with SELECT INTO

It requires 3-part name referencing to operate between databases (cross database). The current database requires only 2-part object name referencing.

```
USE tempdb;
SELECT *, CopyDate = CONVERT(DATE,GETDATE())
INTO Department
FROM AdventureWorks.HumanResources.Department  ORDER BY DepartmentID;
GO
```

```
SELECT TOP (5) DepartmentID, Department=Name, CopyDate  FROM Department ORDER BY DepartmentID;
```

| DepartmentID | Department | CopyDate |
|---|---|---|
| 1 | Engineering | 2016-07-19 |
| 2 | Tool Design | 2016-07-19 |
| 3 | Sales | 2016-07-19 |
| 4 | Marketing | 2016-07-19 |
| 5 | Purchasing | 2016-07-19 |

```
-- SQL drop table - full referencing of table for mistake reduction
DROP TABLE tempdb.dbo.Department;
```

## Combining SELECT INTO with UPDATE

After creating a populated table with SELECT INTO, we perform UPDATE to change a column.

```
USE tempdb;
SELECT TOP 100 * INTO   PurchaseOrderHeader
FROM   AdventureWorks.Purchasing.PurchaseOrderHeader  ORDER  BY NEWID();
GO
```

```
-- The following logic updates dates to different values - multiple value assignment operator
DECLARE @OrderDate DATETIME = CURRENT_TIMESTAMP;
UPDATE PurchaseOrderHeader  SET   @OrderDate = OrderDate = dateadd(day, -1, @OrderDate);
GO
```

```
SELECT TOP (5)  PurchaseOrderID,   VendorID,   OrderDate  FROM   PurchaseOrderHeader;
```

| PurchaseOrderID | VendorID | OrderDate |
|---|---|---|
| 631 | 39 | 2016-07-18 09:03:18.193 |
| 759 | 32 | 2016-07-17 09:03:18.193 |
| 2652 | 33 | 2016-07-16 09:03:18.193 |
| 769 | 80 | 2016-07-15 09:03:18.193 |
| 949 | 30 | 2016-07-14 09:03:18.193 |

```
DROP TABLE tempdb.dbo.PurchaseOrderHeader;
```

**CHAPTER 14:  SELECT INTO Table Creation & Population**

## SELECT INTO Table Create from Complex Query

SELECT INTO table create works from simple to very complex queries.

USE AdventureWorks;

```
SELECT          SalesStaff      = CONCAT(C.LastName, ', ', C.FirstName),
                ZipCode         = A.PostalCode,
                TotalSales      = FORMAT(SUM(SOD.LineTotal),'c', 'en-US'),
                PercentOfTotal  = FORMAT( SUM(SOD.LineTotal) /
                                      SUM(SUM(SOD.LineTotal))
                                      OVER (PARTITION BY 1, 2 ),'p')
INTO   tempdb.dbo.SalesSummary
FROM   Person.Contact C
    INNER JOIN Person.[Address] A
        ON A.AddressID = C.ContactID
    INNER JOIN Sales.SalesOrderHeader SOH
        ON SOH.SalesPersonID = C.ContactID
    INNER JOIN Sales.SalesOrderDetail SOD
        ON SOD.SalesOrderID = SOH.SalesOrderID
WHERE  TerritoryID IS NOT NULL
GROUP  BY C.FirstName,   C.LastName,   A.PostalCode,   C.ContactID
ORDER  BY SalesStaff,   ZipCode;
-- (17 row(s) affected)


-- SELECT 10 rows random, then sort them by name (SalesStaff) - derived table construct
SELECT * FROM
(
        SELECT TOP (10) *
        FROM   tempdb.dbo.SalesSummary ORDER  BY NEWID()
) x          -- x is called a derived table; also dubbed SELECT FROM SELECT
ORDER BY SalesStaff;
```

| SalesStaff | ZipCode | TotalSales | PercentOfTotal |
|---|---|---|---|
| Dusza, Maciej | 98027 | $9,293,903.00 | 11.55 % |
| Dyck, Shelley | 98027 | $10,367,007.43 | 12.88 % |
| Ecoffey, Linda | 98027 | $10,065,803.54 | 12.51 % |
| Eldridge, Carla | 98027 | $3,609,447.21 | 4.48 % |
| Elliott, Carol | 98027 | $7,171,012.75 | 8.91 % |
| Emanuel, Michael | 98055 | $5,926,418.36 | 7.36 % |
| Erickson, Gail | 98055 | $8,503,338.65 | 10.56 % |
| Estes, Julie | 98055 | $172,524.45 | 0.21 % |
| Esteves, Janeth | 98055 | $1,827,066.71 | 2.27 % |
| Evans, Twanna | 98055 | $1,421,810.92 | 1.77 % |

DROP TABLE tempdb.dbo.SalesSummary ;

**CHAPTER 14:  SELECT INTO Table Creation & Population**

## SELECT INTO Table Create from System Procedure Execution

Using OPENROWSET and OPENQUERY, we can make the result sets of system procedures and user stored procedures table-like.

```
SELECT *
INTO  #spwho
FROM  OPENROWSET ( 'SQLOLEDB',
          'SERVER=.;Trusted_Connection=yes',
          'SET FMTONLY OFF EXEC sp_who');
GO  -- (64 row(s) affected) - it varies, depends on the number server connections

SELECT TOP (5) *  FROM  #spwho  ORDER BY spid;
GO
```

| spid | ecid | status | loginame | hostname | blk | dbname | cmd | request_id |
|------|------|--------|----------|----------|-----|--------|-----|------------|
| 1 | 0 | background | sa | | 0 | NULL | LOG WRITER | 0 |
| 2 | 0 | background | sa | | 0 | NULL | RECOVERY WRITER | 0 |
| 3 | 0 | background | sa | | 0 | NULL | LAZY WRITER | 0 |
| 4 | 0 | background | sa | | 0 | NULL | LOCK MONITOR | 0 |
| 5 | 0 | background | sa | | 0 | master | SIGNAL HANDLER | 0 |

```
/* Requirement for OPENQUERY operation on current instance.

DATA ACCESS to current SQL Server named instance can be setup the following way:

exec sp_serveroption @server = 'PRODSVR\SQL2008'   -- computer name for default instance
    ,@optname = 'DATA ACCESS'
    ,@optvalue = 'TRUE' ;

This way, OPENQUERY can be used against current instance. Usually OPENQUERY is used to access linked
servers.
*/
```

```
SELECT   DB_NAME(dbid) AS DB, *
INTO  #splock
FROM  OPENQUERY(HPESTAR, 'EXEC sp_lock');
GO
-- (156 row(s) affected)  - it varies, depends how busy is the system with OLTP activities

SELECT TOP(2) * FROM  #splock ;
```

| DB | spid | dbid | ObjId | IndId | Type | Resource | Mode | Status |
|----|------|------|-------|-------|------|----------|------|--------|
| ReportServer | 52 | 5 | 0 | 0 | DB | | S | GRANT |
| msdb | 54 | 4 | 0 | 0 | DB | | S | GRANT |

# SELECT INTO from OPENQUERY Stored Procedure Execution

The following is the only way to make stored procedure results table-like. The bill-of-materials stored procedure is recursive.

```
USE AdventureWorks2012;
GO
SELECT Name FROM Production.Product WHERE ProductID = 900;   -- LL Touring Frame - Yellow, 50


-- First we test the query execution
DECLARE @RC int;  DECLARE @StartProductID int; DECLARE @CheckDate datetime;

EXECUTE @RC = [dbo].[uspGetBillOfMaterials]     @StartProductID = 900 , @CheckDate = '20080216';
GO
-- 24 rows returned


-- Transform query into SELECT INTO table create  - Single quotes (around date literal) must be doubled
SELECT * INTO BOM900
FROM OPENQUERY(HPESTAR, 'EXECUTE [AdventureWorks2012].[dbo].[uspGetBillOfMaterials]
900,''20080216''');
GO
-- (1 row(s) affected)            -- create table
-- (24 row(s) affected)           -- inserts


SELECT * FROM BOM900;
```

| ProductAssemblyID | ComponentID | ComponentDesc | TotalQuantity | StandardCost | ListPrice | BOMLevel | RecursionLevel |
|---|---|---|---|---|---|---|---|
| 900 | 324 | Chain Stays | 2.00 | 0.00 | 0.00 | 2 | 0 |
| 900 | 325 | Decal 1 | 2.00 | 0.00 | 0.00 | 2 | 0 |
| 900 | 326 | Decal 2 | 1.00 | 0.00 | 0.00 | 2 | 0 |
| 900 | 327 | Down Tube | 1.00 | 0.00 | 0.00 | 2 | 0 |
| 900 | 399 | Head Tube | 1.00 | 0.00 | 0.00 | 2 | 0 |
| 900 | 496 | Paint - Yellow | 8.00 | 0.00 | 0.00 | 2 | 0 |
| 900 | 532 | Seat Stays | 4.00 | 0.00 | 0.00 | 2 | 0 |
| 900 | 533 | Seat Tube | 1.00 | 0.00 | 0.00 | 2 | 0 |
| 900 | 534 | Top Tube | 1.00 | 0.00 | 0.00 | 2 | 0 |
| 900 | 802 | LL Fork | 1.00 | 65.8097 | 148.22 | 2 | 0 |
| 324 | 486 | Metal Sheet 5 | 1.00 | 0.00 | 0.00 | 3 | 1 |
| 327 | 483 | Metal Sheet 3 | 1.00 | 0.00 | 0.00 | 3 | 1 |
| 399 | 485 | Metal Sheet 4 | 1.00 | 0.00 | 0.00 | 3 | 1 |
| 532 | 484 | Metal Sheet 7 | 1.00 | 0.00 | 0.00 | 3 | 1 |
| 533 | 478 | Metal Bar 2 | 1.00 | 0.00 | 0.00 | 3 | 1 |
| 534 | 482 | Metal Sheet 2 | 1.00 | 0.00 | 0.00 | 3 | 1 |
| 802 | 316 | Blade | 2.00 | 0.00 | 0.00 | 3 | 1 |
| 802 | 331 | Fork End | 2.00 | 0.00 | 0.00 | 3 | 1 |
| 802 | 350 | Fork Crown | 1.00 | 0.00 | 0.00 | 3 | 1 |
| 802 | 531 | Steerer | 1.00 | 0.00 | 0.00 | 3 | 1 |
| 316 | 486 | Metal Sheet 5 | 1.00 | 0.00 | 0.00 | 4 | 2 |
| 331 | 482 | Metal Sheet 2 | 1.00 | 0.00 | 0.00 | 4 | 2 |
| 350 | 486 | Metal Sheet 5 | 1.00 | 0.00 | 0.00 | 4 | 2 |
| 531 | 487 | Metal Sheet 6 | 1.00 | 0.00 | 0.00 | 4 | 2 |

CHAPTER 14:  SELECT INTO Table Creation & Population

## Execution of SELECT INTO from Dynamic SQL

T-SQL script demonstrates SELECT INTO execution within a dynamic SQL. Biggest challenge is to get the single quotes right. CHAR(39) use is an option.

```
-- SQL Server 2008 new feature: instant assignment to a localvariable
DECLARE @DynamicQuery nvarchar(max) =
    'SELECT *
    INTO BOM400
    FROM OPENQUERY(' + QUOTENAME(CONVERT(sysname, @@SERVERNAME))+ ',
    ''EXECUTE [AdventureWorks2012].[dbo].[uspGetWhereUsedProductID] 400,
    ''''2007-11-21'''''')' ;

PRINT @DynamicQuery;     -- test query;  this is the static query which will be executed
/*
SELECT *
    INTO BOM400
    FROM OPENQUERY([HPESTAR],
    'EXECUTE [AdventureWorks2012].[dbo].[uspGetWhereUsedProductID] 400,
    "2007-11-21"')
*/

EXEC sp_executeSQL @DynamicQuery;
GO
-- (64 row(s) affected)


SELECT TOP ( 5 ) *
FROM BOM400
ORDER BY NEWID() ;
```

| ProductAssemblyID | ComponentID | ComponentDesc | TotalQuantity | StandardCost | ListPrice | BOMLevel | RecursionLevel |
|---|---|---|---|---|---|---|---|
| 761 | 818 | Road-650 Red, 62 | 1.00 | 486.7066 | 782.99 | 1 | 1 |
| 987 | 823 | Mountain-500 Silver, 48 | 1.00 | 308.2179 | 564.99 | 1 | 1 |
| 990 | 823 | Mountain-500 Black, 42 | 1.00 | 294.5797 | 539.99 | 1 | 1 |
| 765 | 826 | Road-650 Black, 58 | 1.00 | 486.7066 | 782.99 | 1 | 1 |
| 770 | 818 | Road-650 Black, 52 | 1.00 | 486.7066 | 782.99 | 1 | 1 |

```
-- Cleanup
DROP TABLE BOM400;
GO
```

## SELECT INTO Table Create from View

Transact-SQL script demonstrates how to import view query results into a table.

```
SELECT [FullName],
       [SalesPersonID]                                AS StaffID,
       [SalesTerritory],
       COALESCE(FORMAT([2006], 'c','en-US'), '')      AS [2006],
       COALESCE(FORMAT([2007], 'c','en-US'), '')      AS [2007],
       COALESCE(FORMAT([2008], 'c','en-US'), '')      AS [2008]
INTO   #Sales
FROM   [AdventureWorks2012].[Sales].[vSalesPersonSalesByFiscalYears]
ORDER  BY SalesTerritory, FullName;
GO


SELECT *
FROM   #Sales
ORDER  BY SalesTerritory, FullName;
GO
```

| FullName | StaffID | SalesTerritory | 2006 | 2007 | 2008 |
|---|---|---|---|---|---|
| Lynn N Tsoflias | 286 | Australia | | | $1,421,810.92 |
| Garrett R Vargas | 278 | Canada | $930,259.47 | $1,225,468.28 | $1,453,719.47 |
| José Edvaldo Saraiva | 282 | Canada | $2,088,491.17 | $1,233,386.47 | $2,604,540.72 |
| Jillian  Carson | 277 | Central | $2,737,537.88 | $4,138,847.30 | $3,189,418.37 |
| Ranjit R Varkey Chudukatil | 290 | France | | $1,388,272.61 | $3,121,616.32 |
| Rachel B Valdez | 288 | Germany | | | $1,827,066.71 |
| Michael G Blythe | 275 | Northeast | $1,602,472.39 | $3,928,252.44 | $3,763,178.18 |
| David R Campbell | 283 | Northwest | $1,017,402.86 | $1,139,529.55 | $1,573,012.94 |
| Pamela O Ansman-Wolfe | 280 | Northwest | $1,226,461.83 | $746,063.63 | $1,352,577.13 |
| Tete A Mensa-Annan | 284 | Northwest | | $735,983.49 | $1,576,562.20 |
| Tsvi Michael Reiter | 279 | Southeast | $2,645,436.95 | $2,210,390.19 | $2,315,185.61 |
| Linda C Mitchell | 276 | Southwest | $2,260,118.45 | $3,855,520.42 | $4,251,368.55 |
| Shu K Ito | 281 | Southwest | $1,593,742.92 | $2,374,727.02 | $2,458,535.62 |
| Jae B Pak | 289 | United Kingdom | | $4,386,467.42 | $4,116,871.23 |

## SELECT INTO Data Import from Excel

T-SQL OPENROWSET query imports data into a temporary table from Excel. Your Excel library maybe different than the one in the example.

```
SELECT *  INTO ContactList  FROM OPENROWSET('Microsoft.Jet.OLEDB.4.0',
       'Excel 8.0;Database=D:\data\excel\Contact.xls', 'SELECT * FROM [Contact$]')
-- (19972 row(s) affected)
```

**CHAPTER 14:  SELECT INTO Table Creation & Population**

# CHAPTER 15: Modify Data - INSERT, UPDATE, DELETE & MERGE

## INSERT VALUES - Table Value Constructor

T-SQL scripts illustrate the use of INSERT VALUES with Table Value Constructor ( a list of values). Because the text columns are defined as nvarchar the string literals are prefixed with "N" indicating UNICODE literal. Since only Latin letters used, the "N" can be omitted.

```
USE tempdb;
SELECT TOP 0 * INTO dbo.Department FROM AdventureWorks2012.HumanResources.Department;
-- This is necessary because IDENTITY property was inherited in the SELECT INTO
SET IDENTITY_INSERT dbo.Department ON;
GO
INSERT dbo.Department (DepartmentID, Name, GroupName, ModifiedDate) VALUES
(1, N'Engineering', N'Research and Development', getdate()),
(2, N'Tool Design', N'Research and Development', getdate()),
(3, N'Sales', N'Sales and Marketing', getdate()),
(4, N'Marketing', N'Sales and Marketing', getdate()),
(5, N'Purchasing', N'Inventory Management', getdate()),
(6, N'Research and Development', N'Research and Development', getdate()),
(7, N'Production', N'Manufacturing', getdate()),
(8, N'Production Control', N'Manufacturing', getdate()),
(9, N'Human Resources', N'Executive General and Administration', getdate()),
(10, N'Finance', N'Executive General and Administration', getdate()),
(11, N'Information Services', N'Executive General and Administration', getdate()),
(12, N'Document Control', N'Quality Assurance', getdate()),
(13, N'Quality Assurance', N'Quality Assurance', getdate()),
(14, N'Facilities and Maintenance', N'Executive General and Administration', getdate()),
(15, N'Shipping and Receiving', N'Inventory Management', getdate()),
(16, N'Executive', N'Executive General and Administration',getdate());
GO
SET IDENTITY_INSERT dbo.Department OFF;
GO
SELECT TOP 4 * FROM dbo.Department ORDER BY DepartmentID;
```

| DepartmentID | Name | GroupName | ModifiedDate |
|---|---|---|---|
| 1 | Engineering | Research and Development | 2016-08-02 06:35:44.623 |
| 2 | Tool Design | Research and Development | 2016-08-02 06:35:44.623 |
| 3 | Sales | Sales and Marketing | 2016-08-02 06:35:44.623 |
| 4 | Marketing | Sales and Marketing | 2016-08-02 06:35:44.623 |

```
DROP TABLE tempdb.dbo.Department;
```

# INSERT VALUES - Ye Olde Way

T-SQL scripts illustrate the INSERT VALUES for single row insert, the only available method prior to SQL Server 2008.

```
USE AdventureWorks2012;
GO

CREATE TABLE Shift(
        ShiftID tinyint IDENTITY(1,1) NOT NULL,
        Name dbo.Name NOT NULL,
        StartTime time(7) NOT NULL,
        EndTime time(7) NOT NULL,
        ModifiedDate datetime NOT NULL,
        CONSTRAINT PK_Shift_ShiftID PRIMARY KEY CLUSTERED (ShiftID ASC) );
GO

SET IDENTITY_INSERT Shift ON;              -- To force insert into ShiftID

INSERT Shift (ShiftID, Name, StartTime, EndTime, ModifiedDate)
VALUES (1, N'Day', CAST(0x0700D85EAC3A0000 AS Time), CAST(0x07001882BA7D0000 AS Time),
CAST(0x0000921E00000000 AS DateTime))
INSERT Shift (ShiftID, Name, StartTime, EndTime, ModifiedDate)
VALUES (2, N'Evening', CAST(0x07001882BA7D0000 AS Time), CAST(0x070058A5C8C00000 AS Time),
getdate());
INSERT Shift (ShiftID, Name, StartTime, EndTime, ModifiedDate)
VALUES (3, N'Night', CAST(0x070058A5C8C00000 AS Time), CAST(0x0700D85EAC3A0000 AS Time),
CURRENT_TIMESTAMP);
GO

SET IDENTITY_INSERT Shift OFF;

ALTER TABLE Shift ADD  CONSTRAINT DF_Shift_ModifiedDate  DEFAULT (getdate()) FOR ModifiedDate
GO

SELECT * FROM Shift ORDER BY ShiftID;
GO
```

| ShiftID | Name | StartTime | EndTime | ModifiedDate |
| --- | --- | --- | --- | --- |
| 1 | Day | 07:00:00.0000000 | 15:00:00.0000000 | 2002-06-01 00:00:00.000 |
| 2 | Evening | 15:00:00.0000000 | 23:00:00.0000000 | 2018-08-20 19:31:02.293 |
| 3 | Night | 23:00:00.0000000 | 07:00:00.0000000 | 2018-08-20 19:31:02.293 |

```
DROP TABLE Shift;
GO
```

**CHAPTER 15:  Modify Data - INSERT, UPDATE, DELETE & MERGE**

# INSERT SELECT

## INSERT SELECT Literal List

T-SQL scripts demonstrate the insertion of literal records (rows) using INSERT SELECT.

```
USE tempdb;
GO
SELECT TOP 0 * INTO dbo.Department FROM AdventureWorks2012.HumanResources.Department;
GO
-- This is necessary because IDENTITY property was inherited in the SELECT INTO
SET IDENTITY_INSERT dbo.Department ON;
GO
INSERT dbo.Department (DepartmentID, Name, GroupName, ModifiedDate)
SELECT 1, N'Engineering', N'Research and Development', CURRENT_TIMESTAMP  UNION
SELECT 2, N'Tool Design', N'Research and Development', CURRENT_TIMESTAMP  UNION
SELECT 3, N'Sales', N'Sales and Marketing', CURRENT_TIMESTAMP  UNION
SELECT 4, N'Marketing', N'Sales and Marketing', CURRENT_TIMESTAMP  UNION
SELECT 5, N'Purchasing', N'Inventory Management', CURRENT_TIMESTAMP  UNION
SELECT 6, N'Research and Development', N'Research and Development', CURRENT_TIMESTAMP  UNION
SELECT 7, N'Production', N'Manufacturing', CURRENT_TIMESTAMP  UNION
SELECT 8, N'Production Control', N'Manufacturing', CURRENT_TIMESTAMP  UNION
SELECT 9, N'Human Resources', N'Executive General and Administration', CURRENT_TIMESTAMP  UNION
SELECT 10, N'Finance', N'Executive General and Administration', CURRENT_TIMESTAMP  UNION
SELECT 11, N'Information Services', N'Executive General and Administration', CURRENT_TIMESTAMP  UNION
SELECT 12, N'Document Control', N'Quality Assurance', CURRENT_TIMESTAMP  UNION
SELECT 13, N'Quality Assurance', N'Quality Assurance', CURRENT_TIMESTAMP  UNION
SELECT 14, N'Facilities and Maintenance', N'Executive General and Administration', CURRENT_TIMESTAMP  UNION
SELECT 15, N'Shipping and Receiving', N'Inventory Management', CURRENT_TIMESTAMP  UNION
SELECT 16, N'Executive', N'Executive General and Administration', CURRENT_TIMESTAMP;
GO
SET IDENTITY_INSERT dbo.Department OFF;
GO
SELECT TOP 4 * FROM dbo.Department ORDER BY DepartmentID;
GO
```

| DepartmentID | Name | GroupName | ModifiedDate |
|---|---|---|---|
| 1 | Engineering | Research and Development | 2016-08-02 06:35:44.623 |
| 2 | Tool Design | Research and Development | 2016-08-02 06:35:44.623 |
| 3 | Sales | Sales and Marketing | 2016-08-02 06:35:44.623 |
| 4 | Marketing | Sales and Marketing | 2016-08-02 06:35:44.623 |

```
-- Cleanup
DROP TABLE tempdb.dbo.Department;
```

**CHAPTER 15:  Modify Data - INSERT, UPDATE, DELETE & MERGE**

## INSERT SELECT from Table

T-SQL script demonstrates table population with table SELECT.

```
USE tempdb;
SELECT TOP 0 * INTO dbo.Department FROM AdventureWorks2012.HumanResources.Department;
GO
-- This is necessary because IDENTITY property was inherited in the SELECT INTO
SET IDENTITY_INSERT dbo.Department ON;
GO
INSERT dbo.Department (DepartmentID, Name, GroupName, ModifiedDate)
SELECT TOP 15 DepartmentID, Name, GroupName, ModifiedDate
FROM AdventureWorks2012.HumanResources.Department  ORDER BY DepartmentID;
GO
-- (15 row(s) affected)
SELECT TOP 4 * FROM dbo.Department ORDER BY DepartmentID;
```

| DepartmentID | Name | GroupName | ModifiedDate |
|---|---|---|---|
| 1 | Engineering | Research and Development | 2016-08-02 06:35:44.623 |
| 2 | Tool Design | Research and Development | 2016-08-02 06:35:44.623 |
| 3 | Sales | Sales and Marketing | 2016-08-02 06:35:44.623 |
| 4 | Marketing | Sales and Marketing | 2016-08-02 06:35:44.623 |

## SCOPE_IDENTITY() for Last-Inserted IDENTITY Value

The last inserted IDENTITY value can be returned with the SCOPE_IDENTITY() or @@IDENTITY system function (variable). SCOPE_IDENTITY() is better choice since it is within the current connection scope. @@IDENTITY is at server level.

```
INSERT dbo.Department (DepartmentID, Name, GroupName, ModifiedDate)
SELECT TOP 1 DepartmentID, Name, GroupName, ModifiedDate
FROM AdventureWorks2012.HumanResources.Department  ORDER BY DepartmentID DESC;
GO
-- (1 row(s) affected)
```

Alternate is SELECT @@IDENTITY;  @@ variables are system variables.

```
DECLARE @LastID INT = SCOPE_IDENTITY();
SELECT @LastID;   -- 16

SET IDENTITY_INSERT dbo.Department OFF;
GO

-- Cleanup
DROP TABLE tempdb.dbo.Department;
```

**CHAPTER 15:  Modify Data - INSERT, UPDATE, DELETE & MERGE**

## INSERT with Subset of Columns

Only the required columns must be present in the INSERT column list. A column with default or NULL property can be omitted. In the next T-SQL script, ModifiedDate is filled by default with getdate().

```
USE tempdb;
SELECT TOP 0 * INTO dbo.Department FROM AdventureWorks2012.HumanResources.Department;
GO
ALTER TABLE dbo.Department ADD CONSTRAINT DF_Dept_ModDate DEFAULT getdate() FOR
ModifiedDate;
GO
SET IDENTITY_INSERT dbo.Department ON;
GO
INSERT dbo.Department (DepartmentID, Name, GroupName)
SELECT DepartmentID, Name, GroupName  FROM AdventureWorks2012.HumanResources.Department;
GO
-- (16 row(s) affected)
SELECT TOP 4 * FROM dbo.Department ORDER BY DepartmentID;
```

| DepartmentID | Name | GroupName | ModifiedDate |
|---|---|---|---|
| 1 | Engineering | Research and Development | 2016-08-02 06:35:44.623 |
| 2 | Tool Design | Research and Development | 2016-08-02 06:35:44.623 |
| 3 | Sales | Sales and Marketing | 2016-08-02 06:35:44.623 |
| 4 | Marketing | Sales and Marketing | 2016-08-02 06:35:44.623 |

## Capturing Last-Inserted IDENTITY Set Values with OUTPUT

When more than one row is inserted with one statement, the OUTPUT clause can be used to capture the list of just inserted IDENTITY values.

```
DECLARE @LastInserted TABLE (ID INT);
INSERT dbo.Department (DepartmentID, Name, GroupName)
        OUTPUT inserted.DepartmentID INTO @LastInserted
SELECT DepartmentID+1000, Name, GroupName  FROM
AdventureWorks2012.HumanResources.Department;
SELECT TOP 5 * FROM @LastInserted ORDER BY ID;
GO
```

| ID |
|---|
| 1001 |
| 1002 |
| 1003 |
| 1004 |
| 1005 |

```
SET IDENTITY_INSERT dbo.Department OFF;
DROP TABLE tempdb.dbo.Department;
```

### CHAPTER 15: Modify Data - INSERT, UPDATE, DELETE & MERGE

# INSERT EXEC Stored Procedure

Data can be directly inserted from the execution of a user-defined stored procedure or system procedure. We create a table and a stored procedure, then perform INSERT EXEC.

```
USE AdventureWorks2012;
IF OBJECT_ID ('dbo.EmployeeSales', 'U') IS NOT NULL   DROP TABLE dbo.EmployeeSales;
IF OBJECT_ID ('dbo.uspGetEmployeeSales', 'P') IS NOT NULL   DROP PROCEDURE uspGetEmployeeSales;
CREATE TABLE dbo.EmployeeSales
 (
   BusinessEntityID        VARCHAR(11) NOT NULL PRIMARY KEY,
   LastName                VARCHAR(40) NOT NULL,
   SalesDollars            MONEY NOT NULL,
   DataSource              VARCHAR(20) NOT NULL
 );
GO


CREATE PROCEDURE dbo.uspGetEmployeeSales AS
 BEGIN
   SELECT        e.BusinessEntityID, c.LastName, sp.SalesYTD, 'PROCEDURE'
   FROM   HumanResources.Employee AS e
       INNER JOIN Sales.SalesPerson AS sp
          ON e.BusinessEntityID = sp.BusinessEntityID
       INNER JOIN Person.Person AS c
          ON e.BusinessEntityID = c.BusinessEntityID
   WHERE  e.BusinessEntityID > 280
     ORDER  BY      e.BusinessEntityID,  c.LastName;
 END;
GO


--INSERT...EXECUTE user-defined stored procedure
INSERT EmployeeSales EXECUTE uspGetEmployeeSales;

SELECT * FROM  EmployeeSales;
```

| BusinessEntityID | LastName | SalesDollars | DataSource |
|---|---|---|---|
| 281 | Ito | 2458535.6169 | PROCEDURE |
| 282 | Saraiva | 2604540.7172 | PROCEDURE |
| 283 | Campbell | 1573012.9383 | PROCEDURE |
| 284 | Mensa-Annan | 1576562.1966 | PROCEDURE |
| 285 | Abbas | 172524.4512 | PROCEDURE |
| 286 | Tsoflias | 1421810.9242 | PROCEDURE |
| 287 | Alberts | 519905.932 | PROCEDURE |
| 288 | Valdez | 1827066.7118 | PROCEDURE |
| 289 | Pak | 4116871.2277 | PROCEDURE |
| 290 | Varkey Chudukatil | 3121616.3202 | PROCEDURE |

## Insert Into A Table Via The Direct Execution Of An SQL Query With The EXEC Command

SELECT Population = count(*)  FROM   dbo.EmployeeSales;

| Population |
|------------|
| 10         |

```
--INSERT...EXECUTE('string') example
INSERT EmployeeSales
EXECUTE ('     SELECT e.BusinessEntityID, c.LastName,     sp.SalesYTD, ''EXEC SQL STRING''
               FROM HumanResources.Employee AS e       INNER JOIN Sales.SalesPerson AS sp
               ON e.BusinessEntityID = sp.BusinessEntityID        INNER JOIN Person.Person AS c
               ON e.BusinessEntityID = c.BusinessEntityID
               WHERE e.BusinessEntityID BETWEEN 270 and 280
               ORDER BY e.BusinessEntityID, c.LastName ');
GO
-- (7 row(s) affected)
```

Inserted number of rows can be captured for later use. **Capture must be done immediately after the monitored statement.**  Any following statement will change @@ROWCOUNT value.

```
DECLARE @InsertCount int = @@ROWCOUNT;
SELECT @InsertCount;   -- 7
GO
```

SELECT * FROM   dbo.EmployeeSales ORDER BY BusinessEntityID ;

| BusinessEntityID | LastName | SalesDollars | DataSource |
|------------------|----------|--------------|------------|
| 274 | Jiang | 559697.5639 | EXEC SQL STRING |
| 275 | Blythe | 3763178.1787 | EXEC SQL STRING |
| 276 | Mitchell | 4251368.5497 | EXEC SQL STRING |
| 277 | Carson | 3189418.3662 | EXEC SQL STRING |
| 278 | Vargas | 1453719.4653 | EXEC SQL STRING |
| 279 | Reiter | 2315185.611 | EXEC SQL STRING |
| 280 | Ansman-Wolfe | 1352577.1325 | EXEC SQL STRING |
| 281 | Ito | 2458535.6169 | PROCEDURE |
| 282 | Saraiva | 2604540.7172 | PROCEDURE |
| 283 | Campbell | 1573012.9383 | PROCEDURE |
| 284 | Mensa-Annan | 1576562.1966 | PROCEDURE |
| 285 | Abbas | 172524.4512 | PROCEDURE |
| 286 | Tsoflias | 1421810.9242 | PROCEDURE |
| 287 | Alberts | 519905.932 | PROCEDURE |
| 288 | Valdez | 1827066.7118 | PROCEDURE |
| 289 | Pak | 4116871.2277 | PROCEDURE |
| 290 | Varkey Chudukatil | 3121616.3202 | PROCEDURE |

**CHAPTER 15:  Modify Data - INSERT, UPDATE, DELETE & MERGE**

## INSERT EXEC System Procedure

Data can be inserted into a table by the execution of a system procedure. We create a test table with SELECT INTO FROM OPENQUERY. We can also create the table manually if we know the data type of columns.

```
-- DATA ACCESS must be turned on at YOURSERVER SQL Server instance
SELECT TOP(0) * INTO #SPWHO
FROM OPENQUERY(YOURSERVER, 'exec sp_who');          -- will not work with sp_who2 due to duplicate
column name

/*  Table created
CREATE TABLE [dbo].[#SPWHO](
        [spid] [smallint] NOT NULL,
        [ecid] [smallint] NOT NULL,
        [status] [nchar](30) NOT NULL,
        [loginame] [nvarchar](128) NULL,
        [hostname] [nchar](128) NOT NULL,
        [blk] [char](5) NULL,
        [dbname] [nvarchar](128) NULL,
        [cmd] [nchar](16) NOT NULL,
        [request_id] [int] NOT NULL
); */

INSERT #SPWHO   EXEC sp_who
```

The blk column contains blocking spid if any.  A large update for example may block other queries until it completes. The spid of the current session is @@SPID.

```
SELECT * FROM  #SPWHO
GO
-- (42 row(s) affected) - Partial results.
```

| spid | ecid | status | loginame | hostname | blk | dbname | cmd | request_id |
|---|---|---|---|---|---|---|---|---|
| 21 | 0 | background | sa | | 0 | master | TASK MANAGER | 0 |
| 22 | 0 | background | sa | | 0 | master | CHECKPOINT | 0 |
| 23 | 0 | sleeping | sa | | 0 | master | TASK MANAGER | 0 |
| 24 | 0 | background | sa | | 0 | master | BRKR TASK | 0 |
| 25 | 0 | sleeping | sa | | 0 | master | TASK MANAGER | 0 |
| 26 | 0 | sleeping | sa | | 0 | master | TASK MANAGER | 0 |
| 27 | 0 | sleeping | sa | | 0 | master | TASK MANAGER | 0 |
| 28 | 0 | sleeping | sa | | 0 | master | TASK MANAGER | 0 |
| 29 | 0 | sleeping | sa | | 0 | master | TASK MANAGER | 0 |
| 30 | 0 | sleeping | sa | | 0 | master | TASK MANAGER | 0 |
| 40 | 0 | background | sa | | 0 | master | BRKR TASK | 0 |
| 42 | 0 | background | sa | | 0 | master | BRKR TASK | 0 |
| 43 | 0 | background | sa | | 0 | master | BRKR TASK | 0 |
| 51 | 0 | sleeping | YOURSERVER \Owner | YOURSERVER | 0 | AdventureWorks2012 | AWAITING COMMAND | 0 |
| 52 | 0 | sleeping | NT SERVICE\SQLSERVERAGENT | YOURSERVER | 0 | msdb | AWAITING COMMAND | 0 |

```
DROP TABLE #SPWHO
GO
```

**CHAPTER 15:  Modify Data - INSERT, UPDATE, DELETE & MERGE**

## INSERT Only New Rows Omit the Rest

INSERT only new records. If record exists, do nothing. Note: DELETE will not rollback IDENTITY current value. Therefore with repeated testing, the IDENTITY current value will roll ahead.

```
USE AdventureWorks2012;
SELECT COUNT(*) FROM HumanResources.Department;              -- 16


-- All rows exists, no new row insertion
INSERT HumanResources.Department (Name, GroupName)
SELECT Name, GroupName
FROM AdventureWorks2008.HumanResources.Department D
WHERE NOT EXISTS (      SELECT * FROM HumanResources.Department DD  -- Correlated subquery
                   WHERE D.Name = DD.Name
                      AND D.GroupName = DD.GroupName);
GO
-- (0 row(s) affected)


-- Prefix Name with "ZZZ", 16 successful new inserted rows
INSERT HumanResources.Department (Name, GroupName)
SELECT CONCAT('ZZZ', Name), GroupName
FROM AdventureWorks2008.HumanResources.Department D
WHERE NOT EXISTS (      SELECT * FROM HumanResources.Department DD
        WHERE DD.Name = CONCAT('ZZZ', D.Name)   AND DD.GroupName = D.GroupName);
GO
-- (16 row(s) affected)


DELETE TOP ( 7 ) HumanResources.Department WHERE Name LIKE ('ZZZ%');      -- (7 row(s) affected)
```

Only 7 rows will be inserted since the rest are duplicates.

```
INSERT HumanResources.Department (Name, GroupName)
SELECT CONCAT('ZZZ', Name), GroupName
FROM AdventureWorks2008.HumanResources.Department D
WHERE NOT EXISTS (      SELECT * FROM HumanResources.Department DD
             WHERE DD.Name = CONCAT('ZZZ', D.Name)   AND DD.GroupName = DD.GroupName);
GO
-- (7  row(s) affected)


SELECT * FROM HumanResources.Department;    -- (32 row(s) affected)  -- Partial results;
```

| DepartmentID | Name | GroupName | ModifiedDate |
|---|---|---|---|
| 16 | Executive | Executive General and Administration | 2002-06-01 00:00:00.000 |
| 65 | ZZZEngineering | Research and Development | 2018-08-13 08:32:43.133 |

```
DELETE HumanResources.Department WHERE Name LIKE ('ZZZ%');      -- (16 row(s) affected)
SELECT COUNT(*) FROM HumanResources.Department;                -- 16
```

**CHAPTER 15:  Modify Data - INSERT, UPDATE, DELETE & MERGE**

# DELETE - A Dangerous Operation

DELETE is a logged operation. DELETE may be slow from large table with indexes due to index
reorganization. Warning: **DELETE is a dangerous operation since it removes data**. **Protection: regular
database backup and/or creating a copy of the table prior to DELETE with SELECT INTO.**

```
USE [AdventureWorks2012]
GO
-- Create test table with SELECT INTO
SELECT [SalesOrderID]
    ,CONVERT(INT,[SalesOrderDetailID]) AS SalesOrderDetailID
    ,[CarrierTrackingNumber]
    ,[OrderQty]
    ,[ProductID]
    ,[SpecialOfferID]
    ,[UnitPrice]
    ,[UnitPriceDiscount]
    ,[LineTotal]
    ,[rowguid]
    ,[ModifiedDate]
INTO tempdb.dbo.SOD
FROM [Sales].[SalesOrderDetail];
GO
-- (121317 row(s) affected)


-- Increase table population 64 fold
INSERT  tempdb.dbo.SOD  SELECT * FROM tempdb.dbo.SOD;
GO 6
/* Beginning execution loop
(121317 row(s) affected)
(242634 row(s) affected)
(485268 row(s) affected)
(970536 row(s) affected)
(1941072 row(s) affected)
(3882144 row(s) affected)
Batch execution completed 6 times.
Execution time - 00:01.27  */


CREATE INDEX idxSOD on tempdb.dbo.SOD (SalesOrderID, ProductID);
-- Command(s) completed successfully. Time: 00:00:06


SELECT COUNT(*) FROM tempdb.dbo.SOD;  -- 7764288


-- Delete even SalesOrderID records
DELETE FROM tempdb.dbo.SOD WHERE SalesOrderID % 2 = 0;
-- (3925184 row(s) affected)  - Execution time - 00:01:30
```

**CHAPTER 15:  Modify Data - INSERT, UPDATE, DELETE & MERGE**

# TRUNCATE TABLE & DBCC CHECKIDENT

TRUNCATE TABLE command is very fast since it is minimally logged. It also resets IDENTITY column to (1,1). Warning: **TRUNCATE is a dangerous operation since it removes all the data in a table**. Protection: regular database backup and/or creating a copy of the table prior to TRUNCATE with SELECT INTO.

SELECT COUNT(*) FROM tempdb.dbo.SOD;  -- 3839104

TRUNCATE TABLE tempdb.dbo.SOD;
-- Command(s) completed successfully.  Execution time: 00:00:00

SELECT COUNT(*) FROM tempdb.dbo.SOD;  -- 0
GO

DROP TABLE tempdb.dbo.SOD;
GO
-- Command(s) completed successfully

-- Create new test table with SELECT INTO
USE tempdb;

SELECT * INTO SOD FROM AdventureWorks2012.Sales.SalesOrderDetail;
GO
-- (121317 row(s) affected)

-- Next IDENTITY value will be 121318.
DBCC CHECKIDENT ("dbo.SOD");
/* Checking identity information: current identity value '121317', current column value '121317'.
DBCC execution completed. If DBCC printed error messages, contact your system administrator.  */

TRUNCATE TABLE SOD;
GO
-- Command(s) completed successfully.

-- IDENTITY is reset
DBCC CHECKIDENT ("dbo.SOD");
/* Checking identity information: current identity value 'NULL', current column value 'NULL'.
DBCC execution completed. If DBCC printed error messages, contact your system administrator. */

EXEC sp_help SOD;
GO
-- Partial results.

| Identity | Seed | Increment | Not For Replication |
|---|---|---|---|
| SalesOrderDetailID | 1 | 1 | 0 |

**CHAPTER 15: Modify Data - INSERT, UPDATE, DELETE & MERGE**

*Reseeding IDENTITY*

```
-- Without this command, it may not start at 1
DBCC CHECKIDENT ("SOD", RESEED, 1);


-- Populate the table with 5 rows
INSERT INTO SOD
     ([SalesOrderID]
     ,[CarrierTrackingNumber]
     ,[OrderQty]
     ,[ProductID]
     ,[SpecialOfferID]
     ,[UnitPrice]
     ,[UnitPriceDiscount]
     ,[LineTotal]
     ,[rowguid]
     ,[ModifiedDate])
SELECT   TOP (5)
     [SalesOrderID]
     ,[CarrierTrackingNumber]
     ,[OrderQty]
     ,[ProductID]
     ,[SpecialOfferID]
     ,[UnitPrice]
     ,[UnitPriceDiscount]
     ,[LineTotal]
     ,[rowguid]
     ,[ModifiedDate]
FROM AdventureWorks2012.Sales.SalesOrderDetail;
-- (5 row(s) affected)

-- Next value assigned is 6
DBCC CHECKIDENT ("dbo.SOD");
/*Checking identity information: current identity value '5', current column value '5'.
DBCC execution completed. If DBCC printed error messages, contact your system administrator. */

SELECT * FROM SOD;
-- (5 row(s) affected) - Partial results.
```

| SalesOrderID | SalesOrderDetailID | CarrierTrackingNumber | OrderQty | ProductID | SpecialOfferID | UnitPrice | UnitPriceDiscount | LineTotal |
|---|---|---|---|---|---|---|---|---|
| 43659 | 1 | 4911-403C-98 | 1 | 776 | 1 | 2024.994 | 0.00 | 2024.994000 |
| 43659 | 2 | 4911-403C-98 | 3 | 777 | 1 | 2024.994 | 0.00 | 6074.982000 |
| 43659 | 3 | 4911-403C-98 | 1 | 778 | 1 | 2024.994 | 0.00 | 2024.994000 |
| 43659 | 4 | 4911-403C-98 | 1 | 771 | 1 | 2039.994 | 0.00 | 2039.994000 |
| 43659 | 5 | 4911-403C-98 | 1 | 772 | 1 | 2039.994 | 0.00 | 2039.994000 |

**CHAPTER 15:  Modify Data - INSERT, UPDATE, DELETE & MERGE**

# UPDATE - A Complex Operation

UPDATE changes data content at a row and column level (cell). It is a logged operation: deleted row contains previous data, inserted row contains new data. Warning: UPDATE is a dangerous operation since it changes the data in a table. Protection: regular database backup and/or creating a copy of the table prior to UPDATE with SELECT INTO.

Some UPDATEs are reversible, such as some calculated UPDATE, others may be irreversible.

## Checking Cardinality & Changes by UPDATE Prior to Execution

Since UPDATE is replaces previous data, it is very important to check prior to execution that is works correctly. It is quite simple to convert UPDATE into a checking SELECT. We intend to UPDATE the SalesYTD column with the last day sales for each salesperson.

```
USE AdventureWorks2012;
GO

SELECT   sp.BusinessEntityID, SalesYTD,
                [NewSalesYTD]=SalesYTD
        + (SELECT SUM(SODa.SubTotal)
          FROM   Sales.SalesOrderHeader AS SODa
          WHERE  CONVERT(date,SODa.OrderDate) = CONVERT(date,(SELECT MAX(OrderDate)
           FROM   Sales.SalesOrderHeader AS SODb
           WHERE
              SODb.SalesPersonID = SODa.SalesPersonID))
              AND sp.BusinessEntityID =  SODa.SalesPersonID
          GROUP  BY SODa.SalesPersonID)
FROM Sales.SalesPerson sp  ORDER BY sp.BusinessEntityID;
GO
```

| BusinessEntityID | SalesYTD | NewSalesYTD |
|---|---|---|
| 274 | 559697.5639 | 597350.4859 |
| 275 | 3763178.1787 | 4133185.161 |
| 276 | 4251368.5497 | 4534079.5941 |
| 277 | 3189418.3662 | 3527404.588 |
| 278 | 1453719.4653 | 1599132.4735 |
| 279 | 2315185.611 | 2548077.4756 |
| 280 | 1352577.1325 | 1503691.0098 |
| 281 | 2458535.6169 | 2678660.7921 |
| 282 | 2604540.7172 | 3030519.8258 |
| 283 | 1573012.9383 | 1714964.9067 |
| 284 | 1576562.1966 | 1719945.1917 |
| 285 | 172524.4512 | 176721.5652 |
| 286 | 1421810.9242 | 1649155.9058 |
| 287 | 519905.932 | 520578.226 |
| 288 | 1827066.7118 | 1962768.1658 |
| 289 | 4116871.2277 | 4556655.2802 |
| 290 | 3121616.3202 | 3240852.6195 |

**CHAPTER 15:  Modify Data - INSERT, UPDATE, DELETE & MERGE**

## ANSI Style UPDATE

T-SQL supports ANSI UPDATE, in addition T-SQL supports the FROM clause in UPDATE.

```
UPDATE Sales.SalesPerson
SET   SalesYTD = SalesYTD
           + (SELECT SUM(SODa.SubTotal)
             FROM   Sales.SalesOrderHeader AS SODa
             WHERE  CONVERT(date,SODa.OrderDate) =
                      CONVERT(date,(SELECT MAX(OrderDate)
             FROM   Sales.SalesOrderHeader AS SODb
             WHERE
                 SODb.SalesPersonID = SODa.SalesPersonID))
                 AND Sales.SalesPerson.BusinessEntityID =   SODa.SalesPersonID
             GROUP  BY SODa.SalesPersonID);
GO
-- (17 row(s) affected)
```

```
SELECT BusinessEntityID, SalesQuota, SalesYTD, SalesLastYear FROM Sales.SalesPerson
ORDER BY BusinessEntityID;
GO
```

| BusinessEntityID | SalesQuota | SalesYTD | SalesLastYear |
|---|---|---|---|
| 274 | NULL | 597350.4859 | 0.00 |
| 275 | 300000.00 | 4133185.161 | 1750406.4785 |
| 276 | 250000.00 | 4534079.5941 | 1439156.0291 |
| 277 | 250000.00 | 3527404.588 | 1997186.2037 |
| 278 | 250000.00 | 1599132.4735 | 1620276.8966 |
| 279 | 300000.00 | 2548077.4756 | 1849640.9418 |
| 280 | 250000.00 | 1503691.0098 | 1927059.178 |
| 281 | 250000.00 | 2678660.7921 | 2073505.9999 |
| 282 | 250000.00 | 3030519.8258 | 2038234.6549 |
| 283 | 250000.00 | 1714964.9067 | 1371635.3158 |
| 284 | 300000.00 | 1719945.1917 | 0.00 |
| 285 | NULL | 176721.5652 | 0.00 |
| 286 | 250000.00 | 1649155.9058 | 2278548.9776 |
| 287 | NULL | 520578.226 | 0.00 |
| 288 | 250000.00 | 1962768.1658 | 1307949.7917 |
| 289 | 250000.00 | 4556655.2802 | 1635823.3967 |
| 290 | 250000.00 | 3240852.6195 | 2396539.7601 |

## UPDATE from Table in Another Database

UPDATE can be performed with data from a second database. ZorigAdventureWorks2012 is an original read-only copy of the AdventureWorks2012 database. The "Z" prefix is to force it to the end of alphabetical database list in SSMS Object Explorer.

```
UPDATE Sales.SalesPerson
     SET SalesYTD =   (

                      SELECT SalesYTD
                      FROM ZorigAdventureWorks2012.Sales.SalesPerson sp
                      WHERE sp.BusinessEntityID = Sales.SalesPerson.BusinessEntityID
               );
GO
```

```
SELECT  BusinessEntityID,
        SalesQuota,
        SalesYTD,
        SalesLastYear
FROM Sales.SalesPerson
ORDER BY BusinessEntityID;
GO
```

| BusinessEntityID | SalesQuota | SalesYTD | SalesLastYear |
|---|---|---|---|
| 274 | NULL | 559697.5639 | 0.00 |
| 275 | 300000.00 | 3763178.1787 | 1750406.4785 |
| 276 | 250000.00 | 4251368.5497 | 1439156.0291 |
| 277 | 250000.00 | 3189418.3662 | 1997186.2037 |
| 278 | 250000.00 | 1453719.4653 | 1620276.8966 |
| 279 | 300000.00 | 2315185.611 | 1849640.9418 |
| 280 | 250000.00 | 1352577.1325 | 1927059.178 |
| 281 | 250000.00 | 2458535.6169 | 2073505.9999 |
| 282 | 250000.00 | 2604540.7172 | 2038234.6549 |
| 283 | 250000.00 | 1573012.9383 | 1371635.3158 |
| 284 | 300000.00 | 1576562.1966 | 0.00 |
| 285 | NULL | 172524.4512 | 0.00 |
| 286 | 250000.00 | 1421810.9242 | 2278548.9776 |
| 287 | NULL | 519905.932 | 0.00 |
| 288 | 250000.00 | 1827066.7118 | 1307949.7917 |
| 289 | 250000.00 | 4116871.2277 | 1635823.3967 |
| 290 | 250000.00 | 3121616.3202 | 2396539.7601 |

## UPDATE Syntax Challenges

The UPDATE statement in SQL has perplexing and potentially confusing syntax. Typically mastered by expert DBA-s and SQL developers, and the rest of the database community uses it in an insecure manner: never sure if it works as intended. Simple T-SQL examples demonstrate some of the issues with the UPDATE syntax and offer solutions.

First we create a new table for experimentation from the AdventureWorks2012 database and perform a demo inner join UPDATE on the new table.

```
USE tempdb;

SELECT ProductID,
    ProductName = Name,
    StandardCost AS Cost,
    ListPrice,
    Color,
    CONVERT(date, ModifiedDate) AS ModifiedDate
INTO   Product
FROM   AdventureWorks2012.Production.Product
WHERE  ListPrice > 0.0
    AND Color IS NOT NULL;
GO
-- (245 row(s) affected)

SELECT TOP 5 * FROM Product  ORDER BY ProductID DESC;
GO
```

| ProductID | ProductName | Cost | ListPrice | Color | ModifiedDate |
|-----------|-------------|------|-----------|-------|--------------|
| 999 | Road-750 Black, 52 | 343.6496 | 539.99 | Black | 2008-03-11 |
| 998 | Road-750 Black, 48 | 343.6496 | 539.99 | Black | 2008-03-11 |
| 997 | Road-750 Black, 44 | 343.6496 | 539.99 | Black | 2008-03-11 |
| 993 | Mountain-500 Black, 52 | 294.5797 | 539.99 | Black | 2008-03-11 |
| 992 | Mountain-500 Black, 48 | 294.5797 | 539.99 | Black | 2008-03-11 |

We shall proceed and update ALL (no WHERE clause) the rows in the Product table. We increase the ListPrice by 5%.

```
UPDATE Product     SET ListPrice = ListPrice * 1.05;
-- (245 row(s) affected)
```

In this instance a reversible UPDATE.  But not always.

```
UPDATE Product     SET ListPrice = ListPrice / 1.05;
-- (245 row(s) affected)
```

## CHAPTER 15:  Modify Data - INSERT, UPDATE, DELETE & MERGE

## UPDATE with INNER JOIN

The UPDATE uses a table alias from the FROM clause.

SELECT TOP 2 * FROM Product  WHERE Color = 'Yellow' ORDER BY ProductID DESC;

| ProductID | ProductName | Cost | ListPrice | Color | ModifiedDate |
|-----------|-------------|------|-----------|-------|--------------|
| 976 | Road-350-W Yellow, 48 | 1082.51 | 1700.99 | Yellow | 2008-03-11 |
| 975 | Road-350-W Yellow, 44 | 1082.51 | 1700.99 | Yellow | 2008-03-11 |

```
UPDATE p  SET   p.ModifiedDate = DATEADD(HH,1,awp.ModifiedDate)
FROM   Product p   INNER JOIN AdventureWorks2012.Production.Product awp
                 ON p.ProductID = awp.ProductID  AND  p.Size LIKE '4%' ;
-- (91 row(s) affected)
```

## Capturing Affected Rows with @@ROWCOUNT

When we have to know the number of updated  rows, it is best to capture it into local variable and use it from there in the program logic.

```
DECLARE @UpdatedRows int;   -- capture @@ROWCOUNT for subsequent  use in the program

UPDATE p
        SET    p.ModifiedDate = DATEADD(mm,1,awp.ModifiedDate)
FROM   Product p
     INNER JOIN AdventureWorks2012.Production.Product awp    ON p.ProductID = awp.ProductID
WHERE  p.Color = 'Yellow' ;
-- (36 row(s) affected)

SET @UpdatedRows = @@ROWCOUNT;

SELECT @@ROWCOUNT;          -- @@ROWCOUNT already changed
-- 1
SELECT TOP 5 * FROM Product  WHERE Color = 'Yellow' ORDER BY ProductID DESC;

SELECT @@ROWCOUNT;          -- @@ROWCOUNT changed again
-- 5
SELECT @UpdatedRows;          -- local variable kept the UPDATE count
-- 36
```

| ProductID | ProductName | Cost | ListPrice | Color | ModifiedDate |
|-----------|-------------|------|-----------|-------|--------------|
| 976 | Road-350-W Yellow, 48 | 1082.51 | 1700.99 | Yellow | 2008-04-11 |
| 975 | Road-350-W Yellow, 44 | 1082.51 | 1700.99 | Yellow | 2008-04-11 |
| 974 | Road-350-W Yellow, 42 | 1082.51 | 1700.99 | Yellow | 2008-04-11 |
| 973 | Road-350-W Yellow, 40 | 1082.51 | 1700.99 | Yellow | 2008-04-11 |
| 965 | Touring-3000 Yellow, 62 | 461.4448 | 742.35 | Yellow | 2008-04-11 |

## UPDATE with Common Table Expression

UPDATE can be issued through a CTE to UPDATE the underlying table, Product in this case. Prices are increased 5% for products with over $1,000.00 list price.

```
SELECT TOP 5 * FROM Product  WHERE ListPrice > 1000.0 ORDER BY ProductID DESC;
GO
```

| ProductID | ProductName           | Cost      | ListPrice | Color  | ModifiedDate |
|-----------|-----------------------|-----------|-----------|--------|--------------|
| 976       | Road-350-W Yellow, 48 | 1082.51   | 1700.99   | Yellow | 2008-04-11   |
| 975       | Road-350-W Yellow, 44 | 1082.51   | 1700.99   | Yellow | 2008-04-11   |
| 974       | Road-350-W Yellow, 42 | 1082.51   | 1700.99   | Yellow | 2008-04-11   |
| 973       | Road-350-W Yellow, 40 | 1082.51   | 1700.99   | Yellow | 2008-04-11   |
| 972       | Touring-2000 Blue, 54 | 755.1508  | 1214.85   | Blue   | 2008-03-11   |

```
;WITH CTE
   AS (SELECT Price = ListPrice
      FROM   Product
      WHERE  ListPrice > 1000.0)
UPDATE CTE
SET   Price = Price * 1.05
GO
-- (86 row(s) affected)
```

```
SELECT TOP 5 * FROM Product  WHERE ListPrice > 1000.0 ORDER BY ProductID DESC;
```

| ProductID | ProductName           | Cost      | ListPrice  | Color  | ModifiedDate |
|-----------|-----------------------|-----------|------------|--------|--------------|
| 976       | Road-350-W Yellow, 48 | 1082.51   | 1786.0395  | Yellow | 2008-04-11   |
| 975       | Road-350-W Yellow, 44 | 1082.51   | 1786.0395  | Yellow | 2008-04-11   |
| 974       | Road-350-W Yellow, 42 | 1082.51   | 1786.0395  | Yellow | 2008-04-11   |
| 973       | Road-350-W Yellow, 40 | 1082.51   | 1786.0395  | Yellow | 2008-04-11   |
| 972       | Touring-2000 Blue, 54 | 755.1508  | 1275.5925  | Blue   | 2008-03-11   |

Similar data modification with ANSI SQL UPDATE.

```
UPDATE Product
SET   ListPrice = (SELECT p8.ListPrice * 1.05
          FROM   AdventureWorks2012.Production.Product p8   WHERE  Product.ProductID =
p8.ProductID)
WHERE  EXISTS (SELECT * FROM   AdventureWorks2012.Production.Product p8
          WHERE  Product.ProductID = p8.ProductID   AND Product.ListPrice > 1000.0);
```

**CHAPTER 15:  Modify Data - INSERT, UPDATE, DELETE & MERGE**

## Four Methods of UPDATE with GROUP BY Query

UPDATE can be done a few ways with GROUP BY aggregates.

```
USE tempdb;
SELECT Color=ISNULL(Color,'N/A'), ItemCount=0 INTO ProductColor
FROM AdventureWorks2008.Production.Product
GROUP BY Color
GO
-- (10 row(s) affected)
```

```
SELECT * FROM ProductColor
GO
```

| Color | ItemCount |
|-------|-----------|
| N/A | 0 |
| Black | 0 |
| Blue | 0 |
| Grey | 0 |
| Multi | 0 |
| Red | 0 |
| Silver | 0 |
| Silver/Black | 0 |
| White | 0 |
| Yellow | 0 |

### ANSI UPDATE

```
UPDATE ProductColor
SET ItemCount = (SELECT ProductColorCount FROM (SELECT Color=ISNULL(Color, 'N/A'),
            ProductColorCount=COUNT(*)
            FROM AdventureWorks2008.Production.Product
            GROUP BY Color) cg WHERE  ProductColor.Color = cg.Color)
GO
-- (10 row(s) affected)
```

### FROM Clause UPDATE with Derived Table

```
UPDATE pc   SET pc.ItemCount = cg.ProductColorCount
FROM ProductColor pc
INNER JOIN (SELECT Color=ISNULL(Color, 'N/A'), ProductColorCount=COUNT(*)
      FROM AdventureWorks2008.Production.Product GROUP BY Color) cg
ON pc.Color = cg.Color;
-- (10 row(s) affected)
```

## FROM Clause UPDATE with CTE

```
;WITH CTE AS (SELECT Color=ISNULL(Color, 'N/A'), ProductColorCount=COUNT(*)
       FROM AdventureWorks2008.Production.Product
       GROUP BY Color)
UPDATE pc
SET pc.ItemCount = CTE.ProductColorCount
FROM ProductColor pc
INNER JOIN CTE
ON pc.Color = CTE.Color;
GO
-- (10 row(s) affected)
```

## CTE UPDATE

```
;WITH CTE AS (SELECT * FROM ProductColor pc
INNER JOIN (SELECT ColorPrd=ISNULL(Color, 'N/A'), ProductColorCount=COUNT(*)
       FROM AdventureWorks2008.Production.Product
       GROUP BY Color) cg
                        ON pc.Color = cg.ColorPrd)
UPDATE CTE SET CTE.ItemCount = CTE.ProductColorCount;
GO
-- (10 row(s) affected)

SELECT * FROM ProductColor
GO
```

| Color | ItemCount |
|-------|-----------|
| N/A | 248 |
| Black | 93 |
| Blue | 26 |
| Grey | 1 |
| Multi | 8 |
| Red | 38 |
| Silver | 43 |
| Silver/Black | 7 |
| White | 4 |
| Yellow | 36 |

```
DROP TABLE tempdb.dbo.ProductColor;
GO
```

**CHAPTER 15:  Modify Data - INSERT, UPDATE, DELETE & MERGE**

# MERGE for Combination INSERT, UPDATE or DELETE

The MERGE statement can be used to INSERT, UPDATE and/or DELETE all in one statement.

```
USE tempdb;
go


-- Setup 2 test tables
SELECT TOP (5000) ResellerKey,
          OrderDateKey,
          ProductKey,
          OrderQuantity,
          SalesAmount
INTO   FactResellerSales
FROM   AdventureWorksDW2012.dbo.FactResellerSales ;
go
-- (5000 row(s) affected)


SELECT TOP (8000) ResellerKey,
          OrderDateKey,
          ProductKey,
          OrderQuantity,
          SalesAmount
INTO   ResellerSalesTransaction
FROM   AdventureWorksDW2012.dbo.FactResellerSales ;
go
-- (8000 row(s) affected)

DELETE rsc
FROM   ResellerSalesTransaction rsc
    JOIN (SELECT TOP 1000 *
        FROM   ResellerSalesTransaction
        ORDER  BY ResellerKey DESC) x
    ON x.ResellerKey = rsc.ResellerKey ;
go
-- (1010 row(s) affected)

UPDATE TOP (6000) ResellerSalesTransaction
SET   SalesAmount = SalesAmount * 1.1 ;
go
-- (6000 row(s) affected)
```

## *MERGE is a very powerful statement*

```
SELECT TOP (10) *
FROM   FactResellerSales
ORDER  BY ResellerKey,        OrderDateKey,        ProductKey ;
go
```

| ResellerKey | OrderDateKey | ProductKey | OrderQuantity | SalesAmount |
|---|---|---|---|---|
| 1 | 20050801 | 270 | 1 | 183.9382 |
| 1 | 20050801 | 275 | 1 | 356.898 |
| 1 | 20050801 | 285 | 1 | 178.5808 |
| 1 | 20050801 | 314 | 2 | 4293.924 |
| 1 | 20050801 | 317 | 1 | 874.794 |
| 1 | 20050801 | 319 | 2 | 1749.588 |
| 1 | 20050801 | 324 | 2 | 838.9178 |
| 1 | 20050801 | 326 | 1 | 419.4589 |
| 1 | 20050801 | 328 | 1 | 419.4589 |
| 1 | 20050801 | 332 | 2 | 838.9178 |

```
SELECT BeforeFactCount=COUNT(*)
FROM   FactResellerSales ;
-- 5000


-- Ready for the MERGE (update if exists,  insert otherwise)
MERGE FactResellerSales AS fact
USING (SELECT *
    FROM   ResellerSalesTransaction) AS feed
ON ( fact.ProductKey = feed.ProductKey
   AND fact.ResellerKey = feed.ResellerKey
   AND fact.OrderDateKey = feed.OrderDateKey )
WHEN MATCHED THEN
 UPDATE SET fact.OrderQuantity += feed.OrderQuantity,
       fact.SalesAmount += feed.SalesAmount
WHEN NOT MATCHED THEN
 INSERT (ResellerKey,
     OrderDateKey,
     ProductKey,
     OrderQuantity,
     SalesAmount)
 VALUES (feed.ResellerKey,
     feed.OrderDateKey,
     feed.ProductKey,
     feed.OrderQuantity,
     feed.SalesAmount);
go   -- (6990 row(s) affected)
```

### Checking results after MERGE

```
SELECT TOP (10) *
FROM  FactResellerSales ORDER  BY        ResellerKey,    OrderDateKey,    ProductKey;
```

| ResellerKey | OrderDateKey | ProductKey | OrderQuantity | SalesAmount |
|---|---|---|---|---|
| 1 | 20050801 | 270 | 2 | 386.2702 |
| 1 | 20050801 | 275 | 2 | 749.4858 |
| 1 | 20050801 | 285 | 2 | 375.0197 |
| 1 | 20050801 | 314 | 4 | 9017.2404 |
| 1 | 20050801 | 317 | 2 | 1837.0674 |
| 1 | 20050801 | 319 | 4 | 3674.1348 |
| 1 | 20050801 | 324 | 4 | 1761.7274 |
| 1 | 20050801 | 326 | 2 | 880.8637 |
| 1 | 20050801 | 328 | 2 | 880.8637 |
| 1 | 20050801 | 332 | 4 | 1761.7274 |

```
SELECT AfterFactCount=COUNT(*)  FROM  FactResellerSales ;
go
-- 7658

DROP TABLE ResellerSalesTransaction;  DROP TABLE FactResellerSales;
go
```

**CHAPTER 15: Modify Data - INSERT, UPDATE, DELETE & MERGE**

## Using MERGE Instead of UPDATE

MERGE statement can be used in the UPDATE only mode to replace UPDATE.

```
-- Prepare 2 test tables
USE tempdb;
SELECT TOP (5000) ResellerKey,  OrderDateKey, ProductKey, OrderQuantity, SalesAmount
INTO  FactResellerSales FROM  AdventureWorksDW2012.dbo.FactResellerSales;
GO -- (5000 row(s) affected)
SELECT TOP (8000) ResellerKey,  OrderDateKey, ProductKey, OrderQuantity, SalesAmount
INTO  ResellerSalesTransaction FROM  AdventureWorksDW2012.dbo.FactResellerSales;
GO -- (8000 row(s) affected)


-- Alter the test data
DELETE rsc
FROM  ResellerSalesTransaction rsc
   INNER JOIN (SELECT TOP 1000 * FROM  ResellerSalesTransaction
      ORDER  BY ResellerKey DESC) x  -- subquery inner join
   ON x.ResellerKey = rsc.ResellerKey;
GO --(1010 row(s) affected)
UPDATE TOP (6000) ResellerSalesTransaction SET SalesAmount = SalesAmount * 1.1;
GO -- (6000 row(s) affected)


SELECT BeforeFactCount=COUNT(*) FROM  FactResellerSales;
GO -- 5000
```

**-- Ready for the MERGE UPDATE only mode**
```
MERGE FactResellerSales AS fact
USING (SELECT * FROM  ResellerSalesTransaction) AS feed
ON ( fact.ProductKey = feed.ProductKey
   AND fact.ResellerKey = feed.ResellerKey
   AND fact.OrderDateKey = feed.OrderDateKey )
WHEN MATCHED THEN
 UPDATE SET fact.OrderQuantity = fact.OrderQuantity + feed.OrderQuantity,
      fact.SalesAmount = fact.SalesAmount + feed.SalesAmount;
GO -- 4332 row(s) affected)


SELECT AfterFactCount=COUNT(*) FROM  FactResellerSales;
GO -- 5000


DROP TABLE ResellerSalesTransaction;
DROP TABLE FactResellerSales;
```

**CHAPTER 15:  Modify Data - INSERT, UPDATE, DELETE & MERGE**

# CHAPTER 16: The Magic of Transact-SQL Programming

## IF...ELSE Conditional

IF... ELSE is a step toward a bona fide programming language.

```
DECLARE @StringNumber varchar(32) ;
SET @StringNumber = '12,000,000';
IF EXISTS( SELECT * WHERE ISNUMERIC(@StringNumber) = 1)
        PRINT 'VALID NUMBER: ' + @StringNumber
ELSE    PRINT 'INVALID NUMBER: ' + @StringNumber;
GO
-- VALID NUMBER: 12,000,000


DECLARE @StringNumber varchar(32) = '12,000:000';

IF EXISTS( SELECT * WHERE ISNUMERIC(@StringNumber) = 1)
        PRINT CONCAT('VALID NUMBER: ', @StringNumber)
ELSE    PRINT CONCAT('INVALID NUMBER: ', @StringNumber);
GO
-- INVALID NUMBER: 12,000:000


DECLARE @StringDate varchar(32);

SET @StringDate = '2017-03-15 18:50';

IF EXISTS( SELECT * WHERE ISDATE(@StringDate) = 1)
        PRINT 'VALID DATE: ' + @StringDate
ELSE    PRINT 'INVALID DATE: ' + @StringDate;
GO
-- Result: VALID DATE: 2017-03-15 18:50


DECLARE @StringDate varchar(32) = '20116-03-15 18:50';
IF EXISTS( SELECT * WHERE ISDATE(@StringDate) = 1)
        PRINT CONCAT('VALID DATE: ', @StringDate)
ELSE    PRINT CONCAT('INVALID DATE: ', @StringDate);
-- Result: INVALID DATE: 20116-03-15 18:50
```

# WHILE Looping - UPDATE in Batches

WHILE looping can be used to break down large transaction to small batches.  Executing in small batches is safer and does not block other OLTP transactions for a long time.  Blocking can be seen by running sp_who system stored procedure

```
EXEC sp_who;
```

UPDATE of 121,317 rows is batched to 13 batches of 10,000 or less.

```
USE tempdb;
SELECT * INTO SOD
FROM AdventureWorks2012.Sales.SalesOrderDetail ORDER BY SalesOrderDetailID;
GO
--(121317 row(s) affected)
```

```
WHILE (2 > 1)   -- Infinite loop until BREAK is issued
 BEGIN
  UPDATE TOP ( 10000 ) SOD
  SET   UnitPriceDiscount = 0.08,  ModifiedDate = CONVERT(DATE, getdate())
  WHERE  ModifiedDate < CONVERT(DATE, getdate());

  IF @@ROWCOUNT = 0
   BEGIN
    BREAK;
   END
  -- 1 second delay - Very important for other OLTP transactions execution
  WAITFOR DELAY '00:00:01'
 END; -- WHILE
GO
```

```
(10000 row(s) affected)
(10000 row(s) affected)
(10000 row(s) affected)
(10000 row(s) affected)
(10000 row(s) affected)
(10000 row(s) affected)
(10000 row(s) affected)
(10000 row(s) affected)
(10000 row(s) affected)
(10000 row(s) affected)
(10000 row(s) affected)
(10000 row(s) affected)
(1317 row(s) affected)
(0 row(s) affected)
```

```
DROP TABLE tempdb.dbo.SOD
```

# WHILE Loop Usage in Cursors

Transact-SQL logic will visit all databases on the current SQL Server instance using a cursor. NOTE: **cursor solutions do not scale well, first choice is set-based logic if appropriate.**

```
DECLARE @CurrentDB sysname;
DECLARE AllDBCursor CURSOR  STATIC LOCAL FOR
        SELECT  name FROM    MASTER.dbo.sysdatabases
        WHERE    name NOT IN ('master','tempdb','model','msdb') ORDER BY name;
OPEN AllDBCursor;
FETCH  AllDBCursor INTO @CurrentDB;
WHILE (@@FETCH_STATUS = 0) -- loop through all db-s
  BEGIN
/***** PROCESSING (like BACKUP database)  *****/
        PRINT @CurrentDB;
        FETCH  AllDBCursor  INTO @CurrentDB;
  END; -- while
CLOSE AllDBCursor; DEALLOCATE AllDBCursor;


/*.... AdventureWorks
AdventureWorks2008
AdventureWorks2012
AdventureWorksDW2012 .... */
```

Transact-SQL script demonstrates a subcategory cursor.

```
USE AdventureWorks2012;
DECLARE curSubcategory CURSOR STATIC LOCAL  FOR          -- declare cursor
        SELECT ProductSubcategoryID, Subcategory=Name
        FROM Production.ProductSubcategory ORDER BY Subcategory;
DECLARE @Subcategory varchar(40), @PSID int
OPEN curSubcategory
FETCH NEXT FROM curSubcategory INTO @PSID, @Subcategory  -- fetch cursor
WHILE (@@fetch_status = 0)              -- cursor fetch_status
BEGIN -- begin cursor loop
/***** USER DEFINED PROCESSING CODE HERE  *****/
        DECLARE @Msg varchar(128);
  SELECT @Msg = CONCAT('ProductSubcategory info: ', @Subcategory,' ',CONVERT(varchar, @PSID));
        PRINT @Msg;
FETCH NEXT FROM curSubcategory INTO @PSID, @Subcategory;   -- fetch cursor
END; -- end cursor loop
CLOSE curSubcategory;  DEALLOCATE curSubcategory;


/* ... ProductSubcategory info: Bike Stands 27
ProductSubcategory info: Bottles and Cages 28
ProductSubcategory info: Bottom Brackets 5   ... */
```

# T-SQL Transaction

Transact-SQL language has been extended with features beyond ANSI SQL such as variables, IF... ELSE and WHILE. **"Transact" refers to the capability to execute business transactions which require the synchronized update of tables as one or none at all.**

**DELETE from 2 Tables with TRANSACTION Control**
DELETE PRIMARY KEY rows from PK table and related FOREIGN KEY rows from FK table in a single transaction. NOTE: Deleting lots of rows may interfere with online access in an ecommerce database.

Alternate method: define tables with CASCADE ON DELETE action.

BEGIN TRANSACTION


```
-- First delete from FOREIGN KEY table
DELETE OmegaFK
FROM Omega AS OmegaFK
  INNER JOIN Delta AS DeltaPK
   ON DeltaPK.ColApk = OmegaFK.ColBfk
WHERE DeltaPK.ColApk = {single value A} ;
```


```
IF @@ERROR <> 0
BEGIN
        ROLLBACK TRANSACTION;
        RAISERROR('FK delete failed.', 10, 1);
END
-- if no error, delete from PRIMARY KEY table
ELSE
        DELETE
        FROM Delta
        WHERE ColApk = = {single value A};
```


```
-- Commit transaction only if both DELETE-s succeeded
IF @@ERROR <> 0
BEGIN
        ROLLBACK TRANSACTION;
        RAISERROR('PK delete failed.', 10, 1);
ELSE
        COMMIT TRANSACTION;
```

## Stored Procedure with Input & Output Parameters

A stored procedure usually returns a table-like result set from the SELECT(s) in the stored procedure. Scalar value can also be returned with the OUTPUT option.

```
USE AdventureWorks2012;
GO
CREATE PROCEDURE uspQuarterSales      @StartYear  INT,       @TotalSales MONEY  OUTPUT
AS
 BEGIN -- sproc definition
  SET NOCOUNT  ON -- turn off rows affected messages
  SELECT @TotalSales = SUM(SubTotal)
  FROM   Sales.SalesOrderHeader    WHERE  OrderDate >= DATEADD(YY,@StartYear-1900,'19000101')

  SELECT   YEAR = YEAR(OrderDate),
      COALESCE(FORMAT(SUM(CASE
          WHEN DATEPART(QQ,OrderDate) = 1 THEN SubTotal
                END),'c','en-US'),'') AS 'Q1',
      COALESCE(FORMAT(SUM(CASE
          WHEN DATEPART(QQ,OrderDate) = 2 THEN SubTotal
                END),'c','en-US'),'') AS 'Q2',
      COALESCE(FORMAT(SUM(CASE
          WHEN DATEPART(QQ,OrderDate) = 3 THEN SubTotal
                END),'c','en-US'),'') AS 'Q3',
      COALESCE(FORMAT(SUM(CASE
          WHEN DATEPART(QQ,OrderDate) = 4 THEN SubTotal
                END),'c','en-US'),'') AS 'Q4'
   FROM    Sales.SalesOrderHeader soh   WHERE   OrderDate >= DATEADD(YY,@StartYear-
1900,'19000101')
   GROUP BY YEAR(OrderDate)     ORDER BY YEAR(OrderDate);
 END; -- sproc definition
GO
```

```
-- Execute stored procedure with INPUT/OUTPUT parameters
DECLARE @TotSales money
EXEC uspQuarterSales  2007, @TotSales OUTPUT;
SELECT TotalSales = @TotSales;
```

| YEAR | Q1 | Q2 | Q3 | Q4 |
|------|------|------|------|------|
| 2007 | $6,679,873.80 | $8,357,874.88 | $13,681,907.05 | $13,291,381.43 |
| 2008 | $11,398,376.28 | $14,379,545.19 | $50,840.63 | |

| TotalSales |
|------------|
| 67839799.2669 |

# Dynamic SQL Stored Procedure to REBUILD Indexes

The following dynamic SQL stored procedure uses database metadata to loop through all tables in the database, assemble and execute the index REBUILD command.

```
USE AdventureWorks2012;
GO

CREATE PROC sprocAllTablesIndexREBUILD @FILLFACTOR INT = 90
AS
 BEGIN
   DECLARE @DatabaseName SYSNAME = DB_NAME(),
       @TableName   VARCHAR(256);
   DECLARE @DynamicSQL NVARCHAR(max) = CONCAT('DECLARE cursorForAllTables CURSOR FOR
            SELECT CONCAT(TABLE_SCHEMA,''.'', TABLE_NAME) AS TABLENAME    FROM ',
@DatabaseName,
       '.INFORMATION_SCHEMA.TABLES WHERE   TABLE_TYPE = ''BASE TABLE''');
   BEGIN
    EXEC sp_executeSQL
     @DynamicSQL; -- create tables cursor
    OPEN cursorForAllTables;

    FETCH NEXT FROM cursorForAllTables INTO @TableName;
    WHILE ( @@FETCH_STATUS = 0 )
     BEGIN
       SET @DynamicSQL = CONCAT('ALTER INDEX ALL ON ', @TableName,
               ' REBUILD WITH ( FILLFACTOR = ',
                    CONVERT(VARCHAR, @FILLFACTOR), ')'  );
       PRINT @DynamicSQL;  -- test & debug
       EXEC sp_executeSQL
        @DynamicSQL;
       FETCH NEXT FROM cursorForAllTables INTO @TableName;
     END; -- cursor WHILE
    CLOSE cursorForAllTables;   DEALLOCATE cursorForAllTables;
   END;
 END; -- sproc
GO
-- Command(s) completed successfully.

-- Reindex tables with 85% fill factor leaving 15% free space for growth
EXEC sprocAllTablesIndexREBUILD 85;
/*
ALTER INDEX ALL ON Production.ScrapReason REBUILD WITH ( FILLFACTOR = 85)
ALTER INDEX ALL ON HumanResources.Shift REBUILD WITH ( FILLFACTOR = 85)  ....  */
```

# User-Defined Functions

## Table-Valued Functions

A table-valued function returns a table variable, therefore, it has to be invoked like it were a table in a query. T-SQL table-valued function creates a table from a delimited string of values.

```
CREATE FUNCTION dbo.ufnSplitDelimitedString ( @StringList VARCHAR(MAX),    @Delimiter CHAR(1))
RETURNS @TableList TABLE(ID int identity(1,1), StringLiteral VARCHAR(128))
BEGIN
   IF @StringList = '' RETURN;
   IF @Delimiter = ''
   BEGIN
     WITH Split AS                          -- Recursive CTE
        ( SELECT CharOne=LEFT(@StringList,1),R=RIGHT(@StringList,len(@StringList)-1)
          UNION ALL
          SELECT LEFT(R,1), R=RIGHT(R, len(R)-1)
          FROM Split    WHERE LEN(R)>0 )           -- End of CTE
     INSERT @TableList
     SELECT CharOne FROM Split
     OPTION ( MAXRECURSION 0);
     RETURN;
   END; -- IF
   DECLARE @XML xml=CONCAT('<root><csv>',replace(@StringList,@Delimiter,'</csv><csv>'),
                           '</csv></root>');
   INSERT @TableList
   SELECT rtrim(ltrim(replace(Word.value('.','nvarchar(128)'),char(10),'')))    AS ListMember
   FROM @XML.nodes('/root/csv') AS WordList(Word);
RETURN;
END; -- FUNCTION
GO
```

SELECT * FROM dbo.ufnSplitDelimitedString ('New York, California, Arizona, Texas, Toronto, Grand Canyon, Yosemite,  Yellowstone, Niagara Falls, Belgium, Denmark, South Africa, Sweden', ',');

| ID | StringLiteral |
|----|---------------|
| 1 | New York |
| 2 | California |
| 3 | Arizona |
| 4 | Texas |
| 5 | Toronto |
| 6 | Grand Canyon |
| 7 | Yosemite |
| 8 | Yellowstone |
| 9 | Niagara Falls |
| 10 | Belgium |
| 11 | Denmark |
| 12 | South Africa |
| 13 | Sweden |

*CHAPTER 16: The Magic of Transact-SQL Programming*

## Table-Valued Function for PRIME Numbers Generation

Transact-SQL table-valued function generates prime numbers up to the input parameter limit.

```
USE AdventureWorks2012;
GO

CREATE FUNCTION ufnPrimeNumbers ( @Stop INT)
RETURNS @Result TABLE  (Prime INT)
BEGIN
WITH CTE ( SeqNo)
    AS (SELECT 0
        UNION ALL
        SELECT SeqNo + 1
        FROM   CTE
        WHERE  SeqNo < @Stop)
INSERT @Result
SELECT PrimeNo = N2.SeqNo
FROM   CTE N1
        INNER JOIN CTE N2
    ON  N2.SeqNo % N1.SeqNo > 0
        AND N2.SeqNo % 2 > 0
        AND N1.SeqNo < N2.SeqNo
        AND N2.SeqNo > 1
        AND N1.SeqNo >= 1
GROUP  BY N2.SeqNo
HAVING ( N2.SeqNo - COUNT(*) ) = 2
OPTION ( MAXRECURSION 0);
RETURN ;
END;
GO

SELECT * FROM dbo.ufnPrimeNumbers (1000);
GO
-- (167 row(s) affected) - Partial results.
```

| Prime |
|-------|
| 3     |
| 5     |
| 7     |
| 11    |
| 13    |
| 17    |
| 19    |
| 23    |
| 29    |
| 31    |

## Inline Functions

An inline user-defined function, returns table, can be used as a parameterized view.

```
USE AdventureWorks2012
GO


CREATE FUNCTION Sales.ufnStaffSalesByFiscalYear (@OrderYear INT)
RETURNS TABLE  AS
RETURN
SELECT
    CONVERT(date, soh.OrderDate)                                            AS OrderDate
    ,CONCAT(p.FirstName, ' ', COALESCE(p.MiddleName, ''), ' ', p.LastName)   AS FullName
    ,e.JobTitle
    ,st.Name                                                                AS SalesTerritory
    ,FORMAT(soh.SubTotal, 'c', 'en-US')                                 AS SalesAmount
    ,YEAR(DATEADD(mm, 6, soh.OrderDate))                                   AS FiscalYear
FROM Sales.SalesPerson sp
    INNER JOIN Sales.SalesOrderHeader soh
        ON sp.BusinessEntityID = soh.SalesPersonID
    INNER JOIN Sales.SalesTerritory st
        ON sp.TerritoryID = st.TerritoryID
    INNER JOIN HumanResources.Employee e
        ON soh.SalesPersonID = e.BusinessEntityID
    INNER JOIN Person.Person p
        ON p.BusinessEntityID = sp.BusinessEntityID
WHERE        soh.OrderDate >= datefromparts(@OrderYear, 1, 1)
        AND soh.OrderDate < dateadd(yy,1, datefromparts(@OrderYear, 1, 1));
GO
-- Command(s) completed successfully.


SELECT * FROM Sales.ufnStaffSalesByFiscalYear (2007)
ORDER BY FullName, CONVERT(money, SalesAmount) DESC;   --  SalesAmount (string) does not sort
correctly
--( 1476  row(s) affected)  -- Partial results.
```

| OrderDate | FullName | JobTitle | SalesTerritory | SalesAmount | FiscalYear |
|-----------|----------|----------|----------------|-------------|------------|
| 2007-08-01 | David R Campbell | Sales Representative | Northwest | $101,609.29 | 2008 |
| 2007-07-01 | David R Campbell | Sales Representative | Northwest | $93,397.64 | 2008 |
| 2007-04-01 | David R Campbell | Sales Representative | Northwest | $75,104.65 | 2007 |
| 2007-07-01 | David R Campbell | Sales Representative | Northwest | $74,149.95 | 2008 |
| 2007-04-01 | David R Campbell | Sales Representative | Northwest | $73,963.26 | 2007 |
| 2007-08-01 | David R Campbell | Sales Representative | Northwest | $71,283.24 | 2008 |
| 2007-09-01 | David R Campbell | Sales Representative | Northwest | $66,871.84 | 2008 |
| 2007-01-01 | David R Campbell | Sales Representative | Northwest | $63,864.71 | 2007 |
| 2007-11-01 | David R Campbell | Sales Representative | Northwest | $63,339.26 | 2008 |
| 2007-10-01 | David R Campbell | Sales Representative | Northwest | $60,519.95 | 2008 |

*CHAPTER 16:  The Magic of Transact-SQL Programming*

## Scalar Functions

A scalar user-defined function returns a scalar value. It can be used in a query wherever a single value is required.

```
USE AdventureWorks2012;
GO

CREATE FUNCTION dbo.ufnNumberToEnglish (@Number INT)
RETURNS VARCHAR(1024)  AS
 BEGIN
   DECLARE @Below20 TABLE      ( ID  INT IDENTITY ( 0, 1 ),   Word VARCHAR(32) );
   DECLARE @Tens TABLE  ( ID  INT IDENTITY ( 2, 1 ),    Word VARCHAR(32) );
   INSERT @Below20  (Word)
   VALUES('Zero'), ('One'),('Two'), ('Three'), ('Four'), ('Five'), ('Six'), ('Seven'), ('Eight'),
       ('Nine'), ('Ten'), ('Eleven'), ('Twelve'), ('Thirteen'), ('Fourteen'), ('Fifteen'),
       ('Sixteen'), ('Seventeen'), ('Eighteen'), ('Nineteen');
   INSERT @Tens
   VALUES('Twenty'),   ('Thirty'), ('Forty'), ('Fifty'), ('Sixty'), ('Seventy'), ('Eighty'), ('Ninety');
   DECLARE @English VARCHAR(1024) = (SELECT CASE
         WHEN @Number = 0 THEN ''
         WHEN @Number BETWEEN 1 AND 19 THEN (SELECT Word FROM   @Below20 WHERE  ID = @Number)
         WHEN @Number BETWEEN 20 AND 99 THEN
      CONCAT((SELECT Word FROM   @Tens WHERE  ID = @Number / 10), '-',
dbo.ufnNumberToEnglish(@Number%10))
       WHEN @Number BETWEEN 100 AND 999 THEN CONCAT((
          dbo.ufnNumberToEnglish(@Number / 100) ), ' Hundred ', dbo.ufnNumberToEnglish(@Number%100))
      WHEN @Number BETWEEN 1000 AND 999999 THEN CONCAT((
          dbo.ufnNumberToEnglish(@Number / 1000) ), ' Thousand ', dbo.ufnNumberToEnglish(@Number%1000))
      WHEN @Number BETWEEN 1000000 AND 999999999 THEN CONCAT((
          dbo.ufnNumberToEnglish(@Number / 1000000) ), ' Million ', dbo.ufnNumberToEnglish(@Number%1000000))
       ELSE ' INVALID INPUT'  END);
     SELECT @English = RTRIM(@English);
     SELECT @English = RTRIM(LEFT(@English, len(@English) - 1))
     WHERE  RIGHT(@English, 1) = '-';
     RETURN ( @English );
 END;
GO
-- Command(s) completed successfully.

SELECT dbo.ufnNumberToEnglish (9999);   -- Nine Thousand Nine Hundred Ninety-Nine

SELECT dbo.ufnNumberToEnglish (1000001);  -- One Million One

SELECT dbo.ufnNumberToEnglish (7777777);
-- Seven Million Seven Hundred Seventy-Seven Thousand Seven Hundred Seventy-Seven
```

# Dynamic PIVOT Script

Static PIVOT has pretty limited role since it has to be changed when data changes effects the PIVOT range. Dynamic SQL makes PIVOT data driven. Instead of hard-wired columns, dynamic PIVOT builds the columns from the data dynamically.

```
USE AdventureWorks;
GO

DECLARE @OrderYear AS TABLE
 (
    YYYY INT NOT NULL PRIMARY KEY
 ) ;
DECLARE @DynamicSQL AS NVARCHAR(4000) ;

INSERT INTO @OrderYear
SELECT DISTINCT YEAR(OrderDate)
FROM   Sales.SalesOrderHeader;

DECLARE @ReportColumnNames AS NVARCHAR(MAX),  @IterationYear   AS INT;

SET @IterationYear = (SELECT MIN(YYYY)    FROM   @OrderYear);
SET @ReportColumnNames = N'';

-- Assemble pivot list dynamically
WHILE ( @IterationYear IS NOT NULL )
  BEGIN
    SET @ReportColumnNames = @ReportColumnNames + N','
                + QUOTENAME(CAST(@IterationYear AS NVARCHAR(10)));
    SET @IterationYear = (SELECT MIN(YYYY)
              FROM   @OrderYear
              WHERE  YYYY > @IterationYear);
  END;

SET @ReportColumnNames = SUBSTRING(@ReportColumnNames, 2,
         LEN(@ReportColumnNames));

PRINT @ReportColumnNames; -- [2001],[2002],[2003],[2004]

SET @DynamicSQL = CONCAT(N'SELECT * FROM (SELECT [Store (Freight Summary)]=s.Name,
       YEAR(OrderDate) AS OrderYear,  Freight = convert(money, convert(varchar, Freight))
       FROM Sales.SalesOrderHeader soh
       INNER JOIN Sales.Store s
       ON soh.CustomerID = s.CustomerID) as Header
       PIVOT (SUM(Freight)   FOR OrderYear IN(', @ReportColumnNames,N')) AS Pvt ORDER BY 1;');
```

-- **T-SQL script continued**

```
PRINT @DynamicSQL; -- Testing & debugging
/* SELECT * FROM (SELECT [Store (Freight Summary)]=s.Name,
        YEAR(OrderDate) AS OrderYear,  Freight = convert(money, convert(varchar, Freight))
        FROM Sales.SalesOrderHeader soh
        INNER JOIN Sales.Store s    ON soh.CustomerID = s.CustomerID) as Header
        PIVOT (SUM(Freight)    FOR OrderYear IN([2001],[2002],[2003],[2004]))  AS Pvt ORDER BY 1;*/


-- Execute dynamic sql
EXEC sp_executesql  @DynamicSQL;
GO  -- (633 row(s) affected) - Partial results.
```

| Store (Freight Summary) | 2001 | 2002 | 2003 | 2004 |
|---|---|---|---|---|
| A Bike Store | 921.55 | 1637.24 | NULL | NULL |
| A Great Bicycle Company | 142.08 | 114.34 | 15.24 | NULL |
| A Typical Bike Shop | 976.61 | 1529.08 | NULL | NULL |
| Acceptable Sales & Service | 12.58 | 25.17 | NULL | NULL |

# INSERT, UPDATE & DELETE through a View

Underlying table can be modified through a view, thus adding flexibility to security access since a view can be permissioned independently of the table.

```
USE tempdb;
SELECT CONVERT(INT, ProductID) AS ID, Name AS ProductName, ListPrice, ModifiedDate INTO
Product
FROM AdventureWorks2012.Production.Product;
GO -- (504 row(s) affected)
CREATE VIEW vProduct AS SELECT * FROM Product;
GO
UPDATE vProduct SET ModifiedDate = '2018-01-01';
GO -- (504 row(s) affected)
INSERT vProduct VALUES (2000, 'Three-Wheeler Bike', $999.99, getdate());
GO -- (1 row(s) affected)
DELETE TOP (10) FROM vProduct;
GO -- (1 row(s) affected)
SELECT TOP (1) * FROM Product;  -- 322 Chainring       0.00      2018-01-01 00:00:00.000
GO
DROP VIEW dbo.vProduct;
DROP TABLE tempdb.dbo.Product;
GO
```

# Sensitive Data Audit Trigger

Triggers can be used to track sensitive data changes into an audit table. The OUTPUT clause is an alternative, but not exactly equivalent.

```
USE Payroll;
GO


CREATE TRIGGER uTrgEmployeeUpdate
ON Employee
AFTER UPDATE
AS
  IF ( Update(Salary)
     OR Update(SSN) )
  BEGIN
    INSERT INTO CorpSecurityEmployeeAudit
          (auditlogtype,
            auditEmployeeDeptID,
            auditEmployeeID,
            auditEmployeeSalary,
            auditEmployeeSSN,
            auditUpdatedBy)
    SELECT 'PREVIOUSDATA',
        DeptID,
        EmployeeID,
        Salary,
        SSN,
        User_name()
    FROM   DELETED

    INSERT INTO CorpSecurityEmployeeAudit
          (auditlogtype,
            auditEmployeeDeptID,
            auditEmployeeID,
            auditEmployeeSalary,
            auditEmployeeSSN,
            auditUpdatedBy)
    SELECT 'NEWDATA',
        DeptID,
        EmployeeID,
        Salary,
        SSN,
        User_name()
    FROM   INSERTED
  END;
GO
```

**CHAPTER 16: The Magic of Transact-SQL Programming**

## Automatic Timestamp Trigger

Whenever the Person.Contact is updated, the ModifiedDate will be updated to current time by the update after trigger. NOTE: disable/drop other update triggers on this table, if any, for the test.

```
USE AdventureWorks;
GO


CREATE TRIGGER uTrgContactTimestamp
ON Person.Contact
FOR UPDATE
AS
 BEGIN
  IF TRIGGER_NESTLEVEL() > 1     RETURN;
   UPDATE Person.Contact  SET    Person.Contact.ModifiedDate = CURRENT_TIMESTAMP
   FROM   Person.Contact c
      INNER JOIN INSERTED i
       ON c.ContactID = i.ContactID
 END
GO
-- (1 row(s) affected)


SELECT *
FROM   Person.Contact
WHERE  FirstName = 'Kim'   AND MiddleName = 'B'      AND LastName = 'Abercrombie'
GO
-- ModifiedDate: 2000-02-10 00:00:00.000

-- Updating a column will automatically update the ModifiedDate
UPDATE Person.Contact    SET    Phone = '299 484-3924'
WHERE  FirstName = 'Kim'    AND MiddleName = 'B'     AND LastName = 'Abercrombie'
GO

SELECT *
FROM   Person.Contact WHERE  FirstName = 'Kim'    AND MiddleName = 'B'    AND LastName =
'Abercrombie'
GO
-- ModifiedDate: 2018-08-11 07:22:01.157


-- Cleanup
DROP TRIGGER Person.uTrgContactTimestamp
```

# Recursive Product Assembly

Recursive Common Table Expression (CTE) is used to assemble a bike frame based on the BillOfMaterials table.

USE AdventureWorks2012;

```
DECLARE @ProductID int = 831;
WITH CTE(AssemblyID, ComponentID, PerAssemblyQty,  AssemblyLevel) AS
(       SELECT bom0.ProductAssemblyID, bom0.ComponentID, bom0.PerAssemblyQty,
                0 AS AssemblyLevel
        FROM Production.BillOfMaterials AS bom0
        WHERE bom0.ProductAssemblyID = @ProductID
                AND bom0.EndDate is null
        UNION ALL
        SELECT bom.ProductAssemblyID, bom.ComponentID, p.PerAssemblyQty,
                AssemblyLevel + 1
        FROM Production.BillOfMaterials AS bom
                INNER JOIN CTE AS p
                        ON bom.ProductAssemblyID = p.ComponentID   AND bom.EndDate is null    )
SELECT pp.Name AS ProductName, AssemblyID, ComponentID,
        p.Name AS AssemblyName, PerAssemblyQty, AssemblyLevel
FROM CTE
        INNER JOIN Production.Product AS p
                ON CTE.ComponentID = p.ProductID
        INNER JOIN Production.Product AS pp
                ON CTE.AssemblyID = pp.ProductID
ORDER BY AssemblyLevel, AssemblyID, ComponentID;
```

| ProductName | AssemblyID | ComponentID | AssemblyName | PerAssemblyQty | AssemblyLevel |
|---|---|---|---|---|---|
| ML Mountain Frame - Black, 44 | 831 | 324 | Chain Stays | 2.00 | 0 |
| ML Mountain Frame - Black, 44 | 831 | 325 | Decal 1 | 2.00 | 0 |
| ML Mountain Frame - Black, 44 | 831 | 326 | Decal 2 | 1.00 | 0 |
| ML Mountain Frame - Black, 44 | 831 | 327 | Down Tube | 1.00 | 0 |
| ML Mountain Frame - Black, 44 | 831 | 399 | Head Tube | 1.00 | 0 |
| ML Mountain Frame - Black, 44 | 831 | 492 | Paint - Black | 8.00 | 0 |
| ML Mountain Frame - Black, 44 | 831 | 532 | Seat Stays | 4.00 | 0 |
| ML Mountain Frame - Black, 44 | 831 | 533 | Seat Tube | 1.00 | 0 |
| ML Mountain Frame - Black, 44 | 831 | 534 | Top Tube | 1.00 | 0 |
| ML Mountain Frame - Black, 44 | 831 | 803 | ML Fork | 1.00 | 0 |
| Chain Stays | 324 | 486 | Metal Sheet 5 | 2.00 | 1 |
| Down Tube | 327 | 483 | Metal Sheet 3 | 1.00 | 1 |
| Head Tube | 399 | 485 | Metal Sheet 4 | 1.00 | 1 |
| Seat Stays | 532 | 484 | Metal Sheet 7 | 4.00 | 1 |
| Seat Tube | 533 | 478 | Metal Bar 2 | 1.00 | 1 |
| Top Tube | 534 | 482 | Metal Sheet 2 | 1.00 | 1 |
| ML Fork | 803 | 316 | Blade | 1.00 | 1 |
| ML Fork | 803 | 331 | Fork End | 1.00 | 1 |
| ML Fork | 803 | 350 | Fork Crown | 1.00 | 1 |
| ML Fork | 803 | 531 | Steerer | 1.00 | 1 |
| Blade | 316 | 486 | Metal Sheet 5 | 1.00 | 2 |
| Fork End | 331 | 482 | Metal Sheet 2 | 1.00 | 2 |
| Fork Crown | 350 | 486 | Metal Sheet 5 | 1.00 | 2 |
| Steerer | 531 | 487 | Metal Sheet 6 | 1.00 | 2 |

## Percent on Base Calculation

When deriving percent on base, we need to calculate the overall total in a single value subquery to use it as denominator in the percentile calculation.

```
USE AdventureWorks2012;

SELECT YEAR(OrderDate) AS [Year],
    FORMAT(SUM(TotalDue),'c0','en-US') AS YearTotal,
    FORMAT(SUM(TotalDue) /
        (SELECT SUM(TotalDue) FROM Sales.SalesOrderHeader),'p0') AS Percentile
FROM Sales.SalesOrderHeader
GROUP BY YEAR(OrderDate)
ORDER BY YEAR ASC;
```

| Year | YearTotal | Percentage |
|------|-----------|------------|
| 2005 | $12,693,251 | 10 % |
| 2006 | $34,463,848 | 28 % |
| 2007 | $47,171,490 | 38 % |
| 2008 | $28,888,198 | 23 % |

Adding a Grand Total line with ROLLUP.

```
SELECT COALESCE(CONVERT(varchar,YEAR(OrderDate)), 'Grand Total') AS [Year],
    FORMAT(SUM(TotalDue),'c0','en-US') AS [SalesTotal],
    FORMAT(SUM(TotalDue) /
        (SELECT SUM(TotalDue) FROM Sales.SalesOrderHeader),'p0') AS Percentage
FROM Sales.SalesOrderHeader
GROUP BY YEAR(OrderDate)    WITH ROLLUP
ORDER BY YEAR ASC;
```

| Year | SalesTotal | Percentage |
|------|-----------|------------|
| 2005 | $12,693,251 | 10 % |
| 2006 | $34,463,848 | 28 % |
| 2007 | $47,171,490 | 38 % |
| 2008 | $28,888,198 | 23 % |
| Grand Total | $123,216,786 | 100 % |

This page is intentionally left blank.

This page is intentionally left blank.

# APPENDIX A: Job Interview Questions

## Selected Database Design Questions

D1. What is your approach to database design?

D2. Some of our legacy databases are far from 3NF. Can you work in such an environment?

D3. Can UNIQUE KEY be used instead of PRIMARY KEY?

D4. Can a FOREIGN KEY be NULL?

D5. Can a PRIMARY KEY be NULL?

D6. Can a PRIMARY KEY be based on non-clustered unique index?

D7. Do you implement OrderQty > 0 condition as a CHECK constraint or in the application software?

D8. What is a heap?

D9. Can a table have 2 IDENTITY columns, 2 FOREIGN KEYs, 2 PRIMARY KEYs and 2 clustered indexes?

D10. Should each table have a NATURAL KEY or is INT IDENTITY PK sufficient?

D11. How can you prevent entry of "US", "U.S", "USA", etc. instead of "United States" into Country column?

D12. How would you implement ManagerID in an Employee table with EmployeeID as PRIMARY KEY?

D13. How would you implement the relationship between OrderMaster and OrderDetail tables?

D14. The Product table has the Color column. Would you create a Color table and change the column to ColorID FK?

D15. Can you insert directly into an IDENTITY column?

## Selected Database Programming Questions

P1. Write a query to list all departments with employee count based on the Department column of Employee table.

P2. Same as above but the Employee table has the DepartmentID column.

P3. Write an INSERT statement for a new "Social Technology" department with GroupName "Sales & Marketing".

P4. Same query es in P2, but the new department should be included even though no employees yet.

P5. Write a query to generate 1000 sequential numbers without a table.

P6. Write a query with SARGable predicate to list all orders from OrderMaster received on 2016-10-23. OrderDate is datetime.

P7. Write a query to add a header record DEPARTMENTNAME to the departments listing from the Department table. If there are 20 departments, the result set should have 21 records.

P8. Make the previous query a derived table in an outer SELECT * query

P9. Write an ORDER BY clause for the previous query with CASE expression to sort DEPARTMENTNAME as first record and alphabetically descending from there on.

P10. Same as above with the IIF conditional.

P11. The table-valued dbo.ufnSplitCSV splits a comma delimited string (input parameter). The Product table has some ProductName-s with comma(s). Write a CROSS APPLY query to return ProductName-s with comma and each split string value from the UDF as separate line. ProductName should repeat for each split part.

| ProductName | SplitPart |
| --- | --- |
| Full-Finger Gloves, L | Full-Finger Gloves |
| Full-Finger Gloves, L | L |

P12. You need the inserted lines count 10 lines down following the INSERT statement.  What should be the statement immediately following the INSERT statement?

P13. What is the result of the second query? What is it called?
SELECT COUNT_BIG(*) FROM Sales.SalesOrderDetail;      -- 121317
SELECT COUNT_BIG(*) FROM Sales.SalesOrderDetail x, Sales.SalesOrderDetail y;

P14. Declare & Assign the string variable @Text varchar(32) the literal '2016/10/23 10:20:12' without the "/" and ":".

P15. You want to add a parameter to a frequently used view. What is the workaround?

This page is intentionally left blank.

# APPENDIX B: Job Interview Answers

## Selected Database Design Answers

D1. I prefer 3NF design due to high database developer productivity and low maintenance cost.

D2. I did have such projects in the past. I can handle them. Hopefully, introduce some improvements.

D3. Partially yes since UNIQUE KEYs can be FK referenced, fully no. Every table should a PRIMARY KEY.

D4. Yes.

D5. No.

D6. Yes. The default is clustered unique index. Only unique index is required.

D7. CHECK constraint. A server-side object solution (if available) is more reliable than code in application software.

D8. A table without clustered index. Database engine generally works better if a table has clustered index.

D9. No, yes, no, no.

D10. Each table should be designed with NATURAL KEY(s). INT IDENTITY PK is not a replacement for NATURAL KEY.

D11. Combination of Lookup table and UDF CHECK Constraint. UDF checks the Lookup table for valid entries.

D12. ManagerID should be a FOREIGN KEY referencing the PRIMARY KEY of the same table; self-referencing.

D13. OrderID PRIMARY KEY of OrderMaster. OrderID & LineItemID composition PK of OrderDetail. OrderID of OrderDetail FK to OrderID of OderMaster.

D14. Yes. It makes sense for color to be in its own table.

D15. No. Only if you SET IDENTITY_INSERT tablename ON.

## Selected Database Programming Answers

P1. SELECT Department, Employees=COUNT(*) FROM Employee GROUP BY Department ORDER BY Department;

P2. SELECT d.Department, Employees = COUNT(EmployeeID)
FROM Employee e INNER JOIN Department d ON e.DepartmentID = d.DepartmentID
GROUP BY d.Department ORDER BY Department;

P3. INSERT Department (Name, GroupName) VALUES ('Social Technology', 'Sales & Marketing');

P4. SELECT d.Department, Employees = COUNT(EmployeeID)
FROM Employee e RIGHT JOIN Department d ON e.DepartmentID = d.DepartmentID
GROUP BY d.Department ORDER BY Department;

P5. ;WITH Seq AS (SELECT SeqNo = 1 UNION ALL SELECT SeqNo+1 FROM Seq WHERE SeqNo < 100) SELECT * FROM Seq;

P6. SELECT * FROM OrderMaster WHERE OrderDate >='20161023' AND OrderDate < DATEADD(DD,1,'20161023');

P7. SELECT  AllDepartments = 'DEPARTMENTNAME' UNION SELECT Department FROM Department;

P8. SELECT * FROM (SELECT  AllDepartments = 'DEPARTMENTNAME' UNION SELECT Name FROM HumanResources.Department) x

P9.  ORDER BY CASE WHEN AllDepartments = 'DEPARTMENTNAME' THEN 1 ELSE 2 END, AllDepartments DESC;

P10. ORDER BY IIF( AllDepartments = 'DEPARTMENTNAME', 1 , 2 ), AllDepartments DESC;

P11. SELECT ProductName, S.SplitPart FROM Product P  CROSS APPLY dbo.ufnSplitCSV (Name) S WHERE ProductName like '%,%';

P12.  DECLARE @InsertedCount INT = @@ROWCOUNT;

P13. 121317*121317; Cartesian product.

P14. DECLARE @Text varchar(32) = REPLACE(REPLACE ('2016/10/23 10:20:12', '/', SPACE(0)), ':', SPACE(0));

P15. Table-valued INLINE user-defined function.

This page is intentionally left blank.

This page is intentionally left blank.

# INDEX for Beginner Database Design & SQL Programming Using Microsoft SQL Server

## Index of the Most Important Topics

| D |
|---|

---

### Y

---

www.ingramcontent.com/pod-product-compliance
Lightning Source LLC
Chambersburg PA
CBHW080133060326
40689CB00018B/3776